Praise for *Zappa*.

"In Barry Miles's admiring, myth-busting biography, Zappa emerges as an artist compelled to undermine his achievements through an unrelenting blend of immaturity, stubbornness, and misanthropy."

—*The Boston Globe*

"A comprehensive and finely detailed biography . . . Miles traces his life with academic ferocity." —Mitch Myers, *High Times*

"Rebel, performer, and a true musical visionary, *Zappa* is a brilliant and sweeping portrait of an American legend, written by one of rock music's most respected biographers." —*San Diego Reader*

"Barry's Big Book of Bastards is a Butane Bombshell Biography."

—*Creem Magazine*

"Pop culture biographer Miles . . . paints an engrossing portrait. . . . Skillfully weaves together the major beats and minor notes of Zappa's remarkable life . . . hits the ups and downs of Zappa's life like a skilled composer in his own right . . . The result is a penetrating look both at Zappa and at the social and political milieu in which popular rock music stepped to the fore." —*Publishers Weekly*

"Miles, who knew him well, gets closer than anyone to unraveling the enigma of Zappa and explaining his peculiar gifts and neuroses."

—*Mick Brown, The Daily Telegraph*

"[An] excellent and authoritative biography."

—Val Hennessy, *Daily Mail*

"A heavyweight but dynamic look at the life and times of a legend."

—*Daily Mirror*

Zappa

Barry Miles

GROVE PRESS
New York

First published in Great Britain in 2004 by Atlantic Books,
an imprint of Grove Atlantic Ltd., London

Published simultaneously in Canada
Printed in the United States of America

Library of Congress Cataloging-in-Publication Data

Miles, Barry, 1943–
    Zappa : a biography / Barry Miles.
      p. cm.
    Includes bibliographical references (p.) and index.
    ISBN: 978-0-8021-4215-3
    1. Zappa, Frank. 2. Rock musicians—United States—Biography. I. Title.
ML410.Z285.M49 2004
782.42166'092—dc22
  [B]   2004051805

Designed by Richard Marston

Grove Press
an imprint of Grove Atlantic
154 West 14th Street
New York, NY 10011

Distributed by Publishers Group West

groveatlantic.com

21 22 23   10 9 8 7 6

To David Walley, Urban Gwerder, Alain Dister and Mick Farren;
pioneer Zappaists.

Contents

List of Illustrations

Introduction

In 1965 Cucamonga was just a village: a few streets clustered either side of Foothill Boulevard, historic Route 66, where it crossed Archibald Avenue about 75 miles east of Los Angeles. Around 7,000 people were scattered in the suburban desert sprawl that extended all the way to LA and connected the twin towns of Ontario-Upland to the west and San Bernardino to the east. Though this was the mid-sixties, the Cucamongans lived in a fifties time warp. It was a conservative, right-wing village and the male population wore short-sleeved white shirts and bow ties. Even a T-shirt was looked upon with suspicion. Cucamonga had a high school, a court house, a holy-roller church, a malt-shop and a recording studio, Studio Z, built by local boy Paul Buff, but now owned by 24-year-old Frank Zappa.

Business was slack: few Cucamongans wanted to record their bands, even at the very reasonable rate of $13.50 an hour, so Frank had to drive 75 miles to Sun Village in the High Mojave Desert every weekend where he earned $7 a night playing in a bar band. With him in the studio lived his 18-year-old girlfriend Lorraine Belcher and his high-school friend Jim 'Motorhead' Sherwood.

One of Zappa's schemes was for a low budget science-fiction

movie: *Captain Beefheart Versus the Grunt People*, starring Captain Beefheart (aka Don Vliet) and his parents. Zappa had bought $50-worth of stage flats that took up much of the back room of Studio Z, and had painted them with cartoon designs for a rocket ship and a mad scientist's lab. Despite having no money, he had confidently announced a casting call for the movie. This drew the attention of the local police. Tipped-off by the Cucamonga police department, Detective Sgt Jim Willis from the San Bernardino sheriff's office vice squad auditioned for the part of Senator Gurney (the 'role of the asshole', as Zappa put it) and was convinced he had uncovered a vice den.

To Sgt Willis, Studio Z looked like a bohemian 'pad'. The walls were covered with newspaper clippings and memorabilia: a threat from the Department of Motor Vehicles to revoke Zappa's driver's licence, his divorce papers, a still of him on *The Steve Allen Show*, rejection letters from several music publishers, pop art collages and song lyrics. One was 'The Streets of Fontana', a parody of the folk music standard 'The Streets of Laredo', which Zappa used to sing with Ray Collins in the local clubs as a joke.

> As I was out sweeping the streets of Fontana
> As I was out sweeping Fontana one day
> I spied in the gutter a mouldy banana
> And with the peeling I started to play . . .

To Sgt Willis this was no joke. Zappa was clearly a threat to society. He ordered a surveillance team to drill a hole in the wall of the studio and for several weeks undercover police gathered evidence of subversive behaviour.

Then Sgt Willis visited the studio, this time in the guise of a used-car salesman. Attracted by the smart sign over the door (TV PICTURES), he explained that he and the boys were having a little party and wondered if Zappa could make him an 'exciting film' to suit the occasion. Zappa – who was living on peanut-butter sandwiches and instant mashed potatoes scrounged by Motorhead from the blood-donor centre – rapidly calculated that such a film would cost $300 to make. This was beyond the budget of the San Bernardino vice squad, so Zappa suggested that a tape-recording might suffice and would cost only $100.

Willis outlined all the things he would like to hear on the tape (including 'oral copulation') and Zappa said it would be ready the next day. Their conversation was relayed to a police tape recorder in a van parked across the street via a wrist-watch transmitter, like something out of a Dick Tracy cartoon.

That evening Zappa and Lorraine bounced around on the bed to make the springs squeak for a half-hour tape and added gasps, moans and what the police later described as 'blue' dialogue. There was no actual sex. Zappa edited out all the giggles and laughter and then, ever the professional, added a musical backing track. Sgt Willis showed up the next day and offered him $50.

Zappa complained that the deal was for $100 and refused to hand over the tape. At that moment the door burst open and two more sheriff's detectives, plus another from the Ontario police department, rushed in, closely followed by a reporter from the Ontario-Upland *Daily Report* and a photographer. Zappa and Lorraine were arrested and handcuffed. Willis and his team searched the premises while the photographer's flash bulbs went off. They seized every scrap of tape and strip of film in the studio and even took away Zappa's 8mm projector as 'evidence'.

Zappa and Lorraine were taken to the county jail and booked on suspicion of conspiracy to manufacture pornographic materials and sex perversion, both felonies.

It was front-page news in the *Daily Report*: under the heading *2 A GO-GO TO JAIL* they breathlessly described how: 'Vice squad investigators stilled the tape recorders of a free swinging a-Go-Go film and recording studio here Friday and arrested a self-styled movie producer and his buxom red-haired companion.'

Paul Buff loaned Zappa the money to get out on bail and Zappa got an advance on royalties from Art Laboe at Original Sound – who had a Mexican Number One with 'Tijuana Surf' by the Persuaders (Zappa had written the B-side: 'Grunion Run') – to have Lorraine released.

They were arraigned the next week at the Cucamonga Justice Court across from Studio Z.

Before the trial, Zappa's elderly, white-haired lawyer took him aside and asked: 'How could you be such a fool to let this guy con you? I thought *everybody* knew Detective Willis. He's the kind of guy who earns his living waiting around in public rest rooms to catch queers.' Zappa had never heard of anything like it. The idea that there were people employed in the police department to do such things was a revelation.

He and Lorraine – now described as 'a buxom red-haired girl of perfect physical dimensions' by the increasingly excited *Daily Report* – appeared before the judge. At one point in the proceedings, he took them both, along with all the lawyers, into his private chambers to hear the 'pornographic' tape. It was so funny the judge started laughing, which outraged the prosecution. The case was being brought by a 26-year-old assistant district attorney who demanded that Zappa serve time for this piece of filth, 'in the name of Justice!'

The case against Lorraine was dropped and Zappa was found guilty of a misdemeanour. He was given six months in jail, with all but ten days suspended, then put on three years probation. During this time he was not allowed to be in the company of a woman under 21 without a chaperone and, most importantly, must not violate any of California's traffic laws.

The ten days in San Bernardino County Jail had a traumatic effect on Zappa, shocking him out of his innocence and creating the cynical, suspicious persona that defined him throughout his life.

Forty-four men were crammed together in Tank C in temperatures reaching 104 degrees. The lights were on all the time. There was one shower at the end of the cell block, but it was so grimy Zappa didn't shave or shower at all. One morning he tipped his aluminium breakfast bowl over and at the bottom, stuck in the creamed-wheat, was a giant cockroach. He enclosed it in a letter to Motorhead's mother, but the prison censor found it and threatened him with solitary confinement if he tried anything like that again. Zappa was powerless to fight back and sat there imagining monster guitar chords powerful enough to crack open the walls.

By the time he got out, he no longer believed anything the authorities had ever told him. Everything he had been taught at school about the American Way of Life was a lie. He would not be fooled again. He made sure that his pornographic tape was heard by everyone – he remade it time and time again, at least a couple of times on each album, rubbing it in the face of respectable society, making America see itself as it really was: phoney, mendacious, shallow and ugly.

1 Baltimore

Zappa means 'hoe' in Italian, symbol of the back-breaking toil of the Sicilian peasants who had to scratch a living from the dry stony ground. Frank Zappa's father, Francis Vincent Zappa, was born on 7 May 1905 in Partinico, western Sicily, a small town of about 20,000 people. Partinico is twelve miles west of Palermo along a twisting mountain road. An area of astonishing beauty, with Greek temples, Roman bridges, Saracen mosques, Romanesque churches and cloistered monasteries set among olive groves and vineyards, it is also the Mafia heartland.

After the Second World War, the 'Partinico Faction' was the main supplier of heroin to members of the 'Partnership' – the 'Partinico West' families – who controlled Detroit, San Diego, Miami, Las Vegas, Tucson and other cities. Partinico is now dominated by five mafia families and is the capital of *il triangolo d'oro di marijuana*, the 'golden triangle' where cannabis grows in high-tech greenhouses among the vines. But when Francis Zappa was born, the mafia was only just coming into existence.

Family legend has it that he weighed an astonishing 18 lbs at birth. He was clearly healthy and was one of only four children to survive his mother's 18 pregnancies. Francis had a brother, Cicero (later known as Joe) and twin sisters. Sicilian peasants lived in grinding poverty, with all its accompanying ill-health, disease and child mortality. They left in their thousands to find work in America, including Vincent and Rosa Zappa, Frank Zappa's paternal grandparents. They arrived in Baltimore in 1908 on an immigrant boat with Francis and Cicero, their surviving children (sadly the twin girls died in a train crash).

The contrast could not have been greater: Partinico was a sleepy medieval town on the Mediterranean. Baltimore was a noisy Atlantic sea-port: a harbour filled with ships, a mixture of races and nationalities. It must have been a culture shock for Zappa's grandparents. Vincent brought with him the peasant lifestyle of the old country. Frank Zappa: 'What they said about my grandfather was that he never took a bath, used to drink a lot of wine and started every day with a full glass of Bromo Seltzer. And because he didn't take a bath he wore a lot of clothes, and put cologne on. He had a terminal case of ring around the collar; one of those kind of fat Italian guys who would sit on the porch.'

The Zappas were hardworking immigrants determined to make a success and they worked all hours, eating pasta three times a day and saving their dollars and cents. They settled in a house on York Road in north Baltimore and Vincent used his savings to buy a barber-shop on the waterfront by the pier. Little Francis also did his bit. Zappa: 'One of my father's first jobs in life, he must have been about six [actually eight], was standing on a little wooden box in his father's barber shop. He got paid a penny a day to put lather on the faces of sailors.'

The teenage Francis used his hairdressing skills to supplement his allowance while studying at Polytechnic High School. He was a good scholar and told Vincent that he wanted to go to college. This was the immigrant dream and his father dipped into his savings to give Francis $75 – a huge sum in those days. This, combined with his earnings as a bridge-player, enabled him to attend the University of North Carolina at Chapel Hill, where he gained a degree in History.

At college Francis was on the wrestling team and also played guitar in a musical trio. They stood under the windows of the dormitories and serenaded the co-eds with such catchy twenties ditties as 'Pretty Little Red Wing, the Indian Maiden' (a song with questionable lyrics). One of these girls was Nel Cheek. It was a college romance and Francis and Nel were soon married.

In November 1931 they had a daughter, Ann. Francis had graduated that summer and took a job teaching in Rose Hills, North Carolina, but there he encountered prejudice: they didn't like Catholics and they didn't like Italians. There had been mounting problems between Francis and Nel, but the final break came when he decided to take a job teaching in Baltimore. Nel did not want to leave her family and friends in Chapel Hill. They divorced and Ann stayed with her mother.

In 1935 Francis met Fifi Colimore, who liked him, but thought he was more suitable for her sister Rose Marie. She telephoned her at work and arranged for the three of them to meet for tea at the Italian consulate that evening, telling her sister she was going to meet a 'nice man, a college graduate'. They got on well and Francis invited Rose Marie on a date. She met him at his college and watched from the back of the schoolroom while he taught a history class. Afterwards they had dinner in the college bookstore, which had a beer garden. But to Rose Marie's Catholic family, the idea of her dating a divorced man with a child was completely unacceptable and they did everything they could to prevent it.

Frank Zappa's mother, Rose Marie Colimore (known as Rosie), was born on 7 June 1912 in Baltimore, a first-generation American, the tenth in a family of eleven children. Her father, Charlie Colimore, came from Naples and her mother, Theresa, was born in Italy of French and Sicilian ancestry. They owned Little Charlie's, a lunchroom at 122 Market Place, a block from the waterfront, as well as the adjacent confectionery store. The Colimores lived on Market Place, close to the store. Little Charlie's was in the centre of Little Italy and had some pretty tough customers: sailors, stevedores and tug-men. Charlie and Theresa served the usual Neapolitan working-class fare: soup, pasta, fish, grilled or fried brains, fried calves' liver, hog's head, collard greens, sweet pastry or apple fritters and plenty of strong coffee.

Like many of the older immigrants, Theresa spoke little English. She would tell the young Frank Zappa stories in Italian and in his autobiography he remembered the tale of the *mano pelusa* – the hairy hand. *'Mano pelusa! Vene qua!'* she would cry, running her fingers up his arm to scare him. Theresa was a strict Catholic and the church was the centre of her social life. Rosie remembered her childhood as 'horrible' – her mother never picked her up or held her. Perhaps Theresa was scared of getting too close to her children. It was an era of high infant mortality; the pain and anguish of a child's death was too much to bear and she had borne many. Of Rosie's siblings – Frank Zappa's uncles and aunts – one sister died at birth; another, Margaret, died aged two of measles. Yet another, Rose, died shortly afterwards. Brother Louis got involved with a bad crowd and simply disappeared, aged 19, never to be seen again. It hurt to get too close.

Rosie attended the Catholic Seton High School and got on so well with the nuns that she almost joined the order. But her mother sobbed and protested until the idea was dropped. Theresa's plan was for Rosie to remain a spinster and look after her in later life.

Rosie graduated from high school in 1931. She worked as a librarian and helped her mother at home before joining her older sister Mary as a typist at the French Tobacco Company in 1933. She made $17.50 a week – good money in those poverty-stricken days. It was while she was typing invoices and letters in French that she met Francis Zappa.

Theresa was appalled at the idea of her daughter marrying a divorced man, so Rosie and Francis met in secret. They dated for four years until one night, as they stood talking on the front porch, Theresa invited Francis in for the first time. She still wanted Rosie to look after her in old age, so only agreed to their marriage if they lived in the Colimore home. Rosie was 26 and legally independent, but she had been brought up in the strict Catholic ways of the old country and dared not defy her family. So Francis and Rosie were married on 11 June 1939 and moved in with Theresa and Charlie at 2019 Whittier Avenue, West Baltimore.

Frank Vincent Zappa was born on 21 December 1940 at Mercy Hospital in Baltimore. He almost didn't make it. According to his Aunt Mary (Maria Cimino), who was there, the doctor had already delivered about nine babies that day and didn't want to do any more, so he gave Rosie some kind of drug to retard her labour. 'The baby was born breech and was going from bad to worse. At one point it looked as if they might lose both mother and child.' Rosie had to have a blood transfusion. She was in labour for 36 hours and when Frank was finally pulled out by a nurse he was limp, the umbilical cord was wrapped around his neck and his skin was black. Francis was crying, convinced the boy would die.

But Frank recovered and was taken home (Aunt Mary remembered that he had 'such beautiful eyelashes'). His parents only lived at Whittier Avenue for a short time. In 1941 Rosie's father Charlie died after a long illness and Theresa sold the house. Francis was now teaching mathematics at Loyola Blakefield High School, a Jesuit preparatory school in suburban Towson, Maryland, so he moved his family to an apartment in the 4600 block of Park Heights Avenue in the north of Baltimore, an easy commute to the new school and closer to Rosie's sister Mary. Zappa: 'I remember it was one of those rowhouses. There was an alley in the back and down the alley used to come the knife-sharpener man – you know, a guy with the wheel. And everybody used to come down off their back porch to the alley to get their knives and scissors done.'

Frank's younger brother Bobby was born on 28 August 1943. Theresa would care for him while Rosie and Aunt Mary took young Frank shopping with them on weekends at Hecht's, Hutzler's, Stewart's and Hochschild Kohn, a quartet of elite department stores at the junction of Howard and Lexington Streets. He used to wear a sailor suit with a wooden whistle on a string around his neck. Aunt Mary remembered on one outing, when Frank was about three years old, he saw some nuns in the street and said: 'Look at the lady penguins!'

After tea at Hutzler's they would sometimes visit the Lexington Market, close to where Zappa's grandfather Charlie had had his lunchroom. In the forties, hurdy-gurdy men could still be heard in all those East Coast cities with strong Italian neighbourhoods: New York, Baltimore, Philadelphia and Boston. A visit to Baltimore's Little Italy at that time was like a trip to Italy itself.

Much of the Baltimore of the forties has been swept away by the switch to a service economy, the flight to the suburbs and by 'urban renewal'. No more the screech of the street cars taking a corner on their iron rails, their web of overhead cables lacing the streets into long wide rooms or the steam whistles of the red tugboats of the Inner Harbour. Some fragments remain: the sound of wooden mallets breaking apart freshly steamed crabs, the polished marble steps of the distinctive Baltimore rowhouses, the leafy parks, the bay, the shot-tower – Zappa remembered being taken there as a child. It was the tallest structure in the United States until the Washington memorial was erected after the Civil War. Zappa also recalled visiting Haussner's in East Baltimore, the enormous German restaurant with 112 items on its menu and every inch of wall space covered with paintings (though Zappa was too young to appreciate the naked ladies painted by Gérome and Alma-Tadema). Occasionally, the Zappas would also dine in Little Italy.

One of the most hated dishes of Zappa's childhood was pasta with lentils. He claimed that his mother made enough to last all week and that after a few days in the icebox it would turn black. (Rosie hotly disputed this.) Either way, he had a lifelong aversion to pasta. The only Italian food he could bear to eat was pizza. He had an abhorrence of anything with garlic or onions in it, even the slightest trace, which meant he rarely ate in Italian restaurants.

As a child he enjoyed blueberry pie, fried oysters, fried eels and especially corn sandwiches (white bread and mashed potatoes with canned corn on top). As an adult he mostly survived on Hormel chilli straight from the can and 'plump-when-you-cook-'em' hot dogs cooked on the end of a fork over a gas ring. In a restaurant he would order hamburgers, simple steaks or chicken. He was plagued by digestive problems throughout his life.

The position of Italian-Americans in Baltimore was sometimes a difficult one. Prohibition had struck at the heart of Italian family life, where wine is an essential ingredient of a meal, both to drink and to cook with, causing people within the Italian community to import and sell it illegally. At the same time gangsters began to produce and sell alcohol and Italian-Americans were stigmatized by the actions of a few members of their community, mostly based in Chicago near the Canadian border, where much of the alcohol came from.

On a more positive note, in 1926 Baltimore elected the Sicilian Vincent Palmisano to the US Congress, the first Italian to take such high office. When the Second World War broke out, however, many Americans questioned the loyalty of Italian-Americans. Then Italy declared war against America and Italians became enemy aliens. Anyone who had supported Fascism and Mussolini was arrested by the FBI. As a result, Italian-Americans were especially conspicuous in the war effort, with patriotic fundraisers and large numbers of sons of immigrants enlisting to fight.

Francis Zappa's loyalty was clearly unimpeachable, because he next took a job with the Navy in Opa-locka, Florida, working in ballistics research, calculating shell trajectories. Zappa's father would be employed in the defence industry for the rest of his life. Rosie was reluctant to abandon her mother, but her duty was to be with her husband. Frank was a sickly child and his parents hoped the warmer climate would improve his health. They were right. The move to Florida had a tremendous impact: Frank's condition improved almost overnight and he grew 'about a foot' in height.

Zappa told interviewer Rafael Alvarez: 'All my life I had been seeing things in black and white while living in Maryland. And here I was down there and it was flowers, trees, it was great. It seemed like suddenly BOOM! Here's Technicolor.' Opa-locka is a northern suburb of Miami, which during the war housed a large military base. Much of the architecture has an Arabic flavour: houses with minarets and street names like Ahmad Street, Ali Baba Avenue, Sharazad Boulevard and even Sesame Street.

The Zappas lived in military housing for $75 a month and because they were in the Navy they didn't experience the privations caused by gasoline and food rationing. Opa-locka is between Biscayne Gardens to the east and Miami Lakes to the west, and Zappa's memories of Florida included watching out for alligators, because they sometimes ate children. He recalled a lot of mosquitoes and that if bread were left out overnight, it grew green hair. He was only four years old, but he also remembered air-raid drills: every once in a while they had to hide under the bed and turn out all the lights because 'someone thought the Germans were coming'.

Then Rosie developed an abscessed tooth, which for some reason needed to be treated in Baltimore – perhaps through a family friend. However, Francis knew that once Rosie was back with her mother, she would never return, so he packed up the house and transferred to another military establishment at Edgewood, 21 miles north-east of Baltimore. 'Even though I was sick all the time,' says Zappa in his auto-biography, 'Edgewood was sort of fun.' These years in small-town sub-urbia remained his principal memory of his childhood in Maryland.

His father worked as a meteorologist at the Edgewood Arsenal, headquarters of the Army Chemical Center. It was his job to discover ways of predicting the best delivery trajectories and weather conditions for gas warfare, a position that brought with it a top-secret military security clearance and Army housing on the camp. The Zappas moved into 15 Dexter Street in a now-demolished Army housing estate. Zappa had a clear memory of the place: 'We were living in a house that was made out of cardboard . . . They were duplexes made out of clapboard . . . real flimsy stuff, real cheezoid.'

Winters on the Chesapeake Bay were very bad and the thin walls meant the house was always cold, despite a coal fire in the kitchen. In the mornings, before it was lit, Frank and Bobby would warm them-selves by opening the door of the gas water heater to expose the flames. Around Christmas one year Bobby stood too close and the trapdoor flap on his pyjamas caught fire. His father beat out the flames with his bare hands, but neither of them were badly burned.

Zappa: 'In those days they were making mustard gas at Edgewood and each member of the family had a gas mask hanging in the closet in case the tanks broke. That was really my main toy at the time. That was my space helmet. I decided to get a can opener and open it up. It satis-fied my scientific curiosity, but it rendered the gas mask useless. My father was so upset when he found out . . . he said, "If the tanks break, who doesn't get the mask?" It was Frankie up the creek. I was fasci-nated by [poison gas] . . . the idea that you could make a chemical and then all you had to do was smell it and you die . . . For years in grammar school every time we had to do a science report I would always do mine on what I knew about poison gas.' Gas masks remained a source of interest and amusement in later life; for instance, the album *Weasels Ripped My Flesh* (1970) contains a track called 'Prelude to the Afternoon of a Sexually Aroused Gas Mask'.

Francis brought home a lot of laboratory equipment – Florence flasks, beakers, vials and test tubes – for his sons to play with. He also brought home petri dishes full of mercury. Frank would pour the mercury on the floor and hit it with a hammer, making thousands of little blobs explode across the room. Eventually the floor of his bedroom was coated with a grey paste consisting of mercury mixed with dust balls. 'My first interest was chemistry,' said Zappa in 1981. 'By the time I was six I could make gunpowder. By the time I was twelve I had had several explosive accidents. Somewhere around there I switched over to music. I gave up chemistry when I was fifteen. Chemical combinatorial theories persist however in the process of composition.' In fact, although he *knew* how to make gunpowder at the age of six, he merely play-acted mixing the ingredients, dreaming of the day he would really cause an explosion.

When America entered the Second World War, the US Chemical Warfare Service had only one manufacturing installation to make conventional ammunition and toxic chemicals: Edgewood Arsenal, Maryland. Workers developed gas masks and protective clothing, trained Army and Navy personnel and tested chemical agent dispersal methods. The Army had been manufacturing and testing poison gas at Edgewood since 1917 and by the forties the site was contaminated by various toxic agents including sarin, mustard and phosgene.

Frank would often go with his father to catch catfish and crabs for the family table. Even today, Delaware, DC, and Maryland, the states surrounding the Chesapeake Bay, have the three highest rates of cancer in the United States. The bay is contaminated, but local people, especially those on low incomes, still catch and eat the toxic fish, crabs and snapping turtles in the bay.

Most of Zappa's memories of living in Maryland are associated with ill health. He was prone to severe colds, sinus trouble and asthma. 'In my earliest years my best friend was a vaporizer with the fucking snout blowing that steam in my face. I was sick all of the time.' He was also inclined to earaches, which his parents treated with an Old World remedy: pouring hot olive oil into the ear. 'Which hurts like a mother-fucker,' said Zappa. As a young child he often had cotton wool hanging from his ears, yellow with olive oil. His sinus problems were treated by an Italian doctor using the latest technology: pellets of radium which he inserted into Frank's sinus cavities on both sides with the aid of a long wire. The dangers of long-term exposure to low-grade radiation were unknown at the time.

Asthma, recurrent flu, earaches and sinus trouble are all symptoms of exposure to nitrogen or sulphur mustard gas. The fact that these ailments disappeared when the family moved to Florida and recurred when they returned to Maryland suggests that Zappa's childhood illnesses were caused by living in a toxic environment. The toxicity of the Edgewood home was increased by a big bag of DDT powder that Zappa's father brought home from the lab to kill bugs. This, he maintained, was so safe you could eat it. It was later banned as carcinogenic. Frank almost died at birth and was a sickly child; it is likely that the fact that he spent most of his life in the warm climate of Southern California, avoided drugs and rarely drank alcohol prevented a series of disabling illnesses.

Francis Zappa supplemented his income by volunteering for 'patch tests': the human testing of chemical agents. An unknown chemical or agent was spread on his skin and covered with a patch. He was not to scratch it or look under the patch, which he wore for several weeks at a time. Zappa remembered that his father came home each week with three or four patches on his arms or different parts of his body. For each patch he received $10. According to the Department of Veterans Affairs, an estimated 4,000 servicemen and civilian personnel participated in secret testing of nitrogen, sulphur mustard gas and lewisite at Edgewood and other test sites during the war. Later studies showed a relationship between exposure and the development of certain diseases for which veterans were entitled to financial compensation.

The Edgewood years were difficult ones for Frank and he spent much of his time alone in his sickbed. Rosie told Rafael Alvarez: 'The whole time he had to stay in bed and rest he would have all his books on the bed. He was always creating something or inventing; he never liked sports. Every month something new would come for him in the mail.' Frank later took to studying at the local library. He drew a lot (usually Indians and trains) and made puppets, sewing their clothes with a careful hand – a skill that proved useful later when he needed to repair torn clothing on the road.

At Edgewood Frank had three good friends: a Panamanian boy called Paul, whose grandmother used to cook them spinach omelettes; a crippled boy called Paddy McGrath, whose mother made them peanut butter sandwiches; and Leonard Allen, who shared Frank's interest in chemistry. The two of them, in fact, succeeded in making gunpowder at Leonard's house.

Frank, Leonard and their friends would ride their bicycles to the woods at the end of Dexter Road and climb trees. The road ended in a polluted creek where they caught crawdads. When it snowed, the children used flattened cardboard boxes to toboggan down the hill near the project. Frank also had his brother Bobby to play with, though sometimes sibling rivalry got the better of them. Francis was a strict father and Rosie tried not to let him know if the boys had been fighting.

Frank's parents wanted their children to assimilate quickly and made a point of not teaching them Italian. They only used it at home to discuss something in private. Though Frank was just four years old when the war ended, people remembered that Italy had been America's enemy and he came in for a certain amount of bullying. As he later observed: 'World War Two was not a good time to be Italian-American in America.'

Frank was enrolled in Edgewood School on Cedar Drive. His teacher was Mary H. Spencer, who remembered him as 'fairly mischievous, but he wasn't naughty'. His parents were involved with the school and his father launched a campaign to have screens installed to prevent flies getting in to the classrooms. As a result of his efforts the cafeteria was eventually screened.

Frank seems to have been a popular child. His childhood sweet-heart, Marlene Beck, then aged eight, remembered: 'He was a cut-up ... kind of like being the class clown. He was a very nice person, but he was always kind of strange.' Zappa told Kurt Loder: 'I first found out I could make people laugh when I was forced to give a little speech about ferns at a class in school. I don't know what made them laugh, but they laughed, so I thought, "All right, not bad." So I tried to develop it into a – I won't say fern routine ... '

Zappa was about eleven at the time, as his third-grade teacher Cybil Gunther told Rafael Alvarez: 'We had 40 or more in a class and kids could get lost in a crowd. Frank didn't get lost in the crowd, but it wasn't music he was into – he was big on drama. If for any reason I had to leave the room, I could turn to Frank and he would hold the class enthralled with something. I never did figure out what it was, but there was never any trouble with the class because Frank was doing something that never really made any sense to me. It was some sort of drama ... some sort of cowboys and Indians. I don't know that he liked the attention, but he liked what he was doing. I always had the feeling that he was doing it for himself. That it was rather immaterial to him whether people really sat there and listened. But he was happy in what he was doing.'

Zappa claimed his class act was a recreation of the scene in the 1949 Cecil B. DeMille movie *Samson and Delilah*, where Victor Mature pushed over the columns holding up the temple. Frank used cardboard tubes and rolls of linoleum as pillars.

Despite such efforts to be popular, there was one bully at school who kept beating him up. When Frank complained, his father told him he had to deal with it himself, or he would take care of Frank. The next day Frank waited for the bully and jumped on him, pummel-ling him with his fists. Bobby witnessed the attack and shot home to tell Rosie, who ran to the scene and pulled Frank off. Then they went home, put an ice-pack on Frank's knuckles (and on Rosie's forehead) and all ate a pot roast. The Principal telephoned and told Francis that his son was a brute and a troublemaker, but the next day Francis visited the school and gave the principal such an earful that she ran and hid in another room until he left.

Zappa frequently described his family as being poor, but 'parsimonious' seems a better word. In one interview he said that the idea of taking a family drive to see where their grandfather used to cut hair was regarded as 'a rather large waste of money' and he once complained: 'I swear I don't remember a single Christmas present.' Yet childhood photographs show him in a sombrero, seated on a tricycle, and he mentions riding his bicycle when they lived in Edgewood, so he appears to have had the usual children's toys. The Zappas also took the usual holidays, Rosie and the children spending summer at the seaside.

In his autobiography, Zappa recalls living in a boarding house in Atlantic City, where the owners' Pomeranian used to eat grass and throw up something that resembled white meatballs. But rather than actually living there, as he suggests, the Zappas were undoubtedly spending the summer 'down the ocean', as they say in Baltimore (pronounced 'downy eauchin', according to Baltimore film-maker John Waters). It suggests they were never poor, as Zappa's father told David Walley: 'All my life I've made good money. It all went for food, clothing and environment. I've paid for everything I've wanted.'

Francis was fiercely protective of his family and not afraid to use his fists on anyone who criticized them or their background. In his autobiography, Zappa describes how Rosie had to dissuade his father from using his chrome .38 pistol to shoot his neighbour Archie Knight, who had been insufficiently respectful. Francis remained at heart a Sicilian.

Like all Catholic children, Zappa's early memories were of kneeling a lot. He attended Mass with his family on Sundays and took Communion. He was confirmed and went to confession on a regular basis until he was 18. Zappa once said that his mother was from a 'very strict religious family', but he also told Peter Occhiogrosso: 'I didn't come from a family where everybody was kneeling and squirming all over the place in holy water fonts.'

In 1980 he told John Swenson: 'The Baltimore catechism is one of the most absurd things in my recollection. It's so vivid. That little blue and white cover and the stuff that was in there. I used to have to go to catechism class and the nuns would show you charts of Hell. They would flip the page back and show you the fire and monsters and shit in there that can happen to you if you do all this stuff. I'm going, "Hey, this is something. This is really exciting." But you know, I've seen worse monsters in some of the audiences we've played for, and they were probably suffering more than the ones in that fake fire on the poster.' There were also competitions. If you recited certain texts accurately, you were given a relic as a prize. Frank won one: a little card and a package with something sewn up inside it, which he was warned never to open.

Francis and Rosie wanted Frank to be an altar boy and sent him to parochial school, but he only lasted two weeks. He took one look at the nuns in their black vestments and starched white coifs like giant lilies, and revolted. After a nun hit him on the hand with a ruler he refused to go back. 'I lasted a very short time,' he said. 'When the penguin came after me with a ruler I was out of there.'

Zappa was enrolled in the scapular: two small squares of brown woollen cloth, joined by tapes across the shoulders. He was never supposed to take it off, because the Virgin Mary had promised: 'Whosoever dies wearing this scapular shall not suffer eternal fire . . .' Zappa complained to Peter Occhiogrosso: 'How can you do this? These strings are gonna rot from sweat, y'know? You go through life with brown felt stinky things with a picture sewn on one side and some strings that are full of sweat going over your shoulder. You're supposed to wear this under your clothes for the rest of your life? I didn't like that.'

There were other things he did not like. For instance, the way that kneeling to pray crinkled the toes of his shoes ('You could spot a Catholic a mile away'); nor was he prepared to wear the brown corduroy trousers the church favoured. Nevertheless, the young Zappa accepted Catholicism as a significant element in his life and he was devout: 'I just liked it. It felt right for me – I was that kind of kid. Some kids have that mystical bent; they can envision the whole aura of religion and it gets to them. That was my style at the time.'

Zappa's illnesses continued and Francis decided they should settle permanently in a warmer climate. In 1951 he was offered a job at the Dugway Proving Ground in Utah, a division of the Chemical Warfare Service and closely connected with the Edgewood Arsenal. He came home with pictures and asked the family how they would like to live in the desert. 'My father was so nostalgic for where he used to live in Sicily,' said Zappa, 'and the terrain looks like Arizona. It's got that same kind of desert and mountains.' Francis thought it would be a wonderful life, but his family did not. Zappa: 'He showed us more of these cardboard houses . . . I was going, "No, I don't want to go there." But he thought it was nice.' Under pressure from Rosie, Francis eventually decided against it. Instead he took a job at the Naval Post Graduate School in Monterey, California.

By this time, Zappa had two more siblings: a brother Carl (born 10 September 1948) and a sister Patrice, known as Candy (born 28 March 1951). According to Zappa's Aunt Mary, Rosie told her the move to California was not permanent. She had missed her mother and sister while living in Florida and was saddened at the prospect of moving to the other coast. But theirs was an old-fashioned marriage and Francis made all the important family decisions.

The Navy shipped out their furniture and they prepared to leave. Francis bought one of the new Henry J two-door compacts introduced that year by Kaiser. It had a distinctive bullet-like shape, but there is nothing more uncomfortable than sitting in the back seat of a Henry J, as the three children discovered (just a few months old, Candy was on her mother's lap). 'That seat was a piece of wood with covering,' said Zappa. 'To spend 3,000 miles riding in the back of car like that with all your worldly possessions piled on top of you, that is not a terrific experience.'

They left in December 1951, taking the southern route. While driving through South Carolina they saw a black family working in a field. Francis stopped the car, went over to them and gave them every stitch of winter clothing they owned, telling them 'Take it with our blessings.' They were very grateful, but his family began to regret Francis's altruism when they reached Monterey. In northern California it rained constantly and they no longer had any coats. Francis had assumed that all of California was like the Westerns he loved.

2 California

Francis taught metallurgy at the US Naval Post Graduate School on University Circle in Monterey and Zappa attended yet another new school. In his autobiography, he remembers that his father's idea of a weekend outing was to pile into the Henry J and drive 18 miles inland to the lettuce-growing area around Salinas, where they would follow the farm trucks and pick up any lettuces that fell off. Francis was on a reasonable salary, so other factors must account for this level of penury. Possibly his self-published volume *Chances: And How To Take Them* (1966) provides us with a clue to their perpetual poverty.

It was dedicated, somewhat enigmatically, to his wife: 'Whose kindness, patience and understanding has guided me through the many years of our married life. She knows not how to gamble, but she does know when and how to take a chance.' The chapter headings are: (1) Probabilities, (2) Systems, (3) Keno, (4) The One-Armed Bandits, (5) Roulette, (6) Dice or Craps, (7) Poker, (8) Horse Racing and Sports Betting, (9) Black Jack or Baccarat, (10) Miscellaneous Dice and Card games, and (11) Mathematics of Possibilities. Virtually any one of these could lead to a college professor having to grub about in the gutter for damaged lettuces.

Zappa did his best to fit into his new school and overcame his self-consciousness and shyness by reprising his role as the class clown. He was an early developer and the first traces of his famous moustache were already visible on his upper lip: 'I had a moustache when I was eleven, big pimples and I weighed about 180 pounds.'

It was not long before his ever-restless father upped and moved the family to Pacific Grove, a few miles west along the peninsula. A pretty little seaside town, 'PG' (as the locals call it) is famous for the thousands of Monarch butterflies that winter in its trees. It was an easy commute to Monterey and the quiet little town was better for the children.

Intrigued by his father's profession, Frank longed for his own scientific apparatus. He particularly favoured the large-size Gilbert chemistry set that included the wherewithal to make tear-gas, but his parents demurred. Zappa told an interviewer in 1972: 'My father wanted me to do something scientific and I was interested in chemistry, but they were frightened to get the proper equipment, because I was only interested in things that blew up.' Ever resourceful, he experimented with household objects. He had some success with powdered ping-pong balls, which turned out to be 'rewardingly explosive'. He also managed to produce a shower of little orange-yellow fireballs from the packing of some 50-calibre machine-gun bullets stolen from a garage across the street.

In his autobiography, under the heading 'How I Almost Blew My Nuts Off', Zappa fondly recalls one especially satisfying detonation. He gathered some used firework tubes from the gutters after the Fourth of July and primed them with his own special ping-pong ball dust. You could buy single-shot caps for toy guns and Zappa improved their performance by cutting away the extra paper. He sat on the dirt floor of his parents' garage with the fireworks between his legs, pressing the trimmed single-shot caps into the tubes with a drumstick. He pressed too hard, igniting the charge. The resulting blast blew open the garage doors, left a crater in the floor and threw Zappa backwards several feet, though fortunately there was no anatomical damage.

The drumstick had come from Frank's first instrument: a snare drum. In 1951 he joined the school band and became interested in music. Zappa: 'I went to a summer school once when I was in Monterey and they had, like, basic training for kids who were going to be in the drum and bugle corps back in school. I remember the teacher's name was Keith McKillip and he was the rudimental drummer of the area in Pacific Grove. And they had all these little kids about eleven or twelve years old lined up in this room. You didn't have drums, you had these boards – not pads, but a plank laid across some chairs – and everybody stood in front of this plank and went rattlety-tat on it. I didn't have an actual drum until I was 14 or 15 and all of my practising had been done in my bedroom on the top of this bureau – which happened to be a nice piece of furniture at one time, but some perverted Italian had painted it green and the top of it was all scabbed off from me beating it with the sticks. Finally my mother got me a drum and allowed me to practise out in the garage – just one snare drum.'

Zappa played his drum in the school orchestra and his first composition was a solo for snare drum entitled 'Mice'. It apparently dates from the summer of 1953, when Frank was twelve. Zappa: 'We had a year-end competition where you go out and play your little solo.'

He got his first record on his seventh birthday in 1947. It was 'All I Want For Christmas Is My Two Front Teeth' by Spike Jones and his City Slickers – a big Christmas hit that year. Frank liked it so much he wrote a fan letter to RCA Victor asking for a photograph. 'I was expecting a photograph of Spike Jones in the mail,' he told Charles Amirkhanian, 'but instead, I got a photograph of a man named George Rock, who was the actual vocalist on that tune, and he looked like a master criminal. It was, like, a frightening thing to receive in the mail.' In fact a photograph of Spike Jones, with his loud check suit and squashed-up, Mickey Rooney face, might have had a similar effect.

Zappa had a lot in common with Spike Jones: they were both perfectionists who only employed top-class musicians who were good sight readers and who were prepared to endure long rehearsals. Like Zappa's groups, Jones's musicians were expected to perform any crazy idea he might think up. The City Slickers were a comedy group and used a battery of unusual instruments to produce amusing sounds: washboards, pots and pans, doorbells, car-horns, cowbells and football rattles. Later he added pistols, guns and even a small cannon to his arsenal and employed a full-time arms roadie to look after them. As with Zappa's later bands, many of Spike Jones's players were fine jazz musicians and he always longed to produce more serious music. After the war, Jones formed a large dance band named the Other Orchestra to perform his more serious compositions, but it disbanded in 1946 after losing a lot of money (shades of Zappa's 1988 touring band). 'I used to love Spike Jones,' said Zappa. 'He had a lot of special instruments built to do all that stuff, like arrays of car-horns that you could honk that were in pitch. In the early sixties, when I moved to Los Angeles, they were having an auction of that equipment and I would have dearly loved to have bought it, but I had no money.'

In 1953 Zappa's father, exasperated by the cold foggy climate of Northern California, took a job as a metallurgist with Convair in Claremont, about 30 miles east of LA, on the edge of the open desert he had always dreamed of. (Claremont was used by George Lucas as the location for *American Graffiti*.) It was another quiet suburban community. 'Claremont's nice,' said Zappa. 'It's green. It's got little old ladies running round in electric karts.'

Zappa transferred to Claremont High School. The other students were polite, reserved, white conservative types who wore the Californian equivalent of Ivy League clothes and studied hard to graduate in order to go to one of the local colleges. But before Zappa could really settle and make new friends, his father was off again, this time to El Cajon, an eastern suburb of San Diego.

El Cajon was not all that different from Claremont. Francis worked on the Atlas missile project and Frank moved to Grossmont High School. The California climate appeared to be doing him good. His illnesses had disappeared and at 13 he was taller than his father.

Grossmont High was not quite as white middle-class as Claremont, but the majority of the students aspired to San Diego State or Tempe, Arizona, and studied hard for their diplomas. It was a large school with a marching band, cheerleaders, a student government and all the elements of the archetypal American high school that were later celebrated by the Coasters, Chuck Berry, Eddie Cochran, the Beach Boys, Gene Vincent, Gary US Bonds, Dee Clark and scores more.

Frank took part in student activities. He had been interested in art from an early age and at Grossmont High he won a prize for designing a poster for Fire Prevention Week in a competition involving 30 schools. Zappa's entry was headlined NO PICNIC and showed the faces of three disappointed looking children. Beneath it read: WHY? – NO WOODS. PREVENT FOREST FIRE.

Zappa was always very good at art, while his essays such as '50s Teenagers and 50s Rock' for *Evergreen Review* show that he could have been a writer. His parents had no interest in music and there was no radio or television in the house, so the only music Zappa heard as a child came from outside: movie soundtracks, background music to soap operas, the big band music that was still popular in the early fifties, which he heard at friends' houses. Zappa: 'I think the first music I heard that I liked was Arab music and I don't know where I ever ran into it, but I heard it someplace and that got me off right away.'

Then came the big breakthrough. Around the time of his thirteenth birthday, Frank was riding in the Henry J with his parents when 'Gee' by the Crows came on the radio, followed by the Velvets singing 'I'. 'It sounded fabulous,' said Zappa. 'My parents insisted it be dismissed from the radio, and I knew I was on to something . . .' (Incidentally, 'Gee' by the Crows was also Jerry Garcia of the Grateful Dead's first introduction to R&B, so it plays a key role in sixties American music.)

This was the music that moulded Zappa's musical sensibility. R&B was his first and last love. 'I think that one of my main influences, and probably one of the things that turned my ear around since the very beginning, is rhythm and blues,' he said. 'There's just something about it. The earliest, most primitive rhythm and blues. All different styles from Delta stuff to Doo Wop vocal groups. I just loved it because of what was in it. Not because of the nostalgic aroma that goes with it, but musically, because of the sound of it, and because of the feelings that the performers had in that music at that time. It really said something to me. It's something that I've always admired, a musical tradition that should be carried out into the future. I hate to see it go.'

In the summer of 1954 the Zappas acquired a Decca record player from the Smokey Rogers Music Store in El Cajon. It had a speaker on the bottom, raised on little triangular legs, and the pick-up arm needed a quarter balanced on it to ensure accurate tracking. Zappa remembered it as a 'really ugly piece of audio gear'. The record player came with some free 78s, including a copy of 'The Little Shoemaker' by the Gaylords, which had entered the Top 10 in July 1954. Rosie liked to play it while she did the ironing.

Now that he had something to play music on, Zappa bought his first record: a 78 of 'Riot In Cell Block Number 9' by the Robins on the Spark label. (In fact, the A-side was 'Wrap It Up', but the B-side became a classic.) It was a prescient purchase by the 13-year-old Zappa, as the Robins had not yet had their big hit 'Smokey Joe's Café', which prompted Carl Gardner and Bobby Nun to leave and form the Coasters. It showed Zappa's ear for quality. This record also occasioned his first public appearance. Zappa: 'The first thing I ever did in "show business" was to convince my little brother Carl to pretend he was my ventriloquist dummy, sit on my lap and lip-sync "Riot In Cell Block Number 9" by the Robins at the Los Angeles County Fair.'

This same flare for performance led Zappa to entertain his family: 'I used to build models (not from kits, because I couldn't follow the simple instructions). I used to build and sew clothes for puppets and marionettes. I used to give puppet shows using Stan Freberg records in the background.' Stan Freberg did impersonations and cartoon voices. Among his hits were 'Yellow Rose of Texas' (June 1955), and 'Nuttin' For Christmas' (December 1955). Zappa's second record purchase was 'Work With Me, Annie' by Hank Ballard and the Midnighters, the first of a series of records with 'Annie' in the title.

The two greatest influences on Zappa's music were R&B and the work of the French-born composer Edgard Varèse (1883–1965). R&B was on the jukebox and on the radio, but Varèse was virtually unknown to the general public. Zappa first heard of him in an article in a weekly magazine about Sam Goody's record store in New York, saying that

Goody was such a good salesman he could even sell *Ionisation* by Edgard Varèse, which the article described as 'nothing but drums – it's dissonant and terrible; the worst music in the world'. It included a photograph of Varèse that in Zappa's eyes made him look like a mad scientist. To Zappa, naturally, *Ionisation* sounded terrific and he made a note of the record number (EMS 401) and vowed to track it down.

In countless interviews and in his autobiography Zappa always stated that this article was in *Look* magazine, but the only mention of Varèse in *Look* during that entire period was a favourable review of *The Complete Works of Edgard Varèse, Volume One*, which appeared in Joseph Roddy's Record Guide column in November 1950 (when Zappa was nine). 'Varèse is unlike anything else in music,' wrote Roddy, 'and well worth knowing. The recording is excellent.' There was no record number and no mention of Sam Goody (whose store did not open until 1951). Zappa must have been thinking of a different publication. Greg Russo has identified a feature extolling Sam Goody's sales prowess in the 13 February 1952 issue of *People Today* magazine, but it does not mention Varèse. Perhaps one day some Zappa fanatic will unearth the review of *Ionisation* that so inspired him, but until then it remains a mystery.

Next the Zappas moved from El Cajon to San Diego proper and Frank transferred to the newly built Mission Bay High School on Grand Avenue next to the bay. It was a very different experience. Mission Bay was a transient neighbourhood filled with inner-city kids whose fathers worked in the Navy or the naval yards. 'It was definitely juvenile delinquent territory,' wrote Zappa. 'You wore a leather jacket and very very greasy hair. You carried a knife and a chain. If you were really bad, you mounted razor blades in the edge of your shoes for kicking. Also, you made sure you carved up the school's linoleum floor by wearing taps on your soles. If you failed to do any of these things you would (1) not get any sex-action and (2) probably be injured . . . Kids were proud of the violence in their schools. They didn't want to have some ninny school. They wanted a rough school.' Though Zappa did not drive, he was close to the car-club culture: 'In San Diego there were some very ferocious car clubs with these plaques that would drag on the pavement because the cars were lowered all the way around. The status car to own then was an icebox white '39 Chevvy with primer spots.'

The soundtrack to all of this was R&B: 'I used to know a lot of vicious teenage hoodlum-type characters who identified very strongly with that sort of music, because not only did the lyric content match their lifestyle, but the overall timbre of the music seemed to express the way they felt. And it sort of got my stamp of approval, too, so I just went out collecting every one of those records I could find.'

At Mission Bay High it was only girls and younger boys who liked Elvis Presley. San Diego is a good town for the blues and Zappa's circle preferred Howlin' Wolf, Muddy Waters and B. B. King. Frank's friends felt oppressed by everything. Zappa: 'The real gritty slang came from those guys who felt themselves so threatened that they would do everything they could to look hard, even if they didn't get a chance to act hard.'

Though Zappa appears to have been accepted by the leather-jacket set, he still felt like an outsider. In the much-quoted lyrics attributed to Frank in the 1964 rock operetta 'I Was A Teenage Malt Shop', he complained: 'I'm new at your high school, / no teenage girl to call my name / Jus' cause my daddy done work for the Government / I change schools 'till it's a cryin' shame // I'm just a mumbling round your schoolyard, wishin' someone would call my name / Lord I need some friendship 'til it hurts me / Why can't these people feel my pain?' Zappa's memories of teenage loneliness and alienation remained fresh a decade later. They were the kind of sentiments expressed in the blues and R&B records he most related to and he became an avid collector, seeking out obscurities and rarities all over town.

Zappa kept in touch with people from El Cajon, in particular David Franken, a friend from Grossmont High School. Franken lived in a small town called La Mesa, and he and Zappa went to check out the town's hi-fi store. There was a sale on R&B singles. Zappa found a couple of Joe Houston records he wanted and on his way to the cash register he flipped idly through the long-player rack. He found an album with a black and white sleeve of an intense-looking, middle-aged man with wiry hair. He looked like a mad scientist and Zappa thought how great it was that a mad scientist had finally made a record. Then it struck him – here was the record he had been searching for: *The Complete Works of Edgard Varèse, Volume One*, performed by the New York Wind Ensemble, Frederic Waldman conducting.

He returned the Joe Houston records and explored his pockets. Albums were an expensive luxury in the early fifties and Zappa had never bought one before. He asked the sales clerk how much it was.

'The grey one in the box? $5.95.'

Zappa had only $3.80, but he told the sales clerk he had been searching for this album for more than a year. The man had been using the album to demonstrate hi-fi sets, but it actually seemed to deter customers. If he wanted it so much, Zappa could have it for $3.80.

The family record player had never been set to play 33 1/3 before. Frank turned up the volume all the way and eased the stylus into *Ionisation* (1930–1). It was all he had hoped it would be. It is written for 13 percussionists who play 37 instruments, including two sirens, gongs, tam-tams, three different sizes of bass drum, chimes, two anvils, snare drums and a desiccated Cuban gourd. As crash cymbals shook the room, Frank's mother, aghast, forbade him from ever playing it in the living room again. Frank protested that he wanted to listen to it all the way through, so Rosie insisted that he take the record player into his bedroom. She never heard 'The Little Shoemaker' again.

Even to the casual listener, the influence of Varèse (and especially *Ionisation*) on Zappa's music is obvious. The use of blocks of sound, timbre rather than pitch and varying time signatures are all hallmarks of his work. Zappa played the record over and over and read and re-read Stanley Finkelstein's scholarly sleeve notes, puzzling over the more technical musical references: 'Timbre holds a central place in Varèse's musical thinking. To borrow an idea from the title of one of his works, each instrumental timbre has, to him, its own "density" or solidity and weight. It shapes the music in its own characteristic way . . .'

Finkelstein's notes also contained the Varèse quote 'The present-day composer refuses to die,' which Zappa took as his motto. In fact it is a misquotation from the charter manifesto presented by Varèse to the International Composers' Guild on 31 May 1921. Varèse actually said: 'Dying is the privilege of the weary. The present-day composers refuse to die. They have realized the necessity of banding together and fighting for the right of the individual to secure a fair and free presentation of his work. It is out of such a collective will that the International Composers' Guild was born.' Given Zappa's general antipathy towards working with anyone else on an equal basis, it is a curious epigram for him to adopt.

Zappa played the *Complete Works of Edgard Varèse, Volume One* to anyone who would listen. He even marked his favourite passages with chalk in order to find them quickly, which he understood was how radio DJs did it. Zappa: 'What I used to do was play them parts of the Varèse album, and then play them Lightnin' Slim things like "My Starter Won't Work" or "Have Your Way" or I'd play them some Howlin' Wolf . . . Usually that would get rid of the girls and the ignorant boys and what was left over was somebody you could have a conversation with.' But on the whole, his friends tended towards Rosie's view of 'sound set free', as Varèse called it.

Varèse was not as obscure an influence as Zappa thought. Many of his contemporaries grew up listening to *Ionisation*: Phil Lesh of the Grateful Dead, Marty Balin from the Jefferson Airplane and all the members of Soft Machine, for example. The difference being, they heard Varèse in context, whereas Zappa was stuck in suburbia, far removed from those cultural circles where he might encounter the Vienna School.

In his notes, Finkelstein said that Varèse came from the generation of Béla Bartók (1881–1945), Igor Stravinsky (1882–1971) and Anton Webern (1883–1945) so Zappa immediately added them to his list of composers to investigate. The second long-player he bought was a cheap Camden label recording of Stravinsky's *Rite of Spring*, played by the World Wide Orchestra (actually the Boston Symphony Orchestra, conducted by Pierre Monteux, but re-issued under a different name by RCA Victor to avoid paying royalties). 'I loved Stravinsky almost as much as I loved Varèse,' Zappa later wrote.

He made no distinction between these composers and the R&B vocal groups he loved. To Zappa it was all good music: 'What appealed to me in the Varèse album was that the writing was so direct. It was like, here is a guy who's writing dissonant music and he's not fucking around. And here's a group called the Robins, and they don't seem like they were fucking around, either. They were having a good time. Certainly Hank Ballard and the Midnighters sounded like they were having a good time. And although harmonically, rhythmically, and in many other superficial ways it was very different, the basic soul of the music seemed to me to be coming from the same universal source.'

Frank's favourite record in the spring of 1955 was 'Angel In My Life' by the Jewels. To find out why he liked the record so much he took it to Mr Kavelman, his band instructor at Mission Bay High and asked him to explain the attraction.

'Parallel fourths,' came the reply.

It was Kavelman who first played Webern's Symphony Op.21 and some of the string quartets to Zappa. He also introduced him to the principles of twelve-tone music. This is when Zappa first began to write music and it is likely that Kavelman also tried to explain the principles of musical notation to him. Either way, he was a good teacher and Zappa acknowledged his debt to him in his autobiography.

The appeal of seeing notes on the page came originally from Zappa's interest in art. 'I liked the way music looked on paper,' he said. 'It was fascinating to me that you see the notes and somebody who knew what they were doing would look at them and music would come out. I thought it was a miracle.' Zappa had always been interested in graphics, and spent much of his time in school drawing pictures. Musical notation seemed like another form of art: 'I got a C5 Speedball pen and a jar of Higgins India ink and some music paper and, *shit, I could draw those.*'

The difficulty lay in getting somebody to play it so he could hear what it sounded like (a perennial problem for Zappa). In 1992 he was asked if he had been able to hear the music in his head as he wrote it down. 'Absolutely not!' he said. 'I didn't have the faintest fucking idea of what it sounded like. I mean, I was so ignorant. I thought that all you did was you got an idea for the way it looked, you drew it, and then you found a musician who could read it – and that's how you did it. I was literally that naïve . . . Once you understand what the audio result is going to be of that dot that you just drew, then you hear it yourself as a writer.'

Frank joined his first group at Mission Bay High School. They were called the Ramblers and were led by Elwood 'Junior' Madeo, also known as 'Bomba the Jungle Boy' because of his Indian-Italian parentage. Elwood played lead guitar. Zappa: 'He was really excellent and I used to love to hear him play.' Elwood's brother remembered 'Frank was great, but he did often play too loud then . . . It took a while before Frank persuaded El to let him join the band . . . Most of the time they practised in our garage.'

They also rehearsed at the home of the pianist, Stuart Congdon. His father was a preacher and would not allow Frank's snare drum into the house, but Frank was permitted to beat on a pair of cooking pots: 'I'm sitting there trying to play shuffles on these two pots between my legs!' Now that he was in a group, Frank was able to talk his parents into spending $50 on a complete kit: a kick drum, a snare, one floor tom, one 15" Zyn ride cymbal and a little Zyn high-hat. He got them a week before the group's first gig.

It was at the Uptown Hall in San Diego in the Hillcrest district at 48th and Mead. Zappa: 'I remember it well, going to my first gig: I got over there, set up my drums, and noticed I had forgotten my only pair of sticks. And I lived way on the other side of town.' In those days many of the dances in San Diego were promoted by girl gangs who would book the hall, hire the band, hang crêpe paper on the walls and run the box office. The Ramblers' first gig was sponsored by a girl gang called the Blue Velvets who paid them $7 for their efforts. They played covers, mostly Little Richard numbers like 'Directly From My Heart To You' (which later entered the Mothers' repertoire).

Frank played a number of gigs before Elwood decided his performance was not up to scratch. 'He fired me because I couldn't keep a good beat,' said Zappa, 'and because I played the cymbals too much. I wasn't a very good drummer. My main drawback was that I didn't have very good hand-to-foot coordination. I could play a lot of stuff on the snare and the tom-toms and the cymbal and everything, but I couldn't keep an even beat on the kick drum. That was the reason I became no longer employed as a drummer – nobody could dance to it!' Many years later Zappa flew Elwood down from San Francisco to LA several times for recording sessions, so he continued to hold his playing in high regard.

There were a lot of bands in San Diego and Frank saw as many as he could. Zappa: 'It's almost impossible to convey what the R&B scene was like in San Diego. There were gangs there, and every gang was loyal to a particular band. They weren't called groups, they were called bands. They were mostly Negro and Mexican, and they tried to get the baddest sound they could. It was very important not to sound like jazz. And there was a real oral tradition of music. Everybody played the same songs, with the same arrangements, and they tried to play as close as possible to the original record. But the thing was that half the time the guys in the band had never heard the record – somebody's older brother would own the record, and the kid would memorize it and teach it to everybody else. At one point all the bands in San Diego were playing the same arrangement of "Okey Dokey Stomp" by Clarence "Gatemouth" Brown. The amazing thing was that it sounded almost note for note like the record.'

One of the really popular local bands was the Blue Notes, featuring Wilbur Whitfield. Zappa: 'We were all very proud of Wilbur when he escaped from San Diego and went to Los Angeles to record on the Aladdin label.' 'P. B. Baby' by Little Wilbur (Whitfield) & the Pleasers – with its memorable chorus of 'piddly piddly all the time' – was released on 7 May 1957.

San Diego is only ten miles from the border and as well as absorbing black R&B culture, Zappa was influenced by the many Mexicans at school and on the scene. The young Mexican-Americans were Pachucos (a Latino term for juvenile delinquents). They had their own style of clothes and music and drove chopped-down Low Riders. Frank affected baggy Pachuco zoot suit pants with pegged bottoms and grew a little moustache. His speech took on a slightly mocking tone. Even the blacks in Los Angeles absorbed something of a Pachuco accent, as can be heard in groups like the Medallions and the Five Satins, who drawl 'lahrve' for 'love' and extend 'I' to sound like 'Aiiii'.

The 15-year-old Zappa still retained his childhood interest in explosives. He and a schoolfriend experimented with a new mixture and manufactured enough to fill a quart mayonnaise jar with a combination of solid rocket fuel (half powdered zinc, half sulphur) and stink-bomb powder. On Open House night at Mission Bay High, while parents discussed their offspring with the teachers, Frank and his friend took a stack of paper cups from the cafeteria, filled them with the powder and passed them out to their gang, who proceeded to start a number of small, evil-smelling fires throughout the school. Zappa stored the leftover mixture in his locker. The next day Frank found his locker wired shut and during Miss Ivancic's English class he was invited to visit the Dean's office. From there he was escorted to the police station. Rosie had been summoned, arriving with Carl and baby Candy. Frank was hauled over the coals by the San Diego fire marshal. He was suspended from school for two weeks and had to write a 2,000-word essay. After a fortnight Zappa returned with a list of all the R&B records in his possession and all those he hoped to acquire in the near future, catalogued by song title, artist and record label. The school was not amused and he only avoided expulsion because the probation officer was Italian. Rosie convinced him her son was a good Catholic boy really. In any case, her husband was about to be transferred to Lancaster, California, so they would soon be leaving and taking their pyromaniac son with them.

3 Lancaster, CA

In the summer of 1956 Francis Zappa finally realized his dream of living in the desert when he moved his family to Lancaster, California, a town of about 20,000 people 2,300 feet up in the Mojave desert, 80 miles to the north of LA. At the extreme edge of LA county, Lancaster was unincorporated and only became a city in its own right in 1977.

When the Zappas moved there, Lancaster was in the middle of an unprecedented boom. Fuelled by the expansion of the Edwards Airforce base to the north and by Airforce Plant 42 in Palmdale, five miles to the south, the population grew from 3,500 in 1950, to 28,000 in 1960. (It is now almost half a million.) The old time residents were mostly cattlemen or alfalfa farmers; you could always tell High Desert residents because the fine wind-blown sand had pitted their windscreens and scarred their paint jobs. They greatly resented the changes brought by the defence workers – the people from 'down below' they called them, referring to anyone who was not from the High Desert – with their city ways and demands. The newcomers were appalled to find themselves living in a wilderness with none of the usual amenities; nothing to do and nowhere to go. They looked at the farmers and realized they had moved to the sticks. 'One of the worst places I ever lived,' Francis admitted. His son agreed.

Theresa Colimore died and Rosie inherited enough money for the family to buy a tract home. 45438 3rd Street East was a four-bedroom, two-bathroom, stucco bungalow with a low gabled roof on a newly built street on the northern edge of the town near the fairgrounds, so new that they could smell the paint when they moved in. It was a state-of-the-art American suburban home complete with an intercom in every room, a fireplace and a breakfast bar with a set of high stools in the kitchen. The attached garage was side on to the street so you had to turn to get into it. There was a concrete sidewalk, some newly planted shade trees and chain-link storm fencing surrounding each property.

Third Street ended at the north end of the block, at a T-junction with the unimaginatively named East Avenue H 8. Beyond that was the vast emptiness of the Mojave Desert. There was no side-walk on the desert side of the street, just a few telephone poles, car tyres, broken bottles, a couple of beaten up yucca trees and automobile-tracks continuing 3rd Street on out into the open desert. There is a light scattering of wind-blown sand extending out into the street. It is a wide low vista, the almost flat horizon broken only by the occasional utility post, yucca or sagebrush, silhouetted against the intense blue sky. The average summer temperature is in the high nineties and the streets shimmer in a heat haze. Tumbleweed rolls down the empty streets.

With limitless desert all around, the town sprawled in all directions along the usual grid system, and even now many of the blocks contain only one or two buildings. It is impossible to get anywhere without a car except in the few blocks of the original downtown. Three blocks to the west of the Zappa household ran the Southern Pacific Railroad main line, where, if you missed the crossing, you could wait up to half an hour while a three-mile long freight train slowly pulled through the town, bells clanging, whistle wailing, on its way to LA.

Frank had no illusions about it: 'I lived on a tract of little stucco houses. Okies with cars dying in their yards. You know how you always have to pull up a Chevrolet and let it croak on your lawn . . .' This may have happened later, but when they moved in the houses were brand new and the road newly laid. Little has changed in the half century;

the street has not been extended and the neighbourhood appears frozen in a fifties time warp.

Once more the Zappa family found themselves in the difficult position of getting to know new neighbours, and the children had to make new friends. Fortunately, most of the school children were new to the place too, just as everyone was new to the block. Kids played ball on the street and sat on the front porch eating watermelon and spitting the seeds at each other. Zappa's father put up a swing set and built a raised Doughboy swimming pool for them in the backyard. For Zappa, however, life was difficult as he once more faced the loneliness of having no friends.

Francis Zappa's restless and often pointless roaming meant that his family was unable to form any long-term friendships. They grew wary of investing time and emotional energy in getting to know people when at any point he might uproot them again. He never seems to have considered the psychological strain on his family or more likely he did not notice. He always had a job to go to where he fitted right in with the other defence workers and their secret projects, so he never suffered from a sense of dislocation and loneliness. His eldest son, however, grew isolated and introspective.

In later life, Frank claimed to have no friends. His only friends, he insisted, were his family; everyone else just worked for him. And so his childhood experience remained with him for a lifetime. His father's quest for the land of the cowboys caused a permanent emotional blockage: Frank was never able to freely express his emotions and had great difficulty forming intimate, long-term friendships.

Antelope Valley High School (AVHS) on Division Street at the corner of Lancaster Boulevard was within walking distance and it was here that Frank resumed his education. Covered walkways connected the classrooms to protect the students from the fierce sun. Frank was only 15 and had already attended six high schools – the damaging effect on his education was plain to see. In other circumstances a boy of Zappa's intelligence would have gone on to university. As it was, he behaved badly in class and didn't even get enough credits to graduate; they only gave him a diploma to get rid of him.

His way of fitting in was to resume his role as class clown, only in a more disruptive form. He was attracted to the Pachucos, preferring to hang out with the Mexican-Americans rather than aspire to join the Senior Cabinet, wear a suit and tie, and maybe date a girl from the Sewing Club. He became something of a nutty dresser, affecting white socks, Oxford shoes, pleated pants and a salt and pepper sports coat. However, aside from the need for some friends, he was intrigued by the Pachuco lifestyle from an anthropological point of view, always keeping a certain distance, observing their lifestyle and customs as if on a field trip.

Instead of accepting the status quo, he began to question things, with predictable results. Zappa: 'Can you imagine a nation who never questions the validity of cheerleaders and pom-poms? At Lancaster, the cheerleaders had such an importance, boola boola wasn't enough for them; they were running what you call the student government, too. They were just pigs. It was too American for me.' The cheerleaders wore short dresses with bandboy braids across the front and carried batons with a duck head on the end. It is easy to see why Frank couldn't relate to the values promoted by his student government.

In his search for alternative ideas and values he read more, beginning with his father's books, then frequenting the Lancaster County library. One of the subjects under scrutiny was Catholicism. As far as Rosie and Francis were concerned, their son was still devout. He went with them to Mass at Sacred Heart church, a few blocks from his school, and fasted three hours and confessed before taking communion on Sunday. However, much of his spare time was spent reading books on comparative religion, from Buddhism to Zoroastrianism.

At 18 he decided the Catholic Church was not for him. Giving it up, however, was not so easy, and the psychological programming of all those years of churchgoing stayed with him always. He had been taught to think that sex was a sin, masturbation was a sin, sex outside marriage was a sin and even that sex inside marriage was a sin, unless the intention was to conceive a child. Any sexual thought or action made him feel guilty; he had been taught to be ashamed of his body, its natural desires and functions. Had he not seen the charts and maps showing the levels of purgatory and hell awaiting those who disobeyed Catholic doctrine? Zappa concluded it was a medieval control system based on fear and guilt that crippled normal relations between the sexes and was the cause of untold misery and suffering.

His rejection of Catholicism affected him in many ways. His desire to have complete control over his life – his musicians and staff often described him as a 'control freak' – has its origin, in part, in his rejection of the authority of the Catholic church. Much that was juvenile and prurient in his work makes more sense when seen as an over-reaction to Catholic guilt. A lot of his sexually themed songs are virtually incomprehensible to non-Catholics who are not shocked or offended, just puzzled by his obsession with the subject. To Catholics they made sense: it was like shouting 'Fuck!' in church.

Zappa's future identity was rapidly forming as his creativity came to the fore, but he had little opportunity to express it. Had he remained in San Diego, he might have gone straight into another group, but in Lancaster he knew nobody and there only seemed to be cowboy music on the radio. Zappa: 'There weren't any cultural opportunities in Lancaster. You couldn't just go to a concert. There was nothing.' Unable to play music, the 15-year-old Zappa's creativity found another channel. In 1956, shortly after arriving in Lancaster, he began his first experiments with film.

His father owned an 8mm Kodak wind-up cine-camera. Zappa: 'For my first film I tied a piece of clothes line to the view-finder, turned on the camera and swung it around until the spring ran out. I then re-shot the same roll of film several times. Eventually I shot and edited on a short piece of film for the title "Motion".' This type of superim-position of random images was used to critical acclaim by a number of experimental American filmmakers in the early sixties. Zappa was interested in the cinema throughout his life. He made several films and planned many more. Though his work was unorthodox, it was parallel to, rather than part of, the experimental tradition in America.

Frank continued to play his two classical albums. On his sixteenth birthday (not his fifteenth, as he always claimed) he used a $5 gift from his mother to make a long-distance phone call to Varèse. He assumed

Varèse lived in Greenwich Village, the natural habitat for weird composers and artists, and when he called New York information, Varèse was right there in the phone book.

The composer's wife Louise answered and told Frank her husband was in Brussels, but that he should call again in a few weeks, which he did. Zappa: 'I don't remember what I said to him exactly, but it was something like "I really dig your music." He told me he was working on a new piece called *Deserts*. This thrilled me quite a bit since I was living in Lancaster, California, then. When you're fifteen [*sic*] and living in the Mojave Desert and find out that the world's greatest composer, somewhere in a secret Greenwich Village laboratory, is working on a song about your "home town" you can get pretty excited.' Zappa mentioned that he was planning a trip back east and Varèse told him to write when he knew his dates so they could meet.

Zappa had amassed a sizeable collection of R&B records, but was understandably frustrated at not being able to lay his hands on any more in Lancaster. This was the classic era of R&B and Doo Wop with bands like the Platters, the Spaniels, the Penguins, Clyde McPhatter and the Drifters, the Flamingos, the Dells and dozens more breaking into the pop charts. When he had saved enough money, Zappa would make the long trip all the way to San Diego to the store on the ground floor of the Maryland Hotel that sold ex-jukebox Excello releases.

Excello would only supply their R&B releases to stores that took their gospel records as well, which effectively meant they only sold in black neighbourhoods. Zappa: 'In Lancaster there wasn't any rock 'n' roll, unless you listened to it on a record. Most of the people who liked R&B were not the white sons and daughters of the alfalfa farmers or defence workers who lived there. There were a number of Mexicans and a lot of black kids and they liked that kind of stuff. So I put together this racially mixed ensemble that liked to play that kind of music. We banged our heads against the wall just like every other garage band, trying to figure out how to play it. There's no guide book.'

They called themselves the Black-Outs, because several members had the unfortunate habit of passing out after drinking peppermint schnapps, their beverage of choice. There is some dispute about the line-up, but in their first incarnation they probably included Wayne Lyles on vocals and bongos; Johnny Franklin on alto sax; Dwight Bement on tenor sax; Ernie Thomas on trumpet; Terry Wimberly on piano; and Frank on drums. In *The Real Frank Zappa Book*, Zappa gives a different line-up, dropping Bement and Thomas and adding Fred Salazar on horn and Wally Salazar on guitar, along with Carter Franklin, whose instrument we don't know. Johnny Franklin, Carter Franklin and Wayne Lyles were black and the Salazar brothers were Mexican. They were the only R&B band in the Mojave Desert.

The Black-Outs learned ten songs, including 'Kansas City', 'Behind the Sun' by the Rockin' Brothers, Clarence 'Gatemouth' Brown's 'Okie Dokie Stomp', Little Richard's 'Directly From My Heart To You' and André Williams and His New Group (the Don Juans)'s 'Bacon Fat' – also known as 'Diddle Diddle Womp Womp', which Zappa played with the Mothers and with his own lyrics on *Broadway the Hard Way* (1989). Their uniform – every band had to have a uniform in those days – consisted of brown plaid or dark blue lamé shirts and baggy white pegged pants with metal belts that could be used as weapons in case of trouble. In fact, most of the money they made went on the uniforms.

In 1954 a big touring show consisting of tenor player Big Jay McNeely, Joe Houston, Marvin and Johnny and some other R&B acts had played the fairgrounds in Lancaster. Their shows were designed to incite the audience to a fever pitch, with so-called 'shoot-outs' between stars like Houston and McNeely (whose stage antics were legendary). No one in Lancaster had seen anything like it before and it made the authorities very nervous.

The new 'teenage' phenomenon had arrived (there had been no label for that age group in the forties) and the city fathers did not know how to react. Each day they read horror stories in the Los Angeles newspapers about juvenile delinquents, gangs and the dangers of marijuana and, sure enough, along with the R&B groups came an entourage of dope dealers, while the show also attracted teenagers from all over the Mojave. As a consequence, the Lancaster authorities were less than pleased when the Black-Outs arrived on the scene.

It was hard for an integrated group to find gigs in a place like

Lancaster and they spent more time rehearsing than performing. The Black-Outs were not allowed to play at high-school dances, so they had to mount their own events. About 20 miles south of town, to the east of Palmdale on Palmdale Boulevard around 90th Street, there was a black community called Sun Village. They were the people, mostly turkey farmers and their families, who supported the group. The Black-Outs sometimes played dances at the Village Inn and often rehearsed there.

Frank now had a part-time job in a record store run by a woman called Elsie, who promoted the infamous 1954 touring show. Frank asked her to hire the Lancaster Women's Club for a dance on his behalf. Everything went well: tickets were sold, the band rehearsed, posters went up around town. But a day before the show, Zappa was walking along Lancaster Boulevard in the small downtown section of Lancaster at 6 p.m. when he was arrested for vagrancy, presumably to hold him just long enough for the show to be cancelled. He spent the night in jail, but Elsie and his outraged father bailed him out the next morning. 'It was right out of a teenage movie,' said Zappa. 'But the dance went off anyway.'

A large contingent of Sun Valley students turned up and it was a great success. A school friend of Frank's, Jim 'Motorhead' Sherwood, danced with the band. He did 'The Bug' in which he attempted to shake off some horrible creature that was tickling him; he twitched and shook and rolled around the stage trying to get it off. Eventually he managed to throw it into the audience, hoping that some of the girls would pick up on it. Afterwards, the band were loading their equipment into the trunk of Johnny Franklin's blue Studebaker when they were surrounded by a group of white farmers' sons, aspiring varsity men with letter sweaters, who wanted to show the Black-Outs that an integrated group was not welcome in their honky little town. Fortunately a number of Sun Valley residents were still in the parking lot and they immediately produced tyre-irons and chains from the trunks of their cars and advanced upon the white boys, who fled. From that moment on until graduation, relations between the Black-Outs and the lettermen were strained to the point of hostility. 'They didn't like me, and I knew they didn't like me,' said Zappa, 'and I didn't like them.'

All of this caused friction between Frank and his father. Francis objected to what he called 'screaming nigger music' on the radio. Now his son was playing it on-stage in a racially mixed group and getting arrested, which threatened his own security clearance. Band rehearsals caused further altercations between father and son. Frank would telephone Rosie to get her to drive him home after rehearsals and she often stayed up late, waiting for his call. This infuriated Francis, who thought Frank should make his own way home.

This wasn't their only difference of opinion. They argued over religion (Frank's investigations into his faith upset Rosie and angered Francis). They argued over Frank's girlfriend and over Frank's sloppy school work. As an immigrant, Francis had high hopes for his eldest son, and in his eyes Frank was just letting opportunity drift away. Fathers often argue with their teenage sons, but the old Sicilian patriarch was more obdurate than most, and his son equally stubborn.

Zappa continued to experiment with musical composition. He bought a copy of H. A. Clarke's *Counterpoint: Strict and Free* (1928), the second page of which began: 'Never write any of the following successions . . .', then gave musical examples with explanations. 'Numbers 1 and 2 are very harsh. Numbers 3 and 4 are not so harsh and of common occurrence in modern usage.' The intervals were F and A, a major third, expanding to E and B, a fifth. Clarke also said you could not write G and B, a major third, expanding to F and C, a fifth. Frank played them on the piano. 'Why?' he wondered. '*Why* can't we do this? This sounds great!' He never read any further.

Antelope Valley High's record library had a good collection of Folkways recordings: everything from a ceremony in a Zen monastery in Japan to a recording of an Eskimo scraping a hole in the ice to fish. Zappa listened to Tibetan and Arab music, sea shanties and Hungarian gypsy songs. He also got into the new jazz: albums like Ornette Coleman's *Something Else!* (1958) and *Tomorrow Is The Question* (1959), plus Cecil Taylor's *Jazz Advance* (1956) and *Looking Ahead* (1958). It is Coleman and Taylor, and later Eric Dolphy – Zappa especially liked his work on Oliver Nelson's *Blues and the Abstract Truth* (1961) – that provide the basis for Zappa's understanding of jazz. It was their sound he was looking for in later years whenever he demanded a jazz riff or a squealing saxophone solo.

Also in the school library Frank found an orchestration book with examples, including an excerpt from Varèse's *Offrandes*, with a lot of harp notes that impressed him very much. 'You know how groovy harp notes look,' he wrote in 'Edgard Varèse: Idol of My Youth'. 'I remember fetishing the book for several weeks.'

As a drummer Frank was required to play in the marching band at football matches. They had to wear maroon and grey uniforms and strike up the band every time Lancaster scored a touchdown. Zappa: 'The only reason I got trained as a musician was because the school needed a marching band at its football games. It was just another tool to support the sports programme. I never did enjoy sports . . . That really got me thinking, how can you take any of this seriously?' One day, he was taking a cigarette break under the bleachers when he was caught by William Ballard, his music instructor. It was not forbidden to smoke, but to smoke in uniform was a heinous crime and Frank, to his delight, was thrown off the team.

Ballard was actually sympathetic towards Frank and helped him in other ways. Zappa could never properly assess his musical compositions unless he heard them, so Ballard arranged for the school orchestra to play them. Frank wrote out the parts in chalk on the blackboard and, with him conducting, his bewildered schoolmates played their way through 'The String Quartet', a composition that included the pieces known eleven years later as 'Sleeping In A Jar' and 'A Pound For A Brown On The Bus' when they appeared on *Uncle Meat*.

He made sure the results were dissonant. The school used a tuning device that put out a tone. There were two settings: A and B flat. The B flat was used by the marching band and the A was used by the school orchestra. Frank took the first violins and tuned them to the A, then tuned the second violins to B flat, guaranteeing that whatever they played would be dissonant, no matter what notes appeared on the score. There were musical staves painted on the blackboard, and

Ballard let Frank write out enormously dense chords on the blackboard and then tell all the different players which of the notes was going to be theirs. Then he would conduct a downbeat and Frank could hear for the first time what he had written: 'Some of them were so dense it just sounded like wind – there wasn't even any harmony coming out. But how are you going to find out what these things would sound like if you don't get a chance to hear them played by instruments? He saved me a lot of effort in later life just by letting me hear things like that. Of course, the other people in the orchestra thought I was out of my fucking mind.'

Zappa had been introduced to serial music by Mr Kavelman at Mission Bay High, who played him pieces by Berg, Webern, Hauer and Krenek. Serialism, also known as the twelve-tone system, evolved in the early years of the twentieth century as a reaction against the overused musical platitudes of romanticism. Led by Arnold Schoenberg and other post-Wagner avant-garde composers, it rapidly became the principal form of expression of musical modernism. Frank was keen to try it because it seemed so simple. The composer took the twelve notes of the chromatic scale and played them so that none of the notes was repeated until all the others were used. Schoenberg invented the method in about 1922 and it was immediately taken up by his ex-pupil Anton Webern.

To Frank it seemed almost too easy. All he had to do was make sure that he didn't repeat a note until all eleven other notes had been played, nor did he have to worry about what it sounded like because the intrinsic value of the music was determined arithmetically by how well the twelve notes had been manipulated. But he was not to be a serialist: 'I finally got a chance to hear some of it, and I really didn't like the way it sounded, so I stopped doing it.' Nevertheless, the influence of serialism remained and Zappa always referred to Webern as one of his favourite composers.

In those days the saxophone was still the principal instrument on R&B records, but Frank always preferred a good guitar solo: 'The solos were never long enough – they only gave them one chorus, and I figured the only way I was going to get to hear enough of what I wanted to hear was to get an instrument and play it myself.' His father had played the guitar in college and still had one in the house. Frank's brother Bobby had taught himself to play chords on it and Frank had tried to play it, but it didn't feel as good to him as the one Bobby had bought for $1.50 in an auction. Bobby gave it to Frank.

It had an arch-top and a T hole. The base was cracked and the strings were so high off the fretboard that you couldn't play chords on it, so Frank started off playing melodic lines. He liked it because although it was an acoustic guitar, it came close to the wiry tone he enjoyed in Johnny 'Guitar' Watson, especially if he picked it right next to the bridge. Zappa: '[Bobby] learned to play the guitar before I did. He knew chords, so I used to make him play chords in the background while I played lead lines. Once I'd figured out that the pitch changed when you put your finger down on the fret, I was hell on wheels.'

About a year later, Frank decided it was essential that he know chords, so he took his father's guitar away from Bobby and – with Bobby's help and by studying photographs and watching other local bands – he worked out the basic chord changes. Frank added a DeArmond soundhole pick-up, so though it wasn't a real electric guitar, it was at least an amplified guitar. Then he bought a Mickey Baker instruction book and taught himself from that. He had been listening to Johnny 'Guitar' Watson, Clarence 'Gatemouth' Brown, Joe Houston, Guitar Slim (Eddie Jones), Lightnin' Slim (Otis V. Hicks), Matt Murphy and others for years. Now he studied their guitar solos until he had a solid grounding in the blues.

By the new year Frank was happier than he had been on arriving in Lancaster, but he still felt ambivalent about living there. He was frustrated at being 80 miles from LA, the home town of many of his favourite groups: the Cadets, the Robins, the Olympics, the Medallions, the Platters, the Jacks, Don Julian and the Meadowlarks, the Jewels, the Teen Queens, the Coasters, Etta James, Jesse Belvin and Johnny Otis, whose moustache and 'imperial' goatee Frank was in the process of cultivating. On the other hand, he had his own R&B group and even a few friends, including Danny Wally, who lived next door and would join the Mothers in 1975 on slide guitar; and Jim Sherwood ('Motorhead'), who would play saxophone with the original Mothers of Invention.

Frank had even managed to lose his virginity. Zappa: 'It was at her house when her parents weren't home; at my house either my mother or my brothers or my sister were always around. It was really putrid – neither of us had the vaguest notion what to do of course. I never saw her afterward – for some reason she never wanted to talk to me again.' The path through adolescence was a very rocky one in the fifties; there was no sex education and for a loner like Frank it was painful and embarrassing to be in a position where you didn't know what to do or how to behave.

However, he was beginning to cultivate his image. Motorhead: 'Frank used to sit out on the front lawn at the high school when I was a freshman and he had this old beat-up guitar. It was an old acoustic, with the frets really high. It had been in a fire and was all burnt up.' Motorhead was in the same year as Bobby and when Bobby discovered he collected blues records, he introduced him to Frank who now had a part-time job as the buyer in a record shop. Frank embarked on 'a campaign to upgrade the musical taste of the community' by stocking records like 'Tell Me Darling' by the Gaylords and 'Oh What a Night' by the Dells. He also discovered Gilbert's Dime Store, which had a rack of ex-jukebox records at a dime each where he could stock up on Excello records and other R&B rarities. Mr Gilbert let Frank and Motorhead check through each batch of records as they came in.

Best of all, Frank now had a girlfriend and was having sex, though foolishly they did not use any birth control. Zappa: 'I was truly blessed that I had a teenage girlfriend who lived three doors away from me. So, yeah, I was having a wonderful time in high school.' Sadly, it didn't last. 'Eventually the girl I was going out with in high school, her parents decided that we shouldn't be so serious and they moved away so that I couldn't see her any more.' This must have been Sandy, the blonde who used to disappear into Frank's bedroom whenever she came over. Frank's father would station himself at the kitchen table with an eye on Frank's bedroom door.

'Dad didn't like her,' recalled Zappa's sister Candy. 'That was clear.' Francis suspected them of having sex in his house, which, as a Catholic, he could not tolerate; on the other hand, he could hardly burst in and confront them. A few years later, when Frank and Kay Sherman moved in together, Francis would not allow Frank's siblings to visit them because they were living in sin. He only relented when they married.

Meanwhile, Frank was living the proverbial fifties teenage life of sex, sun, Doo Wop records and monster movies: Gene Fowler Jr's *I Was a Teenage Werewolf* was a favourite, along with Roger Corman's classic *Not Of This Earth*, both released in 1957. In his essay '50s Teenagers and 50s Rock', Zappa fondly recalled those days: 'There was this one theatre in Lancaster where, looking down the seats, you'd see a head here, another one there, fine, but then you'd see some huddled lump of blankets or clothes that was moving, and then another and another. And then you'd notice all these bodies jammed in weird positions against the walls – Kama Sutra 375 with a leg sticking up – and the monster was happening on the screen. It was really great!'

He looked forward to lunchtime, because just down the street from the school was a coffee-shop where he would eat a bowl of chilli (his favourite meal) with crackers and a bottle of Royal Crown Cola, while listening to the jukebox. Opal and Chester who owned the place agreed to ask the jukebox supplier to include some of Frank's favourite records, and so, as he told Nigel Leigh for a BBC TV documentary: 'I had the ability to eat good chilli and listen to "Three Hours Past Midnight" by Johnny "Guitar" Watson for most of my junior and senior years.'

Watson's solo on the record was absorbed deep into Zappa's consciousness and several of his phrases occurred in Frank's later work: 'One of the things I admired about him was his tone, this wiry, kind of nasty, aggressive and penetrating tone, and another was the fact that the things that he would play would often come out as rhythmic outbursts over the constant beat of the accompaniment . . . It seemed to me that was the correct way to approach it, because it was like talking or singing over a background. There was a speech influence to the rhythm.' Watson often plays ahead of the beat and takes great risks to resolve a break. He has a hard, unforgiving tone. It is easy to see his influence on Zappa's guitar style.

Frank grew increasingly restless and with the advent of the summer vacation Rosie suggested he make a trip back east to expand his horizons. 'This letter is going to be kind of a questionnaire,' he wrote to Aunt Mary. 'The question being, "Could you find some space for me if I were to come and visit you and Uncle Robert?" . . . The reason for the trip is twofold. Firstly, I would like to see the East again and all the relatives (most of which I probably couldn't recognize by face at all) back there. The second reason is that I think I have invented something new in the way of music (probably not), which I would like to take to the conservatory back there for investigation. If I did come I would not stay long, and I would help out around the house any way that I could, so please consider this request and write soon.'

Robert and Maria Cimino had no children of their own and were delighted to receive him. So Frank made the four-day train journey back to Baltimore where his aunt and uncle greeted him at Penn Station. Zappa: 'My relatives were shocked to see the way I looked. They were all so horrified that I think I was an embarrassment to them. I was accused of rampant drapery.' Zappa arrived in full East LA Pachuco array: Cuban heels, long drape jacket, baggy Zoot suit pants pegged so tight at the ankles that he could hardly get his feet through them, his long greasy black hair combed up into a pompadour, long sideboards, moustache and wispy goatee. To Aunt Mary and Uncle Robert he looked like a juvenile delinquent.

Zappa sat out on the porch at 4805 Loch Raven Boulevard, North Baltimore near Morgan State University, and spent his time trying to meet girls – without success. 'At the time I got back, the girls were very, very Catholic and tended not to be stimulated by people who had my kind of appearance,' he told Rafael Alvarez. He also shocked his relatives by taking a bus to West Baltimore, the black section of town, in search of R&B records. After all, the Orioles came from Baltimore; they were discovered singing on the corner of Pitcher and Pennsylvania and even took their name from the Maryland State Bird.

Frank wanted to show his musical compositions to someone at the conservatory. Aunt Mary was able to set up a meeting with Massimo Freccia, the conductor of the Baltimore Symphony Orchestra. Frank had brought manuscript paper with him and had spent some of his time at Aunt Mary's composing a new piece. 'I was naïve and thought [Freccia] could play it,' said Zappa. Astonished that someone of Frank's extraordinary appearance could write orchestral music at all, Freccia began by questioning his musical knowledge.

'What's the lowest note on a bassoon?' he asked.

'B flat . . . and also it says in the book you can get 'em up to a C or something in the treble clef.'

'Really?' said Freccia, impressed. 'You know about violin harmonics?'

'What's that?'

'See me again in a few years,' said the great conductor.

Shortly after arriving in Baltimore, Zappa wrote to Edgard Varèse, who had suggested they might meet. Baltimore was an easy train ride from New York City and Frank also looked forward to seeing Greenwich Village, home of all the artists and bohemians. He received a reply in tiny neat scientific handwriting:

VII 12th/57

Dear Mr Zappa,

I am sorry not be able to grant your request. I am leaving for Europe next week and will be gone until next spring. I am hoping however to see you on my return. With best wishes

Sincerely

Edgard Varèse

The meeting never took place. Varèse died on 6 November 1965, before Zappa made it to Greenwich Village. He was not the only one to miss meeting the composer. Charlie Parker's widow once told Varèse that Bird had followed him up and down the streets of Greenwich Village for two years, but never had the courage to introduce himself. 'He's the only man I'd willingly be a servant to,' Parker had told her.

Oddly, Zappa never made an attempt to contact Igor Stravinsky, whose work had almost as big an impact on his music. Stravinsky would have been easy to meet as he lived in Los Angeles – not far from the house where Zappa eventually settled – and often appeared in public when his work was performed. He died in 1971.

When Aunt Mary took her nephew to the famous tea rooms in Hutzler's department store, to her great shame he was forbidden entry because he was not properly dressed. However, they kept a seersucker jacket for just such an occasion and he put it on. After a light luncheon he decided to try one of his new cigarettes.

Zappa, who had been smoking for a year and loved tobacco, had just been to a tobacconist selling cigarettes from all over the world. Among his discoveries was a Russian brand. 'Have you ever smelled Russian tobacco?' he asked Rafael Alvarez in an interview for the *Baltimore Star*. 'Ho-ho, boy – I hadn't. It was the most nauseating smell, and the minute I lit it, chairs began moving away while my aunt was trying to be polite. And I'm sitting there with this long, really elegant-looking but vile-smelling Russian cigarette in my hand with a seer-sucker coat on – ha ha ha – having tea with Aunt Mary.' It was not with a certain amount of relief that Aunt Mary and Uncle Robert put their nephew on the train to LA after two weeks.

At the end of summer 1957 Frank entered his senior year. As he approached his seventeenth birthday, a darker side emerged. Wearing sunglasses and with a moustache and little goatee, he slouched along the covered walkways in his sinister blue-hooded parka. He cut classes and spent his time at school playing the guitar. His independent attitude and obscene language brought him into frequent conflict with authority. As Zappa put it: 'I was a jerk in high school and got thrown out quite frequently.'

On several occasions he was reprimanded by Ernest Tossi, the vice-principal. In an interview with David Walley (Zappa's first biographer), Tossi only remembered one occasion when Zappa was actually suspended: 'There was one incident when I had to give Frank a vacation without pay.' This was for being discourteous to a teacher. 'I jerked him out of assembly, he was ready to put on a show.' But Tossi incurred the wrath of Frank's father, who came to the school and shouted his own obscenities at them – this seems to have occurred with alarming frequency.

Tossi could see that Zappa was intelligent and talented and sympathized with his restlessness and frustration cooped-up in a place like Lancaster. Tossi had seen Zappa's IQ test scores and told Walley: 'I know he has the talent of a genius.' Zappa and Tossi became friends and they would often sit talking in Tossi's office long after school finished. On one occasion, Tossi gave Zappa a lift home and he invited him in to see his parents. These are hardly the actions of a hard-core juvenile delinquent. Tossi was not the only teacher to recognize Zappa's uniqueness. His music teacher, William Ballard, had long talks with him about musical composition and serialism and arranged for him to take a special course in harmony during his senior year. This meant going over to the adjoining Antelope Valley Junior College (AVJC), for one hour a week. Or, as a cynical Zappa tells it: 'I was an incorrigible student, and one of the people in the office decided that maybe I would be socially better adjusted if I was given the opportunity to study something I was actually interested in.' Mr Russell, a jazz trumpet player who taught harmony over at AVJC, gave him plenty to do. He made Frank read Walter Piston's *Harmony*. Zappa: 'I could barely make it through the harmony book because all the formulas that you learn there sound so banal.' Frank objected, but Russell was not prepared to argue. If Frank didn't resolve the chords, he got a D.

Frank's quarrel was with authority and society in general, not with his teachers. He even credited Tossi and Ballard on the sleeve notes of *Freak Out!*, the *Bildungsalbum* that summed up his entire life to that point. Frank also developed a friendship with Don Cerveris, who had been his English teacher at Lancaster before leaving to try and make it in Hollywood as a screenwriter. They stayed in touch and Cerveris was to play an important role in Frank's early days away from home.

Don Vliet (later known as Captain Beefheart) was in Frank's year at AVHS, but they didn't become friends until 1958, when Vliet saw Zappa hitch-hiking one day and gave him a lift. 'I couldn't help it,' said Vliet, 'he looked so woebegone.' They were almost the same age (Zappa was three weeks older) and shared musical tastes. It was a friendship of great mutual significance: Vliet gave Zappa innumerable ideas and Frank not only produced Beefheart's greatest album *Trout Mask Replica*, but pretty much forced him to sing in the first place.

Don Vliet lived on Carolside Avenue, a short ride due south of Zappa's place, in a virtually identical house. Mr and Mrs Vliet, known to everyone as Sue and Glen, shared the house with Don's Uncle Alan and Aunt Ione. Unusually for the time, Don's girlfriend Laurie lived in the house with him. Across the street lived his grandmother Anne Warfield, known as Granny Annie. Don's father was a Helms bread man with a route that took him from Lancaster up to Rosemond and Mojave.

Don and Frank would get together after school, usually at Frank's house, and they would listen to records for three or four hours. Then they would get something to eat and try to pick up girls in Vliet's car – a powder-blue '49 Oldsmobile with a clay werewolf head attached to the steering wheel. Having failed in this objective, they would go back to Don's house and listen to more records: obscure Doo Wop cuts by the Spaniels, the Paragons, the Orchids, the Penguins or the great blues masters: Muddy Waters, Howlin' Wolf, Sonny Boy Williamson, Johnny 'Guitar' Watson, Guitar Slim or Clarence 'Gatemouth' Brown. They would eat pineapple buns and sweet rolls left over from Don's father's bread route and periodically Don would scream at his mother, 'Sue! Get me a Pepsi!' She would bustle in, dressed as always in a blue chenille bathrobe and slippers, to wait on her adored only child. Many years later Zappa used this refrain as the basis for his song 'Why Doesn't Somebody Get Him A Pepsi?'

Sometimes these record sessions would go on until 5 a.m. and they would skip school the next day. Zappa: 'It was the only thing that seemed to matter at the time. We listened to those records so often we could sing the guitar leads. We'd quiz each other about how many records does this guy have out, what was his last record, who wrote it, what is the record number.'

Sometimes they would drive to Denny's on the Sierra Highway for coffee, the only place in Lancaster that stayed open after 6 p.m., and stay there talking until 5 a.m. If Don didn't have enough money, he would pull out one of the bread drawers of his father's van and get Laurie to crawl through to the cab and steal a couple of dollars from his change-maker. Then they would pull her back out by the ankles. After coffee they would drive around in the desert in the middle of the night talking – two teenagers, planning their lives.

When Don's father suffered a heart attack, Don dropped out of school to take over his bread route. He didn't enjoy the work. It embarrassed him to pull out the bread drawers in front of all the housewives. Though in interviews Don always claimed he never attended school, he accumulated enough credits to graduate from AVHS – there's a photograph of him in his mortarboard and gown to prove it.

Don complained that Zappa never went out – just played records and wrote music – but in a town where it is too hot to walk the streets after 11 a.m., it is not surprising Frank stayed at home. He still had no car and besides he was busy. In addition to his musical composition and his guitar practice, Frank was getting something of a local reputation for his art. He had won a state-wide art competition with the theme of 'Symphony of Living' sponsored jointly by the Californian Federation of Women's Clubs and the Hallmark Greeting Card Company. Frank received his award for an abstract painting entitled 'Family Room' in the Jack Carr Galleries in South Pasadena, accompanied by his art teacher, Shirley Eilers, and his proud parents. He also received first, second and third prizes for his entries in the Antelope Valley Fair, held at the Fairgrounds at the end of his block.

Mrs Clifford De Wees wanted to exhibit his abstract work at her newly opened bowling establishment on the Sierra Highway: Sands Bowl (now Brunswick Sands Bowl), while Mrs Jones, the curator of the monthly exhibition at the Women's Club, was also planning to exhibit his work.

According to a local newspaper, Frank had been awarded a scholarship to study at Idyllwild Arts Academy that summer, something arranged by Amy Heydorn, his previous art teacher. Idyllwild, an alpine village 45 minutes from Palm Springs up a winding mountain road, had been an artistic community for some time and the Arts Center summer programmes, aimed at furthering the careers of talented high school students, were in great demand. It is unknown whether Zappa actually took the course, but he sometimes mentioned having studied art and graphic design, which was the area he worked in after leaving AVJC. The same article said Frank was also writing a book, but when asked whether literature or music would be his chosen career he replied 'Music.'

He meant orchestral music. Frank had resigned as the leader of the Black-Outs that spring: 'The band stayed together until everybody got to hate each other's guts. After that I left the group and it turned into the Omens.' He had a good run with them. They had played bills with the Titans and the Velvetones, they were a warm-up band for Earl Bostic and Louis Armstrong, and played at an NAACP benefit at the Shrine Auditorium in Los Angeles, later the venue of many Mothers of Invention concerts. One of the evenings Frank organized was with the Black-Outs and the Ramblers (his previous band in San Diego) at the Fairgrounds Exposition Hall in Lancaster. 'Two Big Blues Bands, Continuous Music, Sponsored by Eagles Lodge, 9 til 2' enthused the advertisement. But Frank was tired of playing early Little Richard covers. He quit playing drums, sold some parts of his kit and rented others to a local group called the Blue Notes, and concentrated instead on honing his guitar skills.

Zappa graduated from Antelope Valley Joint Union High School on Friday 13 June 1958 with 20 units fewer than he was supposed to have. They gave him his diploma anyway. Zappa: 'They didn't want to see me back there for another year, and neither did I.' All the family attended the award ceremony, dressed in their Sunday best, to watch Frank go up on stage in his cap and gown. He smiled and waved his diploma at them, but his father looked grim throughout. He thought his son could have done much better.

This was not the end of Frank's education. Francis wanted to enrol him in the Curtis Institute of Music in Philadelphia, one of the finest conservatories in the United States, but Frank refused to go, though he later wrote: 'I have no degree in anything, and never had enough credits to get into a conservatory ... even though I wanted to go to Juilliard at one time.' As it was he found that everyone he knew had gone on to Junior College, including all the girls. He realized that he would not get a girlfriend unless he went to college and as he told Walley: 'There's no loose nook, so I figured, "Let's be practical, lad," so I enrolled at Antelope Valley Junior College.'

It was at AVJC that one of the earliest surviving recordings of a Zappa composition was made. It was a scatological little number called 'Lost In A Whirlpool', taped on a maroon reel-to-reel Webcor in the college audio-visual department one day after school when the room was empty. Frank and brother Bobby played guitars and Don Vliet sang the vocal. The song had its origins in 1955, when Frank was 15, at Mission Bay High School in San Diego. He and two friends, Jeff Harris and Larry Littlefield, used to hang out and make up stories and little skits together. As San Diego is a surfing town with lots of skin divers, they came up with a story about skin diving in the San Diego sewer system and encountering brown, blind fish. It was a typical teenage thing and involved much toilet humour and laughter.

A couple of years later, in Lancaster, Frank told the story to Don who transformed it into a down-home blues about a man whose girlfriend flushes him down the toilet, where he encounters blind, brown fish. 'Ever since my baby flushed me ...' Zappa told Society Pages: 'That's where the lyrics come from. It's like a musical manifestation of this other skin diving scenario.' Don improvises in a wavering high falsetto, only once dropping into his natural growl, while Frank performs his best Johnny 'Guitar' Watson teenage leads.

Zappa only lasted one semester at AVJC. He had no interest in going on to university and in any case, he wasn't staying around. Towards the end of 1958, his father made another peremptory move and decided to relocate the family to Claremont, California.

4 Ontario, CA

Zappa found himself in yet another suburban community, this time about 40 miles east of Hollywood. He was getting closer to his goal. Claremont was the easternmost of a row of communities strung out along the southern edge of the Angeles National Forest before you reached the Los Angeles county line: El Monte, Covina, Pomona, Claremont. Across the line, in San Bernardino Country, the conurbation continued its march eastward with Upland, Ontario and Cucamonga. This sprawl of suburban housing, anonymous business premises, motels, roadhouse bars, gas stations, drag strips and auto shops – known collectively as The Inland Empire – was where Zappa spent the next few years.

The Zappas first rented a house on Saint Augustine Street, then bought a tract home just around the corner on West Oak Park Drive. As usual they knew nobody, though Rosie's insistence on Sunday church attendance gave them a certain entrée. The Ewings lived a few doors down the street and Zappa made puppets with their son, which they entered in the LA County Fair. They soon fell out and Zappa became a solo puppet master – a role he relished for rest of his life.

The tension between Frank and his father only increased when Francis decided his son should become an engineer. He was also tired of being kept awake when Frank threw parties in the living room, dancing to loud R&B. In her family scrapbook, Candy Zappa describes the friction between them as 'becoming unbearable'. Something had to give. They barely spoke to each other and the whole family suffered.

Frank talked about moving out, but his mother urged him to stay. Then Francis had a heart attack, which put him in hospital. It took him a long time to recover, probably not helped by his constant diet of Chesterfield Kings (whatever else father and son disagreed on, smoking was not one of them). As far as Frank was concerned, the best thing about 1959 was the release of three of his all-time favourite monster movies: Ray Kellogg's *The (Attack of the) Killer Shrews*, Roger Corman's *Wasp Woman* and Monte Hellman's *The Beast From Haunted Cave*.

To ease the tension at home, Frank finally acted. The day he moved out, Rosie sat in the kitchen and sobbed for hours. Frank rented a small apartment in Echo Park, an old residential neighbourhood and one of the first developments along the foothills from the original downtown Los Angeles.

Frank hoped to make a living writing film scores. His friend and ex-AVHS English teacher Don Cerveris had been commissioned by producer-director Tim Sullivan to write the screenplay for a low-budget western called *Run Home Slow,* and Cerveris had arranged for Zappa to write the music. Unfortunately the leading lady suffered a miscarriage on the third day of shooting and Sullivan ran into financial difficulties so the project was put on hold for four years. How much work Zappa did on the score is unknown. Normally it is written after the movie has been shot and edited. However, it is possible Zappa had already written some of the themes for it.

He met Terry Kirkman, a multi-instrumentalist who was a year younger and they played a few gigs together, but nothing came of it. Kirkman later got together with Jules Alexander to form The Association and in 1966 had a million-selling hit with 'Along Comes Mary', a song widely thought to be in praise of marijuana. Frank had relied on the Don Cerveris money to survive, but when nothing came of it he had no income and was soon in trouble. In desperation he called his mother and told her he was starving. She despatched Bobby on the bus to Los

Angeles with a bag of toiletries, food, clean clothes and $50 – enough to last for some time. However, not long afterwards Zappa collapsed with a duodenal ulcer and had to return to the bosom of his family. Though the illness was painful, he liked its name and his album *Lumpy Gravy* has a track called 'Duodenum'. He had had stomach problems when he was 16, the result of eating carelessly or possibly all that lunchtime chilli. He was to have digestive problems for the rest of his life, especially on the road, usually caused by his terrible diet.

Though Zappa's first attempt to leave home had been unsuccessful, he continued to question his parents' values, especially their religion. Around this time he made his final break with Catholicism: 'The light bulb went on over my head. All the mindless morbidity and discipline was pretty sick – bleeding this, painful that and no meat on Fridays. What *is* this shit? I think it was possible to do what I've done only because I escaped the bondage of being a devout believer.' As Zappa saw it, the only way to be a good Catholic was to stop thinking. He saw the essence of Christianity in the story of Adam and Eve: the forbidden fruit was on the Tree of Knowledge, the subtext being that all suffering comes from the quest for knowledge. As Zappa put it: 'You could still be in the Garden of Eden if you had just kept your fucking mouth shut and hadn't asked any questions.' He horrified his parents by refusing to go to Mass and would no longer attend confession. Zappa: 'They thought, "Oh my God, oh no. My boy is going to hell. He's going to page three of that big chart in the catechism class."'

At Antelope Valley High School, Frank had been turned on to Zen Buddhism by his English teacher. Zappa: 'I was interested in Zen for a long time. That's what got me away from being a Catholic fortunately.' However, Zappa did not practise sitting or find himself a Roshi. In 1967 he told the *East Village Other*: 'It's my observation that eastern religions are wonderful if you are living anywhere but the United States. The best they can do for you here is, uh, give you a certain feeling of calm, if you can practise meditation and abstinence by yourself, away from everything else that's happening. The real goal of eastern religion, with mystical experience and all of that, those aims are difficult if not impossible to achieve in an industrial society.'

Nevertheless, at the time he found Zen Buddhism to be the most attractive of all the spiritual philosophies he had explored. He still enjoyed Christian music, especially Gregorian chant, and the tune of the Kyrie that was played at his confirmation particularly stuck in his head: 'That lick pops into my head sometimes and I've wound up playing it on the guitar in the middle of solos.' Alongside his R&B albums he had records by the Mighty Clouds of Joy, the Five Blind Boys From Alabama and the Original Staples Singers.

The idea that Frank's Catholic upbringing was responsible for his apparent fixation on sex and use of taboo words was often proposed by interviewers, with predictable results: 'The words I use on-stage are designed for directness of communication rather than as a protest against my Catholic upbringing. If you're gonna talk to somebody, it might as well be in a language they understand.' However, this does not explain why a man in his forties should still want to sing about groupies, blow jobs, underwear, sex appliances and anal sex. He especially rejected any suggestion that there might be psychological factors at work, that is, factors beyond his conscious control, and had a tremendous aversion to psychologists and psychiatrists.

In the spring of 1960 the 19-year-old Zappa enrolled in Chaffee Junior College in Alta Loma, between Upland and Cucamonga. Here he took Miss Holly's harmony course, which required him to learn to play a keyboard, though he never became proficient. Another of his instructors, Joyce Shannon, the head of the music department, remembered that Zappa never seemed to have any money at the time. She would often give him a ride home to Claremont because she lived nearby. She told *Society Pages*: 'He was a very exceptional music student, extremely bright. He had read the text I used on his own, which was amazing to me, because it wasn't an easy book to read and he was contemptuous of a lot of academia. He went out of his way to study both books and musical scores.' Shannon also got a name-check on *Freak Out!*.

Zappa often dismissed his attendance at Chaffee Junior College as yet another attempt to pick up girls, but in fact he was involved in an intense study of musical theory. He even attended a composition class taught by a Mr Kohn at Pomona College, despite not being enrolled there. It was here that he got a programme on the college radio station, *The Uncle Frankie Show* playing his favourite R&B records. Frank also talked, sang and harangued the students. He was taken off-air a week later when they discovered he wasn't a student.

Zappa studied at Chaffee for a semester, then returned after the summer break, stayed for a few weeks and quit. His formal education was over. He had achieved what he wanted: he now understood the rudiments of music and he had a girlfriend, a fellow student called Kathryn J. Sherman. They moved in together that summer and were married on 28 December 1960, a week after Zappa's twentieth birthday. Because he was underage, his mother had to sign the papers.

They lived at 314 West G Street in Ontario, an old house with an attic and a basement. It had hardwood floors, a large dining room and a screened-in porch where they sometime slept. They had lots of cats running about and Kay liked to burn candles. There was a large notice taped over the bedroom mirror which cautioned: TAKE YOUR PILL. Candy Zappa remembered the house as having a lot of character and smelling old: 'That might have been the attraction for Frank too!'

Frank and Kay were a typical newly married couple making a home for themselves. In family photographs she is blonde with shoulder-length curly hair and an open, smiling face. He puts his arm protectively around her shoulder. Frank is gangly-looking, clean-shaven (but with his perennial five o'clock shadow) and conventionally dressed in jacket and tie or open-necked shirt. His hair is slicked back in a flat-top with pronounced sideboards. Candy also remembered that one Christmas Frank dressed all in black, crept down to the Von's on the corner and 'acquired' a large Christmas tree. Not quite a Norman Rockwell cover, but heading in that direction. The only records Candy remembers listening to in that house, for instance, were by the Kingston Trio and Judy Collins.

Kay took a job as a secretary in the First National Bank of Ontario and Frank's artistic ability got him a job at the Nile Running Greeting Card studio in Claremont. Here he designed and laid out advertisements for the cards to be used in trade magazines and worked in the silkscreen department. He wore big rubber gloves and pushed the squeegee across the screen, then pulled off the mylar. The company specialized in silkscreen and made cards that Zappa described as being 'of a floral nature that would likely be considered entertaining by elderly Midwestern women'. He enjoyed it and was good at it.

After a while he talked the owner into letting him do his own line of cards on an experimental basis. He designed a number of them to be printed on a glossy chrome-coat stock, as well as a point-of-sale rack to display them. One card said *Goodbye* on the front and inside was a black hand. Another said *Captured Russian Photo Shows Evidence Of American Presence On Moon First.* Inside was a picture of a lunar crater with *Jesus Saves* written in it. The strangest example of Frank's work was a white card with the word *Farky* on it. Inside was a picture of a pirate. Zappa described that one as 'fairly abstract . . . you have to look at this guy and imagine him saying the word, and then you derive the meaning that was intended.' They were very much in the then-popular *Mad* magazine tradition, though it is easy to see why Zappa abandoned greeting card design.

Money was tight – the greeting card job appears to have been only part time, and Frank tried his hand at a number of others: selling Collier's encyclopaedias door-to-door (he lasted a week), a short stint as a jewellery salesman and a job as a window dresser. At one point he joined a local ad agency writing copy and designing display ads for small businesses. Much of his work was for the Ontario bank where Kay worked.

Frank tried to augment his income by playing gigs. He rented a Fender Telecaster from a music shop for $15 a month. Though it had taken him only four weeks to learn to play 'shitty teenage leads' on his old arch-top F-hole guitar, he had to start all over again with the electric guitar. He was still in touch with Terry Kirkman and they played a few folk-singing dates in the Claremont area, in particular at the Meeting Place in Claremont, which featured such bluegrass acts as the

Kentucky Colonels and the Pine Valley Boys, and folkies like the young Buffy St Marie. Kirkman became the MC and Frank would show up on Hoot Night and try to play folk music. If he had any of those gigs on tape, he never told anyone.

Frank also formed a quartet called the Boogie Men, which consisted of Al Surratt on drums, Kenny Burgan on saxophone, Doug Rost on rhythm guitar and Frank playing lead. In the only picture we have of them, dated May 1961, Zappa is strumming his rented Telecaster. They practised in Frank's garage, where the photograph was taken. The Boogie Men never got a bass player and it is not known if they ever played a paying gig. If they did, it didn't amount to much and Zappa eventually had to return the Telecaster as he couldn't keep up the payments. Like most of these early groupings the line-up was flexible, depending in part on who was available. Though he had only just learned to play the electric guitar, Zappa had no compunction about printing a business card that read: F. V. ZAPPA COMPOSER – MASTER BLUES GUITARIST.

Around this time, the summer of 1961, Frank met Ronnie Williams, whose family had moved to Ontario from Chula Vista, a suburb south of San Diego. Ronnie's father was a furniture salesman in San Bernardino and his mother worked as a waitress in Ed's Café in Ontario. His brother Kenny was away in reform school; 'boarding school' as he called it. Frank got to know them all and was clearly fascinated by the whole family. Ronnie had dropped out of high school and his parents were away all day working, so he had the house to himself. Back in San Diego he had played lead guitar in a band called the Fydallions (1957–9) and either he or Frank had the idea of putting a band together in Ontario. The tenor sax player with the Fydallions was Dwight Bement who had later moved to Lancaster where he played with the Black-Outs. Both Frank and Ronnie liked his playing, and Ronnie invited him to live in his house in Ontario and join the band. Even as late as 1961, Zappa still regarded a saxophone as an essential part of any group. Musically his heart was still in the fifties. Dwight Bement later returned to San Diego where he became the sax player with Gary Puckett and the Union Gap.

Dwight and Ronnie spent their days practising and playing poker. Somehow they got into a curious habit: instead of using tissues they would pick their noses then smear the offending excretion on the windowpane with their fingers in some sort of competition; the 'Green window' project, as Dwight called it. One day Mrs Williams happened to look into his bedroom and was appalled; she demanded its instant removal. In *The Real Frank Zappa Book* Zappa quotes Ronnie's description of this procedure: 'We had to use Ajax and a putty knife to get the damn things off!'

The original Black-Outs had now become the Omens, so Frank and Dwight revived the name. The Black-Outs II consisted of Ronnie and Frank on guitars, Dwight Bement on tenor sax, Al Surratt on drums, Joe Perrino on piano and (probably) Rex Jakabowski on guitar, harmonica and vocals. Motorhead was still living in Lancaster and remembered: 'Frank had formed a few groups down in Ontario and he would come up for battles of the bands all the time. It was kind of a kick.' The Black-Outs II seem to have overlapped with the lounge band that Frank and Joe Perrino played in later in the year, which was seen purely as a money-making operation.

Zappa still thought that the best way to get his music played was to write film scores and in June 1961 another opportunity presented itself: *The World's Greatest Sinner*, one of the most eccentric (rather than experimental) films ever made. It was an independent movie produced, directed, written and starring the great character actor Timothy Carey – 'the ugliest man alive' – veteran of bit parts in everything from *The Wild One* (1954), where he throws beer in Brando's face; *East of Eden* (1955); *The Killing* (1956) and *Paths of Glory* (1957). Brando liked him and used him in *One-Eyed Jacks* (1961). Frank always enjoyed Carey's films, though he preferred the weird crazed ones like *Rumble On The Docks* (1956), a juvenile delinquent movie.

Frank met Timothy Carey at Wallach's Music City in Hollywood while he was working on *Second Time Around*, a western comedy. 'A fellow came up to me and complemented me on my acting,' recalled Carey. 'He said he was a composer and the guy he came with, his next-door neighbour, played the guitar. I said, "What's your name?" He said,

"Frank Zappa." So I said, "OK, I have something for you. We have no music for *The World's Greatest Sinner*. If you can supply the orchestra and a place to tape it, you have the job." And that's what he did.'

The World's Greatest Sinner is the story of a dissatisfied middle-aged insurance clerk named Clarence Hilliard who wakes up one day and decides that he is God: 'We should be Gods, every one of us here, super human beings!' He starts his own church, gets a guitar and fake goatee, acquires an Elvis Presley silver lamé suit and works his audiences into a frenzy with wild, furious, rock 'n' roll shows, throwing himself around the stage, flopping about on his back as if he were having an epileptic fit and diving into the audience. He runs for President, has sex with 14-year-old groupies, seduces an 80-year-old woman for her money and drives a man to suicide. This disjointed, totally anarchic film uses flash forwards, upside down shots, breaks into full colour at the end and is narrated by the Devil, represented by a stentorian-voiced boa-constrictor. Just Zappa's sort of film. Carey began work on it in 1958, shooting most of the scenes in his garage in El Monte. It cost $100,000 in total.

Money was still a problem, so Frank and Joe Perrino – and possibly other members of the Black-Outs II – formed a lounge band known as Joe Perrino and the Mellow Tones. Zappa: 'What you might call a "Tiptoe-through-the-Tulips"-type band, wearing a white tuxedo coat, black pants, black patent leather shoes, hair slicked back, choreography. We played three twist numbers a night, and the rest of the stuff was "Oh how we danced the night . . ."' He would sit on a bar stool and strum four chords to a bar, taking care to keep the volume down, and take requests for 'On Green Dolphin Street', 'Anniversary Waltz' and, of course, 'Happy Birthday'. The line-up consisted of tenor saxophone, bass, drums with Frank sometimes doubling on vibraphone. He had also found the money to buy a Fender Jazzmaster. Zappa: 'Nobody else in the band really knew what the chord changes were to these dumb songs . . . I played places like Tommy Sandi's Club Sahara in San Bernardino, some clubs around West Covina. Really boring, miserable places.' Frank studied the chords until he had all the standards down and took home his $20 a night.

Joe Perrino and the Mellow Tones ran from November 1961 for about nine months until Frank could take no more. He put his Jazzmaster in its case and hid it behind the settee for eight months. The whole experience was memorialized in 'America Drinks and Goes Home' with its boorish drunken shouting and smashing glass.

That summer Zappa auditioned Don Preston for a lounge band – probably Joe Perrino and the Mellow Tones – but after playing together a few times nothing more came of it, though Preston would later join the Mothers of Invention. Preston: 'When I first met Zappa he was kind of a nerd, but he was smart enough to disguise that by street talk and being into R&B.'

By November Frank had completed his score for *The World's Greatest Sinner* and wanted to record it. Ronnie Williams told him about Pal Studio in nearby Cucamonga, owned by a friend of his named Paul Buff. Frank went to check it out and liked it. Recording began that month with Frank playing lead guitar accompanied by an eight-piece rock 'n' roll band that included Dwight Bement (who played keyboards as well as horns) and presumably Ronnie on guitar. Taping continued into December. Zappa drew heavily on his friendship with Joyce Shannon, the head of the music department at Chaffey Junior College, because the remaining portions of the score were recorded there.

On Saturday 17 December 1961 taping was completed at the Chaffey Junior College Little Theater, when the 52-member Pomona Valley Symphony Orchestra conducted by Fred E. Graff played their way through Zappa's carefully prepared charts. Also on the session were the Boogie Men: Zappa on guitar, Kenny Burgan on sax, Doug Rost on rhythm guitar and Al Surratt on drums. Many of the themes used in the score subsequently appeared on albums such as *Hot Rats* and *Lumpy Gravy*, and most notably the beautiful composition 'Holiday In Berlin' on *Burnt Weeny Sandwich*. Frank was not paid for this Herculean effort, but this didn't bother him. He learned a lot from the experience and also got to hear his dots played by an orchestra. As for the recording, which used only two microphones and was mixed directly to mono in a truck parked outside: 'It was rancid,' he said later.

Another piece of music, now known as 'Take Your Clothes Off When You Dance', was recorded as an instrumental at this time at Pal Studio with Paul Buff engineering. Not used in the final edit of the film, the now familiar theme is rendered as a smooth cha-cha with beautifully executed, but unthreatening, jazz solos played by Zappa and five hired musicians, including two horn players. It suggests that Carey's Frenzy Productions must have picked up the expenses for the project, as these studio musicians would have been on union scale.

When Kenny Williams returned from 'boarding school', he refused to move into his parents' house, preferring the garage instead. Motorhead moved in with him. The absence of a toilet was no great inconvenience in the summer, but when winter came they felt less inclined to walk to the house. So they relieved themselves in some glass mason jars left over from the summer's fruit harvest.

Their buddies came over to play poker and the jars soon filled up. Mrs Williams had a large earthenware crock in the garage of the sort used to make dill pickles and, in a special ceremony to see just how much piss they had collected, they emptied all the jars into the crock. Eventually, Kenny decided to live in the house and Motorhead moved in with Frank, who by that time had broken up with Kay and was living in Paul Buff's studio in Cucamonga. Months later, Motorhead was visiting Ronnie and Kenny and they were reminiscing about the old days of living in the garage with the crock of piss. They went out to inspect it and to their surprise there were little white tadpole-like creatures swimming in it. Motorhead stuck a nail in one and some white liquid came out.

Proud of their biological research, they excitedly informed Mr Williams of their discovery, but he was not so enthusiastic. Disgusted and confused, he yelled 'Pour that whole damn crock down the toilet!' Frank was so enthralled by the story he insisted Ronnie and Kenny tape it for posterity on a Wollensak tape recorder he occasionally hired for the weekend for $5. It was the first of his 'anthropological' investigations. He found the story of the snot on the window and the piss in the crock so funny that in 1967 he turned it into a song: 'Let's Make The Water Turn Black'.

In 1961 Zappa's father made yet another of his peripatetic moves, this time taking his family to Sarasota, Florida, where he had been offered a teaching job. Bobby had gone into the Marines in California, so only Carl and Candy accompanied their parents. However, the family complained so much that even though the money was good and the university offered them a beautiful home on campus, Francis gave in to family pressure and moved back to Los Angeles.

At first they stayed with Frank and Kay while they looked for a place of their own, but eventually they moved to 5625 Palo Verde Avenue in Montclair. Zappa and Kay invited their respective parents over for dinner and in many ways led a very conventional, all-American life. The only inkling of what lay ahead was Frank's involvement with music.

He spent the first half of 1962 playing with Joe Perrino and the Mellow Tones: 'Rockin' the town from the bandstand of Tommy Sandi's Club Sahara on E Street in San Bernardino', according to a local paper. Frank is the only one in the photograph not smiling. He stuck with it because he needed the money to finance his other projects. In March Zappa was interviewed by the *Pomona Progress-Bulletin* about *The World's Greatest Sinner*. Under the headline ONTARIO MAN WRITES SCORE FOR NEW FILM the paper described Tim Carey as 'Hollywood's "ugliest, meanest" character actor' and revealed that Zappa played guitar, drums, piano and vibraphone. Zappa described the film as 'arty' and said, intriguingly, 'The score is unique in that it uses every type of music.'

5 Cucamonga

Ever since he used Pal Studio in Cucamonga to record parts of his film soundtrack, Frank had been hanging around the studio. Paul Buff taught him how to multi-track and overdub and explained microphone positioning. Buff: 'I can't remember if I ever charged Frank any money or if he even had any, but we kind of worked together and recorded some jazz things. He went up to Hollywood regularly and tried to sell 'em. And nobody was interested, basically.'

Buff had been to high school in Cucamonga (the city changed its name to Rancho Cucamonga when it incorporated in 1977) and after graduation studied aviation electronics for a year in the Marine Corps. He graduated first in a class of 500. Back in Cucamonga he took at job at General Dynamics – the 'bomb factory' as Zappa would call it – engineering parts for guided missiles. After nine months he quit and aged 21 he borrowed $1,000 and started his own recording studio. He named it Pal after his parents' Pal-O-Mine music publishing company. The first Pal studio was at 8020 North Archibald Avenue, but the neighbours complained about the noise, so he moved to 8040 North Archibald Avenue, just north of the intersection with Foothill Boulevard – the historic Route 66. Paul blacked out the windows and set about building a recording studio from scratch. Buff: 'My credo was

"I've never been in a real recording studio, but I know what is supposed to come out of one." (hit records).'

He bought a lady's dresser for $15 from the Salvation Army, removed the mirror and installed a large metal plate in the middle for the knobs and switches. He then modified a half-inch professional tape recorder so that he could overdub on it, machining his own record-and-erase heads to make a five-track recorder. It was a remarkable achievement for an amateur. Eight-track machines had been available for four years, but were very expensive. (The first eight-track recording to reach the charts was Bobby Darin's million-selling 'Splish-Splash', released in April 1958, the same year in which stereo was introduced.)

Buff bought a Rec-O-Cut lathe with a heated stylus cutting-head, which enabled him to make his own masters and produce acetates. This meant that when he tried to sell recordings he could give record company executives something they could slap straight on the turntable, without having to load a reel-to-reel tape (cassettes had yet to be invented). He could also provide them with a ready-mastered product: all they had to do was press it. Buff improved the performance of his Rec-O-Cut by attaching a Kenwood vacuum cleaner to the ceiling, its ten-foot suction hose taped to the lathe's cutting head to suck away debris. Zappa liked its bizarre look and it became a recurring motif in his work. In addition to renting out his studio, Buff wanted to make his own records. Rather than pay studio musicians he taught himself how to play piano, bass and drums and apparently mastered the saxophone in one weekend, simply because he needed a sax on one of his recordings. Buff played drums with the Sonny Wilson band at a late-night beer bar and for a time he and two members of the band lived in Pal Studio. The studio was L-shaped and had terrible acoustics. Buff: 'We didn't dare put a microphone more than a foot away from an instrument or you heard the room too much. Everything was close-miked and we did definitely pioneer some multi-track recording techniques and overdubbing.' Close-miking changed the way drums were recorded, particularly in surf music.

His big break came on a winter's day late in 1962 when a schoolfriend from Cucamonga High booked a session and arrived with a group of teenagers from nearby Glendora. They were called the Surfaris. They quickly recorded their song and were packing up their gear when Paul reminded them that records traditionally have two sides. They didn't have another song, so while everyone waited they wrote and arranged one on the spot. Forty minutes later they were ready and, after a quick run-through, they recorded 'Wipeout', *the* surf classic and one of the most memorable pop tunes of all time. It reached Number Two in the charts in June 1963. After the success of 'Wipeout' all the surf bands wanted that close-mic sound and Paul was suddenly very busy. However, he still made his own records, hoping to come up with a hit.

The first joint project with Zappa was a cover of the Merle Travis song 'Sixteen Tons', a Number One hit for Tennessee Ernie Ford in 1955. They called themselves The Masters, but as no one wanted to release it, Buff put it out himself on his own Emmy Records label as Emmy 1008. On the B-side was an instrumental co-written by Zappa, Buff and Ronnie Williams called 'Breaktime'. This is the first time Zappa's name appears as a composer of a rock 'n' roll song. Though he had been writing music since he was 14, it was only now, at 21, that he turned his hand to popular music (though many of his 'serious' pieces were later reworked as rock 'n' roll numbers). Most of his early songs were collaborations, though in 1962 he wrote 'Love Of My Life', which he described as one of his first solo efforts.

Most of Frank's collaborations were with singer Ray Collins. Born in 1936 and raised in Pomona, Ray grew up to a radio soundtrack of pop and Doo Wop – Los Angeles had some of the best DJs in the country – as well as the Mexican-American music of East Los Angeles. He sang high falsetto on 'I Remember Linda' by Little Julian Herrera and the Tigers, released in 1957 on Art Laboe's Starla label. (The Art Laboe Show on KPOP was the number one radio show in 1956.) It was good exposure, but just as 'I Remember Linda' was moving up the local charts, Little Julian – who was only 17 or 18 – was arrested for statutory rape. The record died and Herrera's career was destroyed.

One night in 1962 Ray Collins was drinking in a bar called The Sportsman in Pomona when a four-piece band came in and set up;

the management had hired Frank's group. It was probably a variant of The Black-Outs II with Ronnie Williams and Zappa on guitars and Bement on tenor sax, rather than the last days of Joe Perrino and the Mellotones. Collins: 'I heard him playing R&B stuff, which I thought was pretty bizarre, because they were playing pretty obscure things . . . so I eventually asked Frank if I could sing, and he said, "Yeah, great!" And so I got up and sang "Work With Me Annie" and some R&B ballad things.'

Afterwards they talked about R&B and songwriting. Collins: 'I told him about an idea I had for a song. "How's Your Bird?" was an expression that Steve Allen used to use on his TV show.' Frank thought it was a great idea and a few days later he called Ray to say: 'I wrote it. Let's record it!' They went to Pal Studio and recorded as Baby Ray and the Ferns – a reference to another Steve Allen catchphrase: 'How's your fern?'

Frank now knew various independent labels in Los Angeles, many of which were located on 'Record Row', the section of Selma Avenue between Vine Street and Cahuenga Boulevard near the Capitol Records tower. He walked into the office of Bob Keane, owner of the Del-Fi and Donna labels (named after the Greek oracle and the girlfriend of the late Ritchie Valens) with a 'whole handful of tapes' and asked Keane to listen to them 'with an open mind'. Keane gave Zappa the time of day because he was already familiar with the products of Pal, having released two of Buff's productions earlier that year: Terri and Johnnie's 'Your Tender Lips' and Rene and Ray's 'Queen of My Heart'.

Keane played Zappa's tapes and agreed to release some, if not all of the cuts. The first was Buff's 'Slow Bird'/'Blind Man's Buff' released in January 1963, followed in March by 'How's Your Bird?' by Baby Ray and the Ferns. 'Baby Ray' Collins did the vocals and the Ferns were Paul on piano, his business partner Dave Aerni on bass and Frank on everything else. The snorting grunts ('snorks') were provided by Dick Barber, a friend of Bobby Zappa's from Claremont High (he later worked as a road manager for Zappa from 1968 to 1975). Dick was very good on snorks: a pig grunt sound characteristic of many of Zappa's recordings. (The name itself came from a comic book.)

On the flip side of 'How's Your Bird' was 'The World's Greatest Sinner', a last-minute recording made to accompany the film's title sequence, using the same line-up but with someone, probably Motorhead, honking on a baritone saxophone. Another 1962 collaboration with Ray Collins was the beautiful 'Deseri', a Collins number recorded at Pal with Frank on drums and Ronnie Williams on guitar; but it was not released until Ray put it on a Grandmothers album in 1982. It is the perfect vehicle for his high falsetto.

Frank continued his collaborations, the next being 'Love Of My Life' sung by Ron Roman with Frank on guitar and drums. The song is credited to Ron Roman, Zappa and Dave Aerni; but although the later version on the *Ruben and the Jets* album shares many of the same lyrics, Zappa credits it entirely to himself. Given his frequently expressed hatred of love songs, it is an exceptional song in Zappa's repertoire, though one he obviously liked as he performed it a lot.

On 14 March 1963 Frank appeared on the Steve Allen Show on Channel 5. He had been angling to get on the show for some time as a serious musician and also with his jazz recordings, but they weren't interested until he came up with a gimmick: he would play a bicycle, a musical form he called 'Cyclophony'. Borrowing his sister Candy's bike, he demonstrated to an amused Allen all the different sounds that can be produced from the machine by twirling the pedals, strumming the spokes like a harp or bowing them like a violin and letting air out of the tyres. Dressed soberly in a dark suit, Frank seemed in awe of Allen, then at the height of his fame, and a little too anxious to ingratiate himself with him, though he did get Allen to blow through the handlebars. The fully developed Zappa persona had not yet arrived.

His performance certainly irritated Timothy Carey whose movie had premièred six weeks before. Carey: 'That's where our friendship stopped. Steve asked him what films he did. He said he did *The World's Greatest Sinner*, the world's worst film, and all the actors were from skid row. It wasn't true.' Carey said that Frank was just saying that to curry favour. He described how on the opening night at the Directors' Guild, Frank had been in such awe of his surroundings he walked into a window and banged his head. At the première at the Vista-Continental

Theater in Hollywood on 30 January 1963, Carey, ever the showman, appeared in his silver lamé preacher suit with GOD stitched on the sleeves and got the evening off to an exciting start by firing a .38 over the heads of the audience.

In 1960 Art Laboe released what was probably the very first oldies compilation. *Memories of El Monte* was a collection of golden oldies by bands like the Paragons that used to play at Laboe's big dances at the El Monte Legion Stadium. Ray Collins was visiting Frank one day at his house on G Street and Frank told him that he and a friend of his had thought of writing a song using that as the title. Ray had been to a lot of the dances and had even played there with tenor saxophonist Chuck ('Pachuko Hop') Higgins. He sat down at Frank's piano and began playing the 'Earth Angel' changes.

Ray: 'The first line came immediately, "I'm all alone, feeling so blue . . ."' The obvious group to record the song was the Penguins, so Frank took 'Memories of El Monte' to Art Laboe, who loved it. Laboe came up with the idea of adding the names of the Doo Wop groups and having the Penguins impersonate each of them: the Shields, the Satins, the Medallions, Marvin and Johnny and so on, ending with the Penguins' 'Earth Angel'. The song was produced by Frank, presumably at Laboe's own studio, because Ray later complained: 'Art Laboe's always had this thing about people recording R&B ballads too slow, so I think he over-compensated and made "Memories of El Monte" too fast.' Though Cleve Duncan sang lead on both the original 'Earth Angel' and on 'Memories of El Monte', the other Penguins on this session were tenor Walter Saulsberry and a studio group called the Viceroys, the original Penguins having broken up years before. Though only a local hit, it did well enough for Cleve Duncan to reform the group.

Around this time Frank visited Dootsie Williams' DooTone Records on Central Avenue at 95th in Watts, probably in the company of Cleve Duncan. Williams' office was in the enclosed porch of his home. He had recorded the Medallions, the Penguins, Don Julian and his other acts over in the Jefferson Park section at Ted Brinson's studio.

Brinson, who had played bass in several of the big bands, including Jimmie Launceford's, had a small studio in his garage at 2190 West 30th Street near Arlington Avenue. He worked as a mailman, so money was tight and the studio had no soundproofing or control booth, but it did have a new single-track Ampex and a couple of microphones.

This time Frank really was in awe: 'We went down to see Dootsie Williams' place – DooTone Records – we actually stepped into the room where 'Earth Angel' was recorded and it was like going to heaven. There was a piano that appeared to have shrivelled from over-use, a little stumpy piano, the cheapest they could get, the only thing that would fit into that room, and there was enough room to have that piano, maybe five guys standing up around a microphone, maybe an upright bass, maybe one guy hitting a snare drum in the corner, that was about it. I'm sure most of their group vocal masters were done in that little room.'

Though some critics have questioned the depth of Zappa's love for R&B and the Doo Wop vocal groups, the extent of his knowledge, the size of his R&B collection (around 7,000 singles) and his obvious nostalgia for the period confirms that R&B, combined with the School of Vienna composers, never ceased to be the benchmark of his musical appreciation and also the template for his own musical compositions. Something of those beautiful high-falsetto harmonies and stuttering saxophones was always present in his work.

It is worth dealing with these early surf and Doo Wop singles in detail because they inform the whole of Zappa's work; he was enormously influenced by the rough and tumble of the independent record company milieu, the scams and the deals, the quick cash-ins on chart hits, the 'ice-cream' changes made to someone else's song to produce something similar but different.

'Give 'em what they want,' he told Paul Buff, displaying a cynicism that would last a lifetime. Selling cash-ins to Bob Keane and his like gave him an insight into the music business almost unique among performing artists (Lou Reed is notable for starting in a very similar way), but it also distanced him from his musical contemporaries. He found it almost impossible to believe that someone was playing rock and roll for any reason other than to make money. Zappa saw the whole industry as a cynical commercial exercise; as, of course, did people like Bob Keane.

None of Zappa's work from this period is of particular artistic significance. In fact, most of the numbers were rip-offs of previous chart hits, including Frank's next production, Bob Guy's 'Dear Jeepers'/ 'Letters From Jeepers' – a direct steal from John Zacherle's 1958 top-ten hit 'Dinner With Drac, Part 1' on Cameo. It was a spoken 'letter' read over a rock vamp with Zappa playing all the instruments. Bob Guy was the programme director of Channel 13 and hosted *Jeeper's Creepers*, a popular Saturday-night horror movie show that was a particular favourite of Zappa's. He opened the show by emerging from a coffin and 'Dear Jeepers' was designed to capitalize on a regular feature where he read a fan letter to Jeepers. Frank had some hand in the lyrics – perhaps where Jeepers writes to Count Dracula from Cucamonga – but they were mostly from Guy's TV scripts. It was released by Donna in April 1963, just before Guy left the show.

Another April 1963 Donna release was the Heartbreakers' 'Everytime I See You'/'Cradle Rock'. Though Frank and Ray Collins wrote the A-side, it was recorded at the better-equipped Studio Masters in Hollywood, not at Pal, and Frank did not play on it. The Heartbreakers were two 14-year-old Mexican-American brothers from East LA who wanted to follow up their 1962 single 'Corrida Mash'.

This period also saw the first use of the Vigah! label scam. The Pal Studio gang would press 200 copies of a new record on Emmy or Vigah! and put them in San Bernardino record stores on consignment. Then they would get a DJ friend to play it a few times. They knew the radio station called all the record stores at noon on Fridays, so they would go in at 10 a.m. on Friday and anonymously buy all their own records. When the station called, the stores reported great sales and they would end up at something like Number 38 in the local chart with a bullet. Buff: 'Monday morning we headed to Hollywood to promote the news that we had an emerging hit in San Berdoo. The A&R guy would call the station where he would hear, "Yeah, this record's taking off." We would pick up $500 or $1,000 advance, with which to support our music habit for a few more weeks.'

The Pal Studio gang almost had a hit in May with 'The Big Surfer' by Brian Lord and the Midnighters, written by Frank. Brian Lord was a San Bernardino DJ, so airplay was guaranteed. In the song he impersonates President Kennedy judging a dance contest and there are plenty of references to Jackie Kennedy, Bobby Kennedy, press attaché Pierre Salinger and daughter Caroline. This was the time of the civil rights actions to end segregation in the Southern states and the punchline of the song is that the contest winner receives an all-expenses-paid trip as the first members of the Peace Corps to be sent to Alabama. Capitol Records bought it for the large sum of $7,000, but two weeks after 'The Big Surfer' was released Medgar Evers, the Mississippi field secretary for the NAACP was murdered on 12 June at a rally in Jackson. Segregation was no laughing matter. Capitol dropped the record, but Brian Lord continued to play it and it was a local hit in San Bernardino.

Zappa used his share of the proceeds from 'The Big Surfer' to pay $300 (a lot in those days) to stage a mixed-media concert of his orchestral music. It was recorded and broadcast by KPFA-FM, the LA outpost of Pacifica, the non-profit listener-supported foundation. The Pacifica stations supported Zappa's work throughout his life and possibly covered some of the costs towards this event. Billed as 'The Experimental Music of Frank Zappa', the concert was performed on 19 May 1963 by the student orchestra of Mount St Mary's College, a Catholic liberal arts college for women in Brentwood in the Santa Monica Mountains, before an audience of about 50 people. Zappa had already begun giving his works opus numbers in the manner of Webern and the classical composers. Pieces included 'Opus 5 For Piano, Tape Recorder and Multiple Orchestra'; 'Piano Piece From Opus 5'; 'Collage One For String Instruments' and 'Visual Music For Jazz Ensemble and 16mm Projector'. This last piece was written in 1957, when Zappa was first experimenting with film in Lancaster and was accompanied by 8mm films projected on huge screens.

Paul and Paula's 'Hey Paula' was number one in the US charts in February 1963, just waiting for a Zappa-Collins pastiche. With Frank playing all the instruments and Ray Collins singing about teenage skin problems they pressed up copies of 'Hey Nelda'/'Surf Along' as Vigah! 002 and set the machinery in motion. But this time nobody bit. Frank's humour was too close to the bone. The A&R men knew that teenagers were too sensitive about their acne to buy a record on the subject. Zappa's interest in areas normally considered embarrassing or in poor taste was to hinder his commercial career throughout his life.

Both sides of Ned & Nelda's record were written by the Zappa-Collins team and years later Frank praised Ray's role in his career: 'At this time, I was working with Ray Collins, who could sing all this kind of stuff. If you're a composer, you need a vehicle to bring your music to life. If you write for instruments, you need someone who can play it, and if you write vocals, you need somebody who can sing it. It's fortunate that I had Ray Collins, because if I hadn't met him, I wouldn't have had any way to move into that kind of songwriting.' Few people ever received praise like that from Zappa.

They clearly had a good friendship and had a lot of fun together: Zappa remembered: 'Ray Collins and I used to piddle around in Pomona doing gigs where the two of us would do parodies of folk songs. We sang "Puff the Magic Dragon" as "Joe the Puny Greaser" and we played a perverted version of "The Streets of Laredo" called "The Streets of Fontana". We weren't setting out to make any kind of impact on people. We were just doing it for a laugh, to have fun.' They also played the Troubadour on talent night, calling themselves Loeb and Leopold. Zappa: 'We were singing songs about pimples and all kinds of other far-out things and a lot of that was the basis of the things the Mothers wound up doing.'

This was when Francis Zappa and his brother Joe became partners in a restaurant called The Pit on Foothill Boulevard in Upland, between Claremont and Cucamonga. They served standard American coffee-shop fare as well as pasta and Italian dishes. Francis was the cook and Rosie served at the counter. Frank constructed a small stage at the back so that he and Ray could play to the college crowd on Friday nights. He put bamboo curtains over the windows to try and create a little atmosphere, but the fire department made him take them down. Thirteen-year-old Candy Zappa remembers singing with them, songs like 'Long Tall Texan' and 'I'm leaving It (All) Up To You'. She had been playing guitar since she was eleven, encouraged by Frank who told her over and over: 'Just keep working, Candy.'

Paul Buff was still cutting tracks, one of which was the instrumental 'Tijuana Surf'. Buff wrote it and played all the instruments, and Frank did the same for the B-side, 'Grunion Run'. (A grunion is a small fish the size of a sardine. Late at night on Los Angeles' beaches millions of grunions bury themselves in the sand to lay their eggs. Young people gather to watch this spectacle and to go on a Grunion Run is a fifties' LA euphemism for a hot date.) As Zappa and Buff had received no royalties from Bob Keane – and never did – the Hollywood Persuaders (as they now called themselves) took their new record to Art Laboe who put it out on Original Sound. He leased it to the Mexican label Gamma, shortening their name to the Persuaders, and it spent 17 weeks at Number One in the Mexican charts. Zappa had his first hit, albeit only a B-side.

In the summer of 1963 he set up Aleatory Music, the first of his many music publishing companies, in order to control the royalties of the hoped-for hit singles he was writing. (Previously, he had had arrangements with Paul Buff's various companies: Maraville Music, Buffie Publishers and Drive-In Music Co.) At the same time Frank put together yet another group. Called the Soots, it was designed to exploit Don Vliet's extraordinary multi-octave voice.

Zappa: 'I like Don's singing very much, he has an interesting voice, I really like to hear him. But I can remember a time when you couldn't bring him to sing at all, he simply hung back . . . I talked him into becoming a singing star. We quite often drove in his car through the area (Cucamonga). Then he always sang along with the radio. I pressed him over and over: "Come on, man, sing!" But he bickered with a terrible problem – he couldn't sing in 4/4 time, until I finally convinced him not to force himself to sing in 4/4 time, but to create his own music.'

Vic Mortensen, who Frank knew from high school in Lancaster, became the Soots' drummer: 'One night Frank and Don walked in . . . Frank had kinda long hair, if I remember. Don also had long hair. Don was wearing one of those black leather coats he liked to wear. I recognized Frank and we shook hands. He said, "Here's my friend Don." That night we packed up my drums, got on 66, headed east, and went out to Studio Z [as Frank referred to Pal Studio] in Cucamonga.' The Soots were sometimes aided by Janschi on bass and/or Alex Snouffer, another friend from Lancaster, on guitar. Zappa's world was essentially suburban: the only people he knew were from the Pomona Valley and Lancaster; and though he was spending quite a bit of time in Hollywood, making contacts and selling songs, it seems as if he knew he was not ready to tackle the big city.

Among the tracks recorded by the Soots were 'Tiger Roach', a surf-style R&B number typical of Zappa at that period and his first attempt at stereo recording at Pal. He put the band in the studio and mixed them down to a mono track. Don stood with his microphone in the hallway, listening to the leakage through the studio door, flipping through an X-Man comic pinned to a noticeboard and improvising on what he saw around him: 'light switch', for instance. Other Soots tracks included the X-Man-influenced 'Metal Man Has Won His Wings', 'Cheryl's Canon', an instrumental called 'I'm Your Nasty Shadow' and a cover of Little Richard's 'Slippin' and Slidin'', sung by Don in a raw blues shout reminiscent of Howlin' Wolf. Unreleased tracks included Howlin' Wolf's 'Evil' and some Vliet compositions: 'The Grund' and a slow blues called 'Vicious Intentions'. Zappa played fuzz-tone guitar. It was an experiment: he had a Gibson amp and plugged the guitar into the microphone input. Zappa: 'Something bad happened.'

In his hustling around Hollywood, Frank had met Milt Rogers, A&R man at Randy Wood's much criticized Dot Records – the label responsible for doing note-for-note copies of original R&B records, insipid cover versions by white acts like Pat Boone, Gale Storm, Tab Hunter and the Fontane Sisters, for which the original black artists received nothing. Though in later years Frank would join in the criticism, he took his acetates over to Dot for consideration. They had already had a hit with Pat Boone singing Little Richard's 'Long Tall Sally' and perhaps Zappa thought he could get in on the act with something a little more authentic sounding. He gave them 'Slippin' and Slidin'' and two originals, now labelled as 'by the Soots': the instrumental version of 'Take Your Clothes Off When You Dance' and 'Any Way The Wind Blows', on which Frank played all the instruments and Ray Collins handled the vocals. This version of 'Any Way The Wind Blows' was inspired by the 'discussions' Frank and Kay were having about splitting up. 'If I had never gotten divorced,' wrote Zappa, 'this piece of trivial nonsense would never have been recorded.'

Rogers wrote to Frank on 19 September 1963: 'The material has been carefully reviewed and while it does have merit, we do not feel strongly enough about its commercial potential to give you any assurance of a recording.' When Frank telephoned to remonstrate, Rogers exclaimed: 'The guitar is distorted!'

But 1963 was not entirely an *annus miserabilis*. Zappa's friend and high-school English teacher Don Cerveris contacted him to say that the director-producer Tim Sullivan had finally raised the funds to resume shooting *Run Home, Slow*. The film now starred Mercedes McCambridge and was a low-budget western described by Zappa as: 'Something to do with a bad ranch lady, a nymphomaniac cowgirl and a hunch-back handy-man named Kirby who eventually winds up pooching the nympho in a barn, next to the rotting carcass of the family donkey.' Even cult film aficionados agree that *Run Home, Slow* is one of the worst films ever made. However, Frank was able to record the original instrumental version of 'The Duke of Prunes' and a number of 'Run Home, Slow' musical cues at Original Sound studios using session musicians. Although the musicians were paid scale, Frank had to wait until the following year before his $2,000 fee came through.

There were a few more Pal Studio singles: In December 1963 'Hurricane'/'Sweet Love' by Conrad & the Hurricane Strings was jointly produced by Frank and Paul Buff under the name Curry & Irvin – a play on Currier & Ives, 'Printmakers to the American people', whose sentimental-historical scenes hung on suburban walls across the country. The record was released on Daytone, which might be why the producers used a pseudonym. Buff was going into a studio partnership with Art Laboe at Original Sound to build a ten-track recording facility and it is likely he was contracted to produce records only for them. Certainly his next two singles with Frank were done for Original Sound. On 'Mr Clean'/'Jessie Lee', Frank and Paul called themselves Mr Clean; on 'Heavies'/'The Cruncher' they were the Rotations. On 'Mr Clean' Ray Collins did the vocals, Buff's wife Allison sang backing vocals, Frank played everything else except the fuzztone bass, which Paul plugged straight into the board. Buff: 'Zappa loved the sound, I thought it was just ugly noise.' Zappa: 'He had the first fuzztone I ever saw. He had taken the preamp from a phonograph and he was running a Sears-Roebuck bass through it. And it was a great fuzz bass. That was the first time I ever saw anybody do a direct fuzz on a recording.' Along with close-miking, fuzztone was another great Buff innovation (two years before the Beatles used it). Frank also had him use it on a recording of Ray Collins' 'Fountain of Love' recorded around this time.

With Buff at Original Sound, Frank took over Pal Studio. Buff still owned it, but Frank practically lived there, pushing the equipment to its limits trying out new techniques. By the end of the year he did move in, as he and Kay finally separated and filed for divorce. One of the prime reasons was a buxom redhead named Lorraine Belcher.

Ray Collins remembered a pleasant balmy afternoon sitting on the front porch with Frank and Kay listening to the bees droning in the honeysuckle, when who should come wandering up the garden path but Lorraine. She settled herself comfortably into one of the porch chairs and explained how she had recently met Frank in a Hollywood coffee shop and he had promised her that if she ever came out to the Inland Empire he would make her the biggest star of low-budget movies. Kay had finally had enough. Shortly after this Frank called his mother: 'Mom, come and get me. Kay and I are through.'

6 Studio Z

Frank left West G Street towards the end of 1963 and moved into Pal Studio. He packed away his R&B collection and put his vibraphone in storage at Original Sound. Kay stayed on at G Street and for a while Frank still used that address for his business correspondence; so relations must have remained cordial. 'Got married when I was twenty . . . a lovely girl: almost ruined her life,' Zappa wrote in the liner notes to *Freak Out*. The divorce came through early in 1964. Paul Buff was hardly ever at Pal, having married Allison and moved to Hollywood to work with Art Laboe, so Frank changed the name to Studio Z and began a life of 'excessive overdubbage'. Zappa: 'Once I learned how to use the studio equipment I would sit there twelve hours at a time and play all the instruments myself onto the tape, and I'd practise what I was going to do later when I got into a bigger studio. It was a lab for me.'

Frank tried to attract clients into the studio by livening it up a little: he painted the blacked-out windows olive green and turquoise blue. And wrote *Studio Z* on the door in zany teenage lettering, like an Annette Funicello album sleeve. The same lettering was on the windows, which read: RECORD YOUR BAND and $13.50 AN HOUR. Very few customers ventured in.

The rent was $50 a month and Frank could no longer rely on Kay's salary from the bank. Zappa: 'My only source of income was working this barbecue joint up in Sun Village. I'd work there on weekends. It was just a pick-up band, some guys that I knew from high school who lived up there. I would come up, plug in my guitar, play with them.' There was no rehearsal; they were a bar band, taking requests from the audience.

Then in July 1964 the money from *Run Home, Slow* finally came through and Frank found himself with $2,000. He bought a 1963 mustard-coloured Chevy Bel-Aire station wagon (having finally learned to drive) and to buy the Gibson ES-5 Switchmaster that he used on his first three albums. Some of the money paid for his divorce and some went as an advance payment to Paul Buff to buy the lease and contents of 8040 Archibald. In a contract dated 1 August 1964, Zappa got $1,212-worth of equipment, reduced to $1,000 'in consideration of the quantity of articles to be sold'. These included a Steinway upright piano, the Rec-O-Cut lathe, three power amplifiers and a variety of speakers, microphones and other equipment. Frank agreed to pay $50 a month, starting 1 September, plus interest at 8 per cent until the sum was paid off, otherwise Buff retained title to the goods.

In addition, Frank gave Paul his old drum set, his vibes – which were already at Original Sound – and his Jazzmaster guitar. He also took on Buff's debts – the studio had been in difficulties for some time. Zappa and Buff remained distant friends throughout Frank's life and he always acknowledged his enormous debt to Buff in getting started in the business. Buff went on to invent the Kepex Noise Gate and other professional audio devices, including computer-controlled mix-down systems. He moved to Nashville and started a photographic supply company to market his innovative designs for photo-flash units.

One of the first projects undertaken at Studio Z was the first ever rock 'n' roll opera – or it would have been if it had ever materialized. Don Vliet was to play Captain Beefheart, a character in *I Was A Teenage Maltshop*, a libretto Zappa wrote in between trying to make Top 20 surf records. It was inspired by *I Was a Teenage Werewolf,* and the fact that Paul Buff's girlfriend Allison had worked at the maltshop on the corner where they ate.

The origin of Don's new name was revealed by Zappa in his autobiography. It seems that Uncle Alan who shared the house with Don and his parents when Frank still lived in Lancaster, was attracted to Laurie, Don's live-in girlfriend. If she was around, Uncle Alan would leave the bathroom door wide open in order to impress her with the size of his member. As he urinated he would mutter: 'Ahh, what a beauty! It looks just like a big, fine, beef heart.' Just the kind of thing Zappa would remember.

I Was A Teenage Maltshop was a typical Zappa reworking of old material. Ned and Nelda – the dark side of Paul and Paula – were resurrected. Nelda became a cheerleader and the daughter of an old man who owned an unsuccessful recording studio. He had failed to produce a hit record and the evil landlord was going to evict him. Then Ned the Mumbler arrives, 'a teenage Lone Ranger' who attends the local high school and has a group that saves the day. Frank sent the outline and a sample extract to Joseph Landis, the Repertoire Workshop producer at CBS television station KNXT. On 2 December 1964 Landis wrote to Frank that he had read and reread his outline six times, and was 'enchanted with the thought of programming a rock-and-roll opera . . . Unfortunately, we remain unconvinced that the outline submitted can ensure a quality show.'

Not long after buying Studio Z, Frank attended an auction at the F. K. Rockett studios in Hollywood, who were going out of business. All their back lot sets were up for grabs and for $50 Frank bought a flatbed full of enough scenery to make a movie: a two-sided cyclorama, purple for night, blue for day – a kitchen, a library and a building exterior. He squeezed as much as he could into the studio and set to work devising a use for it. However, the flats made the accommodation rather cramped, especially as Frank had been joined by Motorhead who had moved out of the garage at the Williams' house with the onset of winter.

As Frank worked on his screenplay, Motorhead did his best to feed them. He would steal bread, peanut butter and coffee from the

Claremont College faculty lounge and found a source of free instant mashed potato at a blood donor centre. Motorhead: 'Everytime we'd get any money at all, we'd just go buy some peanut butter and a loaf of bread.' It was his job to take the empty soda bottles to the grocery store to cash them in for cigarettes – by now Frank had a runaway habit.

There were no cooking facilities, just an industrial sink. Most of the time they never left the studio, spending their entire time recording and overdubbing, not knowing if it was day or night. Motorhead: 'One day we'd open the door and the sun would be shining and it would surprise the hell out of us.' Taping proceeded as usual and one of the numbers from this period is a song called 'Charva', a mispronunciation of Sharva, the name of Motorhead's girlfriend.

This is when Jim Sherwood acquired the name Motorhead: 'I lived in the studio with Frank for about six months. Frank and I would get a lot of people over there to do things and he knew Ray Collins. Ray would come over and sing. He was working with Jimmy (Carl Black) and Roy (Estrada) who got Frank into the band that eventually led to the Mothers. Ray was always joking with me because I was working on cars and trucks and motorcycles. He said "It sounds like you've got a little motor in your head," so they just called me Motorhead and that seemed to stick. I've always been called that ever since.'

The three-room studio now took on the look of Zappa's later abodes: the walls filled with an assemblage of memorabilia: his divorce papers, a photograph of Frank playing the bicycle on the Steve Allen Show, rejection letters from various record companies and a threat from the Department of Motor Vehicles to revoke his drivers licence, as well as bits of comic book and pop art.

Out of the movie flats he built and painted a two-dimensional rocket ship of the Flash Gordon variety. It was like a cheap Hollywood cartoon of the period, with TEAR ON THE DOTTED LINE and other instructions painted on it. He no longer pinned his hopes on *I Was A Teenage Maltshop*; he would propel Don Vliet to stardom with a low budget sci-fi film called *Captain Beefheart vs the Grunt People*. It was based on Don's parents, Sue and Glen, and involved a mad scientist, space travel and all the usual ingredients of very cheap sci-fi films.

Captain Beefheart occupied Zappa for many years. He repainted all the slats and finished up sleeping in the back of the studio in the set for the mad scientist, Billy Sweeney's laboratory.

In the spring of 1965, desperate for cash as usual, Frank got together a power trio called the Muthers: Frank on guitar, Paul Woods on bass and Les Papp on drums. They played weekends at the Saints and Sinners on Holt Boulevard in Montclair to an audience of Mexican orange pickers entertained by four go-go girls in black fishnet stockings who would jump on the tables. As the Muthers pumped out 'In The Midnight Hour', the band, the go-go girls and the audience were watched over by one policeman during the week and two at weekends.

The Muthers were regarded as freaks because their hair was about three inches long, instead of shaved into a flat-top or crewcut (Frank's father became so energized about it that he wouldn't allow him in the house unless he had it cut). At Candy's suggestion, Frank had stopped greasing it back and instead brushed it forwards like the Beatles.

On the night that the track on the *Mystery Disc* was recorded, a Mexican tried to pull off Frank's moustache. Zappa: 'I used to have to sing with that trio at the Mexican place, but that was mostly blues-type songs. I have a horrible time singing and playing at the same time – just ridiculous. I can barely strum a chord and say one word over it; that's hard coordination for me. I'd never make it in country and western music.'

Studio Z rapidly filled up with people. Frank had invited Lorraine Belcher to move in almost as soon as he had unpacked his R&B singles. She had a friend – a white girl with a black baby – who also needed somewhere to stay. The good Christians at the church across the street were horrified to see this little black baby playing in the dirt on the sidewalk outside the studio, and their fears about Studio Z were strengthened by a feature in the *Ontario Daily Report*. Apparently a strange individual called 'the Movie King of Cucamonga' was making a film called *Captain Beefheart vs the Grunt People*. 'Movie King' could only mean one thing to the local police: he was making pornographic flicks.

One day, while the Muthers were working the Saints and Sinners, the cop on duty came up and casually asked Frank if he would be interested in making some training films for the San Bernardino vice squad. Frank thought it was a great idea. He had visions of showing the police that the transvestites and gays they were busting should be treated with respect instead of the usual rough-'em-up routine. The cop gave Frank his card, but he heard no more from him.

Frank announced a casting-call for the movie, even though he had no financing for it. It was then that the Cucamonga police department tipped off the San Bernardino sheriff's office that they had a pornographer in town. Detective Sgt Jim Willis drove over and auditioned for the film, at the same time taking note of the contents of the studio. Convinced he'd uncovered a porn ring, Willis had Studio Z placed under surveillance – he even had a hole drilled in the wall to listen in on Zappa's activities.

A few weeks later, Willis, disguised as a used-car salesman, stopped by the studio. He wanted a stag film for a party. Frank said he could make one for $300, but Willis balked at the price, so Frank quickly added that a tape recording would only be $100. Willis ran through a list of the sex acts he wanted to hear on the tape and Frank agreed, unaware that their conversation was being relayed to a van parked across the street using a transmitter hidden in Willis' Dick Tracy wrist-watch.

That evening Frank and Lorraine recorded 30 minutes of grunts and moans and made the bedsprings squeak. Frank then carefully edited out the giggles and added a little sexy background music. The following day, Friday 26 March 1965, Willis returned and offered Frank $50. Frank objected that the deal was for $100 and refused to part with the tape. Just then the door slammed open and three policemen burst into the room accompanied by local reporters. Frank was blinded by flashbulbs as Detective Willis slapped on the handcuffs. The police stripped Studio Z of all recording tape and even Frank's 8mm projector. He and Lorraine were bundled into a police car and taken off to the county jail to be charged. Fortunately, Motorhead was out buying hamburgers and Lorraine's girlfriend also escaped being involved.

It was a classic case of police entrapment. Under California law the pornography charge was merely a misdemeanour. However, if two or more people simply discuss doing something criminal, it becomes a conspiracy to commit a crime and is a felony. Zappa was charged with conspiracy to commit pornography, for which the maximum sentence was 20 years.

Paul Buff put up the $1,500 to bail him out and persuaded Art Laboe to advance Frank $1,500 from his royalties for writing 'Grunion Run', to pay Lorraine's bail. Zappa's father, who had recently suffered another heart attack, had to take out a bank loan to pay back Buff. He didn't always see eye to eye with his son, but he wasn't about to let one of the family down. When Willis turned up at the house looking for Frank in the week before arraignment, Francis repeatedly jabbed the detective in the chest, screaming abuse at him, and ordered him off his property.

The local press had a field day: 2 A-GO-GO TO JAIL was the kicker above the front-page story headlined VICE SQUAD RAIDS LOCAL FILM STUDIO in the *Ontario Daily Report*. Their reporter had been in on the raid and had a good look round Studio Z.

Frank's father had hired a lawyer and Frank was advised to plead *nolo contendere* – no contest, the only option for people who can't afford expensive legal representation. 'How could you be such a fool as to let this guy con you?' asked Frank's lawyer. 'I thought *everybody* knew Detective Willis. He's the kind of guy who earns his living waiting around in public restrooms to catch queers.' Frank was still an innocent and had never heard of such people. It came as a shocking revelation.

He was charged for conspiracy and during the trial the judge took Frank and Lorraine into his chambers, along with the lawyers, to listen to the offending tape. It was so funny the judge started laughing, which infuriated the prosecutor, a 26-year-old assistant district attorney who demanded that Frank be forced to serve time for this terrible crime 'in the name of Justice!'

Lorraine was not charged, but Frank was found guilty of a

misdemeanour and given six months in jail, with all but ten days suspended. He was put on three years probation, during which he could not violate any traffic laws or be in the company of a woman under 21 without a chaperone. His criminal record was erased after a year, which is why researchers have found nothing in the records relating to the case, but it exempted him from military service.

As Frank waited to be transported to the San Bernardino county jail, Willis entered the holding tank. 'If you'll give me permission to decide which of those tapes we confiscated are obscene,' he said, 'we'll give you back all the rest of them, erased.' Frank told Willis that he did not have the authority to transform him from a policeman into a judge and that Willis had no right to do anything to the tapes, they were Zappa's property. The case was closed and Zappa was legally entitled to them. But of the 80 hours of tape seized, the police only returned 30.

Frank was learning about the *real* American Way of Life: in Tank C he met a 19-year-old Mexican who had been waiting for three weeks to be extradited to Beverly Hills for jaywalking. It was the worst experience of Zappa's life. There were 44 men crammed together in the cell in temperatures reaching 104 degrees. The lights were on day and night, so the inmates couldn't sleep. Zappa didn't shave or shower the entire time he was in there, the facilities were so dirty. One morning he found a large cockroach at the bottom of his breakfast creamed-wheat. He enclosed it in a letter to Motorhead's mother, but the prison censor found it and threatened him with solitary confinement if he tried anything like that again. He sat there, powerless, seething with anger at the American 'justice' system and playing an imaginary guitar. He dreamed up power chords so loud and ugly that they'd tear the bars right out of the walls, so they could all escape to freedom.

Frank was a different person when he came out. He no longer believed in anything the authorities had ever told him. As far as he was concerned, the entire American education system had failed him; it was a lie from start to finish, the reality was that America was a corrupt, grubby little fascist state. He was determined never to be duped again. Tank C traumatized him for life and in many ways he spent the rest of his career shoving his pornographic tape down America's throat, time and time again. He was determined to show Americans what their country was really like.

Frank's jail term had repercussions for his family. The girls at Pomona Catholic Girls High were told by their good Christian mothers to have nothing to do with Candy, who was shunned by her former friends in case she somehow infected them. Frank's father was so incensed by the affair that he refused to let his son return home. Motorhead's mother took him in while he figured out what to do with his life.

Frank realised that he had to get away from the sticks, but as usual he had no money. However, a few days after leaving jail he received a phone call from Ray Collins. They had not seen each other for a year or so and Ray was working as a carpenter with his brother-in-law. He met some builders working on a bar called the Broadside at 960 East Holt Boulevard in Pomona and through them had got to know Skip, the owner. It was a class joint and Ray took to hanging out there.

Skip hired a band called the Soul Giants to play weekends at the Broadside. The drummer was Jimmy Carl Black, a Cheyenne Indian who put the band together after meeting bass player Roy Estrada at a music pawnshop. Black was pawning some cymbals in order to eat and had posted his name on the board as an available drummer. He and Roy started talking and together they formed the Soul Giants with a guitarist called Ray Hunt, a sax player called Dave Coronada – who became the bandleader – and a singer called Dave. Sometimes Collins would get up and sing with them and unfortunately for Dave, Skip liked Ray's singing a lot better than Dave's. He told the band they could stay, but Dave had to go and Ray would be the lead singer.

In his autobiography, Zappa claimed that Ray [Collins] got into a fight with Ray Hunt and punched him out, which is why the guitarist quit. Frank didn't know the Soul Giants at this time and got the story wrong. There was no fight. Hunt didn't really want to be in the band and took to playing the wrong chords behind Collins. At a band meeting the other members of the group confronted him and he agreed to leave. Collins remembered Zappa and telephoned to see if he'd like to take Hunt's place in the Soul Giants. It came at an opportune time.

Frank joined and together they played their way through the usual standards: 'In The Midnight Hour', 'Woolly Bully' and 'Louie Louie'. The Soul Giants now contained four members of the future Mothers of Invention: Zappa and his old buddy Ray Collins, Jimmy Carl Black and Roy Estrada.

Jimmy Carl Black was born James Inkanish Jr in 1938. Known to Mothers fans as 'the Indian of the group', he was five-eighths Cheyenne. He was conceived on the reservation in Oklahoma, but his mother moved to El Paso, Texas, before he was born. Jimmy played trumpet from the age of twelve, but switched to drums when he joined the Air Force in 1958. He spent several years in Wichita, Kansas, pumping gas and working as a part-time professional drummer before moving to LA.

Roy Estrada was born in Orange County in 1943 and came from a Mexican-American background. He grew up in Santa Ana, not far from the coast, and received his musical education by listening to the local orchestra. He took lessons in bass playing and learned to sing at a very early age. He and a friend formed the Viscounts, initially performing Latin music, but as they began playing after-hours bars, they drifted more towards R&B and blues. Roy augmented this meagre income by sometimes driving a lumber truck, a fact celebrated in 'The Orange County Lumber Truck' on the *Weasels Ripped My Flesh* album. He had just turned 21 when he ran into Jimmy Carl Black at the pawnshop and already had many years of playing R&B behind him.

Zappa: 'I thought it was a spiffy little group and I proposed a business deal whereby we'd form a group and make some money, maybe even a little music.' He thought they were too good to be just a bar band. As long as they played covers, no record company would give them a contract. He proposed that they play original music – *his* original music – and try to make it in the business.

Zappa: 'Initially it was a financial arrangement. When you're scuffling in bars for zero to seven dollars per night per man, you think about money first. There's always the hope held out that if you stick together long enough you'll make money and you'll get a record contract. It all sounded like science fiction then, because this was during the so-called British Invasion and if you didn't sound like the Beatles or the Stones, you didn't get hired.'

Jimmy Carl Black remembered the sales pitch: 'Zappa said, and I quote "If you guys will play my music, I'll make you rich and famous." Well, he kept half of the statement. I'm a hell of a lot more famous than rich. The music was, I would say for the times, pretty experimental. I thought it was interesting, but I couldn't figure out why we couldn't do music that would be played on the radio like the Beatles or the Stones.'

Dave Coronada thought it was financial suicide and resigned from the band in order to take a steady job managing a bowling alley in La Puene. He was right. As long as they stuck to cover versions everything went well, but the moment they launched into one of Frank's numbers people stopped dancing, no one bought any beer and they got fired. Frank encouraged them to hang in there. They moved from one go-go bar to another: the Red Flame in Pomona, the Shack in Fontana, the Tom Cat in Torrance. After playing the Tom Cat ('a really wretched place') they would go to jam sessions at a joint called Lambs.

Zappa: 'At that time the band was known as Captain Glasspack and His Magic Mufflers, and they kept throwing us out. They had this old pig who played the piano who was the Mistress of Ceremonies and she was embarrassed to introduce us when we wanted to get up and rock out. She'd say, "You guys gotta be kidding with a name like that." ... It was a strange time ...

'Eventually we went back to the Broadside in Pomona and we called ourselves the Mothers. It just happened by sheer accident to be Mother's Day [10 May 1965], although we weren't aware of it at the time. When you are nearly starving to death, you don't keep track of holidays.' Frank knew there was no future for the group in scuffling around the Pomona Valley; to make it the Mothers had to move to Hollywood.

Meanwhile, Frank had fallen behind with the rent on Studio Z and the landlord had padlocked the door. With the aid of some wire-cutters Frank got in and held a few rehearsals there before salvaging what he could of his possessions. He often said that he had to leave because the studio was to be demolished in a road-widening scheme, but this is not the case. He was evicted and Studio Z stood empty for more than a year before it was torn down when Archibald Avenue was widened in 1966.

Frank now had a group of good musicians who were prepared to play his music. Zappa: 'I never had any intention of writing rock music. I always wanted to compose more serious music and have it performed in concert halls, but I knew no one would play it. So I figured that if anyone was ever going to hear anything I composed, I'd have to get a band together and play rock music. That's how I got started.' Phase two was to move to Hollywood, which he did that May, getting a tiny cottage in Echo Park and preparing for a sustained assault on the music business.

7 The Strip

Frank moved into 1819 Bellevue Avenue, a tiny stucco cottage with one room, a kitchen and a bath. It was one of six buildings cut into the south side of a steep incline and reached by a long concrete stairway. Zappa called it a 'grubby little place on the side of a hill'. The rent was $70 a month. Frank unpacked his R&B records, tacked up a few old El Monte Legion Stadium posters and called it home. The local Mexican kids would look in through his barred window and call him 'Beardo Weirdo'.

It is a very hilly neighbourhood, which now enjoys a fabulous view of the downtown skyscrapers, which were not there in Zappa's time. At the end of the block, below Glendale Boulevard, is Echo Park with Echo Lake and its pleasure boats and palm trees. It was a cheap, old working-class neighbourhood of small single-storey cottages and the occasional court lived in mostly by Mexicans, Japanese, Filipinos and blacks – much as Aldous Huxley had described it 25 years before in *After Many A Summer*, but now with a scattering of musicians and students.

Frank's first move was to get a job in Wallach's Music City, the legendary, cavernous record store at Sunset and Vine. He worked as a salesman in the singles department and wore a badge saying

MR ZAPPA. It was Wallach's policy that you could get fired if you were seen going to lunch with a staff member of the opposite sex, which really annoyed Zappa. In addition to records, radios and musical instruments, the store sold second-hand singles and albums, and a percentage of his income stayed with his employers. During his first week he only had enough money for the bus fare each day and by payday he was starving. He cashed his paycheck and went to a Filipino food store at the bottom of the hill where he bought rice, a bag of red beans, some spices and a quart bottle of Miller High Life – a lethal combination on an empty stomach.

Meanwhile, he worked at the next phase of the master plan: getting a manager. Shortly after moving to Echo Park he ran into Don Cerveris again, who introduced him to his friend Mark Cheka, a pop artist from the Lower East Side of New York. Though Frank didn't understand his art, he liked Cheka and they spent some time hanging out together. Frank assumed that a manager should be someone older with an artistic background, who appreciated what the group were doing, so he sounded out Cheka for the position. He even persuaded him to make the long drive out to the Broadside in Pomona to see the Mothers play. Cheka knew nothing about managing a group, but he did get them a few gigs. However, the only way to develop a following was to play a regular gig on the Strip, and this was proving to be an elusive goal.

In Los Angeles, the long stretch of Sunset Boulevard known as the Strip had been the happening place ever since prohibition. Now the folk clubs, jazz cellars and nightspots were converting to rock 'n' roll.

Los Angeles is new; in the twenties the Strip was still a dirt track through citrus and avocado fields, subject to flooding and mud-slides in the rainy season. This stretch of Sunset, between Hollywood and Beverly Hills, was outside the Los Angeles city limits, and it flourished as an independent region, only subject to L.A. county laws and the easily-bribed county sheriffs. With the coming of prohibition this 'no man's land' became home to brothels and speakeasies. It was ideally located between the Hollywood studios and Beverly Hills where the stars had just begun to build their homes. By the mid-1930s, Sunset Strip contained the hottest nightspots on earth, including the famous trio: the Trocadero, El Mocambo, and Ciro's. By the beginning of the sixties it was also home to record companies, recording studios and a new generation of clubs.

The Whisky a Go-Go was opened in 1964 by former Chicago vice-cop Elmer Valentine, and modelled on Paul Pacine's famous Whisky au Go-Go in Paris where the discotheque craze began with go-go girls dancing in cages. The opening act was Johnny Rivers, who pulled in the celebrity crowd. The album *Johnny Rivers at the Whisky Au Go Go* spent 45 weeks high in the charts from July 1964, and it was clear to the club's owners that the future for the Strip was in rock 'n' roll. New clubs like the Roxy and the Rainbow opened on the Strip.

Still going on the Strip was Ciro's, for 20 years the headquarters of Marlene Dietrich, Judy Garland, Cary Grant, Clark Gable, and the Rat Pack, but by the sixties it was dead. It reopened as a rock club and, in March 1965, hired the newly formed Byrds as their house band. The Byrds had started as 'Beatle imitators' – Roger McGuinn's phrase – and made a successful synthesis of LA soft country rock and the spikier English invasion group sound. Record producer Kim Fowley explained: 'The whole idea of putting the Byrds on at Ciro's was that all the freaks would show up and the Byrds would be their Beatles. And the theory proved exactly right.'

The Byrds became local heroes and by the time 'Mr Tambourine Man' reached Number One, you couldn't get near Ciro's, the sidewalk was so packed. New clubs and coffeeshops opened all along the Strip: the Galaxy, Gazzari's, the Action, the Fifth Estate coffee house, London Fog – a few doors down from the Whisky – and the Trip, owned by the Whisky's owners.

Zappa and the Mothers were relative latecomers to the LA music scene. They had spent an inordinate amount of time in the far suburbs of East LA and had a lot of catching up to do. The original Byrds were all born in 1942 or 1943, but by the time the Mothers arrived on the Strip, the Byrds were already climbing up the charts. The age difference was not that great, but the Mothers were always perceived as being older by the kids because they *looked* older; and all the other groups had the requisite long Beatles hair.

Some groups wore wigs to achieve the coveted look, but the Mothers never stooped so low. However, it took time to grow shoulder-length hair and Frank's prison haircut was a distinct disadvantage. Roy Estrada and Jimmy Carl Black resisted. They lived in Santa Ana, in conservative Orange county, where it was dangerous to look weird. But Jimmy found a solution: 'If you had a good ski jacket and kept the hood up you could hide your hair when you were in Ronald Reagan's Orange County. When you were in Hollywood you took off the ski jacket and looked like a Hippie. Everything worked out great for me that way.'

To distract from this lack of hair, the Mothers affected a uniform of purple shirts and black homburgs. This made Zappa – with his moustache and goatee and prison haircut still growing out – look more like an Italian village mayor circa 1914, rather than a groovy rock 'n' roll star.

Mark Cheka realised that his management was not going to bring the band fame and fortune and suggested they use a friend of his called Herb Cohen, who actually managed groups for a living. They arranged to meet Cohen at a film party where the Mothers were playing. Cheka was friends with a director called Robert Carl Cohen who had just finished shooting a cheap exploitation movie called *Mondo Hollywood*, an attempt to cash in on the success of *Mondo Cane*. It featured Bobby Beausoleil (later a member of the Manson gang), hair stylist Jay Sebring (later murdered by the Manson gang), Jayne Mansfield and considerable footage of Vito, Karl Franzoni and Szou, a group of dancers who were to become close friends with Frank and the Mothers.

Part of the received Zappa story is that the Mothers played in the film and later, when Herb Cohen tried to get money for their performance, their footage was cut. This was not the case. The Mothers were hired as the entertainment for a huge party thrown by Robert Cohen for the cast and crew to celebrate the completion of principal filming. Cohen filmed the party – stills show Frank in his black homburg – and he inserted a few clips of them after principal shooting. Cohen: 'I also recorded the Mothers that night, but the mike was unshielded and picked up too much crowd noise . . . There are only a few fleeting moments of him and his group, then known as the Mothers in *Mondo Hollywood.'*

Shortly after the *Mondo Hollywood* party the Mothers took on Herb Cohen as their manager and he set to work. That October he got them an audition at the Action at 8265 Santa Monica Boulevard. Six months earlier they had been turned away because their hair wasn't long enough – it still wasn't very long, so they went in wearing their purple shirts and black homburg hats. Zappa: 'We looked like Mafia undertakers. The management of this establishment responded on a visceral level to this packaging and hired us for a four-week tour of duty. That was the start of the Big Time.' In truth, their engagement was probably more due to Herb Cohen's connections than to their outfits. Herb was a good choice for a manager at this stage of their career; he really did know everyone you needed to know to make it on the Strip – and he liked a challenge.

Born in 1933 Herb Cohen had been a marine, a deckhand and fire-man and for a short time a union organizer for the Marine Cooks and Stewards Union. He was in the army for eight months in San Francisco before being discharged as 'incompatible'. He lived with Odetta, the folk singer, and became involved with the folk club scene. In 1954 he relocated to LA and began promoting folk concerts by groups like Pete Seeger and the Weavers. This was the McCarthy era and many of Herb's acts were regarded as out and out communists.

In 1956 he managed the newly opened Purple Onion, putting on folk and blues acts like Theodore Bikel and Sonny Terry and Brownie McGee. Next he ran the Unicorn in LA with Victor Maymudes (later Bob Dylan's trusted roadie and amanuensis). The Unicorn was on Sunset, next door to what would become the Whiskey, and featured live music and poetry. It was a success so Herb opened Cosmo Alley on Cosmo Street, between Hollywood Boulevard and Selma, behind the Ivar Theater. He put on Mort Sahl, George Carlin and in 1959 he was busted for obscenity for one of Lenny Bruce's shows (he won the court case, but the legal fees were steep). Cosmo Alley lost money and Herb decided to take a long vacation.

Leaving his lawyer brother Martin – known as Mutt – in charge of the Unicorn, Cohen roamed through Cuba, Egypt, Algiers, Europe and the Middle East for three years. He supplied arms to Patrice Lumumba in defiance of the CIA who supported Joseph Mobutu as being more likely to protect US business interests in the Congo. Belgium conceded the Congo's independence in June 1960 and Lumumba became the country's first Prime Minister. Within six months he had been tortured to death by Mobutu's soldiers, leaving Herb outside Stanleyville with four trucks filled with guns. This was a little too exciting, so Herb concentrated on the business end, selling arms from an office in Copenhagen.

He returned to LA in 1963, but after eight months he was so bored he moved to New York where he managed folk singers Judy Henske and the Modern Folk Quartet. Zappa met him when he had just returned from the east coast, ready to get involved in the burgeoning folk and rock scene on the Strip. When *Teen Set* asked Zappa who is Herbie Cohen? he replied: 'He's a little Jewish man that nobody likes who always wears nylon shirts – the acme of bad taste, who likes to hit people in the face with his head and has a terrible reputation coast to coast! Our manager – Yeah, Herbie!'

The first thing Herb did was get them to join the Musicians Union – local 47 – mandatory if they wanted to play the Whiskey. It cost them a lot of money, but it meant they could put up their rates (and they needed to with Herb taking 15 per cent). There was an immediate improvement in their situation. Herb got them four weeks at the Action. As Zappa put it: 'Almost overnight we had jumped from starvation level to poverty level.' It also helped that Herb could put them into his own clubs – the Unicorn and Cosmo Alley – if bookings were thin on the ground.

Frank studied the career trajectory of the Byrds and noted that the support of the local freak community – as early hippies were called in LA – was essential to be a success on the Strip. The Byrds were closely associated with Vito and the Freaks: Vito Paulekas, his wife Zsou and Karl Franzoni, the leaders of a group of about 35 dancers whose antics enlivened the Byrds' early gigs.

Vitautus Alphonsus Paulekas was born in 1910, the son of a Lithuanian sausage-maker who settled in Massachusetts. He spent a year and a half in a reformatory at the age of 18 and was busted several times after that, all of which gave him a life-long aversion to the police. He spent six months as a marathon dancer during the Depression and he was already in his fifties when he connected with the rock 'n' roll scene in 1962. He began dancing every two weeks with Jim Doval & the Gauchos at a club on the Strip. He wore his hair in a Beatle cut and his youthful body was betrayed by his lined face and greying moustache.

Three nights a week Vito gave clay-modelling classes to rich Beverly Hills dowagers in his studio at 303 North Laurel Street, a two-storey white stucco Moroccan-looking commercial building on the corner with Beverley Blvd, just around the corner from Fairfax High. Vito's studio was in the basement, reached through his wife Zsou's dress shop. He kept an open house and it was the first crash pad in LA, home to countless runaways, especially young women. He met his wife Zsou when she was only 16. Kim Fowley: 'Vito was in his sixties, but he had four-way sex with goddesses.' His studio was brightly lit with fluorescent tubes and painted like a Mayan tomb. One wall was covered with a collage of newspaper clippings, a political satire of words and headlines about capital punishment, the Vietnam war, marriage and big corporations.

The Byrds needed somewhere to rehearse and Vito offered his studio. It was March 1965 and he was looking for a band to present at an anti-Vietnam war dance. After seeing them rehearse he booked them for the gig. About 200 people showed up and their music proved to be perfect for free-form dancing. From then on the Byrds and Vito and his Freaks were inseparable. Next came the Byrds' first night at Ciro's and Vito and about 15 of his dancers went with them. Ciro's had one of the best dance floors in Hollywood. Karl Franzoni: 'We stepped on the dance floor, and from then on it was music and dance for months and months! All right!' Club owners let the Freaks in free as they were an attraction in their own right.

Even after they had a Number One hit, the Byrds took Vito's gang with them on tour, but inevitably they outgrew the Freaks. Fortunately, just as the Byrds bowed out, two new groups were making their presence known on the Strip: Arthur Lee and Love, and the Mothers.

Zappa's interest in Vito, Zsou and Karl Franzoni was twofold. They provided a ready-made audience of about 35 crazed dancers, which got every evening off to a good start, but he was also intrigued by their brazen lifestyle. He was drawn to Vito in much the same way he was attracted to Kenny and Ronnie Williams back in Lancaster and to Don Vliet's peculiar parents. Zappa's genius – whether dealing with TV evangelists, Freaks or simply describing a kitchen – was to carefully research the character or details of his subject, then to blow it up into epic proportions. Vito was a Hollywood beatnik: he appeared regularly on *The Joe Pyne Show* and in between the bare-breasted girls in the late fifties and early sixties men's magazines.

Zsou, an ex-cheerleader, was a pioneer of the thrift-store look; her shop was filled with tatty lace and velvet from the twenties and thirties, frocks and scarves and sequinned bags. Karl Franzoni: 'She became, in the sixties, THE person of elegant things for freaks to wear. They all bought their clothes from her and when we went out dancing you would see these bright coloured people. Women all wore see-through, no panties, no bras – and that was it. She just wore a dress – you could just look right through her – and that was it – (with) high heels or whatever.'

Vito's best friend Karl Franzoni joined the troupe in 1963. His hair was an aura of tight greasy curls surrounding a bald crown, he had a goatee and an unusually long pointed tongue which he used to shoot out to lick the faces of surprised girls like a gila monster. He wore red tights, garish tops and a cape with an 'F' emblazoned on it which stood, not for 'Franzoni' but for 'Captain Fuck'. He was a sexual predator, forever pinching girls' buttocks and forcing his attentions on them.

Vito and company were attracted to the Mothers because they had similar interests. They began to show up at Mothers gigs to dance, though Zappa's music was never as danceable as the Byrds' and required a lot more concentration. They couldn't just flow with it because Frank was always changing the time signature or introducing spoken parts. Nevertheless, Zappa called them 'the Mothers Auxiliary' and Franzoni, in particular, appears in a lot of group photos from this time. Frank even began to dress like Vito's Freaks, just as he had become a Pachuco in order to run with the crowd.

Frank's anthropological interests intersected with a major political event that summer and resulted in the extraordinary blues 'Trouble Coming Every Day', a timeless rant against racial discrimination and the mindless commodification of news by American TV. He wrote it while watching the 1965 Watts riots live on television. It is a superb piece of journalism – involved, concerned and angry – with a heartfelt shout: 'I'm not black, but there's a whole lotta times I wish I could say I'm not white!'

On 11 August in the neighbourhood of Watts, an LA police officer flagged down and arrested a 21-year-old African-American named Marquette Frye, whom he suspected of driving while intoxicated. A crowd gathered and started taunting the policeman. A second officer was called, who struck out at them with his baton. News of police brutality quickly spread throughout the neighbourhood. It was all that was needed to provoke violence on a massive scale, fanned by a combination of escalating racial tension between the residents and the police, overcrowding and a summer heatwave. The following day residents began looting and burning white stores. The riots lasted six days, leaving 34 dead, more than a thousand wounded, about 4,000 arrested and an estimated $200 million in damage. More than 30,000 African-Americans took part in the riot.

'There's always been a journalistic aspect in my work even from the first album,' said Zappa. 'I would say certainly a song about the Watts Riot, which was on the *Freak Out* album, qualified as some form of journalism, because a lot of people don't even remember what the Watts Riot was, and so, at the point where you make the song, the Watts

Riot was a recent journalistic event... but over a period of years... it just becomes folklore. The fact is Channel 5 in Los Angeles, which showed the pictures of the riot, did have a story about a woman sawed in half by 50-caliber machine-gun bullets from the National Guard that was down there taking care of the riot. And that may be the only lasting monument to the woman who got sawed in half. There's a lot of things like that in songs that go from journalism into folklore.' When *Freak Out!* came out, Frank received a visit from the FBI. They wanted to know just how involved he had been in the riots.

'Trouble Coming Every Day' was not the only song Zappa wrote about the troubles in Watts and the burgeoning hippie scene on the Strip. In his little cottage in Echo Park the ideas came thick and fast: 'In that house I wrote "Brain Police", "Oh No, I Don't Believe It", "Hungry Freaks", "Bowtie Daddy" and five or six other ones. A lot of the songs off the first album had already been written for two or three years before the album came out. And a lot of the new songs were not recorded until the third or fourth album. About 50 per cent of the songs were concerned with the events of 1965. Los Angeles, at that time, in the kiddie community that I was hanging out in, they were seeing God in colours and flaking out all over the place. You had plenty of that and meanwhile there was all that racial tension building up in Watts.'

After playing at the Action, Herb got the Mothers a residency at the Whisky. Johnny Rivers was on tour and they needed someone cheap to fill in. Elmer Valentine did not regard them as a major attraction, as there was not even a poster until their last three days – and that the Mothers had to pay for. The big problem was that no one could dance to their music. The audience was evenly divided between those who yelled for 'In the Midnight Hour' and those who were genuinely interested in the extraordinary sounds the group was making.

This problem was compounded by Zappa's pseudo-Mexican rap. Growing up in the cultural desert of East Los Angeles, the prevailing culture had been that of the Pachuco. Frank had become adept at long Pachuco raps, which he interspersed with the band's numbers. He had perfected their mocking, cynical tone and traces of it remained in his

diction for life. He even had Ruben Sana paraphrase Varèse on *Cruisin'
With Ruben and the Jets*: 'The present day Pachuco refuses to die.' Albert
Goldman wrote about this phenomenon, describing it as 'The character of the "white nigger": the man who deliberately adopts the speech,
dress and life-style of the black ghetto, partly out of enthusiasm for the
vitality of the ghetto and partly out of an angry rejection of the values
of the white world.'

Not everyone was taken with his Pachuco rap. Towards the end
of 1965 Frank decided to enlarge the Mothers' line-up. 'We went to LA,
where we added Alice Stuart,' said Zappa in 1968. 'I had an idea for
combining certain modal influences into our basically country blues
(Muddy Waters, Howlin' Wolf, etc.) sound. Alice played very good
finger-style guitar and sang well, but she couldn't play "Louie Louie",
so I fired her.' Alice, for her part, said that she left after three months
because she couldn't stand Frank 'doing his Chicano rap'.

Alice was replaced by Henry Vestine, described by Zappa as 'one
of the most outstanding blues guitarists on any coast.' Officially hired
on 15 November 1965, Vestine had an encyclopaedic knowledge of blues
and R&B records and he and Zappa spent many happy hours discussing rarities and obscure labels. Another record collector/blues fanatic,
Bob Hite (known as 'the Bear') often joined them. Zappa and Vestine
got on so well that they took a place together in a court on Formosa
Avenue, just below Sunset, a couple of blocks west of La Brea.

One of their neighbours was the singer Victoria Winston and the
area was filled with musicians and movie people (the Warner studios
were nearby). Frank offered several songs to Winston's group, Simon's
Children, but her producer didn't like them. She told Neil Slaven, the
author of *Zappa: Electric Don Quixote*, that she had wanted to do something with a political message, so Zappa may have given her 'Trouble
Coming Every Day'. In the sleeve notes to *Freak Out!* he said: 'I shopped
it briefly all over Hollywood, but no one would touch it.'

It was during the period that Henry Vestine was with the Mothers
that they were signed to MGM-Verve. The group had recorded some
demos at Original Sound, where Paul Buff had now completed his
ten-track studio. Herb Cohen sent these out with little success, except

to give Zappa one of most famous phrases. Clive Davis, head of Columbia Records, replied saying that the Mothers had 'no commercial potential'.

MGM-Verve had just hired a new A&R man and in-house producer called Tom Wilson. In the late fifties and early sixties he had produced avant-garde jazz artists such as Sun Ra, Cecil Taylor and John Coltrane. In 1963 Columbia Records made him Bob Dylan's producer after Dylan's manager, Albert Grossman, pressured them to replace John Hammond. Wilson produced Dylan's *Bringing It All Back Home* (1965) and converted Dylan to rock 'n' roll by overdubbing three of his 1961–2 tracks with electric instruments to demonstrate how his folk music would sound with a rock 'n' roll beat. He also produced Dylan's 'Like A Rolling Stone' single, of which Zappa said: 'When I heard "Like A Rolling Stone" I wanted to quit the music business, because I felt "If this wins and does what it's supposed to do, I don't need to do anything else." ... but it didn't do anything. It sold, but nobody responded to it the way that they should have.'

Wilson, who disliked folk music, applied the same technique to Simon and Garfunkel, overdubbing electric instruments on the previously acoustic 'Sounds of Silence' and giving them a Number One hit. On the strength of this he was hired by Verve as head of East Coast A&R. His first move was to sign the Velvet Underground, producing their first two albums (though the first is credited to Andy Warhol who, in reality, only sat and watched).

In January 1966 Wilson visited the Coast. One evening at the Trip he met Herb Cohen and accompanied him to the Whisky to catch the Mothers. He arrived while they were doing an extended boogie workout of the 'Watts Riot Song'. Wilson was black and probably appreciated the anti-racist sentiments of the song; at any rate, according to Zappa: 'He heard us sing "The Watts Riot Song (Trouble Every Day)". He stayed for five minutes, said "Yeah, yeah, yeah," slapped me on the back, shook my hand and said, "Wonderful. We're gonna make a record of you. Goodbye." I didn't see him again for four months. He thought we were a rhythm and blues band. He probably went back to New York and said, "I signed me another rhythm and blues band from the Coast. They got this song about the riot. It's a protest song. They'll do a couple of singles and maybe they'll die out."'

This scenario is both extremely unlikely and an insult to Wilson's intelligence. He signed very few acts and would not have been so impetuous. Cohen had probably arranged to meet Wilson in the Trip and Wilson had probably already heard the Mothers' demos or at least knew what the word was on the street. Whatever – the important thing was, the Mothers had a record deal.

8 Freak Out!

The groups arriving on the Strip brought with them a new kind of fan: the first rock 'n' roll groupies. Little Richard had panties thrown at him in the mid-fifties and the Beatles in the red-light district of Hamburg had no shortage of girls, but it was not until the mid-sixties, with the English invasion and the dominance of groups rather than solo singers, that large numbers of girl fans offered sexual favours to musicians. Only then was there a rock 'n' roll lifestyle, which involved not just music but clubs, drugs, sex and endless hanging-out in coffee shops and motels.

Ben Frank's at 8585 Sunset, across the street from the Trip, was the gathering place of choice. It looked like a fifties sci-fi space station in a Flash Gordon movie. With 24-hour dining, it was a favoured hang-out of celebrities and movie stars. Vito and the Freaks would eat there, squeezing 15 people into one of the huge booths. Later they would bring in such a crowd after dancing at clubs that the management complained.

One of the Freaks was guitarist Arthur Lee. He got talking to Bryan MacLean, the ex-Byrds' roadie, in Ben Frank's parking lot and they decided to start a group: the Grass Roots, which soon became Love. Lee: 'We started the whole hippie thing: Vito, Karl, Zsou, Beatle

Bob, Bryan and me. Bryan put a ribbon in his hair and people would come to Ben Frank's after we played.' Towards the end of 1965, with so many new clubs and coffee shops, the sidewalks on the Strip were jam-packed with kids, one of the few places in LA where there was a street life: the block around Ben Frank's was the worst with people spilling out into the street.

Franzoni: 'Somebody mentioned a place called Cantor's on Fairfax was going out of business. Nobody was going there. So one night when they turned us out of Ben Frank's – there was a line way into the park-ing lot – I said "Let's go to Cantor's." We went down there. I'd say about 35 people walked into Cantor's. The place was almost empty – and from then on, that's where it was.'

Cantor's deli is at 419 North Fairfax. It was huge. The ceiling still has fifties light fittings and the off-white curved banquets with glass panels where Phil Spector and Lenny Bruce used to hang out. Cantor's specialized in corned beef and hot pastrami sandwiches, though Zappa was pleased to find they also served chilli and beans and quesadillas. But the food was never the attraction at Cantor's: it was the people. Open 24 hours, it welcomed the late-night traffic.

That November, after playing the Whisky, the Mothers moved to the Trip, which had a younger, more adventurous audience who really appreciated what they were doing. Zappa: 'We got lots of requests for "Help, I'm a Rock" and "Memories of El Monte". The trouble was, no one danced during these songs because there's talking in the middle and the audience wanted to listen. Elmer [Valentine] wanted people to dance in his club, because if someone looked in the door and saw an empty dance floor, they wouldn't come in. At least this is what he said. So one night we played both those tunes together for an hour! For a solid hour nobody danced. Immediately after that we were selling pop bottles to get money for cigarettes and bologna.'

Another reason they were fired might be that Zappa said 'fuck' on stage. This was illegal though you could say it in the street. Lenny Bruce made a point of demonstrating this ludicrous point of law while play-ing at Herb Cohen's Unicorn next door to the Whisky. He explained to the audience that there was a word he was not allowed to say on stage, then, using a long microphone lead, he went out of the stage door onto the street and said 'fuck'. The audience laughed and the cops in the audience busted him anyway.

Zappa related to the rebel comedians of the mid-fifties and early sixties who made ironic comments on politics and lifestyle. Comics like Mort Sahl whose 'sick humour' is an antecedent of Zappa's own and who spawned a whole generation of comedians including Woody Allen, Tom Lehrer, Nichols and May and Shelley Berman. Then Lenny Bruce came on the scene and destroyed the last taboos of sex and racism, confronting official censorship head-on in the interests of free speech. Zappa was instinctively drawn to him and, unusually for a man who claimed to have no friends except his own family, described Bruce as a friend, though they barely knew each other. In fact, the first and probably only time Frank met Bruce was when the Mothers opened for him at the Fillmore in San Francisco in June 1966.

Frank had a lot of respect for Bruce and asked him to sign his draft card, but Bruce refused. Zappa saw him as a saint who, despite his incapacitating heroin addiction, continually challenged the authorities over his right to free speech by using so-called 'obscenities' in his act, and took his convictions to the Supreme Court.

It is a common belief that satire is used by the oppressed against their oppressor, but this is not so. Jewish jokes mock Jewish sensibilities. Mort Sahl, Tom Lehrer, Woody Allen and company all mock liberal pieties. It was in this tradition that Zappa focused his satire not on the right wing in power, but upon liberal hypocrisies and lifestyle. His *Have I Offended Someone?* compilation ridicules disco, Valley Girls, Soul Brothers, record company executives, Catholic girls, homosexuals, women's liberation, Satanists, Jimi Hendrix fans, the Musicians' Union and beer-swilling mammary-obsessed adolescents – all easy targets and virtually all from within his own peer group. Only later did he turn his critical eye on Richard Nixon, Ronald Reagan, George Bush, TV evangelists and right-wing censors – with much less effect.

Zappa saw himself as a social critic, but aside from some power-ful early songs about the Brain Police and the Watts Riots, he was more content to mock hippies and groupies than to criticize the Vietnam

War, the American overthrow of democratic governments in Chile and Iran or any of the other excesses committed in his name by his government.

This new breed of humourist (Zappa included) focused their attention on what was happening on a personal level. the rapid growth of liberal attitudes, the civil rights movement, notions of equality, tolerance, personal rights and personal growth extending from the New Age therapies, through feminism and homosexual equality, the sexual freedom movement, to the political extremism of the Weathermen; everything we think of as 'the Sixties'. These 'liberal' ideas continued to spread into the American mainstream.

'America turned to the right politically while becoming increasingly liberated in its personal manners,' Adam Gopnik wrote in the *New Yorker*. 'This left comedians making fun of the pieties while looking past, or not caring very much about, the politics. The personal or apolitical tone of so much post-sixties comedy is, in this sense, not a betrayal but a simple tracking of the scent to the place where liberal pretension has gone, namely the bedroom and the living room. The object of comedy remains the absurdities of the new liberal order – but since its power has been largely relegated to private life, that, too, has become the subject of the comedy.'

Despite the right-wing backlash, 'liberal' ideas were so powerful and all pervasive that everything was questioned, from the sanctity of marriage to the length of a man's hair. Oddly, the sight of a young man with long hair outraged straight Americans more than anything else; it threw into question all their preconceived notions of gender and sexual preference. As 'liberal' ideas of free speech and free expression spread to a wider audience, they became 'dumbed down', until in place of Lenny Bruce, Woody Allen and Tom Lehrer, there was Howard Stern, *Beavis and Butt-Head* and *Wayne's World*. Zappa was to follow the same trajectory, dumbing down his lyrics and stage act to appeal to the lowest common denominator: the Mid-West teenager high on pills and beer who didn't even realize that 'Titties and Beer' was about him.

The early days in Hollywood were difficult for the Mothers and for several months they were on the verge of starvation. Nevertheless, Frank insisted on regular rehearsals. He was still owed money for the score of *Run Home, Slow*, but Tim Sullivan couldn't pay. Sullivan had leased a Hollywood sound stage on Seward Street, a few blocks south of Sunset, and from December 1965 the Mothers used it for rehearsals in lieu of the money owed. Even though the Laurentide Finance Company threatened to repossess Jimmy Carl Black's drum set, Frank still found enough money for tape and kept an Akai running much of the time. A rehearsal fragment showed up on *The Mystery Disc*.

They couldn't even hang out at the clubs unless they were on the door list, because they were not yet famous enough to gain free admission but Frank quickly became known to his fellow musicians. One night, while he was jamming with Arthur Lee and the Grass Roots at the Trip, a long-haired blond in the audience caught his eye. He introduced himself the moment he left the stage. She was Pamela Zarubica (later known as Suzy Creamcheese) who was to bring a little order to his existence over the next six months and introduce him to his future wife.

Pamela was attending Pepperdine College and living with her parents in Inglewood, but was about to make the move to Laurel Canyon. She left home a few weeks later, precipitating a crisis with her parents. Though they were never lovers, Frank and Pamela became close friends and eventually lived together.

At first she cleaned his little house on Bellevue. He paid her $5 a week, which was all he could afford. Sometimes she would have to give him 50 cents to put enough gas in his beaten-up Chevy station wagon for him to get to Laurel Canyon to see her. Frank enjoyed Pamela's company and spent a lot of time at her place, bringing her Chinese cookies from Greenblatt's with chocolate drops on top and drinking endless cups of instant coffee – he preferred it black, which was fortunate because they couldn't afford to buy milk. Pamela told Michael Gray, author of *Mother! The Frank Zappa Story*: 'He tried to teach me that sex didn't have to be dirty and that drugs were pointless . . . we used to have fun together, there was time to talk about things . . .

My God, the boy had talent, was obviously brilliant yet warm and close.' For her part she inspired several songs: Zappa made her catch phrase 'Wowie Zowie' into a song and she gave him the theme for 'You Didn't Try To Call Me'. When her father threatened court action to bring her home Frank contributed $5 towards the cost of a marriage of convenience with someone called Bobby.

On 6 November 1965 the Mothers played San Francisco. On the way to the airport with Ray Collins and Henry Vestine, Frank Zappa smoked one of the dozen or so joints in his life. Ray: 'Frank was, if I remember right, a bit giddy, and maybe paranoid.' Zappa was less than impressed with the hippie scene up north: 'I went up to San Francisco once or twice, but I wasn't interested or influenced by the scene there . . . Whereas in LA you had people making their own clothes, dressing however they wanted to dress. Wearing their hair out, that is, being as weird as they wanted to be in public and everybody going in separate directions – I got to San Francisco and found everybody dressed up in 1890s garb, all pretty specific codified dress. It was like an extension of high school, where one type of shoe is the "in" shoe, belt-in-the-back peggers or something like that. It was in the same sort of vein, but it was the costume of the 1890s. It was cute, but it wasn't as evolved as what was going on in LA. In San Francisco they had a "more rustic than thou" approach.'

No one could accuse Frank of looking rustic. His attire at the 1965 Halloween night performance at the Action consisted of bare feet, khaki work pants, an 1890s one-piece bathing suit and a black homburg with the top pushed in. Zappa also acquired a bright flower-patterned suit of thin cotton, unfortunately a bit short in the leg and rather explicit in revealing his aversion to jockey shorts – he claimed not to own any underwear. He tended to make up for any deficit in the other members' sartorial freakiness by assuming the most bizarre attire possible. In Los Angeles, a city with virtually no sense of fashion, it was actually very difficult to dress in a shocking manner. The best the Mothers could do was look different, but scarily so. Zappa: 'Now I didn't tell the guys what to wear; I merely suggested their mode of dress conform to what we were doing. I felt you couldn't play the sort of music we were playing and look the way some of the guys did: with processed pompadours.'

In February Henry Vestine quit because they were no longer playing the blues in any recognisable form. Zappa: 'He was part of the group for quite some time. But our music kept getting progressively stranger and he couldn't identify with what we were doing.' Jimmy Carl Black remembered him leaving: 'Frank came in with a new score he had just written the night before and presented it to us. Henry took one look at the music and said, "I can't play this shit! I'm quitting, an' I'm gonna go join a blues band!"' He joined Bob Hite to form Canned Heat.

This left Roy Estrada, Jim Black, Frank and Ray Collins, but Collins now decided he had had enough poverty and left the group. Frank hired Jim Guercio, who went on to make a fortune producing Chicago and Blood, Sweat and Tears. Zappa: 'He was part of our group for a while. Also, somewhere along the line, we had hired Steve Mann, who is also one of the top blues guitarists on the West Coast. He wanted to play in the group, but he couldn't make the changes and we got rid of him. Then we hired Elliot Ingber and Ray [Collins] came back in the band and there were five Mothers.' On 1 March 1966 they signed with MGM-Verve.

Frank always insisted that their producer Tom Wilson returned to Los Angeles 'just before' the recording sessions and that it was only then that Wilson realized they were not a blues band. This is clearly impossible as recording contracts invariably spell out what is expected from both parties: a certain number of singles and albums, delivery dates, renewal options and so on. In fact the TT&G recording studio at Sunset and Highland had already been booked for a four-day block from 9–12 March, time in those days to record an album. After the band signed, Wilson had just over a week to plan what to record. The contract was for five albums over two years, with a $2,500 advance. As the group's producer, Wilson would have already reviewed all the available tapes to select a single or material for an album, and some sources say he saw the band perform several times before signing them up.

Zappa's version was: 'He came back to town just before we were going to do our first recording session. We had a little chat in his room and that was when he first discovered that that [blues] wasn't all that we played. Things started changing. We decided not to make a single, we'd make an album instead. He wouldn't give me an idea of what the budget would be for the album, but the average rock 'n' roll album costs about $5,000.'

The Mothers were starving when they arrived at the studio. Frank told Jerry Hopkins: 'The first day of recording we didn't even have money to eat. If Jesse Kay hadn't given us ten dollars, we'd have passed out.' Kay was the MGM accounting representative who made sure they didn't overrun their allotted studio time. Frank ran down to the drive-in restaurant next door and soon the fully-fed Mothers were back at work.

The first track they cut was 'Any Way The Wind Blows', followed by 'Hungry, Freaks, Daddy' and 'Who Are The Brain Police?' According to Frank, Wilson was so impressed he got on the phone to MGM in New York and negotiated a more or less unlimited budget for the project. 'You can do something big,' he told Zappa. The final cost of *Freak Out!* was in the region of $21,000. Zappa was delighted: 'The next day I had whipped up the arrangements for a twenty-two piece orchestra. It wasn't just a straight orchestra accompanying the singers. It was the Mothers five-piece band plus seventeen pieces. We all worked together. The editing took a long time, which ran the cost up.' Frank did most of the overdubs himself, spending three weeks in the studio.

The session musicians were shocked to find they had to play from charts: Frank set up a podium in the middle of the studio and showed up wearing a swallow-tailed conductor's dinner jacket, a red and yellow striped shirt and an Iron Cross. He whipped out his baton from under his coat and rapped on the music stand. 'Hey, we're really going to have to play,' said one of the cello players. 'This beatnik has written some music here!' According to Tom Wilson: 'Frank gave it the full Toscanini and conducted their asses off.' Everything went smoothly as the arrangements were relatively easy.

Too easy for some people. There had been a new addition to the line-up just before recording: pianist Mac Rebennak left Sonny and

Rose Marie Zappa with baby Frank, Baltimore 1941. (Patrice 'Candy' Zappa collection)

Left to right back: Francis Zappa, Frank, Bob, Rose Marie. Front: Carl and Candy, California *c.* 1954. (Discreet Records press kit)

(*Right*) Frank's graduation photograph, Antelope Valley High School, Lancaster, CA, summer 1958. (Discreet Records press kit)

1819 Bellevue Avenue, Echo Park: 'Little house I used to live in.' (Barry Miles)

The Canyon Store, Laurel Canyon Blvd: groupie heaven. (Barry Miles)

Frank, aged 11 and already smoking, Bob aged 8 and Carl, 3 in Edgewood, MD. (Patrice 'Candy' Zappa collection)

The Blackouts *c.*1957. Left to right: Dwight Bement, tenor sax; Ernie Thomas, trumpet; Johnny Franklin, tenor sax; Frank Zappa, drums; Wayne Lyles, percussion and vocals. Terry Wimberly on piano, hidden. (Patrice 'Candy' Zappa collection)

The Charles Street apartment, New York, 1968 with Frank's favourite portrait of Gail on the wall, the Little Prince and the Bible on the shelf. (Linda McCartney © The Estate of Linda McCartney)

Frank with the talking bull on the set of *Head* by the Monkees, Los Angeles, November 1967. (pictorialpress.com)

Cher to join the Mothers. He showed up at rehearsals with a joint in his mouth and his friend Elliot Ingber signalled to him behind Frank's back to get rid of it. Rebennak had assumed from Frank's appearance that he was into drugs. He played on a couple of tracks, including 'Return of Monster Magnet'.

Rebennak: 'Everybody in the studio but Frank was wandering around high on acid. Frank had written me this part to play, five or six notes on the piano over and over – not much different than Sonny and Cher. In the background, a twenty-voice choir croaked out monster sound effects, something like "Gggrrrrrrhhhhrrr!" When I had had about all I could take, Les McCann walked in and I asked him to hold down my chair, telling him I had to go to the bathroom. I walked out of there and never came back.' Rebennak later reinvented himself as Dr John the Night Tripper, a musical voodoo shaman.

Some of Zappa's most important lyrics are on *Freak Out!*: 'It Can't Happen Here' and 'Trouble Coming Every Day', arguably the first recorded rap song. The strangest is 'Who Are the Brain Police?', which came to Zappa in what appears to have been an audio hallucination Zappa: '"Brain Police" was a phenomena because I was just sitting in the kitchen at the Bellevue Avenue house and I was working on "Oh No, I Don't Believe It", which didn't have lyrics at the time . . . and I heard, it was just like there was somebody standing over my shoulder telling me those lyrics and it was really weird. I looked around . . . I mean, it wasn't like "Hey Frank, listen to this . . .", but it was there. So I just wrote it down and figured the proper setting for it.'

Early in the morning of 13 March, Zappa assembled an audience of close to 100 Freaks in the studio in order to record a live version of 'The Return of the Son of Monster Magnet', described by Zappa in the sleeve notes as 'what freaks sound like when you turn them loose in a recording studio at one o'clock in the morning with $500 worth of rented percussion equipment'. Guests included Paul Butterfield, Les McCann, Danny Hutton (later of Three Dog Night) and four cast members from *The Untouchables* TV series. Vito and Karl Franzoni yipped and yelled, while Kim Fowley as chorus leader contributed on 'hypophone' (Frank's word for Fowley's big mouth). Some sang, some moaned, others popped gum into microphones. Tom Wilson celebrated the occasion by dropping acid.

There were a number of problems with MGM-Verve. First, they objected to the name the Mothers. They were fully aware that 'mother' was a short form of 'motherfucker', a term applied by musicians to someone with an unusual facility for playing their instrument. MGM did not want to offend Middle America and insisted the name be changed to Mothers of Invention. The band agreed. Second, Zappa had recorded too much material for a single album. He proposed a revolutionary deal to them: he would take a cut in publishing royalties if they released a double album at a single album price. (There were still four tracks left over, including the complete 1 April sessions involving seven session musicians.) Wilson clearly had a lot of clout at MGM because they agreed.

Frank devoted a lot of time to the sleeve design of *Freak Out!*. Zappa: 'The appearance of a group is linked to the music the same way an album cover is linked to the record. It gives a clue to what's inside. And the better the packaging the more the person who picked up that package will enjoy it.' In the event, the Mothers were in Hawaii when the sleeve was put together and though the outside packaging came out as Zappa wanted, complete with solarized 'psychedelic' photographs, the inside was scrambled: 'I screamed all over the place.'

Despite his irritation with the sleeve, Frank was delighted with the album. He showed up at his family's house dressed as he was on cover in long fur coat and sunglasses, waving a copy of the album, a huge smile on his face. His mother was changing the sheets. The music startled them, but Frank kept nodding encouragingly and no one expressed any misgivings. The whole family – even Francis – went to see the Mothers play at a Hollywood theatre, surrounded by long-haired hippies and freaks.

Freak Out! was the first rock double-album, the first rock 'concept' album and musically it was about as cutting-edge as a rock album could be without being classified as avant-garde jazz or modern classical.

Over the years it has consistently been voted as one of top 100 greatest albums ever made and even today it has not aged, even if the recording quality now seems a bit raw.

The entire album was a celebration of Freakdom, seen at that time by Zappa as the only possible antidote to the relentless consumer culture of America. To press the point home, the album opened with a song written for Karl Franzoni: 'Hungry Freaks, Daddy'. 'What is freaking out?' Zappa asked in the sleeve notes, then explained: 'On a personal level, *Freaking Out* is a process whereby an individual casts off outmoded and restricting standards of thinking, dress and social etiquette in order to express CREATIVELY his relationship to his immediate environment and the social structure as a whole. Less perceptive individuals have referred to us who have chosen this way of thinking and FEELING as "Freaks", hence the term: *Freaking Out*. On a collective level, when any number of "Freaks" gather and express themselves creatively through music or dance, for example, it is generally referred to as a FREAK OUT. The participants, already emancipated from our national *social slavery*, dressed in their most inspired apparel, realize as a group whatever potential they possess for *free expression*. We would like to encourage everyone who HEARS this music to join us . . . become a member of *The United Mutations* . . . FREAK OUT.'

Zappa's sleevenotes exhorted his audience to drop out of school, to forget about the Senior Prom and go to the library instead and 'educate yourself, if you've got any guts.' The tone was slightly hectoring, a little humourless even, with perhaps a hint of the old Sicilian Godfather, despite the massive dollops of parody. Zappa clearly saw himself more as the teacher than one of the gang.

Freak Out! is the work of an outsider. Like a first novel, it is largely autobiographical, covering Zappa's life up until that point, from Cucamonga to the Soul Giants, classical music composition to free-wheeling improvisation. The sleeve notes name-check 179 people: his high-school teachers, old girlfriends, obscure actors, musicians and directors in one of the longest dedications on any album. The music covers all of Zappa's influences, from Cecil Taylor-style piano to Hollywood film scores, Stravinsky and Varèse, backwards and speeded-up tape, sound effects and, of course, Doo Wop. 'Go Cry On Somebody Else's Shoulder' was jointly written with Ray Collins (though not credited as such) back in the days of Studio Z.

Collins: 'I was thinking about my ex-wife, if I remember right So Frank and I were in Cucamonga, and I said, "Oh, I got this idea about 'Don't bother me. Go away. Go cry on somebody else's shoulder.'" He said, "Great!" So I sat down at the piano and started playing it, and Frank joined in . . . And then of course, the spoken part that's on the Mothers' album is all just ad-libbed, right in the studio, about the khakis and the Mexican input.'

Even in this first album, Zappa expresses his discontent with the counter-cultural lifestyle, which he attacked with greater ferocity later. Zappa: 'I look at it as deciding what is real and what is not, and I thought that the counter-culture, at the time, was a commercial joke. By the time the counter-culture was recognized by the US media, it had already been absorbed by corporations. I think that if there's a real counter-culture it should exist. Certainly it did exist in Eastern Europe under the most terrible conditions, with secret police spying on you and all the rest of that. I'm not against counter-culture, I'm against things that are *fake*.'

In April Herb Cohen got the band an eight-day residency at Da Swamp in Waikiki and it was on this trip that Zappa began the habit of staying at a different hotel from the group. Jimmy Carl Black remembered: 'When he toured with the Mothers, Frank stayed in a different hotel than we did. The Mothers were into sex, drugs (not heavy drugs) and rock n' roll. He didn't like it at all, so better to stay away from us. That was OK with us – since we were having a lot more fun than he was, I'm sure. He wrote "Brown Shoes Don't Make It" and "Call any Vegetables" while we were in Honolulu in 1966 before *Freak Out!* came out.'

In May the Mothers shared a month-long double-bill residency at the Trip with all 13 members of Andy Warhol's Exploding Plastic Inevitable, complete with Warhol movies, the Velvet Underground and a prickly Lou Reed. The county sheriff didn't like the sinister look of the

Velvets, and closed the club after three days. Their icy demeanour also went down badly with Vito and the Freaks, who cheered the Mothers and booed the New Yorkers. Three weeks later the same double bill played at the Fillmore in San Francisco (the opening act was Jefferson Airplane), where the Velvets received an even worse reception. Later Lou Reed took it out on Zappa: 'They can't play and they can't write . . . Frank Zappa is the most untalented bore who ever lived. You know, people like Jefferson Airplane, Grateful Dead, all those people are the most untalented bores that ever came up.' It didn't help that on stage Zappa said of the Velvets: 'These guys suck!'

It was to become a lifelong feud and exemplified the differences between New York and Los Angeles. New Yorkers regarded themselves as hip and cool and saw Los Angeles as a plastic commercial wasteland. Certainly, the Velvets' black clothes, shades and night-club pallor represented a level of sophistication impossible to attain in California, where groups wore kiddie clothes and had sun-tans (Californian punks experienced the same problem a decade later). Zappa's growing aversion to all drugs – even pot – guaranteed he would never have 'street credibility', even in California, for as Lou Reed pointed out: 'The west coast bands were into soft drugs, we were into hard drugs.'

Perhaps Zappa and Reed had too much in common: they both began their careers recording Doo Wop and surf records for independent labels; Tom Wilson produced them both; they were on the same label; they were both control freaks who saw their groups as extensions of themselves; and both the Velvets and the Mothers had dancers as part of their act. They were one another's only real competition. Reed was even convinced that Zappa had persuaded Wilson to delay the release of the Velvet's first album to get his out first. In fact, the *Velvet Underground* was not even recorded until May 1966, by which time *Freak Out!* had already being allocated a release date of 27 June (the Velvet's album was not released until March 1967, but through no fault of the Mothers).

This was the period Zappa was most closely involved with a community, largely through living with Pamela Zarubica. Rather than share with Vestine now that he had left the Mothers, Zappa preferred to sleep on Pamela's couch. In mid-May 1966, on completion of the *Freak Out!* recording sessions, using some of his share of the advance money from MGM, Frank finally moved in with her. . Pamela Zarubica's cottage at 8404 Kirkwood Drive, near the corner with Yukka, was a long narrow single-story white wood and glass structure squeezed into a tiny lot, hard up against the lush vegetation of the canyon wall, which left only a narrow sidewalk between it and the road. A huge utility pole stood outside like a maypole, with dozens of cables fanning out across the street.

Pamela was having a brief affair with Ray Elliot, the sax and vibe player with Them, who were playing at the Whisky – and he found himself cajoled into helping to move Zappa's grand piano. John Judnich, Lenny Bruce's amanuensis, installed an elaborate stereo system. Zappa carried in his boxes of R&B singles and settled in.

He was now at the heart of what he would dub the Freak Sanctuary, the narrow lanes leading off Kirkwood Drive and Gould Avenue on the west side of Laurel Canyon, which was rapidly becoming Freak Central.

9 Laurel Canyon

The hills and canyons surrounding Laurel Canyon were to be Zappa's home for the rest of his life, with the exception of an 18-month break in New York, and many people see his music as representing the pace of life of the Hollywood Hills. The same laid-back, softer edge that distinguished Los Angeles Doo Wop from the hard edgy New York R&B characterizes much of Zappa's work, which often hums along like a cruise on the Hollywood Freeway.

Living in the hills was a new experience. Unlike Lancaster and Pomona, the landscape was dense, packed with textures and colours, foliage and rock faces. It also retained some of its desert harshness. The spring rains bring a small landslide to each garden, breaching the retaining walls, and most years a mudslide takes a few houses away. The hills around Kirkland are a maze of tiny canyons: some small, choked with poison oak, yukka, chaparral, aloes and fuchia flower gooseberry. Other are big enough to take a road, small side canyons with steep abrupt sides where dirt roads striped with floodwater sand drifts follow streams or washes to cabins and wooden huts surrounded by deep foliage. Dirt roads peter out into tracks, wide firebreaks follow the contours, offering spectacular views of the city and glimpses of rabbits, coyotes, snakes, foxes and deer, trapped in the mountain range as the city grew around and enclosed them. And everywhere on the roadsides and in private gardens: huge gaudy blossoms, flowering bushes, bird of paradise plants, a blaze of magenta mesembryanthemums, surrounding tiny wooden cottages or duplexes. In the mid-sixties, before being taken over by the rock 'n' roll community, this area was run down, and consisted mostly of garages or stables converted into cheap housing; insubstantial, temporary-looking structures lived in by wannabe actors, bohemians and horse owners. Then, as now, the architecture was dominated by the vegetation: the towering eucalyptus trees, stately royal palms and the indigenous California palm, thickets of red alder, pepper trees and pines making the houses all but invisible: small stucco boxes, filled with Freaks, surrounded by greenery against a Technicolor sky.

Love's Arthur Lee led the flood of musicians into the area. Main Street of the Freak Sanctuary was Ridpath Drive where many of the rock 'n' roll bands lived in houses leased by their record companies; a walk down Ridpath would give all the latest industry gossip. Billy James (former A&R man for Columbia Records and now Jackson Browne's manager) had 20 groups listed on his mailbox and was home at various times to Leonard Cohen, Tim Hardin and Tim Buckley. Doors producer Paul Rothchild lived on Ridpath and his music-listening room was one of the best in the city, attracting everyone from Janis Joplin to Linda Ronstadt, the Byrds and the Paul Butterfield band. John Haeny, also from Elektra Records, had a five-foot hookah plus a studio-quality hi-fi in his living room: frequent visitors included Carole King, Neil Young and David Crosby. Steven Stills met Judy Collins there and fell in love. Elektra's Barry Friedman lived halfway between Rothchild and Billy James. Friedman's house was filled with people and all the beds were pushed together for orgies. David Crosby, Steven Stills and Graham Nash were frequent visitors, as were Warren Zevon and Nico, who once dragged some unfortunate woman off the man she fancied at gunpoint. Friedman once telephoned all his neighbours and arranged for them to drop the needle on the new Stones album at the same time, filling the canyon with music.

This community of musicians developed quickly and soon Love, the Byrds, the Doors, Three Dog Night, the Mamas and the Papas, Peter Tork, the Turtles and many other bands had created their own village of converted garages, cottages and chalets.

The village pump and washhouse was the ramshackle Canyon County store at 2108 Laurel Canyon, which looked as if it had been transported from the old West. Half the people hitch-hiking up and down the canyons were sleeping on someone's floor, on the couch, or looking for somewhere to crash. There were lots of runaways, under-age girls with long Cher-like hair wandering barefoot along the dirt roads in hippie dresses and boys with long Brian Jones haircuts dressed in the LA hippie look introduced by Arthur Lee and Love: fringed jackets, leather waistcoats, pin-stripe pants, cowboy boots. And every-where music: not just rock 'n' roll, but Indian ragas, country blues and – a favourite among Ridpath dwellers – the *Music of Bulgaria* by the Ensemble of the Bulgarian Republic that influenced the harmonies of Crosby, Stills and Nash and which Zappa once announced as one of his favourite records.

Ridpath ran off Kirkwood, but Frank and Pam lived beyond the inter-section, surrounded by canyon walls and vegetation. The area still retains a sense of the village atmosphere of the sixties though these days it is rare to see a bare-footed hippie walking down to the Country Store; they are more likely to take the Porsche. 8404 Kirkwood became the meeting place for the rest of the Mothers, their entourage and an ever-changing parade of girls, roadies and musicians including a hooker called Stephanie whom Frank met in San Francisco and invited down, and the famous Cherry Sisters. Now that he had a record deal, Frank entertained a large number of groupies, but his disapproval of pot-smoking meant they didn't stay long. On *Uncle Meat* Pamela recalls one occasion when Frank went to bed with a girl, but when Pamela entered the room the next morning he was with a different one. Because Frank often used Pamela's bed, it wasn't long before they had given crabs to half of Laurel Canyon, as well as quite a few cases of the clap. Crabs inspired several Zappa songs, including 'Toads of the Short Forest'.

Pamela was a part-time secretary at the Whisky, which meant she had to deal with all the groups. In May the Doors were hired as the house band, supporting headliners like Them, Love, the Mothers and Pamela began a short affair with Jim Morrison. Frank disapproved because they left rolling papers all over the living room and even the odd pot seed or twig. Nevertheless, Zappa was sufficiently impressed by Morrison's music to ask if he could produce them, but the Doors were still looking for a record contract and didn't want to be tied to a producer.

Morrison returned to his old girlfriend and Frank issued an edict: no dope in the house. From then on people would sit outside in their cars, grumbling about him as they got toked up. Frank's memory of Tank C overrode everything else; he had no intention of going to jail because of a few potheads.

Despite being surrounded by drug users, Zappa loved the Freak Sanctuary and told *Teen Set*, with unusually mild sarcasm: 'I live in the middle of the great hallucinogenic wasteland – Laurel Canyon – on one of the hot streets with the rest of the stars . . . lotsa action, having a wonderful time, wish you were here.' His relationship to the counter-culture was always ambivalent, because he disparaged much of what they believed in. He wanted society to change but did not condone the methods used to attain widened consciousness. He fully endorsed many other aspects of the sixties counter-culture, particularly free love, open marriages and group sex. Drugs were unknown territory and Frank hated losing control.

He was intrigued enough to watch Ray Collins take LSD and claimed to have tried pot about ten times, but said that it only gave him a sore throat. The other Mothers enjoyed soft drugs. In fact Frank claimed that at a band meeting around the time when Herb Cohen relieved Mark Cheka of the role of co-manager, some of the Mothers thought 'Let's get rid of that Zappa asshole too' – solely because he didn't take drugs. In his autobiography Zappa quotes Ray Collins as saying: 'You need to go to Big Sur and take acid with someone who believes in God.'

'That was a great meeting,' recalls Collins. 'I wish somebody had recorded it, it would have been a great album. I wanted Frank not to be the leader of the Mothers of Invention, because I didn't like what he was doing with the band, and his control ... I suggested at that meeting that we take any member of the band besides Frank or myself to become leader of the band.' There was never any question of Frank leaving or of not playing his music. It was his autocratic ways that irritated the others, particularly the way he was always going on about their drug use. They wanted him to lighten up. Collins: 'That's when the "take acid and go to Big Sur" came, that's out of context, of course ... what I'm saying is "Take it easy, Frank."'

Jimmy Carl Black: 'Zappa was indeed a very tough bandleader to work with. I will say "with" because in the early days we weren't working *for* Zappa but *with* him. He was the bandleader and I didn't mind that since he was writing very challenging music for the times.' Frank had quickly forgotten that the band already existed before he joined; he regarded it as his.

Tom Wilson was Zappa's main connection to the major record labels and whenever he was in town they spent a lot of time together, plotting and hatching schemes. Zappa didn't see himself as just a recording artist, he had all kinds of plans and Wilson was interested to hear them. In June 1966 he signed Burt Ward to MGM, the actor who played Robin the 'Boy Wonder' in ABC's successful *Batman* TV series. Zappa wrote 'Boy Wonder I Love You' and later that month, with Zappa conducting and Wilson producing, they spent two days at TT&G laying down half a dozen tracks; but the single, with Zappa's song on the A-side, went nowhere.

Another of Wilson's moves was to give Zappa a couple of tracks to arrange for the new Animals album he was producing called *Animalism*. They were 'All Night Long' and Fred Neil's 'The Other Side of This Life'. Neil was managed by Herb Cohen and his publishing was controlled by Frank Zappa Music, a company jointly owned by Herb and Zappa. Eric Burdon did not enjoy working with Zappa, saying it was like working with Hitler. However, he was impressed by Zappa as an individual: 'He's regarded as the leading light of the "freak-out" scene over there. He makes these weird movies and puts the soundtracks on them himself. He showed me one of a guy picking spots on his leg and another with a sequence taken by an infra-red camera of a guy necking with this typical Hollywood blonde.'

In July MGM sent the Mothers to play a series of television shows in Washington, DC, Detroit and Dallas to promote the album. They had Karl Franzoni with them as their 'go-go' boy and one of Zappa's fondest memories was of the look on the faces of the teenage Texan Baptists when they first beheld Franzoni's bulging testicles, barely concealed by his thin ballet tights. Before flying home, Zappa asked Pamela to pick him up at the airport. She arrived with a friend from her office. It was love at first sight.

Adelaide Gail Sloatman was a Californian beauty with long straight hair, huge amber eyes and a Brigitte Bardot pout revealing perfect teeth. On her father's side she was mostly Danish, with some French and Irish thrown in. Her mother's family came from Madeira and from there went to Hawaii to work in the cane fields.

Gail was born on 1 January 1945. Her father was a nuclear weapons research physicist working with the US Navy. When she was 14 the Sloatmans moved to London where they stayed four and half years. She attended what she described as 'a severely Catholic' all-girls school. She was rebellious, but stuck it out. In 1962 she ignored her father's wishes that she go on to university, left home and got a job. Using his connections she worked as a secretary for the Office of Naval Research and Development.

Her flatmate Anya Butler moved in record business circles: she was a secretary and confidante to Chris Stamp and Kit Lambert, who managed the Who. Anya also worked part-time for Shel Talmy, the producer of the Kinks, and persuaded him to watch the Who rehearse. He immediately signed them to his production company and cut 'My Generation'.

Through Anya, Gail found herself in the very centre of London's burgeoning music scene. These were the glory days of the Ad Lib, Dolly's, the Bag O'Nails, Revolution and the Scotch Saint James; of dark rooms where the latest Stax and Motown made conversation virtually impossible; when heiresses and actors, rock musicians and groupies frugged on tiny dance floors and there were late-night jam sessions that sometimes entered rock legend.

Then in 1965, at the height of Swinging London, her father was transferred to New York and Gail had to leave as she was no longer entitled to a work permit. She enrolled at the Fashion Institute of Technology, thinking she might design clothes, then discovered New York's music scene. In his autobiography *Backstage Passes* guitarist and hit producer Al Kooper recalled meeting her. His band, the Blues Project, had hired a charismatic lead singer called Emmaretta Marx, who would bounce on stage halfway through the set and liven things up a bit. Emmaretta brought her own roadie with her, Gail Sloatman, described by Kooper as 'a Jean Shrimpton-ish mod delight ... Gail caused a little friction in the band because everyone fell in love with her at the same time and didn't bother to tell the others.'

Gail's ex-roommate Anya Butler arrived in New York, and the two of them hitch-hiked to Los Angeles where they 'decided to be groupies for a while'. Neither of them wore bras, which, Gail recalls, 'bothered a lot of people'. According to Gail there were two kinds of groupies: those who wanted to marry an English pop star and live in a big country house and those 'who seriously defined themselves as groupies and were devoted to honouring the people who were involved with producing the music. [They] were devotees of particular bands and they would literally service those bands. It was a religious experience for most of those girls. The altar was rock 'n' roll, the guys were the gods and the women were the high priestesses. The idea was that we were exploring sexuality in the sixties – what that meant was there was no pressure to have any kind of intimacy on a spiritual level. Physical intimacy doesn't translate into real intimacy. It was very easy to sleep with somebody and much more difficult to get to know them.' She and Anya became very friendly with the Beach Boys and the Byrds (Gail had a fling with Brian Wilson and Anya eventually married Chris Hillman of the Byrds).

Gail became Elmer Valentine's PA, overseeing the affairs of both the Whisky and the Trip, which made it very easy to get to know the groups. (Jim Morrison, in fact, she had already met. As children of high ranking naval personnel, they used to play together in the same navy kindergarten where, according to Frank, Gail once hit Jim on the head with a hammer.) Gail moved on the fringes of Vito and Karl Franzoni's Freak scene and through them got to know Kim Fowley. She even made a record with him as Bunny and Bear (Gail was Bear), but 'America's Sweethearts' on Living Legend LL 722 went nowhere. (Her relationship with Fowley might account for Zappa's later vituperative remarks about him.)

Gail's first impression of Frank Zappa was that he smelt awful. He also had the clap and was infested with crabs, including his hair, which had not been combed in months. She described him as 'probably one of the grubbiest creatures I'd ever seen.' Nevertheless, she was intrigued and a little intimidated. Soon afterwards she visited the Kirkwood house again for a party. Frank had no shirt on and wore waisted cotton-pique bell bottoms with brilliant red hibiscus flowers all over them. They were too short and emphasized his long feet. She thought he looked like a puppet – almost touching the ground. They spent the night together.

She told *New Yorker* writer Connie Bruck: 'The next morning I rolled over and I saw one eye over the edge of the pillow and the moment I saw that, I heard a voice – I've heard voices all my life . . . and it said, "This is it. If you can't accept this, we're never talking to you again." And I remember thinking, Oh my God! Here's this guy, I think he's extraordinary, it's such a different sensation! I know he hasn't taken a bath in four months and his moustache smells like peanut butter . . . But I thought, "Well, okay." So I think that's the same thing as love at first sight.' To Drew Wheeler at *Billboard* she said: 'He had a compelling glare. He had major magnetic charm.' Frank and Gail had a lot in common: they had both been brought up as Catholics, came from military families and spent their childhood on the move. And both, of course, loved music.

By this time there were a number of people living at Kirkwood, including a groupie called Pepper, whom Frank had introduced to the house, but who was now running after Arthur Lee. There was also a singer called Bobby Jameson whom Frank was working with. He arranged Jameson's song 'Gotta Find My Roogalator', making the session musicians on the backing track sound very like the Mothers.

In mid-July Motorhead showed up needing a place to stay. It was about a month before Gail finally moved in, during which time Frank had other girlfriends, but when Bobby Jameson moved out, Gail moved in.

Pamela found herself drifting away from Frank. They were never lovers and it had been a true friendship of shared intimacies and candid conversations, but Frank was now too busy with his career and with Gail to devote much time to the friendship. Pamela was still a teenager, whereas Zappa was in his mid-twenties, a much older, wiser man in her eyes and something of a guru to her. She was disappointed that his missionary zeal to change society seemed to be fading. She had a stop-gap affair with Johnny Rivers while preparing to leave for England with her friend Vicki. Pepper borrowed Frank's Chevy to take them to the airport but Frank and Gail didn't even bother to come out of the bedroom to see them off on their adventure.

More clubs and stores opened on the Strip and the high-class restaurateurs and merchants who wanted it to go upmarket took exception to the Freaks who filled the sidewalks. Complaints were made and the famously heavy-handed LAPD stepped in. First they imposed a 10 p.m. curfew. Next they raided Cantor's and Gee Gee's restaurant on the Strip one Friday night, arresting 276 young people for blocking the sidewalk and for curfew violations. At Cantor's people leaving with take-aways had their food knocked from their hands and were arrested for loitering. Hundreds of innocent people found themselves in jail overnight, unable to raise the $110 bail.

The police caused more problems at the Great Underground Arts Masked Ball and Orgy (G U A M B O) on 23 July, held to celebrate the second anniversary of the *Los Angeles Free Press* (*LAFP*), the local underground newspaper. The Mothers were the main attraction. Two days before the event, the Aerospace Hall cancelled the booking and GUAMBO was hastily relocated to the Danish Centre. Fifty police and two fire marshalls declared the place overcrowded and restricted ticket sales – more than 2,000 people in masks and costumes were turned away.

On 13 August the Mothers played at 'Freak Out! Son of GUAMBO' at the Shrine Exposition Hall, which had a capacity of 5,000. It was such a success they repeated it on 17 September. Having identified his target audience, Zappa wanted to introduce them to his ideas. He took a four-page insert in the *LAFP* on 9 September 1966 to publish *Freak Out! The Official News of the Mothers of Invention*, using the Mothers' advertising budget from MGM to promote his ideas. It was illustrated with arresting, brilliantly designed photo-collages of the Mothers. Zappa's hope was that his young fans might change the world by seeing through the lies of modern consumer society; but these hopes were dashed when he saw those around him turning to mind-altering drugs. All those idealistic discussions with Pamela seemed to have ended in people just getting high.

The following week he placed another full-page advertizement in the paper, this time as if written by Suzy Creamcheese, with no graphics, just a block of text. It was a poorly written, hectoring statement of Zappa's beliefs, but to the vast majority of Mothers fans (who thought of them as a rock band, not a political party) it seemed pompous and paternalistic.

> This is about the Mothers of Invention. We have watched them grow and with their growth, we hopefully have grown. Their honesty has offended some and been provocative to many, but in any case, their performances have had a real effect on their audiences.
>
> The Mothers' music is very new, and as their music is new, so is the intention of their music. As much as the Mothers put into their music; we must bring to it. The Mothers, and what they represent as a group has attracted all of the outcasts, the pariahs, the people who are angry and afraid and contemptuous of the existing social structure. The danger lies in the 'Freak Out' becoming an excuse

instead of a reason. An excuse implies an end, a reason a beginning. Being that the easiest way is consistently more attractive than the harder way, the essential thing that makes the 'Freak Out' audiences different constitutes their sameness. A freak is not a freak if ALL are freaks. 'Freaking Out' should presuppose an active freedom, freedom meaning a liberation from the control of some other person or persons. Unfortunately, reaction seems to have taken place of action. We SHOULD be as satisfied listening to the Mothers perform from a concert stage. If we could channel the energy expended in 'Freaking Out' physically into 'Freaking Out' intellectually, we might possibly be able to create something concrete out of the ideological twilight of bizarre costumes and being seen being bizarre. Do we really listen? And if we really listen, do we really think? Freedom of thought, conversely, brings an awesome responsibility. Looking and acting eccentric IS NOT ENOUGH.

What WE must try to do then, is not only comment satirically on what's wrong, but try to CHANGE what's wrong. The Mothers are trying.

Suzy Creamcheese
1966

Possibly as a result of discussions with Zappa, Karl Franzoni had written a long rambling letter about the dangers of LSD in the 7 October issue of the *LAFP*, which the paper published under the headline: 'A 'MOTHER' AGAINST LSD.' Zappa was outraged that Franzoni had been referred to as a Mother. He also freaked out at an ad in the same issue by the Zeidler & Zeidler clothing store, which announced, buried in a full page of 'psychedelic' jokes and plugs for roach clips: 'May the good dope fairy shine her love lite on the Mothers of Invention.' He also reacted badly to another ad for a 'Freak-in' at the Shine Exposition Hall, featuring among other groups, the Mugwumps (forerunners of the Mamas and the Papas) and advertising 'The world famous artist and sculptor Vito and his wife, his child, and his entire entourage of dancers and freakers.' This commercialisation of what Frank felt was his scene (but also his copyright) outraged him.

The 14 October issue of the *LAFP* carried a two-page *Freak Out, the Official News of the M.O.I.* with the headline: PHONEY FREAK-INS, ZEIDLER DOPE ADS, & KARL FRANZONI'S LETTER. It began: 'Kindly read this: A Statement of Policy from Frank Zappa, for the Mothers of Invention. Last week's issue of the *LAFP* contained three items in print which, we feel, bear analysis and discussion . . .' Zappa then gave convoluted reasons why no one other than he should hold a Freak-Out, even though Vito was involved and had been holding Freak-Outs long before Zappa even arrived in Hollywood from the suburbs. Zappa complained at even greater length about Zeidler & Zeidler, before moving on to Karl Franzoni.

> THIRD: the article 'A MOTHER AGAINST LSD' by Karl Franzoni
>
> Karl's worthwhile and well-intended <u>letter to the editor</u> was, UNFORTUNATELY, incorrectly labelled as a public statement from a member of our group.
>
> KARL FRANZONI IS NOT A MEMBER OF <u>THE MOTHERS OF INVENTION</u>.
>
> Nor does he claim to be . . .
>
> <u>BUT</u>, FOR THE MOST PART, <u>WE</u> AS A GROUP <u>AGREE WITH HIM</u> IN HIS PLEA FOR A <u>SANE</u> <u>DRUG POLICY</u> (basically: stick it up your ass and fly to the moon) . . .

In the next issue, Zeidler & Zeidler ran a childish, full-page attack on the Mothers, headlined: THE MOTHERS CAN FLUSH IT, commenting on Frank's big nose, his appalling dress sense, lack of humour, and so on. To Frank's consternation, in the same issue Vito endorsed a *Monster Halloween Freak-Off*, advertised as 'Join Saint Vito's Crusade to Freak-off the world.' Frank may have garnered sole use of 'Freak Out', but the Freak-Offs and Freak-Ins were beyond his control. In fact, had Vito been as litigious as Zappa, he might have considered preventing Zappa from using 'Freak-Out' too. As it was, there were dark mutterings about Frank's attempt to control the Freak scene. Embarrassingly, there was another full-page *Mothers Official News* in the same issue of the *LAFP*, in which Zappa grumpily complained about Zeidler and the freak-ins and freak-offs. Headed 'Read This First', it was written in Zappa's characteristic style of capital letters and underlinings, like the religious tracts handed out by mentally ill people on the street:

> Many people have been under the impression that the MOTHERS are engaged in the field of ENTERTAINMENT. This is NOT TRUE. THE MOTHERS ARE STRIVING TO COMMUNICATE WITH (not specifically to entertain) THEIR AUDIENCE . . . no matter how small that audience might be.
>
> WE HAVE DISCOVERED a small, but active AUDIENCE OF DETRACTORS here in LA (consisting mainly of IMPOSTERS who would USURP & CORRUPT a number of CONCEPTS & TECHNIQUES which WE DEVELOPED . . . specifically the 'FREAK OUT' & the LIGHT SHOW NIRVANA) These CHARLATANS and their STOOGES IN ATTENDANCE . . .' etc., etc.

The other Mothers were concerned by Frank's somewhat messianic diatribes. He was attributing opinions to them that they did not hold and more importantly, he was alienating what few fans they had. The letters page of the next issue of the *LAFP* (4 November) ran a letter by Ray Collins saying:

> The opinions expressed by Frank Zappa in his 'Freak Out' newspaper, the Free Press, or any other publications are his own and do not necessarily reflect my opinions.
> Love
> Ray Collins of the Mothers of Invention.

No other rock band has ever addressed its audience in this manner: attributing philosophical, political and even spiritual significance to their music, but also nit-picking about copyright and drug-taking. To most people it smacked of megalomania, paranoia and delusions of grandeur. In fact, Frank's ability to alienate everyone that didn't agree with him was becoming a cause of concern within the group.

An air stewardess has described how the Mothers were once on one of her flights. She noticed that Zappa sat alone, away from the band. Jimmy Carl Black and Roy Estrada gave her a copy of *Freak Out!* and had everyone sign it, except Frank. As the passengers deplaned she stood at the door with the album under her arm. On the way out Zappa noticed it: 'I see you have our album, have you heard our music?' he asked. She admitted that she hadn't, whereupon Zappa extended his middle finger and jerked it in front of her face. 'Here's a preview!' he snapped, then continued down the ramp leaving her shaken and upset. Clearly ordinary working people were not included in the Zappa Master Plan.

This attitude extended most noticeably to his audiences. 'The audiences were hostile to what we did,' Zappa said in 1968. 'They gave us a bad time. Now, historically, groups have felt real hurt if the audience expressed displeasure with their performance. They apologized and tried to make the people love them. We didn't do that. We told the audience to get fucked.'

The mass arrests at Cantor's and GeeGee's were not the only instances of harassment of on the Strip; the police had twice raided Ben Frank's and arrested people for loitering and curfew violations. The Freaks had finally had enough. On the night of 12 November 1966 about a thousand demonstrators protested the tight enforcement of the curfew laws and the closing of Pandora's Box, a popular coffee house on a traffic island at 8118 Sunset (a beatnik hangout in the fifties, now scheduled to be demolished in a road widening scheme).

Marchers dressed in psychedelic finery – headbands, beads and face-paint – and carrying anti-LAPD placards blocked the street, causing massive traffic jams. Protesters (including Sonny and Cher) sat down in the road. The police overreacted. The LAPD moved in from the west and the county sheriff's department unloaded two bus-loads of cops from the east, trapping the demonstrators. Someone was pushed through the plate-glass window of the Liquor Locker and the police, hearing the breaking glass, assumed that looting was taking place and began arresting everyone. More than 300 manacled Freaks were carted off to the West Hollywood sheriff station. The outraged remainder began throwing rocks; others tried to set fire to a bus and a car was overturned and set alight. Peter Fonda was led away in handcuffs.

The police had learned nothing from the Watts riots the previous year. 'We're going to be tough,' said County Supervisor Ernest E. Debs. 'We're not going to surrender that area or any other area to beatniks or wild-eyed kids.' They couldn't keep the Freaks off the Strip, so they decided to stop them from dancing. Debs and Sheriff Peter Pitchess asked the County Public Welfare Commission to rescind the dance permits of the Strip's most popular rock 'n' roll clubs, including the Whisky and Gazzari's.

The Whisky a Go-Go switched to a Motown format, attracting a different, mostly black audience. Ciro's closed, but reopened with a Motown theme in 1967 as It's Boss. Bill Gazzari tried burlesque, but that didn't work. The club closed and was reported to be considering a Motown theme. (Club owners always think alike.) The Galaxy was scraping by, not selling alcohol and therefore attracting younger kids. Now the reactionaries who wanted the 'longhairs' and Freaks off the Strip suddenly found it filled with black people instead – and they disliked them even more. A new licensing policy was quickly pushed through to restore teenage dancing on the Strip again and beginning 4 March 1967, 17-year-olds were for the first time allowed to dance in licensed premises. (It had previously been 18 and upward only.) City officials saved face by withdrawing Sonny and Cher's invite to ride in the Rose Bowl Parade that year. And they demolished Pandora's Box.

Out of these events came one of Steven Stills' most famous songs: 'For What It's Worth', about the riot, was released within a month. Zappa also referred to it by name in 'Plastic People', and Monkee Mike Nesmith wrote 'Daily Nightly', in his words a 'rambling account of the Hollywood street scene at the time when people were meeting at Ben Frank's and Pandora's Box . . . That was a very important corner where people would congregate.' And the outcome of the riot? Someone put out a cheap exploitation movie called *Riot on Sunset Strip*, starring

Aldo Ray, Mimzi Farmer and the Chocolate Watch Band. This was Hollywood, after all.

Despite the success of the Shrine Exposition Hall dances, the Mothers continued to have trouble getting gigs because it was difficult to dance to Frank's songs. Zappa thought an extra drummer might improve things and that summer he had hired Denny Bruce, a classmate of Pepper's at LA Valley College in Van Nuys. Bruce: 'I showed up for an audition with Brian Jones-style hair, and Frank said, "You're hired. I need some young, good-looking guys if I'm ever going to get work in this city. All you have to do is keep a backbeat."' Eventually Zappa accepted the fact that the only way to be hired by a dance hall is to play dance music. He didn't have to play covers, just write some music with a danceable beat.

The Mothers arrived at one Hollywood club with Karl Franzoni, Kim Fowley and dozens of dancers. Before the show Frank asked the owner: 'What is your definition of a great dance song?' The man thought for a long time and said 'Louie Louie'. Zappa told the band: 'Ok, we'll give them "Louie Louie" for 45 minutes, but our version is going to be called "Plastic People".' He transformed Richard Berry's 'Louie Louie' into a new song with the same structure using the old 'ice-cream' changes from Cucamonga days. That night they played 'Plastic People' for the full set, urged on by Fowley, who performed with even more enthusiasm than the band.

Recording the next album, *Absolutely Free*, took place at TT&G for four days in mid-November 1966, with mixing done later in New York. But first there were a number of line-up changes. Denny Bruce developed mononucleosis and was replaced by Billy Mundi. Mundi was not only a great drummer, he could read music. Also that summer Don Preston (whom Zappa had played with a few times in 1961) joined as a keyboard player. Preston was a brilliant catch: he had started his musical career in the military when he was stationed in Trieste with Herbie Mann and had years of experience with the likes of Elvin Jones, Carla Bley and Charlie Haden.

Elliot Ingber was fired, probably for smoking too much grass, and started the Fraternity of Man. Ray Collins remembered one night when

Elliot was trying to tune his guitar and his amplifier wasn't turned on. Collins: 'Frank looked over at him, looked over at me, looked over at the amplifier, and I knew right then that was the last of Elliot Ingber in the band.' He was replaced by Jim Fielder who stayed until February 1967, when he joined Steven Stills in Buffalo Springfield. Bunk Gardner joined on wind instruments and Jim 'Motorhead' Sherwood doubled up as roadie and occasional saxophone and vocals. The core line-up was unchanged: Zappa, Ray Collins on vocals, Jimmy Carl Black on drums and Roy Estrada on bass.

The new songs included an impossible-to-dance-to album version of 'Plastic People', which not only called the LAPD 'Nazis', but also labelled the demonstrators at Pandora's Box as 'plastic people', presumably for letting themselves be pushed around. Frank, of course, had not attended the demonstration. Any fans actually listening to the words must have wondered just what it was he wanted of them. In August 1967 he gave a different definition: 'The insincere assholes who run almost everybody's country are plastic people.'

Similarly, he explained that 'Brown Shoes Don't Make It' 'is a song about the people who run the Government, the people who make the laws that keep you from living the kind of life you know you should lead. These unfortunate people manufacture inequitable laws and ordinances, perhaps unaware of the fact that the restrictions they place on the young people in a society are a result of their own hidden sexual frustrations. Dirty old men have no place running your country.' It is a consummate indictment of government corruption and the vacuous sterility of American consumer society; Zappa at his best both lyrically and musically; a seven-and-a-half-minute masterpiece of more than 20 distinct musical themes skillfully edited into a whole.

'Status Back Baby' combined elements of Doo Wop with a homage to Stravinsky's ballads in its musical interlude. The lyrics, though heavy with irony, are quite likely autobiographical: Zappa complains that the school pom-pom girls whispered things about him when they spent an evening together making posters; they did loads of them while he only managed three. His memory of high school remained acute as he explained pom-pom girls for his British audience: 'A pom-pom girl is a young lady who cuts strips of crêpe paper all week long after school to make an object known as a pom-pom, which is a puffy ball composed of strips of crêpe paper. After she has manufactured her own pom-pom, she will go to the football game and jump high in the air with her pom-pom in her hand shouting, as she does so, these immortal words: "We've got a team that's on the beam, that's really hep to the jive. Come on Tigers, let's skin 'em alive!" Or "Push 'em back, push 'em back. We like it. Sissboombah!" Then they drink beer and get pregnant in the back of somebody's car.'

'America Drinks And Goes Home' was to become another Zappa classic: an unsubtle parody of the type of cocktail music he used to play with Joe Perrino and the Mellowtones, complete with the audience talking over the song, the insincere night-club crooner and the sound of fighting and breaking glass. Herb Cohen played cash register.

After the financial debacle of *Freak Out!*, MGM only allowed Wilson four double-sessions – 24 hours of studio time – to produce the album. As the Mothers were going to be playing New York a week later, the mixing had to be done in MGM's own studio where costs would be considerably lower – and where the band was barred from the company cafeteria because of their long hair. *Absolutely Free* was released in June 1967 and reached Number 41 in the charts. The Mothers were finally part of the business.

10 New York City

Starting Thanksgiving Day, 26 November 1966, the Mothers were booked to play a week at the Balloon Farm at 23 St Marks Place in the East Village – New York's Hippie High Street. This was housed above the Dom, where Andy Warhol's Exploding Plastic Inevitable was originally staged, so there was a certain determination to outdo the Velvets on their home turf. The Mothers were a sensation. The New Yorkers loved them and so did the critics.

'They seized the stage and belted the world's first rock 'n' roll oratorio to an audience that was either too engrossed or too confused to do anything but sit and listen,' wrote Richard Goldstein in the *Village Voice*, 'The Mothers of Invention are to be watched, and leader Frank Zappa deserves your attention.'

New York Times critic Robert Shelton (who essentially launched Bob Dylan's career with a rave review) proclaimed that they were 'The most original new group to simmer out of the rock 'n' roll underground in the last hour-and-one-half . . . perhaps the first pop group to successfully amalgamate rock 'n' roll with the serious music of Stravinsky and others . . . Mr Zappa is no more sinister than a cultural revolutionary bent on overthrowing every rule in the music book.' Shelton quoted Zappa as telling a visitor: 'I am trying to use the weapons of a disoriented and unhappy society against itself. The Mothers of Invention are designed to come in the back door and kill you while you're sleeping ... Sure we're satirists, and we are out to satirise everything. Most of the guys in the band feel that we're going to do something to help.'

LAFP writer Eve Babitz had known Zappa since she was 17 and happened to be in New York when the Mothers arrived. One afternoon they walked down Madison Avenue handing out badges Zappa had made of himself seated at a desk, glaring over the top of his glasses with the slogan: WE WILL BURY YOU! Frank was attired in a neon orange-yellow T-shirt, pink and yellow striped pants, his usual strange bulbous shoes and a monkey-skin coat that came down to his ankles. Eve had arranged for them to meet Salvador Dali at the King Cole Bar at the St Regis, but the doorman would not let Frank in without a tie. He found a silver satin one for Frank to wear and Frank tied it in a bow. Eve reported: 'Dali took one look at Frank from across the room and rose to his feet in immediate approbation. If Frank was not for Dali, Dali didn't care; he was for Frank. So I really had very little trouble introducing them.'

They drank green chartreuse and Frank explained who the Mothers were. He was about to go to a rehearsal and Dali said he would like to watch. They arranged to meet at the Balloon Farm, but unfortunately Herb Cohen was having trouble with the club's management and the Mothers were locked out. When Dali and his wife Gala pulled up in a taxi, Frank, Eve and the Mothers were all sitting outside on the steps. 'When it turned out positively that they weren't going to let us in,' wrote Eve, 'Dali and Gala dejectedly got another cab and went back to the St Regis ... and Frank went back to the Hotel Albert or wherever he was staying to argue with the fucking management who had ruined something that was very delicate and could only happen once. Dali and Zappa alone together in a big empty room with musical instruments.'

The promoters extended their residency to the New Year and the Mothers began to make a little money. Anticipating the cold weather, they had bought second-hand overcoats in LA, but nothing prepared them for a New York winter. They looked like shabby immigrants with their long hair (unknown in New York) and tatty clothes. Cab drivers refused to pick them up, so they had to trudge home every night through the snow. But New York was better than Montreal, where they played the New Penelope club for two weeks beginning 7 January. Zappa: 'It was twenty degrees below zero. We walked from our hotel to the club and the snot had literally frozen in our noses by the time we got to work.' It was so cold their lips and fingers would stick to the instruments. To make matters worse, no restaurant would serve them because of their long hair, so they were forced to eat all their meals at the hotel.

From Montreal they flew back to the coast to rejoin their families. Motorhead brought a girlfriend with him from New York called Joni Mitchell, a Canadian folksinger who had previously been hanging around Greenwich Village with David Crosby. She stayed at the Kirkwood cottage, sitting hunched over her guitar, her beret at a jaunty angle, singing the songs that later appeared on her 1968 debut album *Joni Mitchell* (*Song To A Seagull*).

The scene on the Strip was a mess. The police were now threatening to take away Elmer Valentine's liquor licence unless he stopped hiring long-haired groups, and the magic had gone out of Vito's Freaks. In December Vito and Szou's three-year-old son Godo had fallen through a trapdoor on the roof of their building and died. That evening Vito, Szou and the gang went out as usual; dancing with an even fiercer intensity to assuage their grief, but things were never quite the same. In addition, the release of *Absolutely Free* was held up in the first of Zappa's lifetime of arguments with record companies.

MGM refused to print the 'libretto', as Zappa called it, on the inside sleeve because of the so-called dirty words. This was only a few months after William Burroughs' *Naked Lunch* was finally declared not obscene by the Massachusetts Supreme Court on appeal. Zappa described some of the changes that MGM wanted to make: 'Look what they censored out of it: "She's only thirteen and she knows how nasty". You know what they took out? The word "thirteen", not "nasty". Look: "Magnificent Instrumental, Ejaculation Number 1." They had to cross it out and change to "Climax". [Laughter] You dig? They wanted to change, "I'd like to make her do a nasty on the White House lawn", they wanted to change it to "I'd like to make her do the crossword puzzle on the back of TV Guide"' MGM also objected to a slogan in the back cover collage: WAR MEANS WORK FOR ALL. After protracted legal arguments, Frank published the libretto himself and the slogan was printed in half-tone instead of black; all of which set the release back until June 1967.

Tom Wilson tried to fill in the gap by releasing a single, 'Big Leg Emma', on 10 April. It flopped. Gigs in LA continued to be thin on the ground, so when Howard Solomon offered to present them as a theatrical performance at the Garrick Theater in New York over Easter week, 1967, they jumped at it.

Before that, however, Zappa had been involved in another project. During an eleven-day period in February he wrote the music for *Lumpy Gravy*, a half-hour sound collage with orchestral and small group elements. A&R man Nick Venet at Capitol Records understood from Zappa that although he was signed as an artist to MGM, he was free to write, produce and arrange for anyone he wanted. Venet liked Zappa's ideas and commissioned an orchestral piece. Unfortunately, just when Frank was looking forward to locking himself away in the Kirkwood cottage and devoting all of his time and attention to composing, the landlord's son moved back to LA and Frank had to move: 'I've got a deadline to do the recording session, I've got all this music to write, and I've got no place to do it.'

There was an office adjoining Nick Venet's in the Capitol Tower that had a little piano in it that Frank could use for a few hours each evening until the building closed. He and Gail moved to the Tropicana Motel on Santa Monica Boulevard, so he wrote a lot of *Lumpy Gravy* there, even though there was no piano. And just before the recording sessions he took a short-term rental on a house in Laurel Canyon. Zappa: 'I was writing around the clock, and I had copyists coming over at three o'clock in the morning to pick up chunks of the score and go off and copy the parts . . . The idea of it is just off the wall, to chop up dialogues and rhythm and stuff, and edit them together into an event. It's more of an event than it is a collection of tunes.'

(*Right*) Edgar Varèse as a young man. (Bettman/Corbis)

(*Below*) Igor Stravinsky in Venice, 1956. (Marvin Koner/Corbis)

Varèse and Stravinsky were the two most important classical influences on Zappa's music.

Rose Marie Zappa with her delinquent son. (Patrice 'Candy' Zappa collection)

Frank and Gail.
It was love at first sight.
(pictorialpress.com)

Zappa in his basement studio, April 30, 1979, just months before the
construction of the Utility Muffin Research Kitchen. Left to right: Ahmet,
Dweezil, Moon Unit, (un-named bird), Frank Zappa (seated on his favourite
vacuum cleaner). (Neal Preston/Corbis)

The Vaudeville Band. Frank with Flo and Eddie, with Aynsley Dunbar on drums, in the studio in Los Angeles, May 1971. (Henry Diltz/Corbis)

Zappa with members of the London Symphony Orchestra, London, January 1983. (Michael Putland/Retna)

Zappa could not afford to pay payola so he went along with any publicity that was an offer. This is Zappa in Paris in the early seventies. (Michael Putland/Retna)

Zappa makes an effort to fit in on the Mothers' first trip to London, September, 1967. (Tony Gale/pictorialpress.com)

With William Burroughs at the Nova Convention, New York, November 1978. (Victor Bockris)

Zappa reading from William Burroughs' *Naked Lunch*, NYC November 1978. (Victor Bockris)

Zappa testifying at the Senate Hearing to consider labelling objectionable content in music, May 6, 1985. (Wally McNamee/Corbis)

Zappa as guitar hero on stage at the Fillmore East, New York, 1970.
(Shepard Sherbell / Corbis)

The album was recorded in three days, from 14–16 March in Capitol's Los Angeles studios, using a 50-piece group of musicians – plus Bunk Gardner – under the direction of Sid Sharp. Zappa called them The Abnuceals Emuukha Electric Symphony Orchestra and Chorus. He also managed to record a few useful orchestral parts to use on *We're Only In It For The Money*, which was already in its planning stage. Capitol had spent $40,000 on studio and session fees for *Lumpy Gravy*, designed a sleeve and assigned a catalogue number to the record before MGM's lawyers stepped in. Litigation lasted for a year, resulting in MGM buying the master tape from Capitol, who turned over the original multi-track tapes, but by then – 1968 – Zappa had other ideas. He added vocal parts and radically changed the album before its eventual release in May 1968.

Zappa moved to New York in the days when coffee was still a dime and a subway token cost 15 cents. The World Trade Center had yet to be built and the wanton destruction of 25 city blocks of historic nineteenth-century buildings to make way for it – including the oldest cast-iron building in the world – had yet to begin. SoHo was not yet called SoHo and at night was a dark gloomy neighbourhood of locked warehouses and parked trucks. Musicians and artists were only just beginning to take over lofts as studios and rehearsal spaces and there was only one bar – Fanelli's – in the entire area. The Stonewall Riots were not until 1969 and Christopher Street still had the atmosphere of old literary Greenwich Village. The *Village Voice* office was on Sheridan Square, across from the Paperback Galleries, and the bars were filled with hard-drinking writers and newspaper men.

Gail was already three months pregnant when they moved to New York. At first, she and Frank stayed at the Hotel Van Rensselaer at 13 East 11th Street (it closed in 1973 and was returned to its original use as apartments). They arrived in March 1967 and took a small room on one of the upper floors. They lived on peanut-butter sandwiches from Smiler's Deli around the corner and grapefruit from Gristedes. Gail: 'We made (instant) coffee from the bathtub, because the water that came into the bathtub was so hot you could really scorch yourself. You did not need to boil it. It was frightening.' There were huge cockroaches and it was still so cold they could keep their milk fresh on the window-sill (though they were shocked by how dirty it was when they brought it in). The filth and pollution of New York City came as an unpleasant shock after the fresh air and sun of Laurel Canyon.

Frank was working on the artwork for *Absolutely Free* at a desk by the window and found it impossible to keep it free from soot and smuts. The Con Ed plant on East 13th Street over by the East River would belch thick black smoke from its stacks, which fell as grime all over the Lower East Side and Greenwich Village. Ken Weaver, drummer with the Fugs, lived close to the plant and used to blow his nose into a tissue each morning and mail it to the head office of Con Ed. He urged everyone he met to do the same as a citizen's protest. Frank loved Weaver's humour, and one day the big Texan made him laugh so much he fell off his chair and couldn't get up.

The Easter week residency was so successful that Herb Cohen decided to block book the theatre through the summer. The gross for the five months was $103,000, but the overhead was high: the rent on the Garrick was $1,000 a month and electricity added another $500, so after expenses they each received about $200 a week. It was better than working at the aircraft factory, but not great.

Gail found a third-floor apartment at 180 Thompson Street (since rebuilt) – just around the corner from the Garrick Theater. The rent was $200 – the same as they had been paying in Laurel Canyon. Zappa took a break from rehearsals to see apartment 3-D. The front door was blocked by the hunched figure of a bum who had pissed himself before passing out. The apartment was at the back with a view of a brick wall, but it was bigger than their hotel room: they had a living room with a kitchenette, a bedroom and a bathroom. To make life more cosy, Frank's brother Bobby came to visit, along with two friends, Bill Harris and Dick Barber, whom Frank knew from Studio Z. They lined up each night in their sleeping bags on the living room floor.

There was just enough room for one more person: Cal Schenkel. When Zappa told Sandy Hurvitz (Cal's ex-girlfriend who opened for the Mothers at the Garrick) that he was planning on a *Sgt Pepper* sleeve parody for *We're Only In It For The Money,* she recommended Cal as the only artist who could do the idea justice. The trouble was, Cal lived in Philadelphia. So Cal also ended up on the floor of apartment 3-D.

The Mothers now had a long residency ahead of them. Starting 24 May 1967, it was billed as *'Absolutely Free* – A musical by Frank Zappa, with the Mothers of Invention, presented by Herb Cohen', and even had a hawker outside to try and entice people in. With a secure residency the Mothers were able to relax and experiment. The show was subtitled *Pigs and Repugnant,* and Frank often welcomed the audience with 'Hello pigs!' The show rapidly became an exercise in seeing how many insults and how much abuse an audience could take. People were dragged on-stage and forced to make a speech; young women were brought up and manhandled; two on-stage marriages were conducted.

One big attraction was a large soft stuffed giraffe. Jimmy Carl Black described it: 'These three beautiful girls gave us this stuffed giraffe that was about three and a half feet tall. One day, out of boredom, Ray Collins and I wired that giraffe for the evening's performance with a half-inch clear plastic tube running up its leg and right underneath its tail . . .' Jimmy and Ray waited until a point in the show when people were running all over the stage and the band was whipping everyone into a frenzy. Then they hid behind the piano. Jimmy Carl Black: 'We got about ten cans of pressurized whipped cream from the Café a Go-Go, right down below the Garrick Theater; real pressurized cans. We started squirting those cans down that tube from behind the piano, and they levelled the first three rows of the people in the audience. They had this white stuff flying out of the giraffe's ass, hitting people in the face, and we sprayed at least five cans. People were splitting and Frank was on the ground. He had to stop playing he was laughing so hard.'

It immediately became part of the act. Zappa: 'Ray Collins would go up to the giraffe and massage it with a frog hand puppet . . . and then the giraffe's tail would stiffen and the first three rows of the audience would get sprayed with whipped cream shooting out of the hose. All with musical accompaniment, of course. It was the most popular feature of our show. People would request it all the time.' At the Mothers' 4 July 1967 show, somebody waved the flag, the industrial-strength whipped cream dispenser was cranked up, and a cherry bomb ignited which blew the ass out of the giraffe. As no one ever cleaned the theatre, the smell of rancid whipped cream soon gave the place a special aroma.

Another time they brought 30 people up on stage and some of them played the group's instruments. At the end of the show Frank got them all to sing 'Louie, Louie' and the band crept quietly away and went home, as the audience continued to sing.

There was a system rigged up with a wire running from the light booth at the back of the theatre to the stage and the lighting man would send stuff down the wire. A spread-eagled baby doll would come down the line, perhaps followed by a salami that would ram the baby doll in the ass. Zappa: 'It was all carefully planned and we played the right music for this sort of thing. Sometimes the lighting guy would surprise us, and send eggs or something really messy down the wire.'

They did not start off using props in the act; in fact, it began as an accident. A marine had been killed in the Village and a rumour went round that the marines were planning to invade the Village and beat up all the long-hairs. The Mothers were unnerved when three marines in full dress uniform walked into the Garrick one afternoon during rehearsals. Frank was polite and invited them to sit and watch, which they did. Afterwards they told him they were from the US aircraft carrier Wasp, which was visiting New York Harbour. They were 19 years old and said they liked his music.

Frank asked if they could sing. They knew Dylan's 'Rainy Day Women Nos 12 & 35' (with its chorus 'everybody must get stoned') and 'House of the Rising Sun' by the Animals. Frank invited them to sing on-stage with the Mothers that evening and they were delighted. While Frank ate his early meal across the street at the Tin Angel, the marines practised their songs (Frank made everybody rehearse). That evening the Mothers went on and began the show and the marines waited on the side.

Frank: 'I said, "When I give you the signal, I want all three of you guys to lunge for the microphone and start screaming 'Kill!'" So we played like that Archie Shepp weirdness, with the dissonant chords and all that, and on cue they ran right to the mikes, started screaming "Kill!" The audience just went – they couldn't handle it. Then when it was over, they clapped. So I said to the audience, "Thank you"; and then Ray Collins says to the audience, "Thank you"; and then when I pointed to the marines to have them say "Thank you", the first one walks up to the mike and says, "Eat the apple, fuck the core" [i.e. Corps]. And everyone went "Whew! Oh wow!" And then the second one, he comes up and says "Eat the apple, fuck the core." Point to the third one; he goes up, he says: "Hey, I feel the same way as my other two buddies: Eat the apple, fuck the core. Some of us love our Mothers more." Full-dress blues man.'

Zappa was astonished. They could be court marshalled for what they were doing. But they just said, 'I don't care, man, they can only get you once.' During the intermission Frank asked Gail to go home and get a large plastic doll that someone had given them. The group went back on stage; the marines came back on and sang their songs.

Zappa: 'They go through all that shit and I says, "Now we're gonna have basic training. Uh, ladies an' gennlemen, this is a gook baby; and the marines are going to mutilate it before your very eyes. Kill it!" Tossed it to them, they ripped the arms off, stomped on it, and just completely tore it apart. After they're all done, the music got real quiet, the lights went down, and I held it by the hair and showed the audience all the damaged parts of the doll's body, pretending . . . There was one guy in the front row, a Negro cat just come back from Vietnam, was crying. It was awful and I ended the show there.'

Some people were critical of Zappa's treatment of his audience, but as he said a few months later: 'Music always is a commentary on society, and certainly the atrocities on stage are quite mild compared to those conducted in our behalf by our government. You can't write a chord ugly enough to say what you want to say sometimes, so you have to rely on a giraffe filled with whipped cream. Also, they didn't know how to listen. Interest spans wane and they need something to help them re-focus.'

Besides, Zappa had very little respect for his fans: 'There wasn't too much going on in the Village that interested me. The people who came to see us at the Garrick mostly had short hair, they came from middle-class white Jewish environments, mostly suburban. They came to see our show because we were something weird that was on that street and we were a sort of specialized recreational facility.' It was from these fans that Frank overheard the line: 'Gee, my hair's getting good in the back,' as they tried to grow their hair into a Beatle cut to get the girls.

Part of it was also Zappa the clown. The same gangly youth who liked to entertain his classmates at Edgewood Elementary now acted the fool on stage. He knew he couldn't compete in the looks department with the Byrds or Love, so he constructed a group image of a bunch of ugly old men who could play real good and were funny. It was also a way of attracting an audience.

Zappa: 'Most people like to perceive satire in what I do. I mean that they really aren't into the music; they are too hooked on the pure theatre side of the music. They're listening to a comedy routine and they want to listen to it that way because, unfortunately, a lot of people aren't really equipped to evaluate any other kind of artistic structure . . . for an audience there's nothing easier than comedy.'

But it wasn't just comedy or theatre; Zappa was continuing the tradition of the Happening artists of the late fifties and early sixties: Red Grooms, Jim Dine, Claes Oldenburg, Lucas Samaras and, most famously, Allan Kaprow. Kaprow wrote: 'Not only will these bold creators show us, as if for the first time, the world we have always had about us but ignored, but they will disclose entirely unheard-of happenings and events, found in garbage cans, police files, hotel lobbies, seen in store windows and on the streets, and sensed in dreams and horrible accidents.' If one had to situate Zappa in the canon of American twentieth-century art, this is where he belongs, along with the Happening artists and pop artists like Warhol, Rivers and Rauschenberg. Like them, Zappa responded to the banality of the world around him with sardonic humour. He preferred to express his bitterness through parody, rather than the righteous anger of Bob Dylan and the folk singers of the early sixties or the blind hatred of the heavy-metal brigade a decade later.

Zappa's early work was a cartoon collage of American life, with his own feelings and personality eliminated in the best Andy Warhol tradition. Only later did he begin to introduce diatribes against Nixon, Reagan, Bush, the 'Star Wars' programme, TV evangelists and the Parents' Music Resource Center (PMRC). This cartoon-happening element remained part of his stage act to the very end: even on his last tour he still had a washing line for panties strung across the stage.

The Mothers played good music at the Garrick, wonderful music, sometimes just riffing on some of Frank's beautiful melodies. The music for the show was built around a series of well-rehearsed musical blocks that could be improvised upon and played in any order, according to Zappa's famous hand-signals. Anything could be dropped into this: the band was so tight, they could turn on a dime.

The early shows were opened by flautist Jeremy Steig, accompanied by Sandy Hurvitz. In fact, Sandy was in both groups. She had been walking through the Village with two girlfriends from LA when they saw Zappa. The two Californians yelled 'Cantor's!' and 'Ben Frank's!' to draw his attention, and all three were given free passes for that night's show. Sandy watched it on acid and, after hanging around for a few days, somehow managed to join both Jeremy Steig and the Mothers. Sandy: 'One day Don [Preston] was not feeling well, and a new electric keyboard had arrived. Frank had heard somehow that I played a little and since Don was ill he asked me would I play the keyboard a little bit for him.' She played some of her own songs and Zappa asked her to follow him into his office. 'How would you like to be a Mother?' he asked and Sandy said, 'Sure.'

Zappa introduced her in the middle of the show as 'this strange little person in her mod clothes, who is called Uncle Meat', and she would do a duet with Ray Collins. 'They stand with their arms around each other, rubbing chests and looking tender and mournful,' reported the *Village Voice*. Ray came up with the name 'Uncle Meat' one day at rehearsals and Zappa pounced on it. Sandy: 'After a couple of months of it I said, "Hey, I really don't want to be Uncle Meat!"' So Frank used the name for something else.

In July Jimi Hendrix played the Cafe Au Go Go directly beneath the Garrick and Zappa went to see him: 'He had a whole stack of Marshalls and I was right in front of it. I was physically ill – I couldn't get out; it was so packed I couldn't escape. And although it was great, I didn't see how anybody could inflict that kind of volume on himself, let alone other people. That particular show he ended by taking the guitar and impaling it in the low ceiling of the club. Just walked away and left it squealing.'

Frank invited Jimi to see the Mothers play, and Jimi and his drummer Mitch Mitchell sat in with them. Frank was so intrigued by what Hendrix was doing that he left the stage and sat in the audience to watch him play with the band, indicating a previously unseen level of respect for another musician's work.

Gail continued her search for decent accommodation and in August she found a long basement apartment on Charles Street near 7th Avenue. That summer the garbage collectors went on strike, giving the rooms the unmistakable odour of rotting trash, but there was a cherry tree in the backyard, and it was a distinct improvement on Thompson. They quickly made it their own.

The rooms were soon cluttered with instruments: bongos, a mandolin, guitars. There was a full-length poster of Zappa in the hall and a 16" x 10" blow-up of the portrait of Gail used as a multiple image in *The Real Frank Zappa Book* in the living-room, walls began to accumulate clippings from magazines and newspapers, music sheets, posters and artwork including a Cal Schenkel assemblage, originally intended for an Eric Dolphy album called *Moop Record* – part of an unrealized project Zappa had with Alan Douglas to produce a series of jazz albums – a detail from which was later used as the sleeve for *Burnt Weeny Sandwich*. There was a copy of Saint-Exupéry's *The Little Prince* and other essential sixties reading, including Robert Heinlein's sci-fi classic *Stranger In A Strange Land*, from which Zappa borrowed the word 'discorporate' for 'Absolutely Free'. In the living room was a rocking chair with an antimacassar crocheted with *Why, what pigs?*.

In New York the Mothers were dogged day and night by groupies. They would follow them down the street, exactly 15 paces behind. Cindy, Annie, Janell and Rozzy were really young – aged 13 to I5 – and Zappa thought it was wonderful: 'They really surprised us. They had really groovy minds. More imagination than I've ever seen in girls so young.' But the groupies were not so keen on Gail. Zappa told *Rolling Stone*: 'I have a tape of a 14-year-old going through a fantasy where she was going to kill my pregnant wife so she could get me. It's a little scary, but it's actually very flattering too.' He used them on the *We're Only In It For The Money* sleeve.

Even with Gail pregnant, Frank continued to see other women, including one night spent with Janis Joplin at the Hotel Chelsea. In the morning she asked Zappa if he had been any good the night before – she had been too drunk to remember. Frank left in a huff.

Aside from groupies, several of Zappa's future musicians were regulars at the Garrick shows. Ian Underwood held a Bachelor of Music from Yale and a Masters in composition from Berkeley. He was a multi-instrumentalist; an accomplished woodwind player and concert pianist (specializing in Mozart), he could play organ, clarinet, flute and alto saxophone. After seeing two shows he approached Jimmy Carl Black and said he liked their music and wanted to play with them. Two days later he visited the Mothers while they were laying down tracks for their third album, *We're Only In It For The Money*. His conversation with Zappa was recreated on stage in Copenhagen a month later:

'How do you do, my name is Ian Underwood. I like your music and I would like to play with your group.'

'What can you do that's fantastic?' asked Zappa.

'I can play alto saxophone and piano.'

'Okay,' said Zappa, gesturing to the instruments littering the studio. 'Whip it out.'

He was hired on the spot. Motorhead also became an official

member of the Mothers as baritone saxophonist and percussionist, making it a nine-piece group.

The Mothers spent much of August and September recording *We're Only In It For The Money* at Mayfair, a home-made studio in a converted office space at 701 Seventh Avenue, which housed the only available eight-track facility in New York. At the same time they completed their residency at the Garrick, which ran on intermittently until 5 September. They took off most of August, giving Zappa time to make a quick trip to London – his first trip outside North America – to publicize *Absolutely Free* and their upcoming European tour.

Zappa had calculated every detail of the presentation and marketing of the Mothers in Europe, and in London he told Nick Jones from *Melody Maker*: 'It took us a long time to convince people, to make them realize that they needed to own a Mothers of Invention album in the States. The problem now is to convert this sales approach to the British audience, and I need to know enough about the scene here. I've got to know enough about it to convince the British audiences that they need to know the things we have to say. And what we have to say can be useful to any young person in any country in the world if that person wants to get a true picture of the environment and society that was established by his fathers, and which he'll have to take over. We're the ways and means committee. I'm not talking about hot teenage blood in the street bashing society over the head. It's just a matter of phasing them out.'

This bizarre combination of commercial marketing and revolutionary rhetoric astonished the British press and provoked a certain amount of cynicism. 'We want to gear our product to the local market,' Zappa told David Griffiths of *Record Mirror*. 'We do this in the States too – I find there are regional variations in taste and we try to cater for them.' Griffiths concluded his article by wondering if all the nice things Zappa had said about London were merely part of the 'process of gearing the product to suit the local market'!

It was Zappa's first time in Europe and he seems to have been overzealous in trying to show how professional he was. There was also a semantic problem: the word 'product' was not used in Britain and sounded very crass to the music journalists, who were unaccustomed to musicians talking like managers. The artists were supposed to talk about everyone having fun, or how artistic their work was.

Zappa's use of the word 'product' also shocked Paul McCartney. During a press reception at the Kasmin Gallery, Zappa asked the Beatle on the phone for permission to parody the *Sgt Pepper* sleeve on *We're Only In It For The Money*. It was fine by McCartney, who liked the Mothers, but he told Frank the sleeve image was owned by EMI, not the Beatles. Frank would have to deal with the record company. Afterwards Zappa told Griffiths: 'Paul McCartney was disturbed that I could refer to what we do as product, but I'm dealing with businessmen who care nothing about music, or art, or me personally. They want to make money and I relate to them on that level or they'd regard me as just another rock 'n' roll fool.'

'I never understood why Zappa blamed me for not being able to use the Sgt Pepper sleeve,' McCartney said later. 'I told him I'd write a letter or get Brian [Epstein, the Beatles' manager] to ask them. I don't think EMI would have stopped them, or even could have stopped them.' This issue held up the release of the album, but it is quite probable that MGM-Verve never even approached EMI. If they did, the Beatles would have heard of it, and helped. Subsequently, *Sgt Pepper* became one of the most parodied album sleeves of all time, presumably with no lawsuits.

Zappa had a cynical (perhaps even jealous) attitude to the Beatles and never recognized the enormous contribution they made to rock music. Discussing the sleeve Zappa said: 'When I did the original parody of that it was to point out the fact that at the time the Beatles were only in it for the money. Everybody else thought they were GOD. I think that was not correct. They were just a good commercial group.' In reality, both EMI and Epstein were extremely worried by the new non-commercial direction the Beatles had taken with *Sgt Pepper* which was by no means guaranteed to be a hit. They thought the group would alienate their fans, and EMI even made them agree to pay the cost of the sleeve themselves if the album did not sell more than 100,000 copies. Far from being in it only for the money, the Beatles had made plenty of that and their only concern with *Sgt Pepper* was a stated aim to make the greatest rock 'n' roll record of all time. This was what really irritated Zappa, who felt that his records deserved this kind of accolade.

Zappa gave Cal Schenkel a little sketch of the sleeve of *We're Only In It For The Money*. Schenkel: 'He actually traced the cover and said "I want to find all these people and get them and put them in the picture," and there were like 100 people. We started to try and get people and it was just impossible.' Some people they found in Frank's old high-school yearbook, but many of the people were found images. Unlike the actual *Sgt Pepper* shoot, just the foreground vegetation and the line-up of people and three-dimensional objects were shot. The rest was a collage done afterwards and stripped in, as can be seen by the face of the young groupie Cindy, second from left in the back row, which came unstuck and is blank on the sleeve. The photography was done by Jerrold Schatzburg, a famous fashion photographer, in his studio in the old Tiffany Building at 333 Park Avenue South.

Jerrold Schatzberg: 'Frank had approached me because he had seen the sleeve that I did on the Stones' "Can You See Your Mother, Baby, Standing In The Shadows" when they were in drag, and he had an idea that he wanted to do a combination of that and *Sgt Pepper*. And instead of flowers and wonderful dreams of that sort, he wanted garbage and old food and what you see around on the floor. We both knew Jimi Hendrix and we asked Jimi to come in, so Jimi sat in there as one of the faces. Basically Frank knew pretty much what he wanted.' The shoot took a day and a half and finished late at night. The costumes came from fashion designer Tiger Morse whose Kaleidoscope boutique was the hippest in town. Frank wore a black velvet mini-dress and Gail a blue full-length glittering ball gown. Gail: 'I was obviously very pregnant. Hendrix showed up with a friend, but the photographer very deftly arranged it, placing Hendrix at the end of the row so he could cut the friend out of the shot.' Also in the picture in real life was record producer Tom Wilson, and sitting at Gail's feet was Schenkel himself, clutching a box of eggs – his favourite food. Frank had wanted a bust of Varèse, but they had to make do with Beethoven. Schenkel put a black bar across his eyes to disguise him when MGM insisted that they bar the eyes of anyone living who had not given clearance for their picture to be used.

A couple of days before the Mothers left on their first European tour, Frank and Gail married at New York City Hall, presumably to legitimize the child and to placate their Catholic parents. Gail was nine months pregnant and the recently arranged tour could have been easily timed to allow Frank to be present at the birth, but he appears to have been as coldly unemotional about this as any other matter.

In a green painted marriage cubicle in the tiny 1811 palace that still serves as the mayor's office, a brief ceremony took place. Frank had no pen and had to buy one from a ten-cent vending machine in the hall. He had not thought to bring a ring, either, so he ceremoniously pinned the pen – which had the words *A Present From Mayor Lindsay* on it – on her bulging maternity dress. It was just before closing time and the official punched their card in a time clock mounted on an imitation pulpit. In Zappa's words, 'It was cheezy.'

Zappa was not especially keen on marriage. In December 1966 he had done a spoof interview for teenybopper magazine *Teen Set* in which Michael Vosse asked him if he would like to get married. Zappa said no: 'I've already been married, and it doesn't make it. If I ever was to get married, I'd prefer a sterile deaf mute who likes to wash dishes. There are so many American women who fit that description philosophically I might as well own one. Your dad probably owns one; I'll go watch his!' Three years later he told a British newspaper: 'Gail was a groupie, and an excellent groupie too. It didn't matter to me that she had slept around with other beat men. We got married in New York when Gail was nine months pregnant. It's not because I believe in having a certificate to prove you're married; it's just that in America it's difficult to get into hospital if you're an unwed mother-to-be.'

As Frank left for London he told Gail: 'If it's a boy, call him Motorhead. If it's a girl, call her Moon Unit.' Moon Unit Zappa was born in New York on 28 September 1967.

Before the group tour, Frank reminded the band that he was the spokesman for the Mothers and that no one else was to give any interviews. He was carefully cultivating an image for the band and he didn't want any of the other Mothers messing it up. The voice of Suzy Creamcheese on *Freak Out!* had particularly intrigued British Mothers fans and the Press, so it was decided that a Suzy Creamcheese would have to accompany them.

Pamela Zarubica and her friend Vickie had returned to LA after a year in London and Zappa suggested she might come to New York to look after Gail while he was away. But when he asked if she knew anyone who could act the role of Suzy Creamcheese, Pamela insisted it had to be her. 'How could you take anyone but me?' she screamed down the phone. 'I'm the only one with the brains for the job and besides, I'm the only chick that knows what you wanna do!' So Pamela was going to London with the Mothers. Sandy Hurvitz also accompanied them. 'Suzy Creamcheese . . . was a real bitch,' she recalled. 'Her name was Zarubica – and let me tell you, she was a real Zarubica.'

But first there was some recording to do. If the British wanted Suzy Creamcheese, then she should be on the new album. Frank took Pamela to Mayfair studios where the engineer Gary Kellgren fed her lines and coached her to sound like Jeannie Vassoir, the voice of Suzy on *Freak Out!* While they were at the studio Vickie called to say that Pamela's father had the FBI looking for her and they were about to arrest her for withholding information as to Pam's whereabouts. Frank attached a microphone to the telephone and rolled the tape before Pamela called Vickie back to discuss the matter. Forty-five seconds of their conversation appears on *We're Only In It For The Money*, between 'Mom & Dad' and 'Bow Tie Daddy'.

After that Tom Wilson went home, leaving Frank to record the whispers from engineer Gary Kellgren, threatening to wipe the tapes. Zappa: 'He was a funny guy – a suffering individual during those days, because he had a studio . . . it was kind of a homemade rig, and he was recording 18 hours a day, and he had no private life, no social life. He was just run down. We had to get our album done... He would do, maybe, three or four bands a day, and it was just grinding him down.

He was living on leapers and beer, and so I decided one day to just let him blow off a little steam: I put him out in the studio – I became the engineer and let him talk into the microphone. That's where all the creepy whispering comes from.'

In London Zappa continued the practice of staying at a better hotel than the group. He and Pamela checked in to the recently built and enormously trendy Royal Garden Hotel, next to Kensington Gardens. Immediately afterwards they went to Piccadilly Circus and did some sightseeing, which Zappa would rarely do on his later travels.

That evening they went to the Marquee to see *The Crazy World Of Arthur Brown*. Who guitarist Pete Townshend (who would produce Arthur Brown's 1968 hit single 'Fire') came over and introduced himself and Zappa was delighted to find that in Britain he was regarded as a star; people were offering him drinks and knew *Freak Out!* (for some reason MGM had delayed the release of *Absolutely Free* in the UK by five months). It was still unusual to see American recording artists in London, because the Luddite Musicians' Union insisted that any American playing London had to be matched by a British artist playing the States. So British group the Move were doing an American tour to even things up, their manager being Tony Secunda, who promoted the Mothers concert at the Royal Albert Hall.

Townshend took Frank and Pamela to the Speakeasy, the rock 'n' roll 'in' club on Margaret Street where Marc Bolan and Steve Peregrine Took (Tyrannosaurus Rex) were playing. Never one to miss a chance, Frank had with him tapes of the completed tracks from *We're Only In It For The Money* and a promotional film of the Mothers, which the Speakeasy's D.J. was happy to play. They ran into Noel Redding from the Jimi Hendrix Experience, whom Frank knew from the Garrick. The evening ended when Frank got picked up by Jimi's girlfriend, Kathy Etchingham.

Frank's hotel room quickly became a rock 'n' roll salon: Jeff Beck, Jimi Hendrix and other musicians dropped by, as did lots of groupies, photographers and the cameramen working on the documentary *Uncle*

Meat, which Zappa began shooting that summer. Frank's English secretary Pauline Butcher, who had worked with him on his previous visit, was also there. It was she who demonstrated the 'other uses' of a mechanized doll's foot in the *Uncle Meat* booklet. Some of the confusion and excitement was down to Danny Halperin, an American publicist assigned to help promote the Mothers. He also worked for Osiris, the psychedelic poster company, and he commissioned the notorious photograph of Zappa sitting on the lavatory which was first used by the *International Times*, but which Osiris quickly released as a poster. It was bootlegged all over the world.

The next few days were spent rehearsing for the Royal Albert Hall concert on 23 September, where the Mothers were to be augmented by ten members of the London Philharmonic Orchestra. In the evenings, Frank rapidly became a much feted and celebrated man about town, appearing at all the 'in' clubs. He even compèred for Cream, introducing them at the Speakeasy as a 'natty little combo.' Frank wanted to meet Keith West, whose 'Excerpt from a Teenage Opera' was Number Two in the UK charts. Accompanied by Jimi Hendrix and Jeff Beck, Frank and Pamela paid West a visit. She told Michael Gray that everyone was getting high, except for her and Frank, and for once Zappa didn't appear to mind. In fact, after they left, his first comment was: 'I never met such a nice little group of junkies before.' Zappa knew so little about drugs that he didn't know the difference between hash and heroin.

This led to an embarrassing incident the following day when Frank and Pamela went to see Pink Floyd play the UFO Club at the Roundhouse, the main gathering place for London's underground scene. There were far too many hippies for Zappa's liking but as they were leaving someone rushed up and made as if to shake Frank's hand. Instead he deposited a block of hash in Zappa's palm. Frank looked at it with a puzzled expression. 'What is it?' he asked. The hippies standing round him looked aghast – how could the Head Freak not recognize a block of Lebanese black? Pamela quickly shepherded Frank back to the Royal Garden Hotel.

The Albert Hall concert was a huge success; all the London bands were there, including Hendrix (Frank launched into 'Flower Punk', his parody of 'Hey Joe', when he saw him enter). Frank approached the gig with just the right level of irreverence: 'Ah! I know the perfect thing to accompany this man's trumpet. None other than the mighty and majestic Albert Hall pipe organ!' he intoned as Don Preston climbed up the ranked seats to the second largest organ in the world, and took the controls. (He had spent four hours playing it at rehearsals.) There was silence while Don fumbled about in the darkness for the light switch and he received a rousing ovation when he turned it on.

Zappa: 'You understand that you won't be able to hear the organ once we turn the amplifiers up . . . All right, Don? . . . Whip it on 'em! . . . 'Louie Louie!' They like it loud too, you know?'

Zappa had the audience eating out of his hand for the rest of the evening. The press coverage was good and he suddenly found he was a star in Britain. After London there were concerts in Stockholm and Copenhagen. Tom Wilson, who accompanied them to Denmark, told *Record Mirror*: 'Both Frank and I were extremely impressed by the recording techniques in Copenhagen, and it's on the cards that we may record over there ourselves in the near future.'

The Mothers returned to New York and resumed work on *We're Only In It For The Money*. This time they were in Apostolic Studios, 53 East 10th Street, in Greenwich Village, which offered even more tracks than Mayfair. The studio was named after its prototype Scully twelve-track tape recorder, which gave Zappa many more mix-down possibilities. (Apostolic also had an in-house astrologer and it had been known for sessions to be cancelled because the signs were inauspicious.) Frank block-booked studio time in October and finished the album.

He moved straight on to his next project: the completion of *Lumpy Gravy*, which Capitol had sold to MGM. Frank wanted to make numerous additions and changes. He had already spent a lot of time at Mayfair Studios with Gary Killgren, trying to make sense of the tapes: the Capitol engineers had their own unique recording techniques, which ignored all the usual rules of assigning tracks to different instruments and sticking to it throughout the recording. They even had their own way of splicing tape: they used scissors, which they carried in little leather holsters on their belts.

At Apostolic Frank extended his use of recorded conversation as a musical element. He positioned a pair of U-87 microphones under a Steinway concert grand and covered it with a heavy curtain. He put a sandbag on the sustain pedal (sandbags were used in the bass drum to give it a dull thump) and invited anyone who happened by to sit under there and improvise on topics he would suggest to them over the studio PA. Spider Barbour, whose group Chrysalis was also recording at Apostolic, took part; as did Monica the receptionist; John the studio manager; Gilly Townley, sister of Apostolic's owner; Roy Estrada; Motorhead; and Louis Cuneo, a fan from the Garrick, who had a psychotic laugh like a turkey that particularly appealed to Frank. They all did their best to respond to ponies, pigs, grey smoke and other contrived subjects. A number of these fragments appeared on *Lumpy Gravy*, but much longer sections resurfaced in 1994 on the double CD *Civilisation Phaze III*.

Among the other 'anthropological' items collaged into *Lumpy Gravy* was Eric Clapton exclaiming 'God, it's God! I see God!' – which parodied the *Clapton is God* street graffiti then appearing in London. (Interestingly, Clapton later became a born-again Christian.) Zappa: 'He was just in New York one day hanging out, so I invited him over to the studio to do the rap that's on *We're Only In It For The Money*. People think he's playing on it, but he's not; the only thing he's doing on there is talking.'

That November Frank appeared in an episode of *The Monkees* called 'The Monkees Blow Their Minds'. Mike Nesmith: 'I asked Frank Zappa if he would guest on the show. He said, "I'll only come if I can have your part." And I said, "Well, that's fine. If you come on the show and be me, then I'll be you." So I dressed him up in a shirt and gave him a wool hat so he'd look like me . . . He was very kind. When people hated us more than anything he said kind things about us. He was talking about the music, about how well it was produced . . . He offered to teach me to play lead guitar one time. It was an incredibly groovy thing to do. He worked with me for hours, but I never learned.'

Micky Dolenz: 'He asked me to drum for the Mothers of Invention after the Monkees were finished. Sometimes I wish I had, but I couldn't because I was still under contract.'

All this led to Zappa being offered a walk-on part (literally) in the Monkees' only feature film, *Head*, which was being shot at the time. After a white-suit Broadway musical routine by Davy Jones, Frank makes an appearance leading a large talking bull. He played, or possibly improvised, the role of *éminence grise*.

ZAPPA: That song was pretty white.

JONES: Well, I am white! What can I tell you?

ZAPPA: You've been working on your dancing though . . . it doesn't leave much time for your music. You should spend more time on it because the youth of America depends on you to show the way.

JONES: Yeah?

ZAPPA: Yeah!

THE BULL: Monkees are the craziest people!

Back in New York, Frank block-booked more large chunks of studio time at Apostolic and began work on yet another album: *Uncle Meat*, the soundtrack for the movie of the same name. He had already laid down some tracks before going to work with the Monkees, but from now until February 1968 he spent most of his time in the studio, recording such a wealth of material that fragments would continue to appear on various albums until the end of his life. He hired Apostolic for the entire month of January: 'One hundred and eighty hours – not as much as the Beatles use, we can't afford that,' he told the *Village Voice*. Thus began the habit of spending most of his time in the recording studio, usually working all night.

Each evening he struggled into his brown leather great coat, pulled a red knitted hat down over his ears, and set off for 10th Street. At Apostolic he found a sympathetic engineer in Dick Kunc, who was prepared to put up with such anti-social hours because he loved the music. When the Mothers returned to Los Angeles, Zappa took Dick Kunc and Cal Schenkel with him. With the move to Apostolic came a further line-up change when Billy Mundi left to join Rhinoceros. He was replaced by Arthur Dyer Tripp III, who had performed solo concerts of the work of John Cage and Stockhausen and was fresh from two years as percussionist with the Cincinatti Symphony Orchestra, with whom he toured the world for the State Department.

All the albums recorded in New York are inextricably interconnected: *We're Only In It For The Money, Lumpy Gravy, Uncle Meat* and *Ruben and the Jets*. Right after the Garrick, Zappa began working on a project called 'No Commercial Potential' and this merged with the story of Uncle Meat, which was already being filmed whenever there was enough money to shoot a few more minutes. Cal Schenkel: 'I started working on the story of Ruben and the Jets that is connected with the Uncle Meat story, which is this old guy turns this teenage band into these dog snout people, it was like a story, it's written somewhere. We started that before it actually became Ruben and the Jets. That came out of my love for comics and that style, the anthropomorphic animals, but also it was part of a running story line.' Then it became clear that the anthropomorphic animals would make a good sleeve for *Ruben and the Jets*, so the rest of the story was incorporated into the *Uncle Meat* movie.

Zappa: 'It's all one album. All the material in the albums is organically related and if I had all the master tapes and I could take a razor blade and cut them apart and put it together again in a different order it still would make one piece of music you can listen to. Then I could take that razor blade and cut it apart and reassemble it a different way, and it still would make sense. I could do this twenty ways. The material is definitely related.'

This way of working became Zappa's 'project/object' concept: the idea that each project is part of a larger object, an overall body of work in which every individual piece is changed, if only slightly, by the addition of each new part. This new part could be a film, a record or even, as he once claimed, an interview. He reinforced this 'conceptual continuity' by the re-use of identifiable themes from one album to next, by snatches of monologue which refer back to a previous album, by repeating themes on his album sleeves (the poodle is one: 'Po Po' the poodle being mentioned in one of his very first interviews; Suzy Creamcheese was another), and most of all by reworking earlier melodies or subject matter. It is the 'pattern on the carpet' of Henry James, the conceptual continuity of Ezra Pound's *Cantos*, where each new poem gave new meaning to all the previous work, written over a lifetime to produce a 'map of ever-changing consciousness.' Jack Kerouac regarded all his novels as one big saga and even announced his intention to one day unify the names of all his characters. It is the abandonment of the idea of masterpiece in favour of series: Monet's endless haystacks or waterlilies, each one a different aspect of the same work, rather than one final statement. It is the idea of process: the multiple perspectives of Paul Klee or Pollock rather than the fixed composition of the Renaissance.

We're Only In It For The Money was released on 4 March, but not until Zappa had fought with MGM over it. The test pressing had been censored, including the line about Captain's Beefheart's mother ('And I still remember mama with her apron and her pad, feeding all the boys at Ed's Café'), which the MGM executives inexplicably thought referred to a sanitary pad. Worse still, the equalization had been changed, removing the highs and boosting the bottom and the middle to obscure the words.

Zappa told Jerry Hopkins: 'I'm supposed to sign a paper saying they can release it. I called them up and said, "You can't put this record out!" And they've already pressed 40,000 of them. Then, six or eight weeks later, I got a call about *Lumpy Gravy*. They had just pressed 12,000 of them and they had already been shipped, and I hadn't even been sent a release to sign.' It was probably intentional, then, that MGM neglected to exercise their renewal option on the Mothers' contract, clearing the way for Zappa to start his own label.

We're Only In It For The Money is a remarkable album and still holds up well more than 35 years later. Despite its jolly snatches of surfing music, the tape clips ('I'm Jimmy Carl Black and I'm the Indian of the group!' and 'My hair's getting good in the back'), the speeded-up tape, the chipmunk voices and the parodies of the sensitive flower-power music of Donovan and his ilk, it is a profoundly serious album.

Zappa's view is bleak and filled with foreboding. The lyrics are about lonely, unloved children, fascist trigger-happy cops, materialistic parents who are too busy consuming to notice their children are sad. They condemn frigid American housewives and good ol' boy dads, the anti-sex, anti-life, right-wing militarist society as represented by Governor Ronald Reagan of California.

Frank was given a chance to air his feelings about the music industry when someone foolishly booked the Mothers to play at one of the four pre-Grammy dinners on 29 February 1968, at the New York Hilton. Zappa's mood was not improved by the programme which announced 'Music by Woody Herman; Entertainment by the Mothers of Invention'. Zappa told them straight: 'All year long you people man-ufactured this crap, and one night a year you've got to listen to it . . . Your whole affair is nothing more than a lot of pompous hokum, and we're going to approach you on your own level.' Then, Zappa recalled, 'we played some of the ugliest shit we could do . . . they expected that we play ugly shit.' They were booed when they finished and a lot of people were offended that they had been invited at all.

The Mothers were getting a lot of gigs: in the first three months of 1968 they played Miami, Toronto, Boston, Fullerton California and, on 9 April, they opened for the rapidly disintegrating Cream at the International Amphitheatre in Chicago. Backstage, Eric Clapton intro-duced Frank to Cynthia and Dianne, two chubby brunettes known as the Chicago Plaster-Casters. Their hobby was making plaster casts of the penises of rock musicians.

Dianne sucked the subject's penis until it was hard and Cynthia would then plunge it into a paper cup – or something larger if deemed necessary – filled with dental alginate, which is used to make casts of teeth. This took between 40 seconds and a minute and a half to harden into an exact mould, so care had to be taken both to keep the subject in a state of maximum excitation and to make sure his pubic hair did not become embedded in the alginate, as this could be painful. It took 15 minutes to cut away Jimi Hendrix's pubic hair, but his plaster cast took pride of place in Cynthia's collection.

Frank and Clapton both declined to have their members cast, but

Frank questioned Cynthia closely about her activities and decided her diaries would make a brilliant book. 'It was the most fantastic thing I ever heard,' he told *Rolling Stone*. 'I appreciate what they're doing, both artistically and sociologically. Sociologically its really heavy . . . Pop stars are idolized the same way General Grant was. People put up statues to honour war heroes. What they're doing is making statues of the essential part of stars. It's the same motivation as making statues of Grant . . . I find a sense of humour lacking in pop music generally. All these people take themselves so seriously. They should be able to laugh at themselves. The Plaster-Casters help you do that.'

11 The Log Cabin

In 1915 the cowboy movie star Tom Mix built an 18-room log cabin of eucalyptus and scrub pine as a hunting lodge on the corner of Laurel Canyon Boulevard and Lookout Mountain Drive, where the canyon walls are particularly steep and thickly wooded. The five-acre site had a stream, a small lake and thick woodland. He built caves and artificial grottoes and planted flowering trees and vines. Here he entertained his fellow stars of the silent era (as well as Wyatt Earp). Across the street lived his friend Harry Houdini, the great escapologist, and they built a tunnel under Laurel Canyon Boulevard to connect their homes. A stone staircase led down to the dank artificial cave where the tunnel began, but the passageway had been bricked up by the time Zappa moved in.

Adjoining the log cabin, in the back yard, Mix built his own personal tenpin bowling alley, but the story that his famous horse Tony was buried beneath it is not true. Half a century later, the bowling alley was lived in by Karl Franzoni, who used it as a painting studio. He liked to practise his bowling in the nude, apart from pointed cowboy boots and plastic clip-on curlers in his pubic hair. Franzoni ran the place as a sort of commune. In a vault off the basement lived two other members of Vito's dance troupe: Lucy and Sandra, and in a large closet across from them lived 18-year-old Christine Frka. She was tall, thin and aloof and had huge green eyes. She sewed all her own clothes, including a full-length patchwork coat, and her tiny room was filled with fabrics and scraps of fur and lace.

Early in 1968 Lucy, Sandra and Christine befriended a bunch of young groupies on the fringe of Vito's scene and they would all travel to gigs in the back of Vito's blue VW van. With the exception of Christine, who preferred not to join in their bisexual games, claiming to be frigid, all the girls: Lucy, Sandra, 19-year-old Pamela Miller and her girlfriend Sparky, plus a girl called Beverly would peel off their see-through tops and roll around on the mattress, kissing each others breasts – what Pamela described as a 'slight orgy' – while Vito kept his eye on the rear-view mirror and Karl Franzoni urged them on . . .

Franzoni's commune ended in May 1968 when Frank Zappa, Gail, little Moon Unit, Cal Schenkel, engineer Dick Kunc and Frank's English secretary Pauline Butcher, packed their bags and headed for Los Angeles. Zappa had visited Karl at the log cabin on a previous trip and realized it was perfect for his needs. The estate was owned by an eccentric African-American widow who charged $700 a month. Frank went to see her and shortly afterwards Franzoni, Lucy, Sandra and the girls found themselves with nowhere to live.

The huge basement was an ideal rehearsal space, and as Zappa demanded constant rehearsals it made sense to have his own space rather than rent. Below that was a sub-basement, originally used as a wine cellar. There were two walk-in safes (obviously Tom Mix had a lot of valuables), one of which still had its metal door with a dial and handle, described by Bobby Zappa as being about the size of a service-station restroom. Frank and Gail lived in the main house, where the walls were made from huge logs. Zappa had his piano in the living room, where they entertained guests under a 14-candle chandelier before a huge stone fireplace.

Cal Schenkel had his art studio and living quarters up in the tree house, a separate wing of the Log Cabin; you had to climb up around a giant Eucalyptus tree to get there. The first work he did there was the sleeve for *Ruben and the Jets*. (Later Schenkel got on very well with Earth-mother Sandra, a friendship that resulted in a baby girl called Raven.) Also living there were Pauline Butcher, road manager Dick 'Snork' Barber, Ian Underwood, 'Motorhead' Sherwood and Pamela Zarubica. The eventual roll-call was about a dozen people. The grounds were criss-crossed by paths, steps faced with coloured mosaic and artificial-looking stone archways leading to the grottoes, a series of artificial caves made from concrete and stucco with electric lighting. There was a fish pond and wild, overgrown gardens. It was idyllic.

One day Lucy suggested to Christine, Pamela and the girls that they all drop in on Zappa at the Log Cabin. She knew Zappa from New York, though quite how well she would never tell. While they were all talking to the Zappas, Christine drifted away and began tidying up. When Moon Unit crawled over to her, Christine casually hoisted her onto her hip and carried on cleaning. Gail was so impressed she hired her on the spot as a live-in babysitter.

With Christine living at the Log Cabin, it quickly became the central hangout for the other girls and, away from Vito, they began to evolve their own dance routines. They called themselves the Laurel Canyon Ballet Company and rehearsed in the huge basement whenever the Mothers were not using it. One evening they all arrived at the Log Cabin wearing bibs and giant nappies, their hair up in pigtails, each licking a giant lollypop. Zappa, with his love of the perverse and the bizarre, was ecstatic and insisted they dance on-stage with the Mothers that evening. However, he didn't like their name and suggested they call themselves Girls Together Only or the GTOs.

Unfortunately, the gig was in Orange County, right-wing Republican territory, and no sooner had the GTOs gone backstage than they were ushered into an office where an outraged matron screamed at them because she could see a nipple peeking out from Pamela's bib. They were surrounded by security guards the rest of the evening and not allowed on-stage. All was not lost, however. Later that year, Zappa asked the GTOs to appear with the Mothers at the Whiskey. He suggested they work on their theme song, Julie Andrews' 'Getting To

Know You' (a superb choice for a groupie band). They did two numbers, danced about and received a standing ovation.

The Log Cabin became a home from home for the GTOs and soon they were all living more or less permanently in the artificial fairy grotto on the adjacent hillside. It was perfect, because rather than having to go in search of rock stars, they would come to the house; the downside was Frank's attitude to drugs. When Eric Burdon left the Animals and moved to LA, he first of all rented a room in the Log Cabin. Burdon: 'Tom Mix's cabin was actually a mansion designed to look like a Wild West cabin. It was so big I hardly saw any of the residents, except the Mothers working on their monstrous Harley Davidsons in the courtyard.'

British bluesman John Mayall was given a warm welcome when he arrived in LA, and the track '2401' on his 1968 album *Blues From Laurel Canyon* describes life at the Log Cabin in great detail. He depicts an open, hospitable household, name-checking Gail, Moon, Pauline, the GTOs, Pamela, Christine, Kansas the roadie, and even the Raven wondering if he can have his gun back (the full story of the Raven can be found in *The Real Frank Zappa Book*).

The Log Cabin became an essential stop-off point for all visiting British rock musicians. Mick Jagger and Marianne Faithfull went in July 1968 and, in going to answer the door, Zappa caught a splinter in his bare foot from the rough floorboards. Jagger's first experience of the cabin was to kneel and carefully extract the sharp sliver of wood from Frank's toe. Several members of the Who dropped by that evening, as well as Captain Beefheart with his new guitarist Bill Harkelroad, and they all jammed together on rock 'n' roll classics like 'Be Bop A Lula' in the basement rehearsal room. Beefheart later complained that Jagger had given him a faulty microphone to use, so as not to be overpowered. Another day Eric Clapton came over, but it was not a great success. Zappa: 'He wasn't the jamming type. When I used to live in the Log Cabin I had some amps set up in my basement, and he came over one day and played during one of our rehearsals. But he didn't like the amp; we were using Acoustics then, and he didn't like them.'

Another visitor was Grace Slick from the Jefferson Airplane, whom Zappa wanted to star in his film *Captain Beefheart Versus the Grunt People*. The Jefferson Airplane had asked him to produce their album *Plane Its Pointed Little Head*, but Frank had too many commitments. Nevertheless, one of the first things he did on his return to LA was record Grace Slick at RCA's Hollywood studios performing a song they had co-written called 'Would You Like A Snack?' She was backed by Arthur Tripp, Ian Underwood, Don Preston and Ruth Komanoff. Originally intended for *Crown of Creation*, the other members of the Jefferson Airplane dropped it, thinking that perhaps the world was not yet ready for a song about Grace having her period.

In her autobiography, Grace Slick described the Log Cabin: 'Frank Zappa's house in the canyon, which I visited several times, looked exactly like a troll's kingdom. Fuzzy-haired women lounged in long antique dresses, and naked children ran to and fro while Frank sat behind piles of electronic equipment discussing his latest ideas for orchestrating satirical hippie rock music. Never a druggie, Frank openly made fun of the very counter-culture he was helping to sustain.'

Lumpy Gravy was released on 13 May 1968, just as Zappa and his entourage moved back to LA. Frank always said that this was one of his favourite albums, and it is easy to see why. He had a full orchestra to work with, a twelve-track, state-of-the-art studio to stretch out in, and he was at his creative peak. Some of his favourite songs are on here, including 'Oh No', which appears on no fewer than five other albums. It is also one of his most experimental albums. Discussing 'At the Gas Station' on *Lumpy Gravy*, Zappa told Sally Kempton: 'Cage is a big influence. We've done a thing with voices, with talking, that is very like one of his pieces, except that of course in our piece the guys are talking about working in an airplane factory, or their cars.' *Lumpy Gravy* also contains his most intensive tape collages and cut-ups.

Zappa always had dozens of schemes in various stages of development. While in New York he had pondered a Broadway musical based on the life of Lenny Bruce ('He was a saint') and had planned a monster movie to be made in Japan, as well as dozens of ideas that never got beyond conversations. Though Herb Cohen was with him in New York, Frank's principal collaborator in music-related projects was Tom Wilson. But in December 1967 Wilson's contract with MGM had ended and he had decided to set up on his own as Rasputin Productions.

The Mothers' own contract with MGM-Verve had already expired on 1 October and MGM had not exercised their renewal option, leaving the way clear for Frank and Herb Cohen to start Bizarre Inc., their own 'entertainment combine' consisting of seven divisions among them: Bizarre Records; Zappa's Third Story Music music publishing company; a management division consisting of Cohen's existing artists roster: Tim Buckley, Linda Ronstadt, Fred Neil and the Mothers; and an advertising and PR company called Nifty Tough & Bitchen (NT&B), whose first job was the 'cover concept' for the sleeve of *We're Only In It For The Money*.

NT&B also handled promotion for the album. One innovation was to place adverts in Marvel Comics – the first time an LP had been advertized in a comic book. Bizarre was housed in offices at 5455 Wilshire Blvd and had its own logo, an engraving of a medical pump that Cal Schenkel found in his new studio. To get completely free of MGM-Verve, Frank and Herb had to negotiate a compromise: under the Bizarre logo, MGM-Verve would release a compilation, *Mothermania*, and one final new Mothers album, *Cruising with Ruben & the Jets*, as well as an album by Sandy Hurvitz: *Sandy's Album is Here at Last*.

Mothermania contained mostly previously released material and was the first of a seemingly endless series of Mothers compilations issued by MGM, but this was the only one Zappa compiled himself. The Sandy Hurvitz album was first announced as being by Uncle Meat and the CIA and was to be produced by Frank, with the Mothers providing all the backing tracks, but Sandy proved less malleable than Zappa expected. While recording a song called 'Arch Godliness Of Purplefull Magic' – a title that indicates the kind of personal, introspective, hippie material Hurvitz wrote – she and Zappa got into an argument over Billy Mundi's drum track and Sandy stalked out of the studio. An exasperated Zappa handed over the production chores to Ian Underwood, who had never produced an album. He spent a lot of time recording horn tracks and wiping them the next day. The results were disappointing and Sandy continued her career under the name Essra Mohawk.

As if all this were not enough, Zappa launched himself as a college lecturer and essayist, publishing two pieces in June 1968: 'The Incredible History of the Mothers' in *Hit Parader* and a history of rock 'n' roll for *Life* magazine called 'The Oracle Has It All Psyched Out'.

The Mothers were also touring, though without Ray Collins who quit early that summer. That year they played a month-long European tour, ending with their famous concert at London's Royal Festival Hall with the BBC Symphony Orchestra on 25 October 1968 (Zappa rather begrudgingly released it as a live CD called *Ahead of Their Time* in 1993). In the liner notes he described it as 'a fair – not outstanding – M.O.I. rock concert performance', but he even got the date of the concert wrong. Zappa always resented the popularity of the original Mothers line-up; it irritated him that a certain section of his fans maintained that he never did anything as good or innovative after he broke up the band.

On the European tour Zappa had been writing chamber-music pieces in hotel rooms and airport lounges. He was dying to hear them performed, so when promoter Joe Lustig asked him about an opening act for the London concert Frank suggested hiring members of the BBC Symphony Orchestra to play them. The performance was enlivened by creating a mini-drama around the music. Zappa spent $7,000 (roughly his entire tour profits) to hire the musicians, copy out orchestral parts and pay for rehearsal time, thinking that he would get his money back on a European tour album. He didn't release it for 25 years, but the performance was filmed and large sections appeared in the *Uncle Meat* movie. Some live tracks also turned up on *Weasels Ripped My Flesh* and later *The Mystery Disc*.

For the filmed rehearsal, 15 members of the BBC Symphony Orchestra, the Mothers, a film crew and a baby grand piano all squeezed in to the back room of a pub on Seven Sisters Road. Zappa: 'It was great . . . really great!' The playlet featured Roy Estrada dressed as a Mexican

Pope. He carried a plastic child's bucket inscribed with NO MORE UGLY BABIES and filled with contraceptive pills (actually Smarties), which he threw to the audience (a few weeks before the Pope had announced a ban on birth-control pills). Don Preston was transformed into the Phantom of the Opera and Jimmy Carl Black explained how to get laid – in other words, it was a big-stage version of the sort of funny and entertaining things that went on at the Garrick every night.

England also inspired the title of 'A Pound For a Brown On The Bus', an attractive tune originally written for a string quartet in a music competition that William Ballard, Frank's high-school music teacher suggested he enter. When the Mothers flew in from Amsterdam to play the Royal Festival Hall, they were provided with a coach to take them to the Winton Hotel. The bus had very large windows and during the trip Jimmy Carl Black made a wager with Bunk Gardner: 'I'll bet you a pound you won't Brown Out on this here bus.' Gardner had his trousers down and his cheeks spread across the window before anybody knew what was happening.

As Gardner said later: 'You could always count on Motorhead, Jimmy Carl Black and Roy Estrada. They provided most of the humour for the rest of us and in the early days it was badly needed because of problems in dealing with Frank and the fact that we weren't making much money but we were working a lot ...' The problems were mostly caused by Frank's autocratic approach to the group. 'Frank Zappa was not a particularly fun guy to work for or with, for many reasons,' recalled Gardner. 'He had a huge ego and he was definitely a workaholic who could rehearse hour after hour after hour and then make a critique and criticize after all that hard work, and also display a complete intolerance for anyone making a mistake while playing his music ... I can still remember Frank Zappa walking around in a rage after many concerts because someone fucked up and made a mistake which Frank said was a lack of concentration and being tuned into him.' But the Mothers put up with endless rehearsals because fame and fortune were supposed to be on the horizon.

It seemed the hippie days of the Strip were over. At the beginning of December, Vito, his wife Zsou and new baby Gruvi packed their belongings into a VW bus and set off to start a new life in Haiti. He said they were on their way to dance and hear real drums on the street· 'Baby, when's the last time you heard a bongo in Los Angeles?'

There was nowhere left to dance. The Whiskey had lost its licence and many other venues had closed. 'This city is outlawing all its joy,' said Vito. 'It breathes hot down the neck of anyone who is creative or expressive.' But Vito's decision to move to Port au Prince made some people wonder about his sanity. Haiti was under a vicious dictatorship, complete with secret police, but Vito brushed aside such concerns: 'They don't hassle creative people, and you can dance there all the time. And anyway, I'm not out to change the man.' And so another piece of LA Freak history danced off into the sunset.

Zappa's next album *Cruising With Ruben & the Jets*, released December 1968, confused many people. It seemed to be a pastiche of fifties vocal group R&B. Doo Wop is an acquired taste unless you grew up with it and a lot of people thought Zappa was mocking it. Recorded at Apostolic Studios between December 1967 and February 1968, *Cruising With Ruben & the Jets* was in fact a labour of love. By now Zappa had an enormous collection of fifties R&B records, which he much preferred to any popular music recorded in the sixties.

'They're more than recreations,' he said of the songs on the album, 'they're careful conglomerates of archetypal clichés. For instance, "Fountain Of Love" simultaneously has quotes from background chants sung by the Moonglows, and the opening theme of "The Rite of Spring". It's on the fadeout, but nobody ever heard that as "The Rite Of Spring" because there's like five different levels of musical accompaniment going on, not counting the band. There's all these different vocal parts and they're all clichés, and they're all carefully chosen for nostalgia value and then built into this song with the most imbecile words in the world . . .

'I like that kind of music, I'm very fond of close harmony group vocal – oo-wah rock 'n' roll. I really like it. But the scientific side of *Ruben & the Jets* is that it was an experiment in cliché collages, because that music was just riddled with stereotyped motifs that made it sound the way it did. Not only did it give it its characteristic sound, but it gave it its emotional value. Like there's a real science to playing rock 'n' roll triplets. Not everybody who can play three notes at once on the piano can play rock 'n' roll triplets, and make it sound convincing. There's little weird things in there so there was a lot of exploration done at the time we were putting *Ruben & the Jets* together.

'We scaled down the instrumentation of the group, and I tried to make it sound reasonably modern and also reasonably stereo, so we toyed with the idea of doing a really crappy production on it and making it sound old, but I didn't think I would enjoy listening to it over and over again at all . . . I like a little stereo now and then. I can dig that! We discussed different kinds of background chants and the emotional implications of them. Because I think that they have emotional implications the same as morning ragas and evening ragas and things like that. The type of lyric that you would associate with a song that has a low bass voice prominent is different from the type of lyric you would associate with a song that's sung in two- or three-part harmony with a falsetto over it. So we were tinkering around with all these things.'

It is all the more peculiar that having lavished such care on the sound, Zappa added crisp new bass and drum tracks for the re-release. However, the original album sounded very authentic, though the story that one radio station played it for days thinking it was a genuine fifties recording seems a little far-fetched. After all, on the front cover of the album one of Schenkel's anthropomorphic figures asks: 'Is this the Mothers of Invention recording under a different name in a last ditch attempt to get their cruddy music on the radio?'

Bizarre did a deal with Warner/Seven Arts to distribute their records on Reprise (Frank Sinatra's old label, which Warners had recently bought). Now all they needed was some 'product' to release. It is entirely typical of Zappa that he spent months devising a huge corporate structure worthy of a publicly traded company, then chose to launch it by releasing an utterly non-commercial album. This same attitude led him to constantly complain how much it was costing him to keep the Mothers on the road, while hiring more and more members; similarly, in later years he complained of the cost of putting together a touring band, yet he rehearsed them on full pay for two months, when most bands would have taken just two weeks.

Zappa approached his own label in much the same way that he approached his independent recordings at Studio Z. He knew then what the commercial culture wanted – surf records, 'answer' records that played on the ideas of current hits, novelty records – but he always skewed them so much they were too weird to be chart hits. He launched Bizarre Records with a double-album by Lenny Bruce – *The Berkeley Concert*, an indifferent 1966 performance that concentrated mostly on his legal problems – and *An Evening With Wild Man Fischer*, a double-album by Larry Fischer, a street person recently released from a mental hospital, who sang original songs for a dime on the Strip. There were also spontaneous monologues by Kim Fowley and Rodney Bingenheimer, sometimes assisted by the GTOs.

Warners must have had severe misgivings about their involvement with Bizarre. The distribution deal meant that Warners had to pay Zappa each time he delivered some product, but some people at Warners thought he was abusing the terms of the agreement by coming up with any old thing to release. Zappa had known about Wild Man Fischer for some time (there is even a brief quote from one of his songs, 'Merry-Go-Round', on *Lumpy Gravy*). Live street recordings appealed to Zappa, and *An Evening With Wild Man Fischer* can be seen as an extension of his use of voice collages on the Mothers albums. Wild Man Fischer became the first release on the new Bizarre label when the single 'The Circle' came out in October 1968.

An Evening With Wild Man Fischer was released on 28 April 1969 and was one of the worst-selling albums Warners ever had. Zappa: 'I tried to help Wild Man Fischer and he turned out to be just as crazy as everybody thought he was ... I think he's dangerous to work with ... he used to live in the street, his hair was all dirty, he lived in dirty clothes. I brought him in, my wife shampooed his hair for him – he started breaking the kids' toys and punched the babysitter and left.' This was perhaps unsurprising behaviour for someone who had tried to kill his mother three times and had been in and out of mental institutions. Warners were not pleased with their new artist.

'This guy smells so bad,' said Zappa. 'He comes into the office, and you can smell him and tell he's coming, honest to God. He goes over to Warners and asks for copies of his album and if they give them to him, he goes out into the street and sells them. They're always saying, "Please keep your artists away."'

Cal Schenkel did Larry Fischer's album sleeve, which depicts Fischer with his arm around an old lady. Zappa: 'That's not his mother. We staged that. That's a cardboard cut-out of the grandmother of the photographer who took the cover picture ... We originally wanted blood, but we thought it would be a little bit too gory. I'd like to get a tape of his mother when she called the office. Man, she is weird.'

A more commercial release would have been something by the Turtles. Howard Kaylan: 'We were almost on Bizarre, Frank's record label ... We were having trouble with our record company in 1968 and were talking to Frank and his manager Herb Cohen about getting together, because they would have liked some hits on their label as well, and so we almost got together then.' Howard Kaylan and Mark Volman were to join Zappa's band two years later.

The Mothers were touring throughout 1968. Zappa had them all on salary, a regular fixed advance against profits. The band was run in a very businesslike way. Jimmy Carl Black: 'We had to rehearse five days a week and sometimes six days a week when we weren't on the road. It was like an office job where you have to put in at least 40 hours a week. If you were sick, you could be asked for a doctor's excuse or get docked a day's pay. This was toward the end before we split up. We were making more money and the Mothers were run like a business. That was good because it made us the best band in the world, in my opinion.'

At a show in Cal State at Fullerton that November, Wild Man appeared as their support act. On the same bill was a new Bizarre act, Christine's boyfriend Alice Cooper. Vincent Furnier was a rich kid from Phoenix, Arizona, who rechristened his high-school band (originally called the Nazz) when he decided he was the reincarnation of a seventeenth-century witch called Alice Cooper. They moved to LA in 1968 and under the sartorial supervision of Christine (now Miss Christine) and the other GTOs, Alice was soon strutting the stage as a Supreme Bitch Drag Queen dressed in black tights, a girl's tank top and purple lip gloss. Part of the act involved tearing up newspaper with his teeth and stuffing it into his blouse to make artificial tits. They managed to clear the Cheetah club after three songs on the night of Lenny Bruce's birthday party, and did the same at their next gig. It became the in-thing in LA to go see Alice Cooper and walk out.

Alice Cooper: 'We got an audition with Frank Zappa, and we showed up at his house at seven o'clock in the morning. We got there, set up outside of this log cabin he had, and we started playing. We were dressed like we dressed every day – chrome pants, hair, makeup, everything – and Zappa liked us. He was our hero. Knowing him was like knowing the Beatles. He was so straight. It was shocking.'

Zappa was impressed that the group could clear a room in 15 minutes and offered them a $6,000 advance to sign with him. Two New York hustlers, Shep Gordon and Joey Greenberg, offered to manage the group (though they knew nothing about rock 'n' roll and had never even heard of Zappa). Cooper: 'Zappa in the interim was chomping at the bit for us to sign contracts and record an album so he could meet the terms of his distribution deal with Warners. He also had a new bug in his head: he wanted us to change our name to Alice Cookies. He decided that the only way we had a shot at making it was if we played it as a comedy act. I was insulted. To top it off, he was insisting that his partner in Straight-Bizarre Records, Herbie Cohen, become our manager – making us completely Frank Zappa controlled.'

Gordon and Greenberg would not allow Alice or the band to have any contact with Zappa or Cohen until the contract was signed; Alice couldn't even see Miss Christine. He signed with Gordon and

Greenberg, who signed with Straight (another new label dreamed up by Zappa and Cohen). Zappa originally intended to produce them, but it just didn't work out. His idea to get publicity for the band was to press the first album as mini-discs, packaged in tuna-fish cans – further proof that he didn't understand what he'd got. *Pretties For You*, out on 19 May 1969, was Straight's first album release.

Straight and Bizarre were now owned by a holding company called Intercontinental Absurdities. (Naturally Warners had to pay all over again to get the rights to distribute Straight.) Bizarre had been set up to release the Mothers and any other acts Zappa wanted to produce. Warners had the first option on his productions, but if they didn't bite he was free to release them on Straight, which Warners would distribute. With the new corporate structure came more staff: a book-keeper, two secretaries and Zach Glickman who helped Cohen. There was also too much work for Cal Schenkel (who designed ads to go with Zappa's copy), so he was joined by John Williams.

Projects came and went, thick and fast. One of them was the proposed book and exhibition by the Plaster-Casters of Chicago. Frank had their diaries typed up and in addition he recorded hours of tape with the GTOs and collected all their diaries. He had signed a publishing contract with Stein & Day for a political book, but as the 1 January 1969 deadline approached and he had not written it, he sent them *The Groupie Papers* instead. In 1969 Cynthia moved to LA and signed with Zappa's company.

'I was a keypuncher when he discovered me,' said Cynthia. 'Frank was the first person that called me an artist. What I was doing was so effortless and fun that I didn't think it could be art.' Herb Cohen did, and persuaded her to entrust more than 20 of her casts to him for safe keeping, telling her their value could only increase with time. With her permission he had bronze copies made of the more important ones, for that 'timeless' look.

When Cynthia moved back to Chicago she left the casts in Cohen's safe keeping and it was not until 1991 that she asked for them back, but Cohen claimed they belonged to him. This case – along with the attempt to manage, produce and release Alice Cooper – reveals the rather dubious nature of Intercontinental Absurdities. In Herb, Frank found another Paul Buff. Frank enjoyed the rough and tumble and frankly exploitive deals of the record business. It was only when the record companies used the same techniques on him that he objected.

In the autumn of 1991 Cynthia filed a lawsuit to get her casts back, but it was a further two years before the case reached court. 'I was on the witness stand for about two days, talking dick in a court of law to a very poker-faced female judge,' said Cynthia. 'It wasn't as much fun as it sounds.' Santiago Durango, her lawyer, said: 'They brought in a contract, which Cynthia signed. It agreed to give Herb her diaries that she had kept over the years for the price of one dollar. Herb assumed that because they [the casts and the diaries] were so related, he deserved the casts as well . . . I took the case because of the sheer wrongness of it. It struck me as outrageous. The contract is completely intolerable, to claim right to those documents for the price of one dollar.' Friends raised money and rock bands gave benefit concerts for Cynthia's legal fund in her fight against Cohen. Her lawyers fought the battle pro-bono of costs (estimated at $100,000) and in June 1993 she won back her casts, plus about $10,000 in damages.

Frank liked Laurel Canyon. 'It is the first place I have lived that I feel homey,' he said, though he grew tired of the constant stream of visitors. The Log Cabin had too many people in it and the grounds were too large for him to have any control over what was going on. So Gail began house-hunting again, only this time looking to buy.

In the autumn of 1968 she found the ideal place, in the 7000 block of Woodrow Wilson Drive, a long winding lane running diagonally down the mountainside towards the Strip from Mulholland Drive. The roadsides were thick with trees and exotic flowering bushes and vines. The house was two stories of mock Tudor, set back, high above the street on a curving drive. In the backyard was a staff cottage with a pool and pool hut. Today the property is worth millions and was probably costly even in 1968. The deal with Warners must have brought in a considerable advance payment, though Gail's parents might have contributed something as a wedding gift.

About 18 months after the Zappas moved out, the Log Cabin was destroyed in a (reputedly drug related) fire. Even at the time of writing, more than 30 years later, the huge basement, the remnants of the living-room fireplace and the garden grotto can still be seen in the fenced-off lot, which is covered with vines and undergrowth like a lost temple.

In November 1968 Frank put the GTOs – which now stood for Girls Together Outrageously – on a retainer of $35 a week each and urged them to continue writing songs and rehearsing. His English secretary, the very strict Pauline Butcher, kept time with her pencil while the girls fumbled their way through their hilarious lyrics about the county store, Rodney Bingenheimer, hitch-hiking, soul brothers and groupie life. Frank thought of himself as the groupies' champion, their advocate in a world of obloquy. He told *Rolling Stone*: 'I think pop music has done more for oral intercourse than anything else that ever happened, and vice versa. And it's good for the girls. Eventually most of them are going to get married to regular workers, office workers, factory workers, just regular guys. These guys are lucky to be getting girls like these, girls who have attained some level of sexual adventurousness. It's good for the whole country. These guys will be happier, they'll do their jobs better, and the economy will reflect it. Everybody will be happier.'

The GTOs appeared at the Mothers' Christmas show at the Shine auditorium on 5 December, along with Wild Man Fischer and Alice Cooper; it was if Zappa were assembling his own travelling show. Rodney Bingenheimer dressed as Santa and the GTOs each sat on his lap. Miss Pamela's Christmas wish was to sleep with Mick Jagger. (It came true.)

A week later the GTOs were in the studio with Frank conducting, waving his little baton and Jeff Beck, Nicky Hopkins and Rod Stewart all adding excitement to their off-key renderings. Sleeve shots were taken, the publicity machine cranked up and the GTOs were on the cover of *Teen Set*. Then Miss Cynderella, Miss Mercy and Miss Christine were busted for heroin at the Landmark Motel when the police found a syringe spinning around in a just-flushed toilet. Frank immediately stopped their retainers and put the album on hold.

Uncle Meat, the first Mothers album to appear on Bizarre/Reprise, was released 21 April 1969. *Uncle Meat* was recorded between October 1967 and February 1968 at Apostolic in New York, with a few overdubs added later at Sunset Sound in LA. It is the culmination of Zappa's work in New York and includes some of his most memorable compositions: the 'Uncle Meat Theme', 'King Kong', 'Dog Breath', 'A Pound For A Brown On the Bus' – tunes he played time and again throughout his career, some appearing on five or more albums and which have subsequently been covered by brass ensembles, Renaissance music groups, experimental ensembles and other rock bands.

In March 1969 Zappa began what is regarded as his greatest independent production. Don Vliet had reappeared on the scene fronting Captain Beefheart and His Magic Band, which had started up in 1965 when Alex Snouffer had returned to Lancaster. Though it was technically Snouffer's band, Don was the real leader. When Snouffer started using his middle name, Clair, calling himself Alex St Clair, Don copied him, adding Van to his name to become Don Van Vliet. They played the usual venues around the Pomona Valley – territory Zappa knew well from the early days. The big difference was that Vliet played while high on LSD and pot, whereas the most Frank ever had before a gig was a beer. Captain Beefheart and His Magic Band's first album, *Safe As Milk*, came out in September 1967. *Mirror Man* and *Strictly Personal* followed, but they were dogged by management and record company problems, plus a changing line-up.

When Frank started Bizarre he wanted his old friend on the label and offered to produce an album giving Don complete artistic control. By then, Don was the only one left from the original Magic Band; he had replaced them all with musicians who were about ten years younger than him. Though he intuitively sang extraordinary urban blues, Don knew nothing about arrangements, keys or time signatures and had always been irritated by the fact that other members of the band knew about music and he didn't. With Alex St Clair replaced by 19-year-old Bill Harkelroad in June 1968, Vliet had complete control.

The whole band lived together in an old wooden house on Encenada Drive, a winding mountain road in Woodland Hills on the San Fernando Valley side of the Santa Monica Mountains near the top of Topanga Canyon. Don and girlfriend Laurie had one bedroom, the rest of the band had the other.

He gave the band members new names, loosening their hold on their old identities and making them more susceptible to new ideas (something Andy Warhol had done earlier at the Factory with Billy Name, Ingrid Superstar and others; in fact, a classic brainwashing technique often used by religious cults). Drummer John French even used the term 'brainwashing sessions' to describe Vliet's treatment of the band: 'We all lived together and Don treated everybody in the band like that occasionally – he would single one person out and get everybody on his case. Later on, when I read about Patricia Hearst getting kidnapped, it reminded me – on a much lighter level, of course – of some of the things that Don did with us.' Bill Harkelroad became Zoot Horn Rollo, Mark Boston was renamed Rockette Morton and Jeff Cotton was Antennae Jimmy Semens, drummer John French became Drumbo and finally Vliet's cousin, bass clarinet player Victor Hayden was now the Mascara Snake.

At first they did nothing but arrange new songs. Vliet moved a piano into the house. He didn't know how to play, but as he slammed his hands into impossible ten-finger chords or plunked with one finger picking out the tunes in his head, they were transcribed on to score paper by John French. About a quarter of the songs intended for the new album were whistled by Vliet. Sometimes he just hummed and sang the songs. French: 'He depended heavily on the band to arrange it – to teach it to him, even though he said that he taught his bands every note of the music. He didn't. That's a big story.' He rarely attended rehearsals – leaving the band to hone the material into some sort of musical shape, but once something sounded right to him, he refused to allow them to change it.

Writing 21 songs only took a few weeks, but learning to play them took six months. Extricating Beefheart from his previous record contracts also took Cohen a long time, so throughout the months of rehearsal the band was not actually signed to Bizarre and had no advance. Their relatives sent money and food, but for one month they lived on nothing but soya beans. Sometimes Vliet rehearsed the band for 30 hours straight, then collapsed for 24 hours' sleep. Zappa: 'I used to go there, and they used to rehearse and rehearse, and what they sound like now is what he taught them how to do. I don't know how he did it . . . When they went in to do the tracks for *Trout Mask Replica* they did all the tracks in five hours; and that's doing some of them several times. I couldn't tell the difference between the takes. I mean they were just rehearsed to death.'

Zappa told *Guitar Player*: 'The original plan for the album was to do it like an ethnic field recording. I wanted to take a portable rig and record the band in the house, and use the different rooms in the house. The vocals get done in the bathroom. The drums are set up in the living room. The horn gets played in the garden. And we went over there and set it up and did the tracks that way.' Dick Kunc used a Uher Reporter portable with excellent results, though a suspicious Vliet thought Frank was just being cheap.

Frank hired Whitney studios and the band laid down their backing tracks in one double session, but getting Don's vocals on to those tracks took five days. Zappa: 'It is very hard to work with him, even though he's your friend . . . He had a rhythm problem – he couldn't sing in time with his own tracks. So he took his headphones off and he could hear a little leakage through the window of the control booth so he sang, sort of at random over the tracks. I just left it wherever he wanted to put it. I said, "It's your music, do it any way you want – all I'm going to do is record it for you and mix it the way you want to hear it." The choices were always left up to him. I did everything I could to make sure that there was no tampering with his artistic concept, because I thought that in the past his albums weren't accurate representations of what he was into. It took me maybe two months, three months of my time, completely devoted to that project, trying to get that across for him.'

Trout Mask Replica grew into a double album with snatches of conversation and even one track taped off the telephone as Don sang a new song, 'The Blimp', to Frank while he was in the recording studio working on a Mothers tape. It was Easter 1969 when Zappa finished editing it. He called to say it was ready and the whole band dressed up and drove to his house at 6 a.m. to hear it. Zappa: 'They listened to it, and they said it was the only album that had ever sounded like the band. They went on and on for about four hours saying how pleased they were. Next thing I know, Don's not even coming to my house any more . . . He's such a weird person.'

For the sleeve of *Trout Mask Replica* Cal Schenkel decided to get a real fish head. He rigged it up as a prop and Don wore it. The band, all wearing shades, stood on a little bridge in the overgrown garden of the Encenada Drive house wearing their freak clothes, Don in top hat and overcoat in the hot LA sun. Schenkel was so amazed by the album and the band that he made an 8mm movie of the shooting session; a valuable document of one of the strangest albums ever made. In 1977 Zappa was asked how he enjoyed the music: 'Some of it's pretty hard to listen to.'

12 Bizarre/Straight

On 28 June 1969 the Mothers played the Coliseum in Charlotte, North Carolina, as part of the Charlotte Jazz Festival. Also on the bill were Rahsaan Roland Kirk, Gary Burton and Duke Ellington. Zappa claimed that 'before we went on, I saw Duke Ellington begging – pleading – for a ten-dollar advance. It was really depressing.' After the show, Zappa told the band: 'That's it, we're breaking the band up.' According to Zappa, if Duke Ellington had to beg some assistant for $10, what was he, Zappa, doing with a ten-piece band, trying to play rock 'n' roll? But there is something wrong with this story.

In 1969 Duke Ellington was 70 and fêted wherever he went. Only two months before, he had been guest of honour at the White House to receive the Medal of Freedom and President Nixon had sung Happy Birthday at the piano. In 1969 Ellington was travelling with 18 musicians: usually on well-paid State Department tours. He played the West Indies and Europe (including concerts behind the Iron Curtain) and the previous year he had toured South America and Mexico. Ellington famously ate little but caviar and steak, and on a tour of India he had his filet mignon flown in from the States. It seems extremely unlikely that he was begging for $10, as Zappa claimed in *The Real Frank Zappa Book*.

Don Preston: 'That's not what happened. A lot of stuff in that book is bullshit. It was just his imagination. There were a number of reasons why the Mothers disbanded. One of them was that Zappa was paying us all a salary. Now this kinda sounds stupid to me. He couldn't afford the [Mothers'] salary, but he kept hiring more and more musicians. So anyhow, when he had to pay nine people in the band, it's gonna cost a lot of money. So, don't hire that many. He didn't have to hire nine people ... The other thing was that he used to get very angry when people would respond to the solos more than his compositions. So that was one of the things that was making him angry at the time. The other thing was that we sometimes during a concert would only play three or four songs. The rest would all be improvisation. That's the way the band was working. And working real well that way. We could handle that responsibility and people loved it. It wasn't just jazz, but like all kinds of weird time changes, experimental types of music. So I think he wanted more kinds of control on the music. Lastly, a lot of people were getting laid and he wasn't. That was probably a cause of friction.'

According to Zappa: 'I just got tired of beating my head against the wall. I got tired of playing for people who clap for all the wrong reasons. I thought it time to give the people a chance to figure out what we've done already before we do any more.' In an interview with *Downbeat* shortly before the break-up, he complained bitterly about the audiences: 'Those kids wouldn't know music if it came up and bit 'em on the ass. Especially in terms of a live concert where the main element is visual. Kids go to *see* their favourite acts, not to hear them ... We work on the premise that nobody really hears what we do anyway, so it doesn't make any difference if we play a place that's got ugly acoustics. The best responses we get from an audience are when we do our worst material.'

Don Preston: 'Oh, how can you say that?'

This was a long-running problem that came to a head sometime in early 1969. Larry Kart, the *Downbeat* interviewer, asked if Zappa had a solution to the situation. 'Yeah,' said Zappa. 'I'm not going to tour any more.' A week after finishing the tour, Zappa broke up the band.

Most of the Mothers felt a profound sense of betrayal. Why

break up the band now, just as all the years of struggling, playing the bars of the Pomona Valley, the years on the Strip and half-starving in New York looked like they might be paying off? They were starting to get famous and were regarded as rock stars in Europe. For years they put up with Frank's autocratic ways and endless rehearsals because, as Bunk Gardner explained: 'We were always told "not to worry" when it came time to explain why we weren't making any money – the old cliché about "We are all in this thing together and if we just hang in there through the bad times, we would all eventually have the proverbial fame and fortune." That was the constant message at the band meetings. Unfortunately the end came so soon, and later on the fame was acknowledged, but the fortune completely eluded us.'

The Mothers felt that Zappa had no right to end the band like this, especially as *he* was doing very well. Unlike them, Zappa was making lots of money. His distribution deals, production percentages and publishing royalties had given him a $100,000 house in the Hollywood Hills with a pool and the latest model Buick parked in the driveway. It was little wonder the others felt betrayed. Zappa had now reached a position where he could cut them loose and go it alone. When he joined the Soul Giants, the original idea had been that they would *all* become rich and successful if they played his music rather than covers.

Jimmy Carl Black: 'That's the way Frank is; Frank has got to be king, he's the boss. He's always been that way. When it was us, it was the Mothers of Invention, period. It wasn't Frank Zappa and the Mothers, it was the Mothers. And that's the reason he got rid of us. He couldn't fire us. The only way he could do it was to break the band up. That's what he did . . . We came back off a successful tour and he calls up – we hadn't even been home about five days – and he says, "I've decided to break up the band. You guys have gotten your last check as of last week."'

The Mothers was a partnership with the performance income divided according to an agreement. Zappa wasn't paying their wages, as he always claimed, he was advancing them a regular amount each month against a percentage agreed in their management contract. The fact that he and Herb Cohen now owned both their management company and their record company gave him complete power over the group.

Jimmy Carl Black: 'There were some heavy feelings from the band at the time. It was not the disbandment, but the way it was done. I called Frank on the phone for something or other and after about ten minutes of talking, he said that he had decided to break up the band and our salaries – they were really draws, since according to the contract at the time, we were all partners – had stopped as of last week. It would have been better if he would have given a date, say like six months, and then we all could have made better plans. I felt the same way as the rest of the guys at the time.'

Zappa had worked with these men for years, he knew their families, everything. Jimmy Carl Black: 'To do it that way, that's real cold ... He hasn't got much feeling; doesn't care about people that much. I guess he cares about his family, I would hope he did, I don't know if I would want to be his son though.'

Don Preston observed that 'Zappa obviously likes perfection more than he likes feeling,' and this was in fact the trajectory of Zappa's career. He ended up with a computer that allowed him to replace musicians altogether. He justified breaking up the Mothers by disparaging their musical abilities. 'They could barely perform at all,' he told Neil Slavin. 'Not only that, when they did perform it, they didn't want to perform it.'

In fact, Ian Underwood, Arthur Tripp, Don Preston and Billy Mundi could all read music far better than Zappa, and he borrowed a lot of ideas from the band that he later claimed as his own. Indeed, a year later, while discussing the live album *Weasels Ripped My Flesh* he admitted: 'Most of the music on it – I'd say 80 per cent of it – is group improvisation. Not just accompaniment with solos, but where the group was conducted into a spontaneous piece of music.' In other words, their compositions, not his.

Jimmy Carl Black: 'I don't really believe that he's ever had a band that had as much feeling for the music as the original Mothers of Invention. He's always had good players, but there was something about the band itself. There was a special thing, it wasn't just the music . . . We had fun together; whether Frank had fun with us or not, that was his problem . . .'

The last performance by the original Mothers was at the International Bandshell in Montreal on 18 August, with an appearance the following night on CJOH TV in Ottawa. Zappa's principal reason to have a group was to enable him to hear what his music sounded like. He now knew that, and had an enormous amount of it on tape. At the time of the break-up he had eight Mothers albums ready for release and three months later he had assembled four more. Zappa didn't need the group any more; they were expensive to keep on the road and he was also preoccupied with his record labels and production duties. The band had served their purpose.

He also had a major orchestral piece he wanted to finish and numerous other projects on hand. Frank had always wanted to do his own version of Art Laboe's *Memories of El Monte* compilation and in June he had begun to select the records. Unlike Laboe's commercial *Oldies But Goodies* series, Frank, naturally, wanted to present the strangest, most bizarre R&B singles he could find. Zappa: 'Songs like "Rubber Biscuit" by the Chips. There's no words to it, it's all chanting. The guys are sort of making it up with rhythm accompaniment. Then there's "The Girl Around The Corner", by Lee Andrews and the Hearts: the lyrics to that are just incomprehensible. And "The Drunkard" by the Thrillers on Old Town. A recitation record where this guy tells of the evils of drink and the corruption of a young lad at the hands of a fast crowd and a bottle. Oh man! It's horrible.' Unfortunately, the obscurity of the tracks made getting hold of the masters problematic and, like so many other Zappa projects, this album was shelved.

The house on Woodrow Wilson Drive was perfect for Zappa's needs. It was in an area of tiny ravines and mature trees, secluded and safe. The house had a rather formal living room, in which hung a large oil painting by Ed Beardsley (used on the sleeve of Alice Cooper's *Pretties For You*). In use 24 hours a day, the kitchen was the nerve centre of the house. The walls were covered with newsclippings, handbills, a citation for putting the garbage out by the road too early in the day, weird clips sent in by fans, and around the ceiling hung Frank's collection of hotel and motel keys. There were always people sitting on the stools by the work surface near the phone: Kanzus the roadie or one of the GTOs, Frank's brother Carl (who lived for a time in the changing rooms by the pool) or Moon's nanny Janet Neville-Ferguson, known as Gabby, who had the garden house.

On 5 September 1969 Ian Donald Calvin Euclid Zappa was born – named after Ian Underwood, Don Preston, Cal Schenkel and Motorhead, Zappa's closest friends, three of whom he'd just fired. The staff at Hollywood Presbyterian Hospital would not allow them to call him Dweezil, though at Dweezil's insistence his name was changed legally when he was five. (Dweezil was Frank's name for one of Gail's toes – he loved naming things.) Dweezil spent much of his time strapped into a plastic baby chair on the kitchen work counter watching the people or gazing at the flickering images of a portable black and white TV.

The house had a huge basement that Frank soundproofed and made his studio. On the door to the stairs leading down to his lair was a small black card on which was written: DR ZURKON'S SECRET LAB IN HAPPY VALLEY. The windows were shuttered by patterned screens. The floor was covered by a very thick baby-blue fitted carpet that effectively deadened the room. At one end stood a pair of huge speakers, five feet high, emitting a discernible hiss, and between them, partly covered by a strange Cal Schenkel assemblage of objects (including a car hood), was a hatch through which movies could be screened from an ante-room.

Along one wall were built-in cupboards containing Zappa's 7,000 R&B singles and his enormous tape archive, mostly housed on ten-inch NAB spools and all carefully labelled. The purple walls were covered with concert posters, paintings, news clips and memorabilia, including a framed chipped plaster plaque that said in large white letters ZAPPA'S GRUBBY CHAMBER. There was an antique rocking chair, a settee, an electric organ, an electric clock, and everywhere instrument cases and guitars.

A two-track Scully 280 tape-recorder, exactly compatible with the Scullys at Apostolic stood against the wall at the business end of the room. A small patchboard connected it to a TEAC A1200U and the record player and amplifiers located in a small adjoining record room. Nearby was Frank's coffee percolator where his 'black water' bubbled all day long, ensuring that he was permanently wired on caffeine. On the tape deck was a pack of Winstons, an ashtray for his perpetually burning cigarette, a pair of headphones, a metal editing block and a supply of one-sided razor blades. His Gibson Les Paul was always near at hand, often tangled in headphone leads. He sometimes played with it plugged directly into the tape machine. The floor surrounding the tape deck was littered with little petals of discarded leader tape, like pink and white daisies in a field.

Frank's desk was covered in sheet music. He sat at it all night smoking and drinking black sugarless coffee as he composed or listened to playbacks until 8 or 9 a.m. If hungry, he would go up to the kitchen and root around in the enormous fridge for some hot dogs. He would hold them in the flame on the stove until they were hot, then wrap some bread around them and make his way back to the basement. This gave him the title for the album *Burnt Weeny Sandwich*.

Zappa would entertain visitors by playing fifties singles or selections from his tape archive: 'Here's one which has a crazed groupie from Miami!' or 'Like to hear "Absolutely Free" without the vocal dubs?' All the collage elements used in his albums were carefully labelled – whole spools of snorks, some with echo, some electronically compressed, or of Jimmy Carl Black saying 'I'm Jimmy Carl Black and I'm the Indian of the group' – as well as every stage of mixing or editing each song. Later, when Zappa announced that the master tapes returned by MGM were unusable and he would have to record new bass and drum tracks before some of them could be re-released, there was general astonishment: the idea that Zappa did not have a first-generation safety copy of each of his albums on file was almost inconceivable.

During the first week of June the Mothers toured England and Frank was asked to give a lecture at the London School of Economics – a hotbed of political activism. Frank screened 18 minutes of his new film, *Burnt Weeny Sandwich*, then asked quietly, 'Any questions?' There was silence, so he explained that the film was cut to fit the music and that he had another 20 hours of it in his basement. The students didn't understand what he was getting at and after a couple more questions someone yelled: 'You came here to speak, so speak!'

'I am speaking,' replied Zappa. 'I'd rather talk with you than at you.' But there was a hard core who clearly wanted to disrupt the meeting, and it was difficult to hear him through their shouts. 'Society is trying to do away with dreamers,' he said. 'They want to straighten them out. A dreamer is dangerous if he has an angry dream up his sleeve because it becomes contagious. I am in favour of being comfortable, but everyone has a different idea of what that is. I work towards it in my way and other people do in their ways. There are a lot of Americans who like teenage fairs and Lawrence Welk, now why be a dirty guy and stop them?'

This was not what the students wanted to hear and someone accused him of being 'yet another bourgeois liberal camouflaging his innate reactionary tendencies'. Frank was amused.

'What happened at Berkeley?' asked another.

'What do you want? The hot poop inside story? Do you expect me to have inside information about Berkeley because I live in America? I couldn't tell you what happened because I wasn't there. Demonstrations aren't comfortable and they don't prove anything.'

Nevertheless, largely on the strength of his more political lyrics, some of the audience still regarded him as a revolutionary. He was asked: 'You once said that someone has to do something before America shits on the whole world. What are you doing about it?'

'I'm not sitting there with my finger up the asshole,' said Zappa, which did at least provoke a lot of laughter.

As the question-and-answer period was clearly leading nowhere, Zappa spelled out his views on how to change society: 'The best way to achieve lasting results is to infiltrate where you can. People should go into communications and the military and change them from the inside. I'm afraid that everyone will have a revolution and make a mess of it. They will wave their banners on the streets and brandish sticks and go home and brag about their bruises: "There I was – the teenage rebel." . . . You are not going to solve all the problems in fifteen minutes or ten years. You think "If we win, everything will be great," but who tells you when you're there? The only way to make changes that will last is to do it slowly. People are thrilled with the idea of revolution in the streets. It's this year's flower power. Wait for eighteen months and there will be another fad. I disagree with your tactics. You won't do it wandering around the streets, you have to use the media. The media is the key and you have to use it.'

'Suppose I try and infiltrate,' someone asked. 'What is there to prevent me from being corrupted from the situation I'm working in?'

'There is nothing to stop you from being corrupted. Maybe you aren't the type to infiltrate,' Zappa replied. 'Ultimately, I am a composer. I just happen to care enough about politics to talk to people about it.'

Zappa did not dismiss the effectiveness of all demonstrations; the next day he told an underground newspaper: 'I'm not ruling them out completely. It's the same kids who were going round with beads and all that gear last year who are now saying, "Kick out the jams, motherfuckers." They are at the mercy of the Establishment when they act that way. The Establishment looks at these kids and sees that they're not going to do anything . . . When you have 10,000 people of *all ages* – not just the kids – marching on the Pentagon, then that really does something.'

That summer Frank was working on *Hot Rats*, rehearsing in his basement with Ian Underwood and Roy Estrada, plus Max Bennett on bass, Paul Humphrey and sometimes the hot young jazz-fusion drummer John Guerin. Bennett had played with Quincy Jones and was a Hollywood studio pro. Humphrey was a jazz player and had worked with Wes Montgomery and Lee Konitz. Zappa had picked a dream line-up.

He had also made contact with Johnny Otis, the hero of his youth, who was now working for the Musician's Union. Through Otis they located Don 'Sugarcane' Harris – the Don of Don and Dewey whose 'Leavin' It All Up To You' was one of Zappa's favourite R&B songs. Frank bailed Harris out of jail on a drug bust to play violin. He block-booked the last two weeks of July at TT&G studios and hired Johnny Otis as bandleader. Otis, in black silk socks held up with black calf-suspenders, black shirt, black lacquered hair, and with a voodoo image hanging round his neck, gyrated and sweated, clapping his hands and stomping his high-shine shoes. He also brought along his son Shuggie to play blues guitar. He even explained how to get the correct greasy fifties sound from a saxophone: 'You point it at the wall, it bounces off the ceiling and you put the mic behind the player, pointed up to catch it.'

Zappa first met Otis when he was living in Lancaster: 'I talked to Johnny Otis when I was in high school. I went down and saw his studio on a field trip one day with a few of the guys from the Blackouts – I think it was on Washington Boulevard, DIG records, I saw his echo chamber, which was a cement room and he was into overdubbing and a lot of that stuff even in the early days and he gave us a bunch of records and talked about the business. I've always liked the things that he's done, especially when he was on Peacock. And I dig him as a disk jockey because I liked the records that he played. I thought that he had pretty good taste for rhythm and blues.'

Don Van Vliet sang the vocal on 'Willy The Pimp'. Just as the interview tapes done with Kenny and Ronnie Williams were used for the lyrics of 'Let's Make The Water Turn Black', the words of 'Willy The Pimp' originated in an interview that Zappa taped with Annie Zannas and Cynthia Dobson in New York. Years later, this tape was also released.

Relations between Don and Frank were strained. Don was going through a bad period and the day before 'Willy the Pimp' was recorded, he told Frank he had burned all his lyrics in an uncharac-teristic moment of self-doubt. Frank was devastated. Despite their differences, he had a tremendously high regard for Vliet's work (It later transpired that members of the Magic Band had copies, so all was not lost.)

It was not until late June 1969 that Frank forgave Miss Christine, Miss Mercy and Miss Cynderella enough to resume work on their album. He was bored by the project, which should have happened in the first flush of excitement of Bizarre/Straight, along with Wild Man Fischer and Captain Beefheart. But he had money tied up in it, which he could only get his hands on by providing Warners with the product.

Permanent Damage came out in December on Straight, but the critics couldn't figure it out. It is now a much sought-after sixties cult album, but at the time only the hippest FM stations gave it airplay and it didn't chart. Zappa wasn't surprised: 'I finished their album and my partner in the record company heard it for the first time the night before last and he just shit his pants. He said we can't put that out. He says there's no distributor in the world who would ever take that record.'

That same month *Hot Rats* was released. It went nowhere in the States, but charted in Britain and Holland where it was hailed as a masterpiece (and is even now regarded as the first jazz-rock album). The *Hot Rats* sleeve was designed by Cal Schenkel and featured Miss Christine peering out of an empty swimming pool in an overgrown garden in Beverly Hills, like a zombie rising from a tomb. The memorable image was taken by Ed Caraeff, who did a lot of work for Zappa at the time, including the *Uncle Meat* sleeve.

During the *Hot Rats* sessions Frank played some of the tracks for jazz producer Dick Bock. A few days later Bock brought an acetate by French jazz violinist Jean-Luc Ponty round to the house for Frank to hear. Zappa and Ponty met and Ponty played a fleeting violin part on 'It Must Be A Camel' on *Hot Rats*. The idea of Ponty playing a whole album of Frank's work came up and soon a dream team was assembled, including ex-Mothers Art Tripp and Ian Underwood, future Mother George Duke on electric piano, drummer John Guerin from the *Hot Rats* sessions and Buell Neidlinger on bass, best known for his work with Cecil Taylor and Gil Evans.

The album was 'composed and arranged by Frank Zappa', but

listed Richard Bock as producer. Zappa was not able to credit himself because his Bizarre/Straight deal with Warners gave his own labels his exclusive services. The album was called *King Kong* and featured five Zappa compositions plus one by Ponty: 'How Would You Like To Have A Head Like That?', the only one Zappa actually played on and, in Leonard Feather's opinion, the only track with a real jazz feel. In fact, the whole album lacks energy, largely the fault of the mix, even though Dick Kunc was the engineer. A year later Zappa fell out with Kunc. Zappa: 'I had to let him go . . . [He] was the perfect engineer for the Mothers, but something happened to him. I don't know what.' However, at the time of *King Kong*, Kunc was at the height of his powers, which only makes the muddy sound more inexplicable.

By this time Frank had also completed work on the next Mothers album, *Burnt Weeny Sandwich*, which was released in December 1969. Two R&B obscurities framed the album, which opened with a straight take on 'W-P-L-J' by the Four Deuces (a hymn to white port and lemon juice, a favoured drink in certain circles in 1955 when the record was released). The album ended with 'Valarie' [*sic*], a spirited version of 'Valerie' by Jackie and the Starlites which is nonetheless tame compared with the original majesty of Jackie Rue's uncontrolled hysteria. 'Valerie' was one of the tracks Zappa considered for his oldies compilation.

Critics tend to dismiss Zappa's Doo Wop songs as trivial, but this was the music of his youth. It had a resonance that sixties music never did. It was the musical language he shared with the other members of the original Mothers, the source of a lot of their humour, and much of his music contains oblique references to it. But the musicians in his later bands were a generation younger and no longer shared his musical past. For Zappa, Doo Wop was the archetypal music of teenage innocence. He ignored its commerciality, preferring to see it as the raw, creative expression of young black America.

In many ways Doo Wop is the key to understanding Zappa's work. He wanted to be in one of those bands as a teenager and by playing their songs he was fulfilling a dream. *Burnt Weeny* is something of a musical history of Zappa's life, framed by Doo Wop, followed by a homage to Igor Stravinsky ('Igor's Boogie, Phase One') and some of the most beautiful compositions Zappa ever wrote: 'Holiday In Berlin', 'Theme From Burnt Weeny Sandwich', and the various themes on the almost 19-minute-long 'The Little House I Used to Live In'. The music could only come from Southern California, with its unmistakable consonance with movie music, but it also echoes twentieth-century classical music: 'Holiday In Berlin' following straight after 'Igor's Boogie, Phase Two' could be a ballet – surely no accident? There is also a burning violin solo from Don 'Sugarcane' Harris (recorded during the *Hot Rats* sessions) and a sociological audience clip from the Royal Albert Hall.

In October the Zappas – accompanied by Ian and Ruth Underwood (*née* Komanoff) – took a late vacation in Europe. Ruth played marimba on *Uncle Meat* and three years later would join Zappa's *Petit Wazoo* line-up. She had been a regular at the Garrick shows and one evening she and her brother were waiting outside the Village Gate to hear Miles Davis play when Frank walked past (the Garrick was in the next block). Ruth's brother grabbed him and, to her acute embarrassment demanded: 'You should hear my sister play! She's a great marimbist!'

'Fine,' said Frank, 'bring your marimba backstage and we'll check ya out.'

Shortly afterwards Ruth was in the studio, where she got to know Ian.

Zappa had an unusual assignment in Europe. His friend Pierre Lotez had asked him to co-host the Paris Actuel rock festival, organized by BYG Records. He was offered a fee of $10,000 and all expenses paid. The venue kept changing until it eventually finished up in a large tent in a freezing cold turnip field in Amougies, Belgium, halfway between Tournai and Audenarde. According to Zappa, even the organizers seemed surprised to find that the amplifiers worked when they turned them on. No one spoke English, so Frank's witty remarks were wasted.

He described it as 'the blackest period in my whole life'. For three days in late October he braved biting winds to present Soft Machine, Caravan, Archie Shepp, East of Eden and Aynsley Dunbar's Retaliation. He sat in with many of them including Pink Floyd. Frank also liked the Nice and enjoyed Dick Heckstall-Smith's tenor playing with Coliseum. One reason he was there was to introduce Captain Beefheart and His Magic Band, who stood around freezing in their frocks and capes from the *Trout Mask Replica* sleeve.

Frank sat in with Aynsley Dunbar for a few numbers and four months later, when Frank was in London, he offered Aynsley a job over dinner at the Speakeasy. Frank had played a few gigs to promote the *Hot Rats* album and invited Aynsley to drum in the line-up. Aynsley had just put together a new group called Blue Whale and it would mean giving it up and moving to California. It took him two weeks to decide; Frank sent the air tickets.

Gail met Aynsley at the airport and drove him to the house, where he stayed for the next ten months. He played powerful loud British rock 'n' roll drums; he also brought sex appeal to the band with his Kings Road silks and satins and his Jack-the-Lad British popstar looks. After a few weeks settling into the Laurel Canyon scene, Frank suggested Aynsley set up his drums. 'Show me why I hired you,' he said. Aynsley and Frank got a riff going and in that first day's work they created 'Chunga's Revenge'. During four days in March, Frank and the Hot Rats band (Ian Underwood on keyboards and sax, Max Bennett on bass, Aynsley Dunbar on drums and sometimes Don 'Sugarcane' Harris on violin) recorded ten new songs at the Record Plant, three of which appeared on the *Chunga's Revenge* album released in October that year.

Throughout the autumn of 1969 Frank had been finishing off an orchestral piece, and in the spring he finally heard it performed. He met the conductor Zubin Mehta at KPFA-FM during a radio interview and mentioned that he had an orchestral piece that had been 'sitting around for a while' – would Mehta like to see it? Mehta was too busy, but his orchestra manager liked the score and persuaded Mehta to read it. After three months of talks it was announced that on 15 May 1970 Frank Zappa's 200 Motels would be performed in concert with the LA Philharmonic at Pauley Pavilion, UCLA, conducted by Zubin Mehta.

Zappa described it as the result of three years work: 'It's based on sketches and material that were actually completed on the road or in motels, for one reason or another, and then the final orchestration was done in my house over about three months, just prior to Christmas last year. All I'm interested in doing is hearing what the music sounds like that I wrote in those motels. If I can hear it, then I can write some more.'

The piece was in four movements and lasted for two and half hours, but the second movement, scored for chorus, dancers and a vacuum cleaner, was dropped because it was too expensive. There were problems with the hall acoustics and the fact that a nine-piece electric band is louder than a 96-piece orchestra, even when they play quietly. This meant the orchestra had to be amplified, but the 20 or so microphones would also pick up the band's amplifiers. Two of the six rehearsals were just to balance the sound, but had little effect as there was still a tremendous echo. Nevertheless, as Zappa told the audience: 'When you play music in a hall designed for basketball, you take your chances.'

He also needed a nine-piece electric band – in fact, he needed the band he broke up just a few months earlier. Somehow he managed to persuade something resembling the Mothers of Invention to reform for a 'reunion' tour – which included gigs in Chicago and three sets at the Fillmore East in New York – and to play the Pauley Pavilion: Ray Collins on vocals; Don Preston on keyboards; Ian Underwood on alto sax; Motorhead on baritone sax; Jeff Simmons on bass and vocals; and Billy Mundi and Aynsley Dunbar on drums.

Frank would have naturally liked to record the concert with Zubin Mehta, but the union insisted on the LA Philharmonic being paid full-scale, even if the recording was not released, which for 96 players was just too much. They tried to sell it to the networks, but without success.

As it happened, bootleggers did the job for free and for many years *200 Motels* was available on the Trade Mark of Quality bootleg label.

It was Zappa's evening, from the moment they kicked off with Frank announcing 'All right Zubin, hit it!' to the stage directions for the players who had to snork, grunt and throw confetti; the bass-horn player had to twirl like a drunken elephant and at one point the entire orchestra stood up and walked into the audience, apparently improvising their own pieces. As well as playing snatches of Varèse's Intégrales, Zappa used the occasion for a devastating parody of Jim Morrison's stage act, reworking Morrison's 'The End' with its Oedipal theme of incest and patricide. In Frank's version the son discovers his father 'beating his meat' to a *Playboy* magazine, which he has rolled into a tube and placed over his member. Zappa followed the son's dramatic line: 'Father – I want to kill you,' with the father's urgent reply: 'Not now, son, not now!'

As Frank was still fiddling around with his *Uncle Meat* movie, he wanted to use the reformed Mothers to film much-needed continuity shots. He needed to interview all the band members, past and present: documentary footage that would help to explain the mythology of the band and the music. The famous cameraman Haskell Wexler offered his services free for a week, Frank hired a film crew and lights and bought the film stock, an expenditure of about $12,000 for the week, but two days before shooting, when Frank finally got round to talking to his proposed cast it quickly degenerated into arguments and anger. They were fed up with being used without consultation and for no money.

Zappa: 'Four of the guys decided they wanted to have nothing whatsoever to do with any of the projects. That radically changed my plans for that week's shooting, which I had all blocked out.' Frank quickly wrote a new script, based around Don Preston's monster act. Don used to hunch one shoulder, squint one eye and stick out his tongue like in a monster movie; an act the band dubbed 'transforming'. Everyone did it, but he was the best. Zappa used it as one of the thematic elements of the film. Zappa: 'The idea that somebody turns into a monster and the reasons why he does it – it changes throughout the film. Mostly he turns into a monster whenever he hears the word "royalties".'

Frank had Phyllis Alternhouse (previously Tom Wilson's assistant) fall in love with Don's monster. He also filmed Cal Schenkel, Motorhead and Aynsley Dunbar fooling around in the hardware department of the Hollywood Ranch Market. The film also featured a rubber chicken. Zappa: 'We describe events as "We're using a chicken to measure it." At one point we're measuring the MGM royalties with a chicken. Roy Collins does that. He comes up with a royalty statement, which consists of a certain amount of foam which is expelled from the blowhole of the rubber chicken. He says, "Yes, I think we have some royalties coming now." It's very avant-garde.' Many fans felt that Zappa should have tried to get a refund for his film stock rather than shoot his new script, which drags on far too long.

With the exception of Ian Underwood, Zappa wanted to make a clean break with the original Mothers, so it is surprising he kept the name when he went out on the road with a new group in June 1970. To Mothers fans it was like those fifties revival acts who tour with only one or two of the original band. Comparisons were bound to made and his new line-up was found wanting.

Fans were further confused by the release of *Weasels Ripped My Flesh* in August 1970 as a Mothers of Invention album, featuring live and studio cuts by the original Mothers line-up, recorded between 1967 and 1969. It was the first album Zappa made by ripping up the twelve Mothers albums he had already edited. *Weasels* was distinguished by its award-winning sleeve by Neon Park of a man shaving with an electric weasel, which is literally clawing his cheek to shreds. The album also featured Lowell George, who played on the GTOs album and produced some of the tracks.

Lowell was in the Mothers from November 1968 until May 1969 when he left to form Little Feat (named after Jimmy Carl Black commented on Lowell's shoe size). Little Feat, which also included Roy Estrada on bass, cut several demos for Bizarre/Straight in the autumn of 1969, but they were courted by other labels and eventually Lenny Waronker signed them to Warners. They released a series of critically acclaimed albums, all with sleeves by Neon Park, whose design for *Weasels* Lowell liked so much.

The new Mothers were Ian Underwood on keyboards and alto sax; Aynsley Dunbar on drums; Jeff Simmons on bass and vocals – Simmons's solo album, *Lucille Has Messed My Mind Up*, was produced by Zappa and released by Bizarre that February; George Duke played keyboards and trombone – Zappa loved his celeste and electric piano playing with the LA Philharmonic at the Zubin Mehta concert and asked him to join the band; and on vocals (to the astonishment of many) Frank hired 22-year-old Howard Kaylan and 23-year-old Mark Volman – previously the lead singers with the hugely successful pop band the Turtles. They had finally quit the Turtles after many problems, but unfortunately White Whale Records had them signed both as the group and as individuals, so they were unable to perform either as the Turtles or under their own names.

Mark and Howard had known Zappa for years – the Turtles had appeared on the same bill with the Mothers at the Trip and the Whiskey and they saw the Mothers play the Garrick on several occasions and visited Frank at the Charles Street apartment in New York. Jim Pons, bass player with the Turtles (also shortly to join the Mothers) was a friend of Gail's from her pre-Zappa days on the Strip. Not only that, but Kaylan was Herb Cohen's cousin. Herb gave them tickets for the Zubin Mehta concert and afterwards they went backstage. Zappa told them: 'I'm putting a new band of Mothers together. We're going to go to Europe . . . we're gonna play a bunch of shows and then we're gonna make a movie. Are you interested?' For Mark and Howard it was a brilliant solution to their problems.

Mark Volman said at the time: 'We bring a lot of commerciality to the Mothers and Frank brings us a lot of jump-off points for heavy satire.' Mark and Howard sang their own hits on stage and parodied them as part of Frank's show – a remarkably unselfish contribution considering the Turtles had six US Top 20 hits between 1965 and 1969, including Dylan's 'It Ain't Me Babe' and their biggest 'Happy Together', while Zappa had none. Frank clearly relished the fact that on the inside sleeve of *Freak Out!* he had quoted the Turtles' manager Reb Foster saying: 'I'd like to clean you boys up a bit and mould you. I believe that I could make you as big as the Turtles.' Now he had the Turtles in his band – no doubt a further example of what Zappa called 'conceptual continuity.'

Volman: 'Frank demanded something of us that we had never really experienced in rock 'n' roll, which was fitting ourselves into a band, not just as singers, but as musicians using our voices as musical instruments . . . The notes we had to learn to sing to fit within his chord progressions. It wasn't just taking a song and singing a verse and a chorus where you could pretty much improvise it night to night and have a little fun with it. With Frank, it demanded learning notes, and singing those exact notes, or they wouldn't fit with single notes being hit by a piano, a saxophone, a guitar, and a bass.' It was a tremendous challenge and required many hours of rehearsal.

Howard and Mark sang a high clear falsetto, which meant Zappa could perform songs by the original Mothers such as 'Concentration Moon', 'Call Any Vegetable' or 'Sleeping In A Jar'. But why break up one band, then go through the time and expense to rehearse material with a new band that the audience associates with the earlier line-up, particularly when your latest album features that line-up? Perhaps Zappa did regret disbanding the Mothers, but he was too proud to ever admit it. One of the great attractions of the original Mothers was their crazed humour, something he unsuccessfully tried to replicate over the years.

Mark and Howard brought a different, younger, dumber, more sexually explicit humour to the group. In fact, this is when the accusations of misogyny in Zappa's lyrics and attitude begin. Before then, Zappa had always dealt with sexual themes in a positive manner: he had written about a boy's inability to commit himself to a relationship; criticized stereotypical notions of love; critiqued teenage America boy-girl behaviour; and had even written standard pop love songs – but the underlying message had always been that a healthy sex-life was one of the major cures for society's ills. He said it often: 'You want to get set free onetime? All you have to do is get your pants off, admit that you have your pants off, find somebody of the opposite sex, or, if you wanna be a little bit weird, you can do something else, but do it sexually, that's the only way you're going to set yourself free.' With the Vaudeville Band (as fans dubbed Zappa's new line-up) the definition of a healthy sex life seemed to apply to boys only; it consisted of little more than getting blowjobs and getting laid. Women had dropped out of the picture; they were just there for the guys to feel up and fuck – as in 'Magdalina', which Zappa co-wrote with Kaylan, a supposedly humorous little number based on the idea of someone trying to fuck his teenage daughter. Zappa claimed he was pointing out how wretched and pitiable the man in the song was, but many questioned his writing it at all and that he should find humour in child abuse.

This was the group that divided Zappa's audiences: there was a clear line of development from *Freak Out!* through *Uncle Meat* to *Weasels Ripped My Flesh*, but to many fans the Vaudeville Band was simply dumbing down to make money. Certainly the Frank Zappa who intended to change the world through Freaking Out was long dead.

The theatricality that Mark and Howard brought to the band was utilized by Zappa to create a series of 30-minute sketches which became the centre of the show, more along the lines of Brecht-Weill or Gilbert and Sullivan than Pete Townshend's rock opera *Tommy* (which was too serious for Zappa's liking). Mark Volman: 'He created music, during our time with him, specifically designed for us and our capabilities. Most everything we did with Frank was from live concert recordings and this spontaneous approach worked very well for that era. It was much like improv for a comedian. We would create the foundation of a song and story, and then it would grow into something else as the piece was performed. Each piece would have a structure, but Howard and I were encouraged to add new things with each performance.'

Many of the routines they worked out were extremely funny, like the 'What Kind Of Girl Do You Think We Are?' playlet in which Mark and Howard are groupies who will only have sex with the band if they have a record in the charts. Not only was this based on reality (it happened to Kaylan), but it was done with sympathy and humour, perhaps because Mark and Howard acted out both roles. However, it is a fine line between comic lust and smut, a line many people thought Zappa crossed

Feminism really appeared as a mass movement in 1970, with articles and media publicity culminating in the famous panel discussion at New York Town Hall on 20 April 1971, when Norman Mailer defended his essay 'The Prisoner of Sex' against the objections of Jill Johnston and Germaine Greer. Greer liked Zappa and his music. She proudly called herself a groupie and wanted to transform women into sexual beings rather than sex objects. Other feminists, especially in the early days of the movement, were more extreme.

Zappa viewed feminism with grave suspicion: it threatened his patriarchal Sicilian values and he just didn't see the humour in groups with names like the Women's International Terrorist Conspiracy from Hell (WITCH) with their slogan 'A chicken in every pot and a whore in every home.' All in all, it was not the most appropriate time to release *Just Another Band From LA*. Many people regarded it as puerile and misogynist, while many more thought the joke so shallow as not to deserve repeated listening.

The playlets were a better vehicle for live performance. They had several improvised sections, and it was Mark and Howard's job to create humour based on local references – for instance, the model of the car on 'Do You Like My New Car?' was usually the name of the venue: 'It's a Fillmore isn't it?' They would research the names of local heroes, high schools and recent local news to personalize each show. The album records a show with local LA references, but the same show in New York would be all about New York. Mark Vollman: 'We existed in that band for humour, but not necessarily for the audience's humour, but for *Frank's* humour. When Frank laughed we knew we were funny.'

In November 1970 the new Mothers played four nights at the Fillmore West and two at the Fillmore East in New York, the show of the 13th being particularly memorable: Zappa: 'Joni Mitchell sat in with us last night during the second show and we improvised a thing that was really good. We ended it with her singing "Duke of Earl". Really far out, she came on stage: "Now OK and we're going to improvise this thing . . ." and we did a few chords for her and she started reciting this poem which began: "Penelope wants to fuck the sea . . ." And the audience did a double-take "Yuuunk!" . . . a little hush falls over the Fillmore . . . "Joni Mitchell?"'

Beginning on 1 December, they toured Europe for 17 days. For Zappa the most momentous date was 12 December, when they played the Konzerthaus in Vienna, home of all the composers he loved. Frank had something like an epiphany when he first saw Webern's scores in music-shop windows, and experienced the European lifestyle of cafés and leisurely conversation. He felt himself born in the wrong time and place: he didn't belong in the plastic commercial shallowness of LA, he should have been an intellectual in Greenwich Village in the twenties or in Paris with F. Scott Fitzgerald.

Chunga's Revenge – a mixture of Hot Rats group tracks and the new Mothers of Invention recordings – was released as a Zappa solo album in October 1970. He asked Mark and Howard how they would like to be credited as they sang on six of the tracks. Unable to use their own names, they remembered two roadies with the Turtles. According to Mark, one was a wild flamboyant Spaniard called Carlos Bernal who was always leeching things from the band ('wives, cigarettes, money . . .'), so they nicknamed him the Florescent Leech. The other was Dennis Jones, a real straight-arrow type: short hair, smart and articulate like a Fraternity President, so they called him 'Eddie'. They asked Frank: 'How does the Florescent Leech and Eddie sound?' He laughed and said, 'That sounds really good, let's use it.' Howard was the Florescent Leech and Mark was Eddie. The name was soon shortened to Flo and Eddie.

13 200 Motels

Undaunted by his conspicuous lack of success with the *Uncle Meat* and *Burnt Weeny Sandwich* film projects, Zappa made plans for an even more ambitious film. *200 Motels* began as a project for Dutch television, but quickly grew into something else. That autumn he approached United Artists with a ten-page outline accompanied by a tape of proposed soundtrack music. A few days later he was called to a meeting. Zappa: 'We walked in and the guy says "You've got a deal." Just like that!'

Frank was clearly delighted, even though the budget (originally set at $630,000) was tight. (The final cost was $679,000. Producer Jerry Goode ordered that all the video masters be erased and sold as used stock to help balance the budget. This brought in less than $4,000 and destroyed all the unused scenes and out-takes.) They found they could hire the Royal Philharmonic for £1,000 a session, which for a hundred musicians was amazingly cheap by LA standards.

In London Frank engaged Tony Palmer as the video-director. Palmer had filmed *Goodbye Cream*, their farewell concert at the Albert Hall and was feted for his BBC documentary *All My Loving*, which juxtaposed Vietnam war footage with rock 'n' roll. Palmer had also published *Born Under a Bad Sign*, an enthusiastic book about rock 'n' roll, for which he somehow persuaded John Lennon to write an introduction. It was clear to many there would be a titanic clash of egos, and friends warned Frank that Palmer would not readily bow to his demands, but he didn't know anyone else with Palmer's experience.

The whole movie was to be recorded on video and then transferred to 35mm film. Palmer had been the first to use video in this way with his Cream documentary, and it was only the second time it had been done. They wanted to film at Shepperton studios, but Roman Polanski's *Macbeth* took up every available stage, so production was shifted at the last minute to two sound stages at Pinewood, where work began building Cal Schenkel's sets. The original concept was for the orchestra to live on an artificial mountain, but the cost was too great so they settled on Camp Untermunchen, a music concentration camp sponsored by the US government situated at the end of the main street of Centreville.

The story line, such as it was, concerned a rock 'n' roll band on the road and how touring can drive you crazy. This enabled Frank to use an early version of the groupie routine that appeared on *The Mothers, Fillmore East, June 11* and embellish it with the sort of group antics he had been recording on his portable Uher for so many years. Group members often complained that Zappa recorded their conversations and reused the material as his own, and in *200 Motels* Zappa turned this very situation into a sketch.

It would have taken months to get the Mothers to learn their lines and act convincingly, so it was much easier to let them respond spontaneously to set-up situations. The script was based on their own conversations in the first place. Frank: 'The lines that are in this film are based on things I've heard people say for years, all the way back, to the very beginning.' However, though much of the dialogue was improvised, the main roles were scripted.

The actor Theodore Bikel (best known for his role as Tevye in *Fiddler On The Roof*) used to be in business with Herb Cohen; they opened the Unicorn on Sunset Strip together. Herb arranged for Bikel to see Frank, who went over to his hotel and explained the plot of *200 Motels*. Frank wanted Bikel to play Rance Muhammitz, the manager of the group. Usually an actor will not accept a role without reading the script, but there was no script. Bikel: 'He was so persuasive that I agreed to do the film on the basis of the presentation alone.'

In December Frank and his entourage flew to London. 'I figured it would be fun to do it over there,' he said. 'I would like to see what it feels like to live someplace else, the only time I got out of the country has been when I was working and I remember when I moved from Los Angeles, which I really feel is definitely home base, it changed me so much to live for a year and a half in New York. Not all of it for the better. It was weird to get another perspective. I think there might be another change if I go and live in the country in England for a while, see what that would be like.' In fact, as his friend and roadie Howard Parker put it: 'It was Woodrow Wilson Drive, W11.' (The Notting Hill postcode.)

Frank rented a house in Holland Park where he lived with Gail, Moon, Dweezil, the children's nanny Janet Ferguson, and Miss Lucy Offerall. It was as close as you could get to a Los Angeles environment, given the English weather. Motorhead came to play Lonesome Cowboy Burt and Dick Barber was brought over to play a lovelorn industrial vacuum cleaner, throwing in a few snorks as well. Don Preston came to do his transformer act. Ex-GTO Miss Pamela, who was already living in London, played a reporter, and even Cynthia Plaster-Caster turned up. Ruth Underwood added percussion to some of the tracks. Had Karl Franzoni been there, Zappa might have been filming his own *This Is Your Life*.

Theodore Bikel received several shocks on his arrival: 'The set swarmed with groupies who were only too eager to do anything – and I mean anything – to please Frank and the band. A few of them had been cast in the movie as – what else? – groupies. The trouble was that a couple of them failed to pass the medical examination that every film company requires. The girls were emaciated to a dangerous degree; some had a drug habit or had otherwise plainly abused themselves in pursuit of whatever gratification. Despite the doctor's refusal to give them the required clearance, Frank used them anyway.'

Bikel also balked at the idea of playing a nun in drag (the role was offered to Mick Jagger, who also turned it down) and was surprised to discover there would be several Frank Zappas in the film: Frank was directing operations and the band, so only appeared in the film as a conductor or instrumentalist. There was a stuffed model of Zappa, which sometimes made do as a stand-in, but most of the time his role (Larry the Dwarf) was played by Ringo Starr, who dressed exactly like Zappa, complete with Zappa wig, beard and moustache.

Ringo set the tone of the film by announcing at the beginning: 'He made me do it. He wants me to fuck the girl with the harp . . .' The girl with the harp turned out to be Ringo's old friend Keith Moon dressed as a nun and peering maniacally through the strings. The original harpist (and two trumpeters) had walked out, refusing to sing 'Penis Dimension', but had unwisely left her instrument behind.

Ringo more or less read his lines from cue cards and never got into the part, perhaps because he had a bad cold throughout. Nevertheless, it was a welcome relief from the court case that was running at the time between Paul McCartney and the other three Beatles. McCartney didn't trust Allen Klein, the new manager brought in by the others, and wanted to dissolve the partnership.

Keith Moon was recruited because he had been in the Speakeasy with Pete Townshend one evening and Frank happened to be at the next table. Moon: 'Frank leaned over and said, "How'd you guys like to be in a film?" We said, "OK, Frank." And he said, "OK, be at the Kensington Palace Hotel at seven o'clock tomorrow morning." I was the only one who turned up.' He enjoyed rolling about in a bedroom with Janet Ferguson and Miss Lucy (both topless) and being chased through the orchestra by Ringo dressed as Zappa.

Jeff Simmons had a major role, but at the first script run-through at the Kensington Palace Hotel on 18 January his girlfriend persuaded him that he really should be an important blues player and not fool around with a comedy band. (Even this conversation was taped by Zappa, who released it on *Playground Psychotics* in 1992.) Jim Pons, the bass player with the Turtles, was flown over to replace him in the group. Wilfred Bramble – who played Paul McCartney's grandfather in *A Hard Day's Night* (1964) – was hired as a replacement for the acting role. After a week, on the last day of rehearsals, he found the obscenities he was required to utter and the general chaos too much, and suddenly ran screaming through the sound stage and never came back.

Filming began the next day and they needed an actor. They were all assembled in a dressing room when Zappa said in desperation: 'The next person who walks in is it – what the fuck!' They waited in anticipation. The door opened and in stepped Martin Lickart, Ringo's driver, who had gone to buy tissues for Ringo's cold. He looked the part with his long English popstar hair and his West Midlands accent, and he was even an adequate bass player, having had a band in Stourbridge. 'You're the one!' they said.

Taping took five days (28 January–5 February) and, as predicted, Zappa and Tony Palmer did not get on. Palmer expected to be the director and when he found out Frank intended to direct he threatened to resign. The producer Jerry Goode managed to persuade him to stay to direct the video cameras, leaving Zappa to direct the actors and musicians. It did not help that Palmer had flu that week and was also in the midst of a divorce. At one point Gail overheard him say he would wipe the tapes if something was not done his way. Zappa: 'He seemed to be a fairly ill-tempered individual even on a good day.'

Although Zappa insisted on directing, he knew very little about the mechanics of filmmaking and the studio was in chaos. 'I had participated in many films before this one,' recalled Bikel, 'and was used to the fact that often you find yourself in the midst of organized chaos. This was different; it was unorganized disarray.'

There was an unpleasant undertone of manipulation in the way the film was put together. Zappa clearly took a perverse delight in making everyone sing 'Penis Dimension', a big production involving opera singers, the Mothers, the orchestra and Janet and Miss Lucy. No one seems very enthusiastic, and even Flo and Eddie do not appear particularly ardent in singing this number. Once a chart-topping act with a massive female fanbase, they had been reduced to singing Zappa's puerile lyrics. They sounded like a bunch of giggling schoolchildren saying all the dirty words they know: 'Dick, cock, penis, wee-wee . . .' Janet and Miss Lucy clearly think their lines are pathetic, and the orchestra just finds the whole thing distasteful. It is all slightly embarrassing – not because they are embarrassed to do it, but because they seem embarrassed for Frank, who is making them do it.

They filmed until the last minute of the final day, then cast and crew attended a party to celebrate. But Zappa had organized the shooting schedule so poorly that he had only shot a third of his original script. At the completion of photography, Palmer asked for his name to be removed from the film, lest it damage his career. Again he was persuaded to stay (no one else knew how to edit videotape) and he agreed, but only if he retained some measure of control. Once he began to play with the special effects, he asked for his name to be reinstated. Palmer: 'The whole operation threatened to descend into chaos. Still, I needn't have worried nor underestimated the infinite talents of Zappa, because when we finally got to editing stage, he decided to take over that too.'

They had 24 hours of videotape to edit, which they took into Television Recordings, Europe's largest VT editing studios, and reduced to 96 minutes in ten days. Though Frank obviously had some say over the editing, Palmer probably made it into a more accessible film. Zappa and Palmer managed to find enough linking shots to paste together something resembling a narrative. 'In 200 Motels I want to make sure that the concept tracks from beginning to end,' said Zappa, but most audiences found it utterly incomprehensible.

Zappa's love affair with England had gone sour. After the awful January weather and frequent rows with Palmer there was another set-back. The Royal Philharmonic Orchestra had agreed a £20,000 fee, which included the live film soundtrack and a concert to be held at the Royal Albert Hall on 8 February 1971. But the Albert Hall's lettings manager, Marion Herrod, insisted on reading the 'libretto' for the concert and found it wanting. 'There were words I did not want to be spoken at the Albert Hall,' she told *The Times*. She cancelled the concert.

Frank and Herb had already spent £5,000 in preparing the show and sold 4,000 tickets. It was a clear case of breach of contract. Zappa: 'The woman who runs it is insane. She's an old lady, very prudish and very sick. She gave us a list of twelve words we couldn't say on stage. One of them was "brassière", so you know where she's at. There's about a dozen other bands that are banned from the Albert.'

Frank and the Mothers stood at the doors to give people their money back and apologize to those ticket holders who did turn up. Foolishly, Herb decided to sue the Albert Hall, little realising that the British Establishment would never let him win. The idea of spending six months in London was scrapped, the Holland Park house was returned to its owners, and by April Zappa was back in Whitney Studios in Glendale adding overdubs to the *200 Motels* soundtrack album.

There had been enormous changes in the way rock music was presented since the Monterey Pop Festival in 1967. The managers of the most successful groups saw no reason why their acts should play two sets a night for a week when they could get more money playing a festival or stadium gig. It meant the fans would no longer see big acts in intimate settings, but the music business is driven by greed, and the bands supported their managers. It was the end of an era.

When Bill Graham was offered use of the Metropolitan Opera House in New York he thought the Band would suit such a prestigious venue. But when he explained to their manager, John Taplin, that it was a unionised house with high overheads, so the Band would expect to make £50,000 for eight shows, Taplin said, 'Bill. Do you expect my boys to work for a lousy fifty grand a week?' Graham had had enough. He organized a series of farewell concerts and in June he closed both Fillmores. The Mothers, who were on the road again, were hired for two sets a night on 5 and 6 June 1971 at the Fillmore East.

John Lennon had just moved to New York and was being shown the sights by *Village Voice* columnist and broadcaster Howard Smith. When Smith said he was going to interview Zappa, Lennon said: 'Wow, I always wanted to meet him. I really, really admire him.' Smith was puzzled and asked why. 'He's at least *trying* to do something different with the form,' said Lennon. 'It's incredible how he has his band as tight as a real orchestra. I'm very impressed by the kind of discipline he can bring to rock that nobody else can seem to bring to it.' Smith invited John to come along. 'I'd *love* to meet him,' said the ex-Beatle. They took John's silver Lincoln Continental to 1 Fifth, the hotel-apartment block on the corner of Fifth Avenue and 8th Street where rock bands often stayed.

Frank opened the door.

'I brought somebody along,' said Howard Smith.

'Oh hi, glad to meet you,' said Frank, absolutely deadpan.

The other Mothers, however, leapt up off their seats and rushed forwards to be introduced. Later that day, on Howard Smith's talk-show on WPLJ, John said: 'I don't know why I should have believed it, because I should know better, having had all that guff written about me, but I expected a sort of grubby maniac with naked women all over the place, you know – sitting on the toilet. The first thing I said was, "Wow, you look so different. You look great!" And he said, "You look clean too" – he was expecting a couple of nude freaks.'

Howard told Albert Goldman that Lennon was very deferential to Frank: 'John acted like "I may be popular, but this is the real thing." Yoko acted like Frank Zappa had stolen everything he had ever done or even thought from her. Frank completely ignored her. When Howard suggested that John and Yoko might like to join Frank on stage that evening, it took Frank a moment or two to realize this was a good idea.

The second show ran until the early hours. It was 2 a.m. on Sunday. Zappa had just completed a third encore and people were starting to leave their seats, when the stage lights went on again and an astonished audience realized who was on-stage. They stood on their seats and screamed while Frank scowled at them. John and Yoko were nervous wrecks and it took about a gram of cocaine to get them on stage. At first all went well as they ran through the Olympics' 1958 song 'Well (Baby Please Don't Go)' (the B-side of 'Western Movies'), which Lennon used to sing at the Cavern Club, though it was marred by Yoko's unrelated yowls. Her wailing also messed up 'King Kong', which Zappa quickly terminated. They fell into a simple blues jam over which Lennon, followed by Flo and Eddie, chanted the word 'Scumbag', while Yoko did her thing.

Don Preston, who guested on Mini-Moog that night, had fond memories of this gig: 'At one point in the concert, one of the things that was very striking was that John started imitating Zappa by conducting the band with hand signals. I thought that was hilarious. And he was doing a really good job of it.' After a while, Frank asked the audience to join in and at some point someone placed a black bag over the wailing Yoko. Lennon leaned his guitar against a speaker to produce continuous feedback and she continued shrieking for some time after the band left the stage. For years afterwards Yoko apparently complained that John had abandoned her in the bag.

The concert was released as *The Mothers, Fillmore East – June 1971* on 2 August, a mere two months later. Frank had hoped to use some of the John and Yoko material and over lunch in an Italian restaurant they had agreed they would both have copies of the tapes to do anything they wanted with. But Frank refused to deal directly with Lennon's manager, Allen Klein, who had a reputation for obfuscation and mendacity, and permission didn't come through on time.

John and Yoko, however, used the tapes for their live bonus album that came with *Some Time In New York* annotating Cal Schenkel's hand-scribbled sleeve to make the cover. At the same time John and Yoko claimed copyright on the entire jam, giving 'King Kong' the new title 'Jam Rag' (British slang for a tampon). Frank was exceedingly annoyed.

The half-hour rock playlet that could be modified to include local personalities and places on tour had been a great success. It had provided the Mothers with limitless opportunities to parody other rock groups from the Seeds to a wicked take-off of the Who's *Tommy* in the middle of 'Bwana Dik'. Perhaps Zappa borrowed the idea of an ever-changing operetta from Stravinsky, whose *The Soldier's Tale* was designed to be transposed into any time period and to suit any nationality. As Stravinsky wrote: 'Place names [in the operetta] are imaginary; these and other regionalisms . . . were to have been changed according to the locale of the performance, and, in fact, I still encourage producers to localize the play.' Zappa narrated *The Soldier's Tale* when it was performed at the Hollywood Bowl in 1972 with Lukas Foss conducting.

Zappa wrote a new playlet, *Billy the Mountain,* a virtually unintelligible fantasy about a mountain that gets a royalty cheque for all the postcards that have been sold with his image. He decides to celebrate by taking a vacation in New York and on his first day's travel he levels Edwards Airforce Base (where Zappa's father had worked). *Billy the Mountain* shows every sign of being knocked off in a hurry and not even read through, yet it is quintessential Zappa. In the recorded performance Zappa almost lovingly lists the far-flung dormitory communities of Los Angeles: Torrance, Hawthorne, Lomita, Westchester, Playa Del Rey, Tujunga, Sunland, San Fernando, Pacoima, Sylmar, Newhall, Canoga Park, Palmdale, Glendale, Irwindale, Rolling Hills, Granada Hills, Shadow Hills and Cheviot Hills. He remains at heart, resolutely suburban. This is his material: the great cultural wasteland of the Californian suburbs.

Zappa celebrates their tackiness, their ugliness and lack of taste. Urban sprawl, with its monotonous box-like housing, relieved only by strip malls, drive-ins and roadhouses, has no sense of place. Zappa's use of this no-place explains why Americans and Europeans respond to him in very different ways. Regarded as a genius in Europe, he suffered neglect at home.

Europeans saw him, to a certain extent, as a pop artist – as in pop art rather than pop music. Steeped in history, Old Europe romanticized American consumer culture, so much less varied than its own. American life was predictable and uniform: Coca Cola, hamburger chains and coffee shops were identical from city to city. As the Holiday Inn claimed: 'The best surprise is no surprise at all.' Everything was mass-produced. American roads were nearly always on a regimented grid, whether the topography allowed for it or not – San Francisco being the best example of a wonderful site ruined by the imposition of a grid.

The identity granted to even the smallest European village by its architecture is replaced in America by a standardized environment of fast-food chains, motels and gas stations identical to those in the next community, and those in towns thousands of miles away. Some sense of place is provided by billboards for local enterprises and local radio and TV advertising which takes the role of aural and visual architecture. Zappa loved Cal Worthington, the singing cowboy used-car dealer whose immensely long TV commercials appeared on the *Late, Late Show*. 'People in fifty years' time should have documentation of monsters like Cal Worthington,' he said.

He absorbed it all, the tackier the better. In *Billy the Mountain* the agent delivering the royalty cheque arrives in a large Cadillac El Dorado, 'leased from Bob Spreen . . . ("Where the freeways meet in Downey!")' – though a few lines later the Caddy mysteriously turns into a Lincoln. Another character stops for some 'Aunt Jemima Syrup' and some 'Kaiser Broiler Foil' at Ralph's on Sunset Strip, where 'No prices are lower prices than Ralph's.' From his earliest recordings, Zappa was always a pop artist; with Ned and Nelda he parodied a song in the hit parade and made it his own, like Warhol painting Campbell's soup cans.

Zappa responded to the pace of Southern California and understood its metabolism; perhaps even a touch of the Mediterranean from his Sicilian ancestry. His music could only come from LA; it has the laid-back rhythm of California car culture, the cadence of the freeways, of cruising, of an architecture designed to be seen on the move from a car window. In LA cars are fetish objects, although Zappa did not get his driving licence until he was 21. When it expired he never bothered to renew it, so Gail or one of his staff would drive him everywhere.

Zappa found corresponding rhythms within himself to echo the sounds of the suburbs. He sometimes writes musical pictures, like Virgil Thomson's orchestral portraits: the hypnotic gentle driving rhythm interrupted from time to time by a musical event, a time change, a fragment of conversation or musical blip, like switching freeways, missing the traffic lights and having to stop, or passing a cluster of commercial buildings on one of the long highways heading from LA to the Inland Empire. Zappa finds clarity in the urban sprawl, the widely spaced buildings with their scraggy palm trees against a huge blue sky and the massive, ever-present billboards, and he is able to create beauty out of it. As Zappa told an interviewer: 'I get to know a lot about the city and the people travelling in from the airport. The billboards and road signs give me a pretty good indication of what the mentality of the people is.'

In this he most resembles the painter Richard Diebenkorn, who began his Ocean Park series of abstract paintings and drawings in the late sixties. He was acutely affected by his environment, but found a vocabulary of colours and shapes in the Ocean Park sector of Venice, then a nondescript, run-down beach community of residential and light industrial buildings. Zappa also collaged and mixed his elements to make them his own, but his was a ruthless, flat, accurate portrayal, seen without emotion, viewed as if he had no thoughts and no moral or aesthetic prejudices about what he saw; his was a sociological, almost zoological approach.

This is not to say that Zappa actually liked Los Angeles. 'Talk about a boring place,' he said. 'It's horrible, really bad. You see it the most when you've just got off the plane and drive to your house. The architecture is so ugly in Los Angeles, so banal, it's so wrong, the colours are all wrong, everything is wrong. It just looks cheap and shitty. It's like they call it Squatters' Village with all different kinds of ugly buildings next to each other, interspersed with billboards advertising people's albums and movies and used-car lots. That's all there is, it's really bleak.'

Yet he was able to transform it into truly beautiful music. Others have written songs of the suburbs. David Byrne's memorable Talking Heads track 'The Big Country', for instance, describes the freeways, suburban housing, baseball diamonds and the supermarkets and concludes: 'I wouldn't live there if you paid me.' Zappa, however, continued to live there, a grouchy old curmudgeon of the suburbs – albeit very expensive suburbs.

Zappa: 'I don't have any guests coming to my house unless they're working for me. I'm really not interested in the world of Los Angeles. I hate the place . . . New York is the best place in the world – as far as I'm concerned [but] the real estate is too expensive. To have the same square footage and the facilities I have in Los Angeles would cost a billion dollars.' This was not true. His place on Woodrow Wilson Boulevard was worth a fortune and at that time he could have bought an enormous loft building in SoHo or Chelsea for relatively little money.

Zappa's problem with New York was the downtown art scene. Inevitably, he would have been drawn into the high-art world of happenings, experimental music, loft concerts and gallery openings. But he knew nothing about the visual arts and was not all that conversant with contemporary experimental music – his interests pretty much stopped with the Second World War. He would have been a small fish in a big pond, whereas in the cultural wasteland of LA, even though he rarely went out, he was a very big fish in a small pond.

Billy the Mountain was recorded live at Pauley Pavilion at the University of California, Los Angeles (UCLA) on 7 August, and released on *Just Another Band From LA*. Backstage at the gig Zappa bumped into 16-year-old Nigey Lennon, author of the memoir *Being Frank: My Time With Frank Zappa* (1995). Nigey had met Frank a year or so before when she sent a tape to Bizarre Records. He asked if she still played and took her home. They played music in the basement and he invited her to the Mothers' next gig in Berkeley, on the pretext of being an understudy in case any of the group members collapsed from road fatigue. As she didn't know the material and had not attended any of the rehearsals it was a feeble excuse, though she was academy trained. Nigey soon found herself sharing Zappa's bed at the Berkeley House Motel.

Though Frank was always quick to describe every abnormal act, unusual preference or sexual eccentricity of the members of his band, presented under the guise of anthropological studies, he kept the details of his own sex life very private. In her witty memoir, however, Nigey reveals Zappa's interest in group sex, voyeurism and the use of appliances – all the things he sang about. Sex was only slightly less important to Zappa than music: 'it permeated everything he did on an unconscious level,' recalled Nigey, 'from his voice, to his hand gestures, to his guitar playing.' She felt that he was serious-minded, even solemn, but 'at the same time I distinctly sensed that there was an element of madness in his refusal to accept any boundaries whatsoever, sexually or otherwise. He could find erotic possibilities in the least likely situations – the more absurd, the better; the further he could push the envelope, the better he liked it. And all the while he was pushing it, he was laughing . . . not too loud, but very deeply.' Frank could laugh even while having sex.

He clearly regarded Nigey as more than a one-night stand, because he took her with him on the American tour, risking jail. She was under-age (17 to his 30) and Chuck Berry had done two years under the Mann Act for transporting a minor across a State line. Nigey performed with the Mothers at several concerts, trading guitar licks with Frank.

The tour made its way across America: Seattle, Spokane, Portland, Atlanta, Chicago, Denver, Miami, reaching New York on 11 October, where they were to play two sold-out concerts at Carnegie Hall. But things went wrong at the Holiday Inn: Nigey was put out when Frank introduced a sophisticated redhead to their bedroom and someone in the band called Gail to inform her of her husband's latest romance. Nigey boarded the next plane to LA, while the Mothers flew on to Toronto.

Meanwhile, back at Woodrow Wilson Drive, the nanny Janet Ferguson had moved out to be replaced by Miss Pamela: 'I held kitchen court as the zany nanny, making cinnamon toast, dancing half-naked round the table with Keith Moon. I had never really thought of Moon and Dweezil as children anyway, since Frank and Gail treated them as equals from day one. The munchkins even called their parents Frank and Gail.'

200 Motels premièred at the Doheny Plaza in Beverly Hills on 29 October to 'mixed' reviews: the *LA Times* proclaimed it 'a stunning achievement' and 'a minor classic', whereas Tony Palmer, writing in the *NME* said it was the worst film in the history of western cinema. After publicizing the film launch, the Mothers' tour continued in Europe. They had a punishing schedule and it is easy to see why touring really can make you crazy: Stockholm (19 November); then Aarhus in Denmark (20 November); two shows in Copenhagen (21 November); then Odense (22 November); then Dusseldorf in Germany (23 November); then Berlin (24–25 November) and Hamburg (26 November); the next night Rotterdam; the next night two shows in Frankfurt; the next night Munich; the next night Vienna . . .

After each gig the road crew had to break down the equipment, load it onto the trucks and drive through the night to the next venue. Several trucks broke down in the cold weather. One week a truck froze in a blizzard near Malmo, on the Swedish coast. Dick Barber: 'Scared the daylights out of the road crew, because they thought they were gonna freeze to death 'cause it was real cold at night. They managed to get it fixed and they were a day late getting to Copenhagen.' The Mothers had to perform in Odense with rented equipment: a couple of stacks of Marshalls and a little PA system. The promoter offered the audience a refund, but nobody left. Frank told the band to relax and, for the first time, allowed them to have a few drinks before going on stage. 'Just be loose and have a good time, and give 'em a good show,' he said. Barber remembered it as 'a real high-energy fun night'.

On Saturday, 4 December 1971 the Mothers arrived from Milan to play the Montreux Casino in Switzerland. The concert was held in the faded glory of the casino's ballroom, the last event of the season before it closed for the winter. Frank had suggested that Flo and Eddie deliver some of their lines in German for their German concerts. Zappa: 'I tried to convince Mark and Howard that it was a good idea to learn these things phonetically, because most American groups, if they go and play in another country, make no attempt to communicate in the native language.' (It seemed to have escaped Frank's attention that Montreux is in the French-speaking part of Switzerland.) So large sections of *Billy the Mountain* were performed in German, including the prescient lines: 'Sheets of fire, ladies and gentlemen / *Lachen von Feuer* / Sheets of real fire/.'

In the last few minutes of Don Preston's synthesiser solo on 'King Kong' – the encore to a 90-minute set – flames broke out on the third row of the balcony; someone had fired a Very pistol and the flare had lodged in the ceiling, short-circuiting the electrical wiring. The Mothers could see the sparks and fire from the stage, but it didn't look serious, so they carried on. But the audience panicked. People in the front row climbed on stage and pushed past the band, heading for the exit. Frank tried to calm the audience of 3,000, which was well over capacity, by referring to Arthur Brown's hit single 'Fire': 'FIRE! Arthur Brown, in person!' Then, speaking slowly: 'Well if you just calmly go toward the exit, ladies and gentlemen. Go toward the exit, calmly. Please calmly, calmly towards the exit.'

The band left the stage and watched from the wings as part of the burning balcony broke away and fell on the seats below. Then they realized it was serious. Smoke billowed out and people started scrambling over the seats. The owners had chained the exit doors because people had been trying to get in, even though the hall was full. The Mothers' driver led them downstairs to a kitchen area safe from the crush of the crowd. But the smoke still reached them – it was an old building and burning fast. There was no exit where they were, so the quick-thinking driver smashed a glass wall with his fist and led them to safety. In less than two minutes they were standing in the street.

Only outside did they realize the seriousness of the situation. The flames had caught hold and, shortly after they had escaped, the heating system had exploded, blowing several people through a window, including a Mothers roadie. Fortunately there were no fatalities. The band returned to their hotel and Frank stood on the veranda and watched as the casino burned to the ground, along with all his guitars, three synthesisers and an organ; equipment valued at $50,000, but fortunately fully insured.

The English band Deep Purple were in the audience and had booked the casino ballroom for the following three weeks to record an album. They returned to their hotel and watched from the safety of the restaurant as flames rose hundreds of feet into the air and sheets of fire erupted from the building like solar flares, fanned by the wind from the surrounding mountains and blowing a plume of smoke far out across Lake Geneva. Bass player Roger Glover grabbed a napkin and scribbled down the lines of 'Smoke On The Water', one of their greatest hits.

The next day, as the Mothers walked through the smouldering rubble of what used to be the stage, Frank uncharacteristically allowed them to vote on whether to continue the tour. They still had several weeks of sold-out concerts remaining, but it meant starting from scratch and hiring or borrowing new instruments, lights and sound equipment. They voted to continue. Frank had apparently wanted to abandon the tour and cut his losses, but he understood that with Christmas drawing near, the band wanted to earn as much as possible. The French and Belgian leg of the tour was cancelled and they went straight to London where they were due to play four shows on 10 and 11 December at the Rainbow Theatre, the old Finsbury Park Astoria and the site of the Beatles' Christmas Shows.

Perhaps because of this, Zappa chose to do 'I Want To Hold Your Hand' as the encore when they returned to the stage at the end of the first show. Just as he was announcing it, a young man leapt up onto the stage and violently shoved Zappa off. He fell ten feet into the orchestra pit and lay unconscious in a heap, his leg buckled under him, blood pouring from his head. There was confusion as the packed audience of 3,000 stared in disbelief and the members of the group filed on-stage for the encore to find that Zappa had mysteriously disappeared. The culprit jumped off the stage, but the audience quickly collared him and turned him over to the Mothers' roadies who, in between screaming at him, administered a beating. Frank was rushed by ambulance to the nearby Royal Northern Hospital and treated for a broken rib, paralysed wrist and fractured ankle. X-rays were taken to determine the possibility of a skull fracture and no pain-killers were allowed until the extent of his head injuries had been fully determined.

There were chaotic scenes outside the Rainbow as the audience for the second set mixed with the audience from the first. Rumours circulated that Frank had been killed and for about an hour nobody knew what was happening. Eventually the crowd dispersed, none the wiser. The police arrested Trevor Charles Howell, a 24-year-old labourer, and charged him with assault and malicious intent to commit bodily harm. He was released on £100 bail to appear in court ten days later.

That same day, 11 December, amid chaotic scenes, Frank was transferred to the private Weymouth Street Clinic, just off Harley Street. Herb Cohen grabbed one press photographer's camera and smashed it on the ground, but the Rainbow's manager John Morris, who once ran the Fillmore East in New York, later gave the photographer a check for £100 to forget about it.

The remaining engagements were cancelled and the band were told privately that Frank might never be able to play again. The Mothers were allowed to visit him before they returned to the States. Mark Volman: 'We went in and there was Frank on his back, arm in a sling, one leg in a cast on a sling in the air. His head was bandaged like a mummy. You couldn't see his hair or his moustache, just his lips where they had cut a hole in the bandages, and his eyes, which followed us to the foot of the bed. And then he said: '"Peaches En Regalia' – one, two, three . . ." We died laughing. It was the sorriest of jokes. But it was his way of saying, "It's okay."'

On 8 March 1972, Howell pleaded guilty and was sentenced to a year in jail. At first he claimed to have done it because 'My girlfriend said she loved Frank.' Then he said he had been irritated by Zappa's performance. 'The group were treating the audience like dirt. They were not giving value for money.' A week later, Zappa instigated a high court action for damages against both Howell and the Rainbow's owners.

Despite many visits from friends (a jetlagged Gail had to shoo away two rival girlfriends when she arrived at his sickbed), Frank Zappa spent a miserable Christmas in London and was not able to leave the clinic until mid-January. He recuperated in Hawaii but had to spend the next four months in plaster up to his hip. He was now convinced that Britain was not the place for him.

14 Waka/Jawaka

Nineteen seventy-two was a difficult year for Zappa, though a productive one. Months after the accident, he was still in a wheelchair and his leg refused to mend. Though he learned to hobble around using crutches, his doctors thought it would be best to break it again and reset it, but this idea did not appeal. He was given a leg brace, and when the leg finally healed it was slightly crooked and shorter than the other. He was often in pain; the damaged leg throbbed and his lower back ached. The damage to his neck caused his voice to drop by half an octave; something he was rather pleased about.

He spent almost all of his time in the confines of his dimly lit basement studio, tapping out lyrics with one finger on his IBM Selectric typewriter or composing with his guitar. Sometimes he would use the piano to work out a melody that didn't fit easily on the guitar, but his keyboard skills were limited to searching for notes with one finger – even though Dr Zirkon's Secret Lab was now equipped with a $70,000 eight-foot long Bosendorfer concert grand.

While in his wheelchair he wrote a musical called *Hunchentoot*. Like his other musicals it was never realized, but much of the music was recorded with the 1973–74 band and released on *Sleep Dirt*, which featured 'Flambay', 'Spider of Destiny' and 'Time Is Money'. 'Planet Of My Dreams' had to wait until *Them Or Us* for release.

Lying idle in a hospital, Frank had clearly been listening to a lot of jazz fusion. Miles Davis's extraordinary *Bitches Brew* was released early in 1970. Featuring John McLaughlin on guitar, Joe Zawinul on electric piano, as well as Chick Corea on electric piano and Wayne Shorter on soprano sax, it spawned a whole new genre of music. Zawinul and Shorter went on to found the hugely successful Weather Report, releasing their first eponymous album in 1971. Corea also went into fusion with a series of albums often featuring ex-Miles Davis sidemen, and eventually formed Return To Forever.

Frank had written some new music that especially suited this style. It was a direction he had previously touched upon, particularly with the *King Kong* album with Jean-Luc Ponty and his Hot Rats line-up. Now he assembled his own fusion group, usually known as the Grand Wazoo Orchestra, using Mothers George Duke and Aynsley Dunbar, and Alex Dmochowski, bass player from Aynsley Dunbar's Retaliation, as the rhythm section, plus a collection of LA session musicians: six woodwind players, four brass players plus Sal Marquez on trumpet, two percussionists and Tony Duran on slide guitar.

Duran's involvement arose from a parallel project. Frank had been approached by Ruben Ladron De Guevara to ask if he could use the name Ruben and the Jets for an R&B/Doo Wop revival band. Frank loved the idea and offered to produce and engineer the whole thing. He suggested Guevara bring in Motorhead as a sax player, and Motorhead introduced them to Tony Duran. Duran not only joined Ruben and the Jets as a songwriter, lead guitar and slide player, but was appropriated by Zappa to play in his new Grand Wazoo line-up. The resulting album, *Ruben and the Jets For Real!*, was recorded at Paramount Studios in Hollywood simultaneously with his Grand Wazoo Orchestra in April and May 1972.

It sounds strangely inauthentic, possibly because of the inappropriate organ. Fans bought it for the track written by Zappa, 'If I Could Only Be Your Love Again', where a fragment of his vocal can be heard, and for his ringing signature solo on an extended version of 'Dedicated

To The One I Love'. For 'conceptual continuity', Cal Schenkel added a tiny reproduction of the car from the cover of *Just Another Band From LA* to a hamburger bun in the double-spread photograph of the band.

Now that he had a slide guitar, Zappa brought in 'Sneaky Pete' Kleinow on pedal steel guitar and even forgave Jeff Simmons enough to let him play Hawaiian guitar and sing. Don Preston came in on Mini-Moog and piano. It wasn't a serious attempt at a fusion band and the results vary in styles – all of them Zappa's. When the band is playing the chart everything is fine, tight and well rehearsed, but the essence of jazz is collective improvisation and these were studio musicians, many of whom had not previously met, so there was no sense of camaraderie. They had not previously jammed so the extended improvisations broke down into something simple that everyone was comfortable with. In addition, Aynsley Dunbar is a brilliant rock 'n' roll drummer, but his style is hardly the 'gut-bucket funk' required to prevent fusion from drifting into vapid noodlings, as happened with some of the better-known fusion bands in the mid-seventies.

Nevertheless, there were some exceptional melodies such as 'Waka/Jawaka', which sounded really good played on a brass line-up, the horns playing a fast riff as the rhythm track; and there was 'Big Swifty', a 17-minute epic that occupied the whole of a side on the original *Waka/Jawaka* LP. It was organized in an interesting way. Zappa: 'The restatement of the theme is actually derived from a guitar solo on the album which Sal Marquez took down on paper. After about an hour of wheeling the tape back and forth, Sal managed to transcribe this rhythmically deranged chorus ... After he'd written it out, we proceeded to overdub three trumpets on it, and, presto! An organized conclusion for "Big Swifty"!'

The same sessions produced the next album, *The Grand Wazoo*, a more unified selection of numbers, ending with 'Blessed Relief', an exceptionally beautiful melody providing a perfect vehicle for the line-up. Zappa was pleased with the results and, though he had produced the Paramount sessions from his wheelchair, he now set about touring with a big electric band. Zappa was back on the road.

Not all the players were available due to prior commitments, but by restricting the number of venues he assembled a 20-piece orchestra and hired rehearsal studios at 150 North LaBrea to prepare them for touring. As well as music from the *Waka/Jawaka* album they played older, better-known songs like 'Penis Dimension', 'Dog Breath Variations', 'Uncle Meat' and 'Revised Music For A Low-Budget Symphony Orchestra'. Zappa: 'What we really have here is an electric symphony orchestra. Aside from the recognisable pieces which are rock-oriented, there are two or three semi-symphonic-type pieces, which are of a humorous nature simply because of the subject matter. But we're not going to have people jumping around on stage or falling down with tambourines and saying zany stuff – we're not supplying that this season.'

Though billed as the Mothers, the only recognisable names were Ian and Ruth Underwood; most of the others were studio musicians who, by definition, were not accustomed to going on the road. Zappa wrote that the 'concert presentation will be informal, reasonably straightforward and non-theatrical, as very few of the Wazoo's members exhibit the normal pop musician's ability to function efficiently while garbed in fringes, feathers or festoons.'

However, he did make one concession to showmanship and placed Earl Dumier in the front row of the woodwind section, 'making it possible for the first time to view a grown man with a mod haircut, struggling against the forces of nature to extract accurate intonation from an amplified Eb Contrabass Sarrusophone.' Zappa conducted the ensemble wearing blue jeans, torn to fit over his leg brace.

Frank hated situations where he was not in complete control and a month in hospital, followed by months in a wheelchair with his leg in a cast, had not put him in the best of moods. Even before the accident he and Gail had been going through a rough patch and some members of the Mothers thought he was trying to get rid of her; but she held her ground, even when Nigey Lennon moved into the basement studio.

Nigey's Gibson 335 had been destroyed along with all the other equipment in the Montreux Casino fire and Zappa contacted her when the insurance money came through. She started showing up at all the Grand Wazoo rehearsals instead of job-hunting and in the end her exasperated parents threw her out. Frank invited her to live in his basement workroom. He worked all night, while she tried to sleep on the settee, then he would disappear upstairs for a few hours sleep in the morning.

Things were clearly bad between Frank and the family. The children and Gail were forbidden to enter his little kingdom, and Nigey spent a whole month there without seeing them. She sometimes heard them, however. There was one argument with Gail in which the normally quiet-spoken Zappa actually raised his voice, after which he ran downstairs to the basement in a rage.

Nigey: 'Frank's energy was perverse. He loved being "bad" – and doing whatever he wasn't supposed to be doing. In a very real sense, he turned the polarity of negative energy around and it kept him going, gave him a sense of purpose in life. He was a Catholic, what can I say?'

Grand Wazoo rehearsals moved to the Glendale Civic Auditorium and the electric symphony orchestra – billed by Zappa as the Mothers of Invention/Hot Rats/Grand Wazoo – played the opening concert of their tour at the Hollywood Bowl on 10 September. Zappa: 'The Wazoo has probably earned its place in the Rock and Roll Hall Of Fame for the simple reason it is the only "new" group in rock history which has known from the start that it will not be as successful as the Beatles, and has also known throughout its history the exact time and place that it will split up: after the Boston show, in the dressing room, on September 24th.'

The band did three European concerts: the Deutschlandhalle in Berlin, the Oval Cricket Ground in London and the Hourast Halle in The Hague. After two nights at the Felt Forum in New York they completed the tour at the proscribed time at Boston Music Hall. Nigey had moved out of the basement when the tour began and, significantly, Gail accompanied Frank on the road, even posing with him for photographers.

The Grand Wazoo tour grossed $97,000 and the expenses were just under $100,000. As Zappa was travelling with Gail plus a costly personal bodyguard, to lose a little over $2,000 for the luxury of touring Europe with a 20-piece orchestra seemed like a bargain to him. Zappa's bodyguard became a permanent fixture on-stage and at nightclubs or restaurants. Realistically, he had no need for one provided stage security was good; not even Mick Jagger employed a bodyguard. The incident at the Rainbow had really shaken Zappa's confidence.

He decided to take a stripped-down version of the Grand Wazoo line-up on a full-length tour. For this Petit Wazoo he prepared a new repertoire, including instrumental versions of 'The Duke of Prunes' and 'America Drinks And Goes Home', as well as 'Farther Oblivion', which introduced new material that would later appear in the 'Greggery Peccary' playlet. There was also another unusual piece called 'Tycho Brahe', described in Greg Russo's Cosmik Debris as Zappa narrating the biography of the sixteenth-century Danish astronomer over a four-chord progression. It is entirely possible that Zappa was a fan of this astronomer, but it is more probable he was riffing on the name of his fuzz/octave divider pedal, the Tychobrahe Octavia, as used by Jimi Hendrix and others to get that classic octave up/fuzz sound. The Tychobrahe Parapedal, Pedalflanger and Octavia were very highly regarded at the time, though only a few were manufactured and the company was short lived.

The Petit Wazoo went straight into rehearsals with a ten-piece line-up, nine of whom had been in the Grand Wazoo. They opened in Montreal on 27 October, with Tim Buckley (managed by Herb Cohen) as the opening act, and from there they toured the United States until 15 December, playing more than 20 shows.

Zappa had never formally broken up the Mothers, but after waiting around for several months without hearing from him, Mark Volman, Howard Kaylan and Jim Pons decided to go on the road. They still couldn't use the Turtles name, so they got a record contract from Columbia Records as Flo and Eddie. Aynsley Dunbar joined them as a member of their backing band for a short period, but returned to work with Frank on studio projects like *Waka/Jawaka* and *The Grand Wazoo*. While relaunching their career and promoting their new album, Mark and Howard made a few comments about Frank stealing their material, which did not go down at all well. Zappa: 'I'm extremely disappointed in their behaviour, because there was a time when I thought they were my friends.'

According to Gail, Mark and Howard were virtually the only musicians that Frank ever regarded as friends, so their 'betrayal' must have cut deep. Kaylan: 'One of many parts of [Zappa's] great, great genius is his ability to take the best from his musicians, and recycle it, and put it out again . . . as "Frank Zappa music". This makes some of his musicians very, very angry, because they wrote this part out, or they said these things first. They tell it to Frank. Frank hears it, likes it, writes it down, makes it a song, and the author of the song is now Frank Zappa.'

This complaint was made by many members of his bands. Motorhead: 'Frank's special talent [was] for taking bits and pieces from all over the place and incorporating them into his own work. When we were on the road, Don Preston had taped lots of things; any little thing, like a saying on the bus or an in-joke, became part of the compositional project.'

Tom Fowler: 'He gets too much credit for the things the guys around him contributed. He gets more than he deserves on a lot of the stuff . . . If you take out all the other guys' contributions to a song like "Inca Roads" it's not going to be "Inca Roads" anymore. On half of that stuff it's not going to be there because he didn't think of it.'

Frank saw himself as running a school for musicians, providing a supportive environment to bring out the best in each player and stretching them by writing material specifically tailored to their abilities. He gave examples: 'Bruce Fowler's highest practical note on the trombone is an E-flat above the treble clef, which is the same highest note as an alto flute – fairly unique guy. How often to you get to use that if you're a trombone player? A drummer like Vinnie Colaiuta is capable of playing all these unbelievable polyrhythms, but if he gets a studio gig, that's the last thing in the world they want to hear on their record. You know, "Just give me that fuckin' fatback." . . . But a strange thing happens when they get in the band: they complain about being asked to do things that are hard. And then after they leave, they brag about being in the band.'

Zappa undoubtedly appropriated ideas from his musicians, but they were often ideas they would not have had without Zappa's input. Here he paralleled Andy Warhol who did exactly the same thing at the Factory, encouraging everyone to contribute ideas, which later appeared as Warhol paintings or films, though in Warhol's case he paid his studio assistants for new ideas for paintings.

In 1973 Zappa spent 183 days on tour, exactly half the year – 26 weeks in hotels, tour buses and airports. He loved it; he was a real road rat. Straight after Christmas 1972 Frank was back in rehearsal, this time at 5831 Sunset, at North Bronson, near Vine, the headquarters of DiscReet. Zappa and Cohen had a new record company with a rehearsal studio at the back of the offices. Warners' contract with the Bizarre and Straight labels was about to expire and, as usual, Herb used this as an excuse to completely reorganize their corporate structure.

Ian and Ruth Underwood were not involved in the Petit Wazoo. They were trying to break free of Frank's influence, and his name was not allowed to be mentioned in their North Hollywood home. (If absolutely necessary, Zappa was referred to obliquely, rather like Voldemort in *Harry Potter* 'He who cannot be named.') However, the Underwoods were the best players Zappa knew and he could be very persuasive. They soon found themselves re-entering his world for yet another tour. The Petit Wazoo had done a good job, but Frank now felt it was time to return to vocals and a more commercial show.

On 23 February, after a month of salaried rehearsals, yet another incarnation of the Mothers of Invention went on tour, beginning in Fayetteville, North Carolina. They took a break in mid-March to record some sessions at Bollix Sound, Inglewood, the studio owned by Ike and Tina Turner (the latter's career had not yet made its spectacular revival). On 19 and 20 March, Frank, George Duke, Tom Fowler and

Ralph Humphrey recorded 'Dirty Love', 'Dinah-Moe Hum', ' Montana' and three other tracks.

Zappa: 'I wanted to put some back-up singers on the thing, and the road manager said, "Well, why don't you just use the Ikettes?" I said, "I can get the Ikettes?" and he said "Sure." But you know what the gimmick was? We had to agree, Ike Turner insisted, that we pay these girls no more than $25 per song, because that's what he paid them. And no matter how many hours it took, I could not pay them any more than $25 per song per girl, including Tina. It was so difficult, that one part in the middle of the song 'Montana', that the three girls rehearsed it for a couple of days. Just that one section. You know the part that goes "I'm pluckin' the ol' dennil floss . . ."? Right in the middle there. And one of the harmony singers got it first. She came out and sang her part and the other girls had to follow her track. Tina was so pleased that she was able to sing this thing that she went into the next studio where Ike was working and dragged him into the studio to hear the result of her labour. He listened to the tape and he goes, "What is this shit?" and walked out.

'I don't know how she managed to stick with that guy for so long. He treated her terribly and she's a really nice lady. We were recording down there on a Sunday. She wasn't involved with the session, but she came in on Sunday with a whole pot of stew that she brought for everyone working in the studio. Like out of nowhere, here's Tina Turner coming in with a rag on her head bringing a pot of stew. It was really nice.'

Once again, Zappa was accompanied on tour by Nigey, who wrote the chorus parts on 'Dirty Love'. She overdubbed three back-up vocal parts, but her voice just wasn't funky enough to do them justice. They played them to Tina Turner who listened through then said, 'Ssshit man, I could do that blindfolded with a broomstick up my ass.' It took one pass for Tina to get the harmonies right, and three more to sing each of the three vocal parts in one take each. Regrettably, Ike refused to let Zappa credit her on the album.

'Montana' became a popular concert number, partly because of the sheer absurdity of it. It fared less well outside the States, because

Europeans did not know what dental floss was. Zappa described the song as about 'the idea of travelling along the empty wasteland with a very short horse and a very large tweezer, grabbing the dental floss sprout as it pooches up from the bush . . . grabbing it with your tweezers and towing it all the way back to the bunkhouse.'

'Montana' appeared on *Over-Nite Sensation*, along with 'Dirty Love' and 'Dinah-Moe Humm', two sexually explicit songs that earned Zappa more opprobrium than almost any others. In 'Dirty Love' the narrator encounters a groupie whom he treats entirely as a sex object, specifically saying that he was not interested in her love ('sweet devotion') or feelings ('cheap emotion'), he is only interested in his sexual satisfaction. For Zappa, that was all there was to sex: as long as everyone had an orgasm, everything was all right. 'Dirty Love' concludes with the young woman having sex with her poodle. It probably never occurred to Zappa that this description of bestiality might offend people.

'Dinah-Moe Humm' is a Zappa fantasy about a woman who makes a $40 bet that he can't make her come. It transpires that what really turns her on is watching Zappa fuck her sister. Zappa took a somewhat prurient interest in such stories, but it is important to see the songs in the context of the times.

Having been jailed in 1965 for making a mildly suggestive tape, Zappa was a great believer in the First Amendment to the Constitution which guarantees freedom of speech. In the fifties even Aristophanes' *Lysistrata* had been banned in the States, but throughout the sixties a seemingly endless series of court cases finally gave Americans the right to read John Cleland's *Fanny Hill* (1748), D. H. Lawrence's *Lady Chatterley's Lover* (1928), Henry Miller's *Tropic of Cancer* (1934) and *Tropic of Capricorn* (1938) and William Burroughs's *Naked Lunch* (1959), against the ferocious opposition of conservatives, puritans and self-appointed censors.

Ralph Ginzberg was given a five-year sentence for publishing *Eros* magazine, which contained a tame, rather tasteful photo-essay of a couple making love. No sexual organs were shown, but the man was black and the woman was white. It was 1964 and the South was still segregated. Lenny Bruce was literally hounded to death by the censors, especially the powerful Catholic Church, which did not like his riffs about Cardinal Spellman. Sometimes it seemed that half of Bruce's audience consisted of plain-clothed cops taking notes.

The Living Theater were harassed so much they left the States to live and perform in exile; underground film-maker Jack Smith's *The Beautiful Book* was deemed obscene; coffee houses and bars lost their licence if anyone said 'fuck' on stage; pubic hair could not be shown in magazines or in movies. Louis Malle's beautiful film *The Lovers* was banned despite only fleeting love scenes, as was the Swedish film *I Am Curious – Yellow*. Every tiny step towards freedom of expression resulted in long and expensive lawsuits. Zappa followed these developments with the keenest interest and his 'questionable' lyrics have to be seen against this background of a constant and ongoing struggle against the fundamentalists and censors.

Why were 'Dirty Love' and 'Dinah Moe-Humm' so offensive, when it was acceptable for Donna Summer to simulate orgasm on 'I Feel Love' or Jane Birkin to do the same – though slightly less graphically – on 'Je T'Aime (Moi Non Plus)', which was a UK Number One in October 1969? Those who struggled against censorship thought that no subject should be out of bounds, no matter how controversial or personal, no matter how racist or sexually explicit.

The censorship cases had largely been about confessional literature, beginning with the 1956 trial of Allen Ginsberg's *Howl & Other Poems*. Nevertheless, this tendency for the private to become public continued. It was considered radical in 1964 for Lenny Bruce to discuss underarm hair; and a couple of years later Zappa was already singing about sexual diseases. If it existed, thought Zappa, he had the right to write about it. He saw himself in part as a journalist, reporting on life as he saw it and he believed that anything the band said or did in the privacy of the dressing room could – and should – be shouted from the rooftops.

Zappa was a social reformer, filled with righteous anger and a sense of profound outrage at the state of his country. He looked deeply into the murky side of society, but refused to look at himself. He appeared to have no insight into Frank Zappa at all and strongly objected if anyone tried to decipher his feelings. Fascinated by the fantasies and fetishes, STDs and deviations of his band members to an almost voyeuristic extent, Zappa preferred not to reveal the details of his own private life. His emotions were buried under a carapace of cynicism and misanthropy. He knew that people should be in touch with their emotions, it was a free-flowing sexuality and psychic energy, that was the basis of Freaking-Out as a therapy. But Zappa was never capable of the confessional revelations of, say, Allen Ginsberg, who wrote about his homosexuality when it was still illegal.

Zappa's songs about anal sex, group sex, exhibitionism, blow jobs, sexual devices and other controversial subjects were usually couched in the third-person or sung by somebody else. Yet he always told interviewers the lyrics were rooted in his own experience, as if part of him longed to be more candid. The original Mothers were revered precisely because Zappa was naming the unnameable and telling it as it is. He was seen as a natural successor to the Beat Generation of Ginsberg, Kerouac and Burroughs. But Zappa's intimate revelations diminished as he lost faith in Freaking-Out. At the end of his life, there were no Zappa songs about dying of prostate cancer to match Ginsberg's death-bed poetry and obviously shouldn't have expected any: Zappa's lyrics were ultimately unimportant; it is the music that will last.

However, in 1973 Zappa was at the cutting edge of saying the unsayable: 'It used to be that I would write specific things about obvious social phenomena that a large number of people could identify with because they had seen it in action. But these days such weird things have happened to me as a person that I'd rather put some of those down and do it that way. That's why I have songs like "Penguin in Bondage" and "Montana". I write about the things that are part of my personal experience.'

In the aftermath of the 1966 Supreme Court ruling that anything that could be shown to be of 'redeeming social importance' was not obscene, cinemas began to test the limits. In 1967 *I Am Curious – Yellow* was banned, but won on appeal in 1968. The first films to show hard-core material were documentaries about the recent legalisation of pornography in Denmark: John Lamb's *Sexual Freedom In Denmark* and Alex de Renzy's *Pornography in Denmark: A New Approach* (both 1970). They showed night-club acts, the making of hard-core films, interviews with naked people and a hard-core film being watched by some Danes. They also showed erect penises, something previously totally forbidden in American films. Nobody could deny that these films had socially significant content: they were investigations into how the Danish public had reacted to the lack of censorship.

Soon cinemas were flooded with knock-offs: *History of the Blue Movie* (1970), *The Casting Call* (1970), *Case Histories From Krafft-Ebing* (1971) and so on. Then *Deep Throat* opened at the New Mature World Theatre on Times Square in the summer of 1972. It was the first full-length, full-colour, hard-core feature film ever to be shown. Though heavily championed by Al Goldstein in *Screw* (one of many new sex magazines) it might have gone unnoticed had the authorities not tried to close it down. The trial gave *Deep Throat* excellent publicity and although the cinema owners eventually lost the case, by the time the New Mature World Theatre was closed down in March 1973, *Deep Throat* had been seen by more than a quarter of a million people in New York alone and had grossed upwards of a million dollars.

Frank was fascinated by these developments. That same month, March 1973, he recorded 'Dirty Love' and 'Dinah-Moe Humm'. He saw these songs as sex-positive, a further strike for sexual liberation. Like the first commercially available hard-core porn films, the message was that as long as everyone came, everyone was happy.

Over-Nite Sensation also contained 'I'm the Slime', a return to the political critique of 'Who Are The Brain Police?' and 'Trouble Coming Every Day'. The 'slime' in question is oozing from the television set. Frank describes television content as vile and pernicious, brain-washing the American public until they are a country of zombies who do as they are told: eat the processed junk food that is advertized, and think what the government wants them to think, all dished up as mind-numbing sit-coms, soap operas and game shows. 'I'm the Slime' is one of the finest political rock songs ever written.

However, Zappa's message is undermined by the fact that American television and the consumer culture were his raw material.

Take a song like 'Stink Foot' on the *Apostrophe (')* album, which Zappa described as being 'inspired by the Mennen foot spray commercial where the dog keels over after the guy takes his shoes off. Do you know how hard it is to write a song about something like that?' His use of this type of subject matter demanded audience-familiarity with the source material and also ensured built-in obsolescence. Some of these songs now sound seriously dated.

He was soon back with Tina Turner and the Ikettes to do overdubs. They were already recording material that would appear on the album after next. Zappa had a good line-up and he was on a roll so he kept on recording. After a 21-city American tour, they played Western Australia, giving a concert in Hawaii en route. Zappa met a young lady in Australia whom he liked enough to bring back to Los Angeles and install in an apartment, but the affair seems to have ended before the Mothers set out for Europe.

The European line-up was slightly different: trumpet player Sal Marquez had asked Zappa for a per diem: the daily allowance normally given to musicians when they are touring to make up for the fact they are incurring extra costs by having to take all their meals out and pay hotel bar prices for their drinks. Marquez: 'He got all upset, claiming that he never paid his groups this way. "Not even $15?" And he said, "No man, I've never done it and I'm not going to start. You can hand in your music too." And that was it. I was shocked. I thought he liked me.' Per diems were absolutely standard in the music business. Once again we glimpse the hard-nosed capitalist lurking in Zappa's first generation-immigrant mentality.

The new line-up consisted of Jean-Luc Ponty on violin; George Duke on keyboards and vocals; Ian Underwood on alto sax; Bruce Fowler on trombone; Ruth Underwood on percussion; Tom Fowler on bass; and Ralph Humphrey on drums. The European tour was exhausting, with concerts in Sweden, Finland, Norway, Germany, France, Italy, Switzerland, Belgium, Holland and Britain where they played Liverpool and Birmingham as well as Empire Pool, Wembley in London on 14 September. Zappa was writing all the time they were on the road.

It was a largely instrumental set, with Frank conducting and very little in the way of humour or audience participation. Fans who expected to see something along the lines of the Flo and Eddie show were disappointed and even Zappa found the tour rather dull: 'This was not a theatre-type group. I would say that that was a pretty solemn assemblage of musicians, right there. It was my experience on that tour that in spite of everybody being a good musician and they all had super ability to do all those fantastic things they were, uh . . . boring. In fact I was amazed they could even relate to each other, they were so boring. When you have a group that gets on a bus and plays chess; I mean when there were three separate chess tournaments going on inside the band in places where you should be out going after women, and being crazy? That's not exactly what I had in mind. But it's hard to find musicians who are really skilled when they're also crazy.'

This was the essential dichotomy of Frank's groups: he wanted skilled musicians, but he wanted them to behave like a teenage rock 'n' roll band so that he could have more vicarious experiences to write about; but his music was not hard, driving rock (there were too many time changes), so he was never going to get any really hard rockers. More to the point, he asked his musicians not to use drugs, which ruled out many promising applicants for the line-up. The fact that most of them did anyway cannot have escaped his notice; though he usually stayed in a more luxurious hotel than the band and he was extremely ignorant about drugs, so perhaps they were able to hide it from him.

When he was not on the road or in the studio Frank was in the office. By September 1973 DiscReet was in business: Zappa, Cohen and their business partner Zach Glickman had a new deal with Warners, who had world distribution for the label. Their first two releases were Tim Buckley's *Sefronia*, which went nowhere, and the Mothers' *Over-Nite Sensation*. Controversial songs like 'Dinah-Moe Humm' helped propel the album to Number 32 in the *Billboard* charts. Zappa had his first gold album, which only confirmed his view that you can never dumb down enough to satisfy the American public.

He appeared to use DiscReet simply as a vehicle to release records and to produce an income stream; all other aspects of the company were in the hands of Cohen and his partners. It is hard to imagine Zappa signing any of the acts that Herb now loaded the label with: Christopher Bond; Brenda Patterson, formerly with Black Oak Arkansas; Growl; the Whiz Kids; Denis Bryant; Kathy Dalton, who had some success with 'Boogie Bands and One Night Stands'; and Ted Nugent and the Amboy Dukes, who did two albums with DiscReet before going on to make a fortune for Epic.

After the success of *Over-Nite Sensation*, Frank moved quickly to release a follow up – taken from the same series of recording sessions – called *Apostrophe (')*. He wanted a January release, but was persuaded to wait until a proper advertising campaign could be mounted. *Over-Nite Sensation* was a chart hit, but a vinyl shortage prevented it selling as well as it might have done. Warners put extra effort into promoting *Apostrophe (')* and when it was released in April it entered the *Cashbox* Top 20 at Number 18.

Apostrophe (') was promoted in 30-second TV adverts designed by Zappa and Cal Schenkel, featuring a frenzied DJ shouting over an animated video skit. Zappa: 'We tried to place them in conjunction with monster movies, because with our material that's our audience.' The comedy track 'Don't Eat the Yellow Snow' was edited down and remixed for a single which reached Number 86 and helped push the album into the Top 10, Zappa's second gold album. The combination of dumbed-down humour with extremely sophisticated playing meant that the music was often overlooked.

Jean-Luc Ponty left before the winter 1973 tour, citing musical differences. Ponty: 'It was a very interesting experience at the beginning, because Zappa took out all the very complex instrumental music that he had stashed in his desk for a long time, since it was too sophisticated for the previous members of the Mothers. He had written music that was very influenced by Stravinsky, so he wanted to put together a group of excellent instrumentalists. But the public lost interest quickly, and he had to go back to satire and more commercial rock. That wasn't what I wanted to do, so I left after only seven months. He didn't take it well at all and we parted on very bad terms.' Ponty, who regarded himself as a jazz violinist, was not interested in playing songs like 'Montana' and said so. Frank took it as an insult to his music, which he refused to admit had become more commercial even if it was still hard to play.

He went on the road with a 'Tenth Anniversary of the Mothers' tour for which the band had to learn all the old songs. But numbers like 'Wowie Zowie' and 'Let's Make The Water Turn Black' just didn't sound right played by anyone other than the original Mothers line-up, and Don Preston was the only member of the old group to rejoin for the tour. In fact, the Mothers had gone through several more changes.

The touring group at the end of 1973 – the one on the *Roxy & Elsewhere* live album – consisted of Napoleon Murphy Brock on tenor sax and vocals; George Duke on keyboards and vocals; Bruce Fowler on trombone; Ruth Underwood on percussion; Tom Fowler on bass; Ralph Humphrey and Chester Thompson on drums. Jeff Simmons had joined (again) to assist Zappa on guitar and vocals and Don Preston was back on keyboards.

Ian Underwood had left, but Ruth stayed on. Her conservatory background meant that she played with extreme accuracy, allowing Zappa to attempt pieces of formidable complexity. However, she was the only member of the group who would not take solos, something which for most rock musicians is the sole purpose of being on stage. This led to Zappa using her in a different manner, almost playing her as an instrument. In the *Musician* magazine tribute to Zappa after his death Ruth wrote: 'I was ready to dedicate myself completely to Frank's music. He really knew what buttons to push, emotionally and musically. He was a remarkable referee. He knew how to synthesize people's personalities and talents. That's a very rare gift. He wasn't just a conductor standing there waving his arms; he was playing us as people! I became a perfectionist.'

The 21-city, tenth-anniversary tour ended just in time for Zappa to be back in LA for the birth of his second son on 15 May 1974. Ahmet Emuukha Rodan Zappa had a difficult birth and was in intensive care for the first days of his life. His names came variously from Ahmet Ertegun, head of Atlantic Records, which Zappa and Gail had used as the name of an imaginary servant. Gail: 'We'd snap our fingers and say, "Ahmet? Dishes. Coffee please."' Emuukha was the orchestra from *Lumpy Gravy*; and Rodan, the name of a popular Japanese movie monster from 1957.

Frank's father did not live to see his new grandson. He died of a heart attack on 7 April 1973. Frank heard the news after doing a show at the Circle Star Theater in Phoenix, Arizona. His parents were living in Valley Village, between North Hollywood and Studio City, a short drive from Frank and Gail's house, though Frank saw little of them. He did occasionally invite them to concerts, sending a limo to pick them up. His mother objected to the obscenity and stopped going, but Candy Zappa reports going with her father and seeing the look of pride on his face at his son's success in this strange new world.

Zappa rarely mentioned his father, but though relations between them were cold, he held him in respect. They shared a number of traits and were both control freaks. Francis Zappa clung to the patriarchal Italian family structure and it infuriated him when his son mocked his authority. Similarly, though Zappa brought up Moon Unit, Dweezil and Ahmet in an atmosphere of total freedom, the house still revolved around him and his needs. The one thing his children were afraid of was disturbing him.

15 On the Road

A pattern was now firmly established in which Zappa toured for about half the year and spent the remainder in his basement studio, working through the night writing, arranging and editing. Zappa: 'When I'm home, I have a work schedule that goes like this. If I'm not rehearsing I spend about 16, 18 hours a day down here [in the studio] writing music; typing, working on film . . . and if I'm not here, I usually do about 10, 14 hours in the studio, seven days a week, until rehearsal schedule starts. The only thing I would see as a worthwhile interruption would be 100 per cent concentration on a feature film.'

As usual, Frank had many different projects in various stages of development. One end of the enormous workroom was devoted to a film-editing suite and in the spring of 1974, after editing the *Roxy and Elsewhere* album, he began editing music to fit a short clay-model animation made by Seattle film-maker Bruce Bickford. It was not film music in the usual sense, because Zappa was using live Mothers recordings taken from concerts.

Zappa: 'I got the work print and edited that without sound. Then . . . I put the [Mothers] tracks on, and it worked. It's so unbelievable . . . when you think what it would take to actually score a film like that, and last night I put on this music, which was something constructed for completely different purposes, spontaneously at another location and another time, and I put them together and they worked perfectly.' It was another example of 'conceptual continuity', Frank's belief that everything he did – concerts, albums, even interviews – was a part of a larger creative whole.

The *Roxy and Elsewhere* double-album reached Number 27 in the charts. Zappa spent more than $30,000 filming the Roxy shows – over three nights, 9–12 December 1973 – but he didn't release the footage, even though it would have helped publicize the album. Riding on his chart success, he went back on the road on 28 June for a month-long tour of the US and Canada, followed by a month in Europe where they recorded two sets at the Kulttuuritalo in Helsinki, Finland. These were not released until 15 years later as a double CD, the second of the *You Can't Do That On Stage Anymore* series in October 1988.

On Halloween, 31 October 1974, after the second of two dates at the Felt Forum in New York, Zappa threw a party to celebrate the tenth anniversary of the Mothers of Invention. Labelle sang 'Happy Birthday' and guests included James Taylor, Carly Simon, Bianca Jagger and Dory Previn. Aside from the conspicuous absence of any members of the original Mothers of Invention, it was an enjoyable occasion. For Frank the most interesting guest was Louise Varèse, the widow of his hero. The year ended with a New Year's concert at the Long Beach Arena, but most of December was spent rehearsing a new expanded line-up at DiscReet for more recording in the new year.

Zappa's 1975 spring tour was cut short when after four years the case of Bizarre Productions versus the Royal Albert Hall finally opened in Number Seven Court of the Law Courts in the Strand in front of Mr Justice Mocatta on Monday, 14 April at 10.30 a.m. Among the dusty leather-bound law books and huge piles of paper, a stereo system had been set up and Judge Mocatta appeared startled when he was handed a copy of the *200 Motels* album.

'What's this?' he asked.

'It is a long-playing record, your honour,' explained the Queen's Counsel, setting the tone for much of the case. After the opening arguments, the judge listened to *200 Motels*, his head in his hands. He complained that he couldn't hear the words properly and after reading the lyrics he refused to allow the track 'Penis Dimension' to be played in court.

Frank took the stand on the second and third days. He wore a conservative brown suit, a white shirt and what appeared to be an old-school tie. He did his best to take part in the action he had initiated, though it was clearly almost beyond his comprehension. The proceedings went very slowly to allow the court stenographer to take them down in longhand. Zappa had a very soft voice and on occasion the judge had to ask him to speak up.

'Is a groupie a girl who is a member of a group?' asked the judge.

Zappa shook his head. 'No. She is a girl who likes the members of a rock-and-roll band.'

The counsel for the defence had brought along a large dictionary of American slang, but it did little to bridge the culture gap between Zappa and Judge Macotta.

'When I started this case,' the judge told Zappa, 'I knew very little about pop and beat music. I knew it was to do with rhythm, banging, and an infectious atmosphere. I didn't know it was anything to do with sex or drugs.'

Zappa assured him that most pop music had some kind of sexual connotations.

The Albert Hall contract gave them approval of the type of material to be performed there. One of the arguments that Bizarre put forward was that if the hall management had told them in advance, Zappa would have been prepared to change the lyrics to satisfy Ms Herrod's objections, but he had not been consulted. In order to prove that he could have done this at short notice, Frank's counsel handed him the script of 200 Motels and, falling into Zappa-speak, asked him to 'render the lyrics suitable for a socially-retarded audience'. Frank scribbled away furiously, adapting anything that might appear offensive. In a slow, flat deadpan voice he read out one of the amended lines: 'The places she goes / Are filled with guys from Pudsey / Waiting for a chance / To buy her a sudsy.'

'Pudsey?' asked the judge.

Frank's counsel came to his aid. 'Pudsey, Yorkshire, m'lud. It's produced some fine cricketers, I believe.'

Zappa and Cohen should never have attempted such a case. It was the year of the *Oz* trial, when an underground magazine was prosecuted for depicting Rupert the Bear sporting a large penis drawn by Robert Crumb. It was the longest obscenity trial in British history and the three defendants were jailed, but freed on appeal. Britain had much tougher obscenity laws than the States and there was no way the court would find in favour of anyone writing obscene lyrics. The court found the Royal Albert Hall in breach of contract, but did not award Bizarre the £8,000 damages they claimed or award any costs. Bizarre's legal fees came to £20,000. Zappa's opinion of Britain, already tarnished after the Rainbow Theatre attack, sank to an all-time low. However, the case did provide him with enough material for a whole chapter of his autobiography.

While in London, Zappa gave interviews from his suite at the Dorchester to promote his forthcoming album *One Size Fits All*, which he described as having 'some story-type songs, but it's pretty much rock-and-roll oriented. You could actually dance to this record.' The album's release had been delayed for contractual reasons: he wanted to release it on Warners and not through DiscReet. Clearly problems were brewing, but he was careful to explain: 'Basically, DiscReet is a company that in the past has released my records and as far as me producing things for it is concerned, I've avoided it very carefully. I figured my time was better spent working on things for the Mothers, and my efforts on behalf of other artists, producing their records, are seldom appreciated.'

One Size Fits All was released in June 1975 and included some of Zappa's more lasting songs: 'Inca Roads' was recorded at a KCET-TV special at Culver City Studios in LA, with a guitar solo dropped in from the 7 August show in Helsinki; he liked the instrumental 'Sofa No 1' so much he included it on five other albums, while 'Sofa No 2' appeared on six. These are beautiful pieces which account for Zappa's high standing among other musicians. *One Size Fits All* was well received, reaching Number 26 in the charts, and featured two interesting guests: Johnny

'Guitar' Watson, who played on two tracks and Captain Beefheart playing harmonica under the name of Bloodshot Rollin' Red.

Don and Frank had made up. Only a year before Zappa had told a journalist: 'Captain Beefheart is an asshole. We went to high school together, and back then Don van Vliet was a pretty good guy. I gave him his start in music, but I never see him anymore.' When asked why he allowed him to guest on *Hot Rats*, Frank said: 'That was before he turned into an asshole. He's not creative anymore.' Now he had hired him as a Mother and they had already played a couple of dates, beginning at Claremont College. Zappa: 'He's happy. It's fantastic! It's probably the best way for him to perform, because he's really not a bandleader. He doesn't have the business sense or the self-discipline to keep a band going and this really gives him an opportunity to cavort. This is a different dimension of responsibility for him, too. Now he has to discipline himself in order to remember lyrics and perform things consistently, so that the band can have cues to relate to.'

After giving his testimony at the lawcourts, Frank flew to the States and within hours was back on stage with the Mothers to continue their six-week spring tour. Chester Thompson was no longer in the group, which now consisted of Bruce Fowler on trumpet; Napoleon Murphy Brock on saxophone and vocals; Terry Bozio on drums; Tom Fowler on bass; George Duke on keyboards; Captain Beefheart on harmonica and vocals and Denny Walley on guitar and vocals. Walley used to live next door to Frank in Lancaster. Zappa: 'He was about ten years old. Now he's all grown up and plays slide guitar real good. So him, me, and Captain Beef' sit around and have some great discussions. It's nice to have some people in the band who are not only disinterested in chess, but who share a common interest in other forms of recreation.' Frank had still not got over the Petit Wazoo tour.

Zappa: 'There really has never been any animosity on my part. He asked for help. Any idea of a feud between us is quite pointless.' Frank still believed very much in Don's abilities: 'The way he relates to language is unique. The way in which he brings my text to life. Of course he has problems. His memory causes him trouble. He won't be separated from his sheets of paper that have his words written on.

He clings to them for dear life. He also has a literacy problem. He can hardly read. He also has trouble staying on a beat. Captain Beefheart has no natural rhythm. He does have this thing inside him. It's dynamic and he wants to express it. In a voice like Howlin' Wolf.' On the last dates of the tour, 20–21 May at the Armadillo World Headquarters in Austin, Texas, the album *Bongo Fury* was recorded using the Record Plant remote. Released in October 1975, it included two songs written by Vliet – 'Sam With The Showing Scalp Flat Top' and 'Man With The Woman Head' – a rare honour and an indication of Zappa's respect for his old friend.

Zappa and Beefheart got into some very esoteric collaboration while on tour, resulting in such songs as 'Debra Kadabra', which opens *Bongo Fury* and is a reference to an ill-timed trumpet line in Chano Urueta's 1961 Mexican sci-fi movie *The Brainiac*. Zappa: 'Oh God, it's one of the worst movies ever made; not only is the monster cheap, he's got a rubber mask that you can see over the collar of the guy's jacket and rubber gloves that don't quite match up with the sleeves of his sport coat. When the monster appears there's this trumpet lick that isn't scary. It's not even out of tune, it's just exactly the wrong thing to put there, it doesn't scare you . . . That's what that song is about and when you hear in the background DA-DA-DA-DA-DAHH, that's making fun of that stupid trumpet line that's in that movie . . . When he's saying "Make me grow Brainiac fingers", that's what he's referring to, because Vliet and I have both seen that movie and it's so fucking stupid.'

'Debra Kadabra' also refers to an unfortunate incident from their high-school days when Vliet had an allergic reaction to the Avon cologne his mother used to sell. It also has a shoe reference: Vliet was very choosy about his shoes and the GTOs even wrote a song about them. The album sleeve shows him wearing a pair of sandals, while Zappa wears resolutely high-shine brown shoes (though on tour he sometimes affected a pair of shoes colourfully painted by Karl Franzoni who was now the Commissioner of Parks and Recreation in Santa Rosa, California).

Zappa came in for criticism by including a song called 'Poofter's Froth Wyoming Plans Ahead', about the forthcoming 200th birthday of the United States and the frenzy of commercial excitement it was causing. He had no idea that 'poofter' was English slang for homosexual and had borrowed the word from Howard Parker, the English roadie who gave him the Strat that Hendrix burned at the Miami Pop Festival.

Predictably, by the end of the tour Zappa and Don had fallen out. Don sat on stage drawing when he was not singing, as if he was not really a part of the group; he could not learn the words and read them from pieces of paper that he kept in his ever-present carrier bags. In short, Beefheart was not destined to be a long-serving member of the Mothers. Jimmy Carl Black, who sat in with the band in El Paso, recalled: 'By the time Frank Zappa and Don Van Vliet got to El Paso they weren't even speaking to each other anymore. Seems that Don Van Vliet was drawing too many pictures of Frank in his drawing book and Frank didn't like it. I saw some of the pictures and I thought they were pretty funny. Frank didn't. That is where Beefheart hired me to join the Magic Band, and I did.'

In September 1975 Frank returned to the other end of his musical spectrum. Instead of the long melodic guitar solos of the Bongo Fury tour, he played two nights at Royce Hall, UCLA, with a 37-piece symphony orchestra and the Mothers' rhythm section. Billed as Frank Zappa with the Abnuceals Emuukha Electric Symphony Orchestra conducted by Michael Zearott, the evening included the première performances of 'Pedro's Dowry' and 'Bogus Pomp', as well as other 'unusual items for guitar and orchestra'. A recording of these pieces was released in May 1979 as *Orchestral Favorites* (and later in the *Läther* box set). Unlike Zappa's experience with Zubin Mehta, the orchestra had been specially put together for the event and was really engaged with the music. After they played 'Pedro's Dowry' for the first time, the orchestra broke into spontaneous applause.

The viola soloist Pamela Goldsmith described how she was hired by the cello player Jerry Kessler to join an amplified string quartet to play with Zappa. She was trained in eighteenth-century performance practice, so this was the first (and only) time she had used a pick-up and an amp. She had a combination volume control and wah-wah pedal and had to play barefoot so that she could feel the pedal. She used it to try and get vibrato during rehearsals and Frank came running over yelling, 'That's it! You have to use that!' For the performance, he placed the string quartet right at the front edge of the stage, all dressed in formal eveningwear – except for Pamela's bare feet.

She told Bill Lantz: 'He definitely wrote for individual players, writing more and more difficult passages until you would hit your "wall". I remember finally saying to him, "Frank, I can't play that any faster." Then he said "Okay" and that was that. Everyone was apparently relieved that I was not intimidated by him (only by the electronics) . . . The music was highly complex and difficult, but challenging and fun to play. Michael Zearott conducted – the meter changes were so difficult and frequent – quite wonderfully as I recall. In fact everyone was in top form, rising to the occasion of this incredible collection of players.'

The concert was held on 17 and 18 September before an audience of 1,500 people each night. The second performance was recorded but not used, though there was a recording session, closed to the public, earlier in the day. The pieces were all recorded again on the 19th, this time without an audience. The eventual album cost Zappa $120,000, though with tickets at $5.50 and $6.50, he did not see much in the way of a return at the box office. However, it was clearly a remarkable event for him and the players.

Legal issues took up more of Frank's time in the summer of 1975 when he and Herb sued MGM for $2 million for withholding royalties on the five Mothers of Invention compilations they had released (plus eleven more unauthorized ones in foreign territories).

On 27 September the last line-up to be called the Mothers of Invention took to the road, playing two shows in Ljubljana, Yugoslavia, in the middle of a gruelling 49-city tour of the States and Canada, which included the now obligatory Halloween concert in New York and ended with a New Year's concert at the Forum in LA with Captain Beefheart and Dr John. After ten days' rest, they then set off on a 16-country tour of Australia, Japan and Europe that would last until 17 March 1976. The

Mothers of Invention played their last gig in Bilbao, Spain. Frank did not want to drop the name, but in May, shortly after the tour, he fired Herb Cohen, who had been with the group virtually since their beginning, claiming that Cohen and Mut, his lawyer brother, were stealing money from DiscReet. The subsequent lawsuit meant Zappa couldn't use the Mothers of Invention as a name.

In October 1976 MGM made an out of court settlement in which Zappa received $100,000 and ownership of all his master tapes. MGM would receive a 3 per cent royalty on any future use of the tapes. Unfortunately, by the time the settlement was reached, Zappa was engaged in his lawsuit with Cohen, so the money was frozen until that case was settled. He hired Bennett Glotzer as his new manager.

Trouble had been brewing at DiscReet for some time. It was Cohen's decision to sign Kathy Dalton and Growl that prompted Zappa to negotiate a separate recording contact with Warners. He felt he had lost control of DiscReet and did not agree with Cohen's signings. All of his assets were frozen and he could not rescue his film and tape archives from the DiscReet warehouse until the case was finally resolved in 1982.

Another bone of contention concerned Captain Beefheart's new album *Bat Chain Puller*, which Zappa described as being 'his best album since *Trout Mask Replica*'. It was produced by Don himself and by Kerry McNab, the remix engineer on *One Size Fits All*. Zappa: 'One of the reasons I argued with Herbie was because he used my royalty cheques to pay for the production costs of Beefheart's album when I was away on tour.'

Beefheart was signed to Virgin Records in England, who wanted to release the album, but Herb wanted Virgin's delivery advance to be paid to him, whereas Frank thought he should get it as he had paid for the production. Though he loved *Bat Chain Puller*, Zappa refused to send Virgin the master tapes. 'I can't do anything until this Herbie thing is cleared up,' he said. 'Herbie is holding out for a settlement.' Zappa was convinced that he and Virgin would be sued by Cohen if they tried to release the album before the case was decided. However, when Beefheart was recording his final album, *Ice Cream For Crow*, in 1982 – after the Cohen case had been settled – Frank refused Don's request to let him use half of the tracks from *Bat Chain Puller* on that album. To Beefheart this was proof that Zappa cared nothing for art and was only interested in money and power; was in fact behaving just like the big record companies that he had always railed against. *Bat Chain Puller* had still not been released when Zappa died.

Many of the winter tour concerts were taped and used as the basis for Zappa's next album: a method he was to adopt throughout his career. The bands were so well rehearsed they could play the songs flawlessly and the added excitement of a live venue gave them an extra edge that studio recordings often lack. Using live basic tracks, Zappa then over-dubbed extra material in the studio or dropped in particularly good solos from other performances.

By spending so much time on the road (accompanied everywhere by John Smothers, his huge bodyguard), Zappa's world-view narrowed. After the adrenaline rush of being on stage he looked for the usual backstage and hotel diversions, but most groupies were scared of him, intimidated by Smothers, put off by his anti-drug stance, and regarded him, at 35, as rather old. He hung out more with the band and shared their interest in pornography.

When he did get groupies, they often had rather extreme interests. One rumour that dogged Zappa all of his life was that in a gross-out competition he had eaten shit on-stage. This calumny was inadvertantly spread by Ed Sanders of the Fugs, who told several groupies Zappa was into coprophilia. It was completely untrue, but news spread fast in the groupie community and Zappa was sometimes confronted by strange girls who had saved their faeces for him in a bag, which they brought along to the concert. The Mothers seemed to attract such girls, like the masochistic groupie in 'Carolina Hard Core Ecstasy'. The weirdness of it all certainly fascinated Zappa and was used by him as the basis of many of his songs. (Not all of his road songs were about weirdness. 'Find Her Finer' on *Zoot Allures* seems to be a straightforward explication of touring pick-up technique, possibly based on experience.)

The road remained Zappa's main source of material. 'Ms Pinky' is a good example. Zappa had a fan in Finland called Eric who would appear backstage with a shopping bag full of gifts. Zappa: 'One time he showed up with presents; candy and his favourite Finnish pornographic magazine, a publication called *Kalle*. It had the worst pictures you've ever seen. There's a problem with lithography when you don't get your colour balance right. Things either go too red or too blue. Well, split pink is one thing, but split pink that looks infected is another. And when the people are homely . . .' *Kalle* had ads for what Zappa called 'lonely-person devices'. There was one for Pinky, a life-size plastic head with its mouth wide open, eyes shut and a short haircut. Zappa: 'I thought: "Hmmmm, anyone who's gonna buy a plastic head just to give himself a gum job is Right Out There."' When they reached Amsterdam Zappa sent Smothers to the red-light district to buy one to use on-stage. Zappa was delighted: 'It was even worse than I had imagined.' Ms Pinky's throat was made of sponge rubber and had a vibrator in it with a battery pack and a two-speed motor. A plastic bulb stuck out from her neck, making the throat contract when it was squeezed. In Zappa eyes it was perfect subject matter for a song.

The strangest and most out-of-character piece on *Zoot Allures* was 'The Torture Never Stops', a more or less straight narrative description of a Hollywood/Gothic dungeon, complete with screams. Bruce Bickford was making clay models of castles with dungeons for his animated films and this track may have originally been designed to go with them. Though men were more likely to find themselves in a medieval dungeon, this was more of a basement in the Hollywood Hills, so Zappa used women's screams, provided by Gail and a friend. This gave the piece an uncomfortable edge – were they screams of sexual ecstasy or pain, or both?

The graphic moans and groans were a clear reference to the sex tape that put him in jail, just as the dungeon itself might have been tank 'C' of the San Bernardino jail in 'San Ber'dino' on *One Size Fits All*:

44 men in tank 'C' with only one shower. It was a permanent hurt for which he was forever seeking retribution.

One of Zappa's finest works appeared on *Zoot Allures*: he liked 'Black Napkins' so much it can be found on six other releases. The composition had been around for a year or more, but he finally named it 'Black Napkins' in 1975 at a Thanksgiving dinner in Milwaukee. Zappa told Susan Shapiro: 'Sliced turkey roll with the fucking preservatives just gleaming off of it, and this beat-up cranberry material. The final stroke to this ridiculous dinner was the black napkins, sitting next to the dishes. That really said the most about the dinner.'

Normally Frank used graphics on his album sleeves, but *Zoot Allures* has a picture of his current line-up (even though, with the exception of Terry Bozzio, they didn't play on the record – each track on the album had a different line-up). Perhaps Zappa wanted to show off his youthful new band: he looks old enough to be their father. Frank stands in the centre of Gary Heery's picture, an improbably large bulge in his tight flares supporting his claim not to own any underwear.

Zoot Allures, originally titled *Night of the Iron Sausage*, but changed for sound commercial reasons, came out on 29 October 1976. It sold more than 110,000 in the first week, which was good business considering how little promotion Warners gave it. The album had been delayed by what Zappa called 'paper-shuffling, pin-head diplomacy, executive dancing, fear of high places, Cro-Magnon negligence, and such,' on the part of Mo Ostin, head of Warners' record division.

One problem was that Frank couldn't get his 30ips master-tape of *Zoot Allures* from the Record Plant. Even though he was chairman of the board of DiscReet and president of the company, they wouldn't release the tapes unless Warners indemnified the studio against any legal action that Herb Cohen might take against them. Warners agreed, but only if Frank indemnified them. Zappa: 'Can you believe it? An individual artist having to indemnify one of the biggest record companies in the world so that they can bring his record out?' So Frank mastered the album from his own 15ips safety copy. He always took home safety copies after each recording session. 'When I go home after

20 hours in the studio,' he said, 'what am I gonna listen to? Bob Dylan records?'

That August, to the considerable surprise of many of his fans, *Good Singin' Good Playin'*, a Zappa-produced album by hard rockers Grand Funk Railroad, was released. The band had wanted to get Zappa to produce an album for them for several years, but their management thought the idea too weird, so it was not until 1975 that they put the idea to him. Frank liked them. Grand Funk drummer Don Brewer told *Crawdaddy* magazine: 'His whole viewpoint on what rock 'n roll is all about is basically the same as ours. You go in and do exactly what you do live, without overproduction. Keep it as simple as possible and really bring the balls out of this thing. He was totally different from what we expected. Frank Zappa's basic image to the world is that someplace in the 1960s he was doing so much acid that he freaked out. But he's a very straight cat and he's not ego-ed out.'

Zappa: 'All I did was in a documentary way make a record which tells you exactly what they really sound like. For the first time on record, you can hear Grand Funk Railroad . . . and they're fantastic, fantastic with an F three times taller than you! . . . They're great and I like them as people.' Sadly, on the first day of overdubs the band split up, even though Zappa was up until 4 a.m., trying to persuade them to stay together. *Good Singin' Good Playin'* was their last and worst-selling album.

Frank offered Don Brewer a job with his band, but after jamming with them at Cobo Hall in Detroit and giving the idea careful consideration, he decided not to. It is hard to see how anyone could have shared the drummer's seat with Terry Bozzio, unless Zappa was thinking of having someone to keep the beat, while Bozzio improvised all over the time pattern. Zappa: 'In Bozzio's case the drum is hardly ever the instrument that keeps the beat. Since that guy discovered lipstick it's tap your foot or die. Now I love Bozzio, he's one of the most brilliant drummers I've ever worked with but, I'm sorry, sometimes he goes nuts . . . If you don't calculate with Bozzio what the time is before you start playing, you're up shit creek . . . He gets very passionate and carried away while he's playing.'

Zappa enjoyed heavy metal and it was around this time that he hung out with Ozzy Osbourne and Black Sabbath. It culminated in Zappa compèring their 6 December show at Madison Square Garden. He had always had a certain fondness for playing at very high volume in echoing hockey rinks – you could almost see the air bending as the speakers pumped out the sound. While attending his grandmother's funeral when he was a child he had been struck by the way the flames of the candles moved and swayed in response to movements in the air of the church. He often referred to his own guitar solos as 'air sculptures', solid structures existing in space as well as time, slicing and carving the air.

In September 1976 Zappa hit the road again, touring under his own name with one of the smallest line-ups ever: Ray White on guitar and vocals; Eddie Jobson on keyboards and violin; Patrick O'Hearn on bass; Terry Bozzio on drums and vocals and with Bianca Thornton on keyboards and vocals – though she played only a few dates before quitting; she couldn't stand the way Zappa's audience kept calling for her to undress. No matter how Zappa tried to defend his sexist lyrics, his audience took them at face value.

Frank could not afford a bigger line-up – in fact, he warned them they might not get paid. The musicians said they would stay on the road until their savings ran out. The tour lasted six months (September 1976 to February 1977), with two months in the States and a short break in December, then, after a few West Coast dates, to Hawaii, New Zealand, Australia, Japan and Europe. Touring was the only way Zappa could make money – all his other assets were frozen by the lawsuit with Herb Cohen.

Warners gave minimal tour support, not wanting to get entangled in the breakup of DiscReet or to be seen as taking sides between Herb and Frank. Their press release for the tour included an interview (edited by Zappa) in which Frank described his new music as 'Bionic Funk'. Discussing the new line-up he said: 'All of them auditioned for membership in open competition with many other fine singers and players. I find this to be the best way to select members for the group.'

He described 21-year-old Eddie Jobson as 'bringing to the group a sort of damp English charm, smothered in rosy-cheeked appeal.' Jobson was still technically a member of Roxy Music, but the band had stopped touring. He met Zappa when Roxy Music supported the Mothers in Milwaukee, where Jobson had briefly jammed with Frank on-stage. Zappa contacted him later and invited him to sit in for a week or so of Canadian dates. Jobson: 'I went round with him for a week and just played. In the sound checks and in the dressing rooms we'd just set up some amps and just play and learn some of his things . . . He'd sort of say maybe five minutes before he was due on-stage, "It'd be nice if you played along tonight." You know, there's ten thousand people out there and he tells you like five minutes before and you just have to go on-stage and jam. He goes into a riff that you've never heard before in your life and just points at you, and you have to do a solo. And you just have to solo on it for five minutes! And then he told me to go on keyboards again at one point and he did that number again with the finger and I had to do a synthesiser solo on a synthesiser I'd never seen before. And that's his way of checking you out.

'That's his strength, he stretches his musicians beyond their capabilities all the time. And then when it comes to a performance he'll just relax it slightly to a point where people can actually play what he wants . . . Such outrageous stuff, so technical, so difficult, and you've got to remember it all as well. You've got to learn it fast because Frank gets impatient if you don't.'

The smaller line-up gave Frank more opportunities to play solos. Zappa: 'With a larger group you have to play less – there are a lot of people waiting in line to play solos. That's one of the reasons I've got a smaller group now, because I happen to like to play solos, and I happen to think I'm in a specialized category from the stuff I play, and I don't think there's any reason why I should have to wait in line [laughs]. I have some stuff to say, and I'm going to get out there and do it.'

Though the group was small, Frank still travelled with a relatively large road crew, including a sound mixer, a monitor mixer, a drum roadie, a guitar technician (for a time he had Klaus Wiederman who used to work for Stockhausen), a lighting designer and operator plus his assistant, two truck drivers, a keyboard tuner and maintenance man, a power distribution man, Larry the roadie and John Smothers the bodyguard.

The Halloween concerts at the Felt Forum were a great success; this year's surprise came in the second set when Smothers sang 'Muffin Man'. Frank would say a verse and Smothers would sing it. Frank's brother Bob was in the audience with his wife and several friends, and when someone threw a bra on-stage, Frank threw it at Bob who had to duck to avoid it. Later, Bob's wife took some home-made cookies backstage.

Zappa's annual Halloween concerts in New York were one of the highlights of his year and always well received by the Press. When he discovered Warners had bought only 15 tickets for journalists, Frank hung a banner across the backdrop reading: WARNERS SUCKS! Zappa: 'They say I owe them four more albums. I'm trying to decide whether or not I'll hand them four more right after this tour, 'cause I got 'em, I got more than four. And they know that. If Warners keeps fucking around like this they're gonna get a little present when I get home. One of the tapes is an orchestra album . . . [but] if I do that, they'll definitely shit all over this record. I'm giving Warners a fair chance, I'm saying: "Perform on this album. This is my first release for Warners, not DiscReet; it's not subsidiary, it's not a little independent record company." It's "Hey, I'm on your mainline label, now what are ya gonna do about it?" So far they've done diddly shit.'

Threatening Warners with an orchestral album rather than presenting it as worth releasing was hardly the best way to get the company behind him; however, it shows that *Orchestral Favourites* already existed at this point, an important fact in the convoluted story of the release of the four-album box set *Läther*, most of which had not yet been recorded.

16 Dr Zurkon's Secret Lab in Happy Valley

Zappa had become accustomed to using live tracks as the basis for most of his albums, often just keeping the rhythm section – with its live-performance feel – and overdubbing new instruments or solos, or dropping in solos from other concerts. But now his tape archives were frozen. Though he had several thousand tapes at home, they were mostly from a much earlier period.

His contract with Warners expired in the summer of 1977 and though he still owed them four albums, he began looking for a new label. With his tapes, his films and his royalties frozen – including the settlement money from MGM – Frank was forced to rely on touring for an income. He was not short of money (Gail still drove a Rolls-Royce), but he could not afford weeks of studio time without a recording contract.

In July 1977 Frank's case against Herb Cohen reached the Superior Court. Frank asked for DiscReet to be dissolved on the grounds that Herb mishandled the firm and appropriated assets. He told the court that Cohen and his brother, the attorney Martin 'Mut' Cohen, misled him in the three-way agreement in which Zappa recorded for DiscReet. Zappa's deal was for him to get 12 per cent of the retail price royalty paid by Warners, of which 9 per cent of 90 per cent of the money was paid to him, the remainder reverting to DiscReet, of which he owned 50 per cent.

When Frank and Herb began having problems – presumably over Beefheart's *Bat Chain Puller* – and got into litigation, Frank claimed that Herb paid his lawyers $10,000 from DiscReet's assets to make a case against him. Frank also maintained that DiscReet bookkeeper Dolores Barnett was given $2,500 to pay personal bills without his approval and that Herb used a secretary at DiscReet for his own personal business. Frank asked for the corporation to be dissolved and a receiver appointed to salvage as much money from it as possible.

In March 1977, on his return from the European leg of his tour, Zappa gave Warners four albums: *Studio Tan*; *Hot Rats III*; *Zappa's Orchestral Favorites* and a double-album, then called *Live In New York*. He no longer owed them any more 'product' (a double-album counted as one). The contract stipulated immediate payment by Warners of $60,000 per album, a total of $240,000.

Live In New York was the first release and for this Frank provided the entire package, complete with sleeve notes written by himself, a cover photograph of snow-bound Tenth Avenue taken by six-year old Dweezel, and 17 stage shots by Gail – a real family effort. He also changed the album's name to *Zappa In New York*. It was to be released on DiscReet on 1 July. The sleeve notes and package design for the other three albums would follow nearer their release date.

Zappa: 'Because I'm a nice person, pursuant to my contract, I delivered the four units that I owed them. I walked in and gave them the tapes and the contract says that as soon as I hand in the tapes, they hand me the money, which was somewhat crucial since I had paid for the tapes out of my own pocket – studio expenses I'd already fronted. I expected reimbursement for the four completed albums. They said, "Give us ten days to listen to this to make sure that it's not just Frank and a guitar," even though the contract didn't say they had ten days. They didn't hand me the check, what am I going to do? Ten days are up; no check. Thirty days; no check. Sixty days, no check. Lawsuit time!'

Frank sued Warners for breach of contract. They had not paid for any of the albums – even *Zappa In New York*, which was on their release schedule – so Frank assumed the copyright reverted to him. He had found two possible labels. Capitol (the US branch of EMI) was a strong contender, but it turned out they pressed for Warners and were unlikely to jeopardize their relationship with such a major client. The other was Mercury-Phonogram, who wanted to start a new label with Zappa.

Frank took the two and a half hours of 'product' and resequenced it as a four-album box set called *Leather* (later retitled *Läther*). He cut and added some things, dividing the denser orchestral pieces up over the eight sides. A four-album box set was then unknown in the rock 'n' roll world. George Harrison had a best-selling triple-album *All Things Must Pass* in November 1970, but the Beatles had recently split and it also included a hit single, 'My Sweet Lord'. However, Mercury-Phonogram were very keen to do business with Zappa and this was the price they had to pay to get him on board.

They planned to launch *Läther* on Halloween, 31 October 1977, as the first release of Frank's new Zappa label. Three hundred box sets were manufactured before Warners put a stop to it, not on the grounds of breach of contract, but because *Läther* had material in common with *Zappa In New York*. Clearly Zappa thought Warners had no intention of releasing *Zappa In New York* or he would not have used those tracks on *Läther*.

So the *Läther* project fell through, but then Warners began to object to material on *Zappa In New York*, an album they hadn't even paid for. They regarded passages on two tracks – the homo-erotic references to Angel guitarist Punky Meadows on 'Titties and Beer' and on 'Punky's Whips' – as libellous and refused to release the album unless changes were made. Frank began yet another lawsuit, as Warners did not have the right to tamper with the records he gave them. Zappa: 'They don't have the right to resequence it, censor it, edit it, rename it; I have complete control of the artwork.'

But Warners ignored his objections and unknown to Frank planned to release *Zappa In New York* in a censored form, editing 'Titties and Beer' and dropping 'Punky's Whips'. These delays meant the album did not appear until March 1978, nine months after the original release date. Warners were in such a hurry that the initial release used the wrong tape and the uncensored version went out to critics and some stores. When the censored version appeared with twelve-and-a-half minutes removed, Zappa was furious.

Läther was not released until after Frank's death, but high-quality bootlegs had been circulating among fans. One day in December 1977, an angry Zappa took the Mercury-Phonogram test pressings of *Läther* to the radio station KROQ-FM. Appearing on Jerry Kay's show, he gave listeners advance warning to set up their tape recorders, then played all two and a half hours of it. When *Läther* finally appeared in 1996, Gail's sleeve notes said: 'As originally conceived by Frank, *Läther* was always a 4-record box set. One more time for the world, *Läther* was always a 4-record box set.'

Läther probably *was* conceived as a four-record set, but its components – *Orchestral Favorites* in particular – existed separately before *Läther* was constructed. It was common practice for Frank to assemble and disassemble albums; he loved experimenting with the format. He was always planning double albums – such as the original concept for *Hot Rats* – as well as ten- or twelve-album box sets. It was entirely typical of him to come up with *Läther* if he thought someone – Capitol or Mercury – would release it.

All of this meant that for 17 months (including all of 1977) Zappa had no new albums. Instead he concentrated on his latest obsession: getting his music copied into proper musical notation. In June 1977 he hired David Ocker, a clarinettist who had studied composition and was interested in contemporary music. Ocker: 'Frank needed someone who could copy, edit and otherwise manipulate his difficult written music; which was laying in piles all around his studio the first day I met him.' Ocker thought it was a regular Hollywood job: to write out a score ready for a recording session the next day; instead he left the house with eight different projects and was to work with Zappa for the next seven years.

There were no new albums until *Zappa In New York* finally appeared in March 1978. Of all Zappa's records, it was probably the most vilified for its sexist and sexually explicit lyrics. It opens with 'Titties and Beer', a simple modern fable in which a biker sells his soul to the Devil for titties and beer. Compared with many of Zappa's songs it was stupid rather than offensive.

When Frank wore a bra on stage for 'Titties and Beer' and sat on a stuffed poodle's face, imitating a woman, the critic Susan Shapiro accused him of 'womb envy'. She felt insulted by 'Titties and Beer'. Zappa: 'That particular song was born to be a classic because it has everything in it that America loves, and that's beer and tits.' Shapiro told him that she didn't like either of those things and she represented 51 per cent of the population. Frank admitted that he didn't like beer either, but added: 'You should see the response to that song in Texas. It's stunning. Tits are amusing.'

Shapiro was not to be placated and wondered if he had any qualms about singing the song. This put Frank on the defensive: 'Look if you're gonna grow those things and go out and buy brassières to make 'em stick out even more you deserve what you get! . . . If you don't like 'em you can have 'em chopped off. There are some cases where people bind 'em down. If you wanna de-emphasise yourself go right ahead. But if you got 'em, you gotta appreciate that all those other people who got different plumbing view those appurtenances in a way other than you view 'em.'

When Shapiro objected that this sounded like something out of the fifties, Zappa replied: 'You think the fifties are dead? I think they never went away. Especially as far as tits go.' He remained utterly unreconstructed, stuck in a fifties time warp as far as women were concerned.

Two instrumentals follow 'Titties and Beer', including 'I Promise Not To Come In Your Mouth'. In Rob Reiner's rockumentary *This Is Spinal Tap* (1983), Nigel Tufnel is complimented on a beautiful Bach-like melody he has just played on the piano and asked what it is called. 'Well,' he says, 'this piece is called "Lick My Love Pump".' They might well have borrowed the joke from Zappa, who consistently gave offensive names to instrumentals that might otherwise have entered the classical music repertoire. 'I Promise Not To Come In Your Mouth' is a perfect example: a quiet, delicate melody that began life as 'Läther' is given an offensive title for no other reason than to offend.

It is a self-destructive trait that reveals a deep-seated insecurity. Zappa was also testing his audience: if they can get past the title and still appreciate the music, then perhaps Frank can trust their opinion. It was another of the barriers he set up between himself and the world. He was always the lonely kid in the unfamiliar schoolyard, testing people to see if they could be trusted. He often complained that his music was not played outside the rock world, but he purposely sabotaged his more classical work.

Warners cut 'Punky's Whips' from the album, fearing it was libellous. In addition to wearing a devil mask and bondage gear for 'Titties and Beer', the unfortunate Terry Bozzio also had to act out homo-erotic fantasies on this track which, to the surprise of the New York audience, was introduced by Don Pardo, the NBC announcer whose voice was instantly recognisable. He introduced the acts on NBC's new comedy programme *Saturday Night Live* and enjoyed himself so much performing 'I Am The Slime' with Zappa that he agreed to join them for their four-day stint at the Palladium. (Also on the *Saturday Night Live* show was John Belushi, who sang 'Purple Lagoon' with them.)

'Punky's Whips' concerned Bozzio's alleged attraction to Edwin 'Punky' Meadows, lead guitarist with Angel, a boy band discovered by Kiss. The infatuation was based on a picture of Punky pouting that Bozzio had found in a Japanese rock magazine. Punky found the song amusing and wrote to Bozzio saying how much he liked it, but this did not deter Warners.

The track that even Zappa's most ardent fans find hard to defend is 'The Illinois Enema Bandit'. (Interestingly, this track did not appear on Zappa's compilation *Have I Offended Somebody?*, perhaps because it was genuinely offensive, unlike most of the other tracks.) The song celebrates the true story of Michael Kenyon, who, in the course of committing armed robbery, would sometimes give his victims an enema. Zappa finds the whole idea of Kenyon tying up his terrified victims and sexually assaulting them terribly amusing and takes great delight in describing the 'pitiful screams' of 'college-educated women'.

All Zappa's deep-seated problems with women come out in this song. His limitations are revealed. Though based on fact, he rewrites the court case so that the victims clamour for Kenyon's release. The subtext is that all victims of sexual assault secretly love it. The humorous, celebratory tone of the song reveals someone threatened by female sexuality; the old Sicilian patriarch in Zappa hated it when educated women, often more intelligent than him, dismissed his Stone Age attitude.

Zappa would never understand the women's liberation movement; not only did it threaten his fundamental beliefs, but as with many other things, he wasn't even prepared to listen. Around this time he told journalist Tony Bacon: 'There is a new piece we're working on in the soundchecks at the moment, it's called "Lady", although I only have a first few words of it. It goes something like, "I've been looking for a woman I can treat like a dog / So I can call her Lady, Lady, Lady / Lift her leg." It's one of those sort of things that suits Bozzio's voice.'

Zappa first began to vilify his audiences at the Garrick Theatre. Though his prime consideration was to entertain and give value for the money (he was always aware of the commercial angle, regarding a performance as a commodity that the audience consumed), he also tried to educate them along the way. He lectured them on the evils of Warners or television evangelism, Richard Nixon and other topical subjects. Later in his career he set up voter registration booths at his concerts and got thousands of his fans to register.

Zappa always approached his audiences as an older, wiser patriarch: 'Uncle Frank' would set you straight. Though he was only a few years older than the members of the Rolling Stones, Led Zeppelin or the Who, he came from essentially the same generation. But he was more comfortable being 'Uncle Frank': keeping a superior distance from the audience and, most importantly, staying *in control*. In 1977 he introduced a concert in Louisville by telling the audience: 'So what we're gonna do now is sing a song with real easy-to-understand lyrics, real stupid chords, and a real simple beat. That way we can reach you people.' He felt that if he antagonized them enough, they might rebel against their manipulative bosses, teachers and parents or even the government. Sometimes he succeeded, creating life-long fans who finally found someone able to articulate their confused suspicions. This was Zappa at his radical best.

Zappa: 'Most people come to my concerts because they wanna see something; they wanna have something done to them. I had 3,000 people at the Berkeley Community Theater doing jumping jacks in 1968. I said, "OK, now you're gonna get up and exercise, you people look like you're too tired. C'mon, get up." I had 'em outta the seats. The house lights were on. I stopped the music. They kept on doin' it. Then I said, "OK, listen, this is what just happened. I told you to stand up and exercise and you exercised, is that right?" "Yeah, that's right!" "I tell you to do anything you'd do it, wouldn't you? That's the way the government operates. They tell you to do something and you do it. You're out there doin' jumping jacks, now isn't that stupid?" And all the while they're still jumping, they're waiting for the punchline. So we started playing again, the lights went down and the show resumed.' He felt he was doing them a favour: 'You're telling them the truth. How can they hate you for that? OK. I played a prank on them. Such pranks are pulled every day, and far worse. Forget politics. One of the most depressing pieces of manipulation I saw was the Sly Stone segment of the "Woodstock" film, that kind of bogus hysteria.'

But no audience ever seemed to satisfy Zappa. He looked down on them if they were too stoned and rowdy to appreciate the complexity of his music, but he also condemned English audiences because they sat still and listened instead of getting up and dancing (though a surprising number of the live recordings he released were made in England, where possibly he felt he had to put a little bit extra into his performances). In the end, however, Zappa could never respect his audiences – if he did, he might have to listen to their criticism.

This applied even more to critics, so he made a point of being a difficult interviewee (except for female interviewers, whom he often hoped to see again later) and never disguised his contempt for journalists. He even had an aphorism that he rolled out: 'Rock journalism is people who can't write, interviewing people who can't talk, for people who can't read.' He reserved his special fury for the British rock press, because they were irreverent and put funny headlines on his interviews and generally deflated his idea of his own importance. The *NME*, *Melody Maker*, *Sounds* school of journalism didn't exist in America. He had fallen out with *Rolling Stone* years before, but gave long interviews to professional journals such as *Guitar* and *International Musician*, where the discussion revolved safely around amplifiers and string gauges.

Thanks to Bob Dylan, the Beach Boys' *Pet Sounds*, the Beatles' *Sgt Pepper* and, of course, *Freak Out!*, rock 'n' roll was now regarded as an art form. By the end of the sixties, largely because of the social comment in his songs, Zappa was generally recognized as leading the avant-garde of rock. He was admired as a parodist and a sceptic, an ironical social critic who broke new ground in musical form and lyrical content. Then, about the time of *Roxy and Elsewhere*, the music critics detected a change of direction in favour of more simplistic lyrics and popular subject matter. They felt the music had been dumbed down for commercial reasons. Zappa disagreed. This was the root cause of much of his antipathy toward critics.

Zappa had put together yet another new band, this time for the US and Canadian tour that began on 8 September 1977 and ran until New Year's Eve. Terry Bozzio and Patrick O'Hearn were joined by Adrian Belew on guitar and vocals; Tommy Mars on keyboards and vocals; Peter Wolf on keyboards and Ed Mann on percussion and vocals. This was followed, as usual, by a winter European tour, starting in London on 24 January, after rehearsals at Sheraton movie studios. Sound-stage rehearsal space in LA cost $375 a day, which was especially irksome because Zappa owned a large, fully equipped rehearsal studio in LA that he couldn't use because of the lawsuit with Herb Cohen.

In September Warners released *Studio Tan*. Because he was suing them for the delivery money, Frank had not provided any sleeve notes or artwork. Warners got comic artist Gary Panter to design a sleeve, but the album lacked the usual line-up details and notes. It included a 20-minute ballet in the tradition of *Billy the Mountain* called 'The Adventures Of Greggery Peccary', which became a firm favourite among Zappa's new generation of admirers, though older Mothers fans dismissed it as yet more trivial nonsense.

Studio Tan also included an extended instrumental, 'Revised Music For Guitar And Low-Budget Orchestra'. It is an extraordinary tour de force and a good example of the complexity of Zappa's music. He played his solo on an Ovation gut-stringed acoustic with pick-ups plugged straight into the board. Bruce Fowler then carefully transcribed the solo and doubled it by overdubbing four trombones in harmony, including all the bent notes, to give an effect which is clearly a guitar, but with a brassy sound. Both this and the opening track featured the Royce Hall, UCLA Abnuceals Emuukha Electric Orchestra from 19 September 1975.

Warners followed *Studio Tan* with *Sleep Dirt* in January 1979. Zappa was justifiably aggrieved: 'This time they changed the name of the album. It was originally called *Hot Rats III* . . . They haven't paid me any royalties on the last three albums, they have all these tapes and they've released them, they have one more set of tapes to release, and they don't have publishing rights to any of the songs on it, that's why there's no information on there. They don't even have the master tones for the tapes. All these things have been mastered without the reference tones for the tapes and they've all been wrong . . . So far they have deleted, they've re-packaged, they've hired somebody to do artwork for the thing and probably charged my account with his services and put ugly covers on the thing and not paid me any of the publishing or artists royalties on these albums!'

The final album to clear Zappa's contractual obligation with Warners came out in May 1979. *Orchestral Favorites* was a purely instrumental album consisting entirely of five pieces from the 1975 Abnuceals Emuukha Electric Orchestra concert at Royce Hall, UCLA. With no sleeve notes, terrible cover art and no publicity, it did very badly. Most fans knew of Zappa's problems with Warners and were merely waiting for him to join a new label.

On 31 November 1978 the pop-punk band Blondie played at the Ukrainian Ballroom in New York on the first night of the Nova Convention to celebrate the work of William Burroughs. Zappa was in the audience with Jane Friedman, Patti Smith's manager, who was also doing publicity for him. James Grauerholz, Burroughs' assistant, knew Jane and introduced himself. He explained that Keith Richards had been billed to appear on the closing night, but had just dropped out; he thought that appearing on-stage with the author of *Junky* might have an adverse effect on the verdict on his recent heroin bust in Toronto. Grauerholz was anxious to find a replacement rock star and asked Frank if he would fill in. Frank agreed, saving the day.

He liked Burroughs' *Naked Lunch*, its humour so close to his own, and chose to read the 'Talking Asshole' routine. On the closing night at the Entermedia Theater on Second Avenue and 12th Street, Patti Smith threw a tantrum backstage because she had to follow Zappa. Grauerholz managed to mollify her by explaining that Frank was doing it for Burroughs, not to show her up. She retreated to her dressing room as Frank went on stage and gave a fine reading to an audience composed largely of the downtown art/punk scene that he so often disparaged. Had he lived in New York he would have inevitably become involved in this scene and been less culturally isolated in later years. There were plenty of composers and musicians in New York who would have been stimulating company. And after all, it was his favourite city.

Zappa enjoyed talking backstage with Burroughs and even pro-posed adapting *Naked Lunch* into a Broadway musical. This idea developed and they had several meetings in the following months, one of which took place after Frank took Burroughs to see a performance of *The Best Little Whorehouse In Texas*. Sadly nothing came of it, but they kept in touch and in February 1984 Frank sent a dozen long-stemmed roses to the Limelight Club in New York for Burroughs' seventieth birthday party.

By the end of 1978, studio costs had risen to $20,000 a week and Camden, a new studio just opening in New York, was charging $30,000. In addition to the high costs, all the studios were booked up for months in advance. Frank finally decided it would be more economical to build his own studio. Crucially, instead of moving to the artistic hub of New York's SoHo, he committed himself to Los Angeles.

A 60-foot long, 32-foot wide, two-and-a-half storey building was erected at the side of the house, complete with two live echo chambers in the basement, housed in thick-walled concrete tanks. Another echo chamber was built in the studio proper that could be closed off with a door. Frank may have been famous, but he could not afford this sort of expenditure. 'I'm getting a loan from the bank,' Zappa explained, 'just like any other schmuck does when he builds something.' Nor was he skimping on the materials. 'I'm going to have all new science-fiction equipment, it's going to be the tits! . . . It's a personal studio. It's not zoned for any commercial enterprise, it's for my own work, like a laboratory. I've started buying instruments to put in it. I already have a huge collection of synthesisers – I mean huge. I just got a nine-foot six-inches Bosendorfer that goes down to a low C, that's nine extra notes, which comes in very handy if you're recording things at half speed.'

As so much of Zappa's work used live recordings, it was important to get good clean recordings of concerts, though not until 1982 could he afford to buy a mobile recording truck – in effect, a second studio. Meanwhile, the Utility Muffin Research Kitchen (UMRK) was completed on 1 September 1979, and Frank got straight to work.

He was finally independent with his own studio and record company; distribution of his records (and anyone else signed to the Zappa label) was provided in the USA and Canada by Phonogram. Outside North America, Frank's work was distributed by CBS and other artists on the label by Phonogram. While the Utility Muffin Research Kitchen was under construction, Zappa flew to London to sign the deal with CBS and also to record Lakshmirnarayna Shankar, the first artist he signed to the Zappa label.

Though he rarely used violinists in his line-ups, Zappa loved to hear them playing his work. First there was Jean-Luc Ponty, and now he turned his attention to Shankar. Shankar had played with Zappa on several occasions, including the 1977 New York Halloween show, and now found himself in London, co-writing songs with Frank. They recorded at Advision ('primitive') and at George Martin's AIR Studios ('about like New York studio quality'). Mixing was done at Richard Branson's new London studio, the Town House.

The album, *Touch Me There*, featured four songs co-written by Zappa and Shankar, including the title track and another called 'Dead Girls of London', inspired by the frigid reception Frank had encountered while trying to pick up girls at Tramp after recording sessions, the only place he could find in London that served meals at 2 a.m. Tramp was a Eurotrash hangout filled with footballers, minor European royalty, TV compères and wealthy businessmen. Going back to Frank Zappa's hotel room was not regarded as a good career move. Van Morrison provided the vocal on 'Dead Girls of London', but predictably Warners refused permission for Zappa Records to use his services. Frank had to sing them himself and overdub later. Artists often use a pseudonym when record company permission is unlikely to be forthcoming, and this was an obvious case for one.

In mid-January Frank found Bebe Buell drinking champagne alone in the first-class compartment of a plane from London to Frankfurt. She was on her way to join Rod Stewart in Rio de Janeiro. Frank tried to get her to join the band and stay with them in their Frankfurt hotel. He issued dire warnings about what would happen to her in Rio and told her to forget all about Rod Stewart. 'Zappa was a very straight guy,' she recalled. 'There was nothing romantic about his interest in me. He had been responsible for putting together one of the first all-female rock bands in the United States, the GTOs, and it's more than likely that if I had taken his advice, I would have found myself singing in a band much sooner than I did.' Of course, Frank used the same pick-up line on Nigey Lennon.

The spring tour took in eleven European countries, beginning in Britain and ending in Switzerland; after two gigs in Japan, Frank was back in the studio, working on what would become *Joe's Garage Acts*

I, II and *III* at Village Recorder in LA. But the constant touring and marathon studio sessions – plus the stress of his lawsuits against Cohen and Warners – were taking their toll. He was completely exhausted and was forced to lay off the group and cancel his summer tour.

Sheik Yerbouti, Zappa's first album on his own label, was released on 3 March 1980. The title was taken from the current Number One hit, K.C. and the Sunshine Band's '(Shake, Shake, Shake) Shake Your Booty' – a tortured pun exacerbated by Lynn Goldsmith's cover portrait of Zappa dressed as an Arab Sheik. It got Zappa Records off to a good start, reaching Number 21 on the *Billboard* charts (very good for a double-album) with a single, 'Dancin' Fool', reaching Number 23.

The track 'Rubber Shirt' was Zappa's first conscious use of what he called 'xenochrony': he would select a number of different tapes – all at the same tempo – and play them simultaneously to create a track in which the relationship of the instruments to one another is totally random. David Ocker recalled: 'There's a tune called "Rubber Shirt" which is a combination of three solos – guitar, bass and drums [Zappa, O'Hearn and Bozzio], which Frank combined in the studio using tape transfers. He was really excited about this, and he played it for me, saying something like: "The solos just seem to work so well together." I doubt it was an accident – my guess is that he tried a variety of different combinations of those tracks till he found the one way he liked the best.' Xenochrony was to play a big part in editing his future albums, introducing unexpected new combinations and textures.

Sheik Yerbouti was the usual mix of smutty lyrics, parodies and brilliant music. 'I Have Been In You' parodied Peter Frampton's 'I'm In You'; while 'Trying To Grow A Chin' parodied both the Who's *Tommy* and the Eagles' 'Hotel California'. Adrian Belew did his Bob Dylan vocal on 'Flakes', which always made Zappa crack up on-stage. Such references became more and more frequent in Zappa's work and were often wickedly accurate.

He sang on many of the tracks and had sung a lot more ever since his fall at the Rainbow had lowered his voice. Generally speaking he tailored his songs to the vocal style of his singers. Zappa: 'Just like the real world – you can't write something that somebody can't sing.'

There was an added problem of persuading them to sing, as many of his vocalists disliked his subject matter. Ray Collins, for example, was one of the best vocalists Zappa ever worked with. Zappa: 'He was good – he didn't enjoy singing them – in fact one of the reasons he left the group was that he didn't like the songs – he hated them.'

Sheik Yerbouti includes several controversial songs, including 'Bobby Brown Goes Down' and 'Jewish Princess'. The former was attacked by gay rights groups for being homophobic, and by feminists for being sexist. It was both, but Zappa naively believed that if you parodied something, that made whatever you said all right. The song is about Bobby Brown, a college jock who sleeps with a 'dyke' called Freddie. She has been influenced by the women's liberation movement, which is 'creeping all across the nation' like a plague. This encounter turns Bobby into a homosexual and, as this is a Zappa song, he gets into S&M, so that Zappa can sing gleefully about the 'tower of power' and 'golden showers'.

Oddly enough, this track was a big hit in Sweden where no one understood the references. In an interview with Swedish Radio Zappa explained that a 'tower of power' is 'a S&M device that they sell at a store in Los Angeles. Its a small stool, to sit on, that has this spindle that comes up, that sticks up your asshole and it has straps on the legs of the stool where you're supposed to put a person's ankle into the straps on the edge of the stool. And they actually sell this thing there and it's called the Tower of Power.' Then he explained what a 'golden shower' was, concluding: 'So you get the idea that Bobby Brown in this song as the result of following the advice of women's liberation, has wound up sitting on a stool with a thing up his ass while somebody pisses on him. And that's why I think that it's unusual that the song is so popular here. I mean, when I go to a disco and see people dancing the Bobby Brown, I had to laugh . . . The story of Bobby Brown may not be some-thing that happens every day in Sweden, but I wouldn't be surprised if there are a few Bobby Browns out there. And somebody should write about them.'

References to homosexuality were increasing in Zappa's work. The track 'Broken Hearts Are For Assholes' parodied stereotypycal gay behaviour, but was balanced (Frank no doubt thought) by an ending about anal sex with a woman – to show that they could be assholes too. It is basically one of Zappa's schoolyard get togethers with all the little boys saying dirty words: 'Corn hole', 'fist-fuck' and giving the finger to Detective Willis. It was a big hit in non-English speaking countries like Germany and Norway.

'Jewish Princess' brought Zappa up against the Anti-Defamation League of B'nai B'rith (ADL), a powerful Jewish lobby group who filed a protest with the Federal Communications Commission (FCC) to have the record banned from airplay (a rather pointless exercise, as Zappa's album tracks never received airplay anyway), claiming that it contained 'vulgar, sexual and anti-Semitic references which leave very little to the imagination'. Zappa defended himself: 'I am an artist and I have the right to express my opinion. I'm not anti-Semitic. The Jewish princesses I've played this song for think it's funny . . . producing satire is kind of hopeless because of the literacy rate of the American public.'

Because of the power of the ADL, 'Jewish Princess' received more press than any other Zappa song. In *Relix*, Zappa said: 'The ADL is a noisemaking organisation that tries to apply pressure on people in order to manufacture a stereotype image of Jews that suits their idea of a good time. They go around saying that other people are saying things that produce stereotype images of Jews. What they're really about is manufacturing a freeze-dried, totally perfect image of a Jew. It's an organisation paid for by Jewish people. Their job is to make sure that everybody who is not a Jew will always perceive Jews in just this one, special, perfect way. This is wrong . . . There's all different kinds of Jews.'

In *High Times* he warmed to his theme: 'I used to think that Jewish people had a sense of humour before I got that letter from the ADL . . . Let's face it, there's all different kinds of Jews, there's all different kinds of Italians, there's all different kinds of everything. And it's a good thing that there are . . . Let's face it, there were Mexicans at one time who did wear sombreros and sleep against the cactus – as much as those organisations would like you to believe that such a stereotype could never exist. I personally know people of the Negro persuasion who eat watermelons and pork chops. As we all know, there are Jewish people who jerk off and there are Jewish people who grow their nails out weird and have their zits blasted off. These are facts. Let's face the facts. This is the real world.'

The ADL had in fact unwittingly given the song, and *Sheik Yerbouti*, far more publicity than they would normally have received. Zappa was interviewed about it for months. He never backed down: 'Open hostility is the only way to go. I'm taking off my gloves. My lawyer has called them up and demanded an apology. I haven't stalked controversy – controversy has stalked me.' He told *Bam* magazine: 'Hey, you know what I say to those people? "Go fuck yourself!" One other thing I want to point out: I don't think that most Jews feel that way about that song . . . Who knows how stupid these people want to be? I mean, can't they take a joke? I can't help it if these people were born without a sense of humour and can't laugh at themselves. The things that are said in "Jewish Princess" are absolutely true and correct. Anybody who has ever known a Jewish princess understands the song and sees that what's going on there is accurate reportage of the way they are and the way they act. I'm not here to decide how they got that way or whether it's good or bad.'

He told *Playboy*: 'I'm a journalist of a sort. I have a right to say what I want to say about any topic. If you don't have a sense of humour, then tough titties . . . I didn't make up the idea of the Jewish princess. They exist, so I wrote a song about them. If they don't like it, so what? Italians have princesses too.'

In a way the song was a return to familiar territory: the character of Suzy Creamcheese who, though not named as Jewish, was undoubtedly a Jewish Princess. Zappa had often described himself as a reporter, a journalist or even an anthropologist, recording the minutiae of everyday life in Southern California. In this respect, the Jewish princess was just another of the fauna to be named, held up and described like a newly-discovered Amazonian tribe or a new species of fish.

Zappa was the namer in the family: children and pets were always brought to him to be named and he had a name for everything: Gail's toes, his guitars and amplifiers, even the tour bus: Phydeaux III. Many of Zappa's songs are to do with holding things up and naming them. It is what the art critic Dore Ashton calls the 'simple game of naming things, one at a time.' The infant explores its new world and examines everything in it, holding it up and exclaiming 'Look!' Zappa does the same, only with kitchen utensils, TV ads, catch-phrases developed on the road, diseases (sexual and otherwise) and national stereotypes – though in many cases what he holds up is not what most people want to see. Like Burroughs' *Naked Lunch*, Zappa's work shows you what's wriggling naked on the end of the fork. Also like Burroughs, sometimes it's just there for fun or to shock, rather than part of some crusade to enlighten people.

Zappa played with ideas of sexual identity and gender differences; albeit often crudely and with little finesse, but he was not an intellectual and his chosen audience needed everything spelled out in capital letters. He also explored the underlying violence of human relationships, as most vividly expressed in S&M; he took on role-playing and fetishism, deconstructing them on-stage in skits and sketches that most closely resembled the Happenings of the early sixties. Again, Zappa parallels developments in the art world: in the sixties the traditional barriers between audience and stage were broken by the Living Theater and playwrights like Jack Gelber (*The Connection*), LeRoi Jones (*The Toilet*) and Michael McClure (*The Beard*). Zappa is closest to the Happenings of Allan Kaprow, Claes Oldenberg, Carolee Schneemann and Robert Whitman. An evening at the Garrick with the original Mothers had much in common with an evening with Charlotte Moorman the naked cellist.

One might regard Zappa as a fellow-traveller of the pop artists; there are similarities between his work and that of Roy Lichtenstein, Jim Dine, Robert Rauschenberg and Andy Warhol – particularly Warhol's early paintings of Dick Tracy, Superman, Popeye, refrigerators or advertisements. The phenomenal growth of what is now called popular culture since the Second World War produced an environment of television, paperbacks, glossy magazines and Technicolor movies. The pop artists took this familiar shared visual experience of twentieth-century consumer society – the comic books, advertisements, the packaging of household goods – and elevated them to the level of fine art by taking them out of context so that we could see them, as if for the first time.

Zappa does the same with the aural landscape of radio and TV ads, commercial jingles and popular songs. It is the transubstantiation of everyday objects, like Marcel Duchamp's 'ready-mades'. In the context, Zappa's songs about VD, crabs, S&M, anal sex and the like are pop art: they break down the boundaries of accepted and acceptable taste, so that by the seventies anything and everything was a fit subject for art, even what had previously been regarded as art's antithesis. It was a characteristic of the pop art movement not to romanticize or beautify their images: there was no nostalgia for a fantasy fifties or an impossibly glamorous Hollywood. They were working in a no man's land between art and everyday life.

Like Allen Jones, Zappa deals with previously forbidden subject matter, although there is no erotic element in Zappa's use of sexual themes. When Zappa holds up something for our attention he is not passing judgement, he is merely saying it is there – why can't we admit it is there? This is a pop art statement. Peter Schjeldahl, writing in the *New Yorker*, said: 'The naked efficiency of anti-personal artmaking defines classic pop. It's as if someone were inviting you to inspect the fist with which he simultaneously punches you.'

Similarly, Susan Sontag's definition of Camp can easily be applied to Zappa's songs: 'Camp is generous, it wants to enjoy. It only seems like malice, cynicism . . . it relishes rather than judges.' Zappa remained something of a romantic: he claims to find beauty in a parking lot, in chirpy commercial jingles, in TV tyre ads. He not only tolerates the banal and stupid, the sleazy and the meretricious, he celebrates it. Zappa approaches all that is cheap and vulgar as Michelangelo approached a seam of marble in Carrera: inspecting it, caressing it, joyful in his discovery. (Recall his genuine delight when he found Miss Pinky.) Zappa's motives were not always conscious, of course. As Freud pointed out, sometimes a cigar is just a cigar . Some things Frank just found funny. Often he wrote songs about subjects simply because he was attracted to them: sexual deviation and life on the road, for instance, were subjects of such overwhelming fascination to him that he returned to them again and again. As his next album – naturally a three-album set – was to prove.

Joe's Garage had a slick commercial texture and was aimed directly at the high-school audience. It showed little consideration for his earlier fans now in their late twenties or thirties. Zappa: 'Some of them still come to the concerts, but usually they don't because now that they have wives, kids, mortgages, day jobs and all the rest of that stuff, they don't want to stand around in a hockey rink and be puked on by some 16-year-old who's full of reds. So consequently, our audience gets younger and younger.'

'It started out to be just a bunch of songs,' said Zappa. 'But together, they looked like they had continuity. So I went home one night midway through recording, wrote the story and changed it into an opera. It's probably the first opera that you can really tap your feet to and get a couple of good laughs along the way.'

When Zappa originally planned the record in January 1979, it was conceived as a Broadway musical for that autumn, but as usual his plans changed. He next came up with a movie and a book. Eventually it was released in September as a single album, followed two months later by a double-album, as the cost of a triple album would have priced him out of the market. *Joe's Garage* was recorded in LA at Village Recorders, studio B and Ken-Dun studio D – it was the last time he would have to hire expensive studio time. The line-up consisted of Warren Cucurullo on rhythm guitar and vocals; Denny Walley on slide guitar and vocals; Ike Willis on lead vocals; Peter Wolf on keyboards; Tommy Mars on keyboards; Arthur Barrow on bass and vocals; Ed Mann on percussion; Vinnie Colaiuta on drums; Dale Bozzio on vocals; Al Malkin on vocals and Craig Steward on harmonica.

The opera was inspired by the fact that the Islamic Revolution in Iran had made music illegal. Zappa follows the story of Joe, a young rock 'n' roller in the States where, although music is tolerated, it is regarded as the cause of most of society's ills. The title track is a rather nostalgic story of a bunch of young guys jamming in a garage – shades of Frank practising in the garage in the G Street house in Ontario.

In an effort to achieve balance, 'Catholic Girls' was as insulting to that group as 'Jewish Princess' had been to some Jews. Then Zappa gets on to his favourite subject; groupies. Mary the Catholic girl becomes a 'Crew Slut' – a derogatory term dating back to the Big Band era – and then appears at a wet T-shirt night. The perils of life on the road are rhapsodised in 'Why Does It Hurt When I Pee?' – a question frequently asked by road manager Phil Kaufman. Joe finishes up in jail and contents himself with imaginary guitar solos, much as Frank did in San Bernardino County Jail. This is a cue for 'Watermelon In Easter Hay', which contains some of Zappa's most beautiful guitar playing on record. The album ends in a big finale with all the band and chorus singing 'A Little Green Rosetta' – about the bag used to make piping on muffins; a typically obstruse Zappa subject for a big production number.

Joe's Garage was the most autobiographical album Zappa had made since *We're Only In It For The Money*, but here the events were universalised. Zappa: 'I've been in a garage, but so have a million other people. That's a highly romanticized, fantasy garage situation, you know, where the teenage girls all walk in and clap their hands and dance and stuff. Well, it ain't like that in a garage. No matter how much beer you drink, it's still out of tune, and there's only so many hours a day you can strum that E chord. That's an idealized garage that is probably more accessible to other people's idea of the garage. If I wrote a song about the way it really was in the garages I played in, it would be totally disgusting . . . I'm talking about a character named Joe and there are a lot of Joes out there who have trouble with record companies and run up against bullshit every day.'

As usual many of the songs were about sex, including one about sex with a robot. This apparent sexual obsession, which occurs on album after album, prompted rock critic Karl Dallas to ask Zappa if he ever acted out the things portrayed on his albums. 'No, none of it,' said Zappa. He then described his own sex life: 'It's not ordinary and it's not mundane, but it does not involve golden showers and appliances. I enjoy what I do in the glandular arena. I have a lovely wife and four children, a mortgage, the works.' He did not mention all the groupies he met on the road, which was where he had learned about most of these things in the first place.

Joe's Garage contains some of Zappa best music, but like most rock operas the song transitions are intrusive and irritating. Only the most ardent fan would want to listen to Zappa whispering the plot line in the voice of 'the Central Scrutiniser' through a small plastic megaphone more than once. The actual monologue is at times interestingly conceived, embodying direct quotes from the aural environment of LA: 'Add water, makes its own sauce' comes from a TV ad, while 'The white zone is for loading and unloading only . . . if you have to load or unload, go to the white zone . . .' comes from the pre-recorded, endlessly repeated announcement at LA International Airport. Frank obviously found his links amusing, and cracks up several times while delivering his monologue – he found the word 'plooking' especially comic.

Joe's Garage was one of the first albums to involve extensive time-shifting of the musical elements. Zappa: 'Ninety percent of the guitar solos on the *Joe's Garage* album were from live shows, pasted on studio tracks. In the studio they called it "Ampex Guitar" – I had all these quarter-inch tapes of guitar solos that I liked from the '79 tour, and I'd go through my files, see what key a certain solo was in, and just experimentally hit the start button on the playback machine and lay it onto the multi-track . . . We'd wiggle the pitch around to make sure it was in the right key.' Zappa would take two or more musical passages that were recorded separately – perhaps a rhythm track from one concert and a guitar solo from an entirely different song, recorded at a different concert – and combine them. Zappa: 'It's not gonna land exactly. It takes a certain amount of experimentation to get a musically pleasing result with that. It's not going to work every time you try it.' The exquisite solo on 'Watermelon In Easter Hay' was the only solo on the entire album not constructed that way.

Once Zappa moved into the Utility Muffin Research Kitchen it became more or less his permanent abode. The 24-track mixing board faced a couch and a pair of speakers. An adjoining room and one wall of the studio were shelved and filled entirely with boxes of tapes. In the corner stood an easel holding an oil painting of Jimi Hendrix. Cal

Schenkel's collage, used on the sleeve of *Burnt Weeny Sandwich*, hung on one wall and on another was a giant poster from Richard Nixon's unsuccessful campaign for governor of California. Coffee and a carton of Winstons were in easy reaching distance. The UMRK was up and running.

17 Days on the Road

The early eighties were a curious time in Zappa's career: on the one hand he achieved many of his life-long aims; numerous performances of his classical music resulted in wide acceptance of his work in contemporary music circles. On the other, though his albums sold well, his live audience began to drift away. He attributed this to the influence of punk, but that did not impact on the hardcore fans of the Rolling Stones, Pink Floyd or the other sixties bands. It is more probable that the younger generation could not relate to 'Uncle Frank' collecting panties from the audience and conducting dance contests from the stage. Zappa was out of touch with the young people he had so pointedly tailored his live shows for. Not all of them, of course, but as the empty seats increased in number, he played more shows abroad and toured less in the States.

His records had never been so popular. The recently released *Joe's Garage* was his fastest-selling album, while *Sheik Yerbouti* was his best-selling album to date. In fact, it received two Grammy nominations for Best Rock Vocal Performance (Male) for 'Dancin' Fool' and Best Rock Instrumental Performance for 'Rat Tomago'. His interest in film continued unabated and his new manager Bennett Glotzer was finally able to raise enough money to complete the latest extravaganza. *Baby*

Snakes was largely composed of live concert footage ('A movie about people who do stuff that is not normal'). It premièred on 21 December 1979 at the Victoria Theatre in New York to less than ecstatic reviews, probably because of the extended footage featuring an inflatable sex toy. Typical of this criticism was Tom Carson's piece in *Village Voice*: 'Once, Zappa built a satirist's career on the idea that all of life was just like high school; now it turns out that all he ever wanted, apparently, was a high-school clique of his own – and on the evidence of *Baby Snakes* he's found one.' Zappa was unfazed by the criticism. Foreign critics were more sympathetic and in 1981 *Baby Snakes* won the Premier Grand Prix at the First International Music Festival in Paris.

The two-hour, 43-minute film featured some extraordinary animation sequences made from modelling clay by Bruce Bickford, who jumped over Zappa's fence with two rolls of film under his arm in 1971 and had been on his payroll since 1973. Zappa: 'He talks real slow – as he states in the film he has had some contact with chemical alteration of his consciousness and his speech pattern is probably related to the fact that he's been chemically modified . . . Maybe he'll change some of his habits. I think it's definitely a good investment to support him.' Bickford lived by himself like a hermit surrounded by little clay figures in a house at the end of a dirt road in a wild part of Topanga Canyon, enclosed by rocks and trees. Zappa paid his bills and gave him a salary. Bickford spoke like the people under the piano on *Lumpy Gravy* and joined Zappa's pantheon of anthropological discoveries.

Zappa: 'For some of the more complex parts in there he could shoot only four frames in a day. And remember 24 frames go by in a second. If it takes him one day to shoot four frames of something complicated, it'll take him six days to shoot one second of complicated stuff. So, what you see in the film is a product of about three years' work to give you a half hour of animation. But not all the stuff he does is complicated. One scene in there – where he takes the little hat and puts it on the man's head that's standing on the little chair and then the man shrinks – that was shot in one evening.' Bickford's work was noticed by critics, even if *Baby Snakes* was poorly received. Zappa kept him on the payroll, eventually releasing *The Amazing Mr Bickford*, written, produced, directed by Zappa, with music by Zappa and footage of Bickford dating back to 1978, when he had a studio in Santa Monica. Originally scheduled for release in January 1988, it finally appeared on video in 1990; one of Frank's long-term projects that actually came to fruition.

After a few line-up changes, a new Zappa band began rehearsals: Ike Willis on guitar and vocals; Ray White on guitar and vocals; Tommy Mars on keyboards; Arthur Barrow on bass and David Logeman on drums, replacing Vinnie Colaiuta. On 25 March 1980 they set out on a 33-city tour, often playing two sets a night. After a ten-day break they continued through 32 cities in Europe, ending in Munich on 3 July.

That gave Zappa the summer months to work in the UMRK on his next album and to rehearse a new band for his winter touring season, which began on 10 October and lasted until Christmas. For this tour Steve Vai was added on guitar, Bob Harris on keyboards, trumpet and vocals, and Vinnie Colaiuta returned as drummer.

There were no album releases in 1980, possibly because Zappa had fulfilled his requirement of Zappa Records 'product' to Phonogram and CBS and was waiting for his contract to expire at the end of the year. At that time he started yet another record company, Barking Pumpkin Records, distributed by CBS and named after Gail and her smoker's cough. The logo consisted of a Halloween pumpkin with a speech bubble saying 'Arf!' and a startled cat whose speech bubble reads 'Oh Shit!' in Japanese.

The first release was *Tinseltown Rebellion*, a double-album taken largely from live recordings at the Berkeley Community Center and London's Hammersmith Odeon, with sections from other live concerts edited in along with one studio track. The CBS press release contained a rather belligerent note from Zappa to the reviewers: 'Over the years it has become fashionable to despise what I do. Well, folks, I am not going to go away . . . and neither will the various works of art which regularly get disapproved of. Now, here's what you do: get smart, phase up with reality, this is good stuff . . . it might not be PUNK . . . it might not be NEW WAVE . . . it might not be whatever trend you are worshipping at the moment, but it is good stuff nonetheless, so, check it out.' Zappa blamed punk for his dwindling live audience, but it gave him a perfect subject for a song and he made a wonderful return to his old form in the title track, attacking the insincere, plastic, hypocritical punk bands of Sunset Strip who would do anything to attract the record company executives looking for the next big thing: play as badly as possible, sell their bodies, dress in ugly clothes.

Tinseltown Rebellion opened with a long series of controversial and sexist songs, beginning with 'Fine Girl', which was also offensive to blacks. It was a parody of black male attitudes to women, if the use of the word 'de' instead of 'the' and 'wit' for 'with' was intended to invoke an Afro-American accent; the woman in question carried water from the well in a bucket on her head; presumably the good old days back in Africa. The song concluded that what the world needed was more women like that. It's hard to see the point of such a song which, if it really was a parody, went over the heads of the majority of Zappa's fans. More likely it was an unconscious expression of Zappa's violent dislike of the women's liberation movement.

The next track was 'Easy Meat', another derogatory attack on women. Although Zappa claimed to be in favour of the sexual revolution, he constantly came up with songs like this or 'Crew Slut', which betray a deeply ingrained double-standard. If women asserted their sexuality they were 'sluts' or 'easy meat'.

This attitude is all the more troubling because Zappa regarded himself as a trailblazer in bringing a new honesty about sexual relations to the public debate; as he was, to a degree: 'American sexual attitudes are controlled as a necessary tool of business and government in order to perpetuate themselves. Unless people begin to see through that, to see past it to what sex is really all about, they're always going to have the same neurotic attitudes. It's very neatly packaged. It all works hand-in-hand with the churches and political leaders at the point where elections are coming up. They always promise to clean up smut in the neighbourhood. In order for them to clean up smut, smut must exist. Through schools and religion, the concept of smut is manufactured . . . From a business standpoint, as long as these attitudes have been built into the American mind, they can pose a girl in an evening gown next to a transistor radio and somehow that makes the radio more interesting, makes it work better, makes it fun. Or they'll use red cars. Or designs that include triangles.'

The real problem lay in the fact that Zappa insisted sex was simply a mechanical release of energy and bodily fluids: 'entertainment of a glandular nature'. He did not link it to feelings, emotions or – a word he claimed to despise – love. It is possibly no accident that this same album included a new version of 'I Ain't Got No Heart' from *Freak Out!*, in which he denies the very existence of love. Gail bluntly told George Petros: 'Frank did not do love.' She explained to Victoria Balfour that their relationship survived because 'Frank and I try to talk to each other as little as possible. We make an effort not to speak.'

It difficult to assess Zappa's more blatantly sexist work: was he really just following in the footsteps of his mentor Lenny Bruce, who would walk on-stage in the early sixties and say 'Are there any niggers here tonight?' then, after looking round, continue 'Oh, between those two niggers sits one kike . . . Uh, two kikes. That's two kikes and three niggers and one spic . . .' and so on through 'micks' and 'guineas' and 'greaseballs' and 'Yid Polacks', until the words had been drained of their offensive meaning. There was certainly a conscious intent on Zappa's part to do just this, but unconscious factors seemed to get in the way.

Tinseltown Rebellion continued with Zappa's rap to encourage women to throw panties on-stage (something Elvis and Tom Jones didn't have to *ask* their audiences to do, they needed no encouragement), which involved a lot of sniggering on Zappa's part. Women were the subject of the album. On 'Bamboozled By Love' the male speaker discovers his woman giving someone a blow job and sings about how he is going to bang her head against the wall, make her bleed and finally bury her under the lawn; the level of hatred in this song is really quite extraordinary. Was it an investigation into psychotic jealousy (a traditional blues and R&B theme)? Or was it based on a real-life event? Perhaps it was a mixture of the two. Gail: 'Almost everything he wrote with a story line was based on fact. He was an observer of human nature.'

The so-called toilet humour on the album received the most attention. In the view of many critics, Zappa continually sabotaged his most interesting songs by giving them smutty lyrics or titles. Zappa: 'That misunderstanding basically derives from this fact: people who deal in rock 'n' roll criticism are all part of the machinery that thrives on the idea that the largest number of units sold equals the best music. And if somebody does something without wanting to sell billions of platinum units, then this is incomprehensible to the average rock 'n' roll critic, because they believe that anybody who doesn't play the same game is crazy or dangerous or both. So they can't compute the idea that maybe the concept of the song that they perceive as a perfectly acceptable, viable, nice little rock 'n' roll ditty that they think was sabotaged – maybe the sabotage is the actual information in the song, and the rest of the stuff surrounding it is something that will attract the attention of the people who need to hear that other information. It's the carrot on the end of the stick to make you experience that other information. The part in the song that turns out to be weird to those particular critics is the part that's important, and the other stuff is just something to set you up for that little twist that's in there. Without the set-up, the twist doesn't work, and oftentimes the compositions are designed to lead you right down the primrose path until you hit the brick wall.'

This is the most convincing explanation for his constant return to toilet humour: Zappa the cynic, the teacher, the iconoclast and misanthrope was continually rubbing his audience's face in the dirt. 'I don't think I'm getting more cynical,' he said. 'I've just got more evidence to back up my cynicism. Where in the past I might have only guessed that people were horrible, today I can prove it.'

Zappa's approach to his music was very far removed from that of his rock 'n' roll contemporaries. His mentor was Igor Stravinsky and Zappa shared his belief that music was not the correct vehicle for emotional expression. Stravinsky abhorred Romanticism and Zappa did not believe in romance. He considered love songs to be dishonest and manipulative, using certain musical devices to manufacture cheap emotion.

Zappa: 'I don't want to go and see somebody's deep inner hurt in a live performance. I don't want to hear their personal turmoil . . . See, I take a real cold view about that stuff. I think that music works because of psycho-acoustical things – like the way in which a line will interact with the harmonic climate that's backing it up. And all the rest of it is subjective on behalf of the listener. Maybe you wanted to hear a sad trumpet solo, but it wouldn't be sad unless the notes he was playing were interacting in a certain way against the background. The best test is: if it was a 24-track recording, take the same trumpet solo, change the chord progression behind it, and see if it sounds sad any more: people see and hear what they want to see and hear. If you're in the mood or have a deep, personal need for sad music or soul-searching or sensitivity in that stuff, you'll find it wherever it is. You'll go into an art gallery and be totally amazed by the things you see, whereas I might go into the gallery and go "Hah?" This is a gross example, but say a person buys a Kiss album and listens to it and has a moving experience from it. I mean, are they wrong?'

Stravinsky put it even more bluntly in his notorious epigram: 'I consider that music is, by its very nature, essentially powerless to express anything at all, whether a feeling, an attitude of mind, a psychological mood, a phenomenon of nature, etc . . . Expression has never been an inherent property of music. That is by no means the purpose of its existence. If, as is nearly always the case, music appears to express something, this is only an illusion and not reality. It is simply an additional attribute which, by tacit and inveterate agreement, we have lent it, thrust upon it, and as a label of convention – in short, an aspect unconsciously or by force of habit, we have come to confuse with its essential being.'

Zappa inhabited a cold, hard world. Fortunately, this was ameliorated by his love of stupid pop songs played in hockey rinks. For several years he had been working on an album composed of nothing but his guitar solos, which he intended to sell by mail-order only. He described it as being 'just for fetishists. For those who want to hear my guitar work, that's the album for them.' By the time it came out in May 1981 *Shut Up And Play Your Guitar* had grown to three albums, available separately: 'I have been waiting to do it for a long time. And a lot of people thought I was crazy for spending the time to do it. But, right now that group of albums is selling better than *You Are What You Is* and *Tinseltown Rebellion*. We went into a profit position after two weeks on the market.'

Between each track Zappa introduced short examples of his trademark collages of vocal fragments and ambient sound. At first he edited the tracks together with no vocal texture, but the results felt flat with one solo after another and no interruption. Structurally, the vocal collages served as punctuation. Zappa: 'Just to give your ears a chance to stop hearing a fuzz tone for a minute and hear another texture and then set you up for the next thing.'

The tracks were all from live concerts, rather than studio recordings. Zappa told *Guitar Player* magazine: 'I find it very difficult to play in the studio. I don't think that I have ever played a good solo of any description in the recording studio. I just don't have the feeling for it. And up until the time I got my own studio, I was working in commercial ones where you have to pay anywhere from a hundred to two hundred dollars an hour for the time. There you don't have the luxury of sitting and perfecting what it is that you're going to play, whereas if you have a collection of tapes made over a period of a few years – which I do – you can go through that stuff and find musical examples that achieve some aesthetic goal that you're interested in achieving.'

The albums proved to the critics that Zappa was a consummate guitarist. His compositions were all done on the guitar, not the piano, so they tended to be built from repeated notes and had a lack of long chords. His approach to the guitar solo was one of risk-taking and experimentation. Unlike most famous guitarists, he would take enormous risks to see where a certain idea led; sometimes they were successful and you could almost hear the audience gasp in amazement, other times they were dead ends, resolved by a return to the chord base.

Not for Zappa the flashy, grunting, phallic thrusting of the seventies and eighties heavy metal bands. Nor did he impress audiences with his speed: to play fast did not necessarily mean you were any good, and often disguised the fact you were not. Nor did he tootle around with the high notes as if they were difficult to play. For Zappa each solo was a musical composition and the audience got to watch the creative act as it happened: 'I go out there to play compositions. I want to do compositions instantly on the guitar. I want to take chord change or a harmonic climate and I want to build a composition on the spur of the moment that makes sense, that takes some chances, that goes someplace where nobody else wanted to go, that says things that nobody else wanted to say, that represents my musical personality, that has some emotional content that speaks to the people who want to hear that kind of stuff . . .

'I look forward to every gig because I know I'm going to be able to play at least eight solos during each show. I can get eight chances to decorate a piece of time canvas and I crave it, I really crave it. To me, if every one of those things was written down as I played it I would be just as happy to sign my name to it as a musical composition that I would sit down and write on a table, 'cause that's what I'm doing, I'm a composer, it's just that instead of a pencil I'm using a guitar.'

Throughout the seventies, to make up for lack of airplay and record company payola, Zappa had subjected himself to a relentless schedule of interviews to promote his albums and concerts. While the other members of the tour group were getting over jetlag, Zappa was doing an interview every half hour with the local press. It was little wonder he developed such a hatred of music journalists.

In the eighties he realized he could just give a few longer interviews to sympathetic journalists from specialist magazines like *Guitar World*, *International Musician* or *Downbeat*. Though he still did television, he felt a good deal more relaxed – as did the Press. The idea of waiting an hour or more before being ushered into Zappa's hotel room, under the baleful eye of his bodyguard, and then being given 30 minutes before

Smothers drew his finger across his neck and it was time for the next interviewer, was something few music journalists relished. It was a formal dance, and in Britain in particular Zappa often felt he came out the loser.

It probably didn't help that he usually began the interview by saying England was dreadful, English audiences were lousy and English music journalists unprofessional and ignorant. These attacks were always published – as he presumably intended – which did not endear him to the readers. The journalists knew he was just trying to wind them up and that Zappa would be lost if he ever stepped outside the Hyde Park Hotel. He might as well have been in Moscow or Prague for all he knew about London or Britain. They soon learned that he always bridled if they criticized America, so that became a way of enlivening a dull interview.

From the very earliest days of touring, Zappa had almost always stayed at a different, usually better hotel than the group. He gave various reasons: he had to have a suite in order to give interviews and deal with business (though there were very few interviews during the early days of the Mothers) or that he needed the peace and quiet to write music (he was never without score paper) or to write new arrangements for the show. But perhaps the most important reason was that he never wanted to see the inside of cell again: hence the ban on drugs. He told *High Times*: 'If you're travelling around with a band that says in their lyrics some of the things that I say, it would be best if you didn't give a government agency the opportunity to take you away for potential infringement of some peculiar regulation . . . I'm very adamant about it . . . Once they're in their own house or off the front line of what's going on, they may still be collecting salaries but, if they're not doing a live show and they're not recording, what they do with their own bodies is their own business. But once they're on the tour or in rehearsal or in recording, they have to be on top of it.' Otherwise they were out, as some group members found to their cost.

The 1981 tour supported yet another new album, *You Are What You Is*, which included three song-cycles on Zappa's usual themes: the futility of relationships, groupies and TV evangelists ('The Heavenly Bank Account' is Zappa in fine form). It also saw the welcome return of Jimmy Carl Black: 'He called me up and hired me. He paid me for that one, good too. He put me up at the Sunset Marquee Hotel, picked me up in the Rolls every morning to go to the studio. He can't sing country and western like I can. I guess that's the reason he did it, I don't know. He wanted a Texas sound on it, and me being from Texas, I can supply that. But once again, I was only supposed to do the one song and I wound up doing four or five, just like *200 Motels*, but for the same money. The money didn't get any bigger.'

As usual, Zappa toured Europe in the spring, but this year things went badly: the concert at the Ostseehalle in Kiel, Germany, was cut short by Zappa when audience members threw objects at the stage; two other concerts in Germany were cancelled. The concert in Mannheim lasted only ten minutes before being halted by a downpour. Two concerts in France were cancelled, one after the soundcheck, and Zappa ended the Geneva concert when objects were thrown at the stage. Worst of all was the last show of the tour in Palermo, Sicily, on 14 July, which was stopped after 60 minutes when a full-scale battle developed between the audience and police firing teargas. Three people died.

The concert was held at the mafia-controlled Stadio Communale La Favorita and all the security appeared to be made men. Italy had beaten West Germany 3-1 to win the Football World Cup on 11 July and the fans were still celebrating, so the police were out in force. The army had also turned up. Frank watched in astonishment as a soldier knelt in front of the stage and shot a tear-gas canister into the crowd. Zappa: 'From what I could see from the stage, some of the kids in the audience started shooting back at the cops. I didn't find out about the deaths until later.' They played for as long as they could with tear gas swirling across the stage, fearing that things might get worse if they stopped. After the show they were trapped backstage while the audience fought with the police and the army. Earlier that day Frank had visited nearby Partinico, where his father was born: 'I got a pretty good idea of what my Sicilian roots are like after seeing the town of Partinico; it was pretty grim.'

This was the time of President Reagan, the Contras and the American overthrow of the democratically elected government of Nicaragua. Anti-American feeling ran high in Europe and unfortunately for Zappa some of his audience regarded him as a symbol of America. Disenchanted with diminishing audiences at home and unruly audiences abroad Frank did not play live again until July 1984. 'That was our last European tour,' he said. 'It's too expensive to play, too expensive to travel around, and with the anti-American sentiment around, it is hard to go on-stage and do what you do with the emotional freight that is attendant to European attitudes toward American foreign policy. When we first started to go to Europe in the sixties, there was some of that, especially in Germany, with all the student activism and all that crap. We had a bunch of riots then. But then it died down. And now it's back. Anyone who is an American is *only* an American.'

In 1981 Zappa was approached by Joel Thome, conductor of the Orchestra of Our Time, to participate in a tribute to Edgard Varèse. Zappa was delighted to use his name to help draw an audience and got the venue changed from the Whitney Museum of American Art to the larger Palladium, the one-time opera house where he held his annual New York Halloween show. 'The kids that come may be a little rambunctious,' he told *Rolling Stone*. 'But I've always had a good rapport with them and talked to them like they were my neighbours.' He said he saw his role as 'comic relief', introducing each piece before it was performed, rather than playing or conducting: 'I was there to be a host and to help draw people to the concert and I think I did my job.'

A large, well-behaved crowd attended the concert on 17 April and responded to the music of Varèse with enthusiasm. The composer's 90-year-old widow Louise, the guest of honour, described Zappa as 'a lovely person' and told *Rolling Stone*: 'He's very serious about Varèse's music, you know.'

Zappa and Varèse had much in common. They both shared the view that traditional instruments, electronic instruments and non-musical sounds – street sounds, conversations – recorded on tape, were all equally valid as vehicles for composition. Neither of them rejected traditional instruments – Varèse objected when described as a composer of *musique concrète*. Varèse had a great interest in choral music – he founded choral societies and conducted huge choirs. He was also an authority on pre-Bach classical music and supported the use of period instruments. 'I even consider it desirable that we should revive the instruments for which Monteverdi, Lully and their predecessors actually wrote,' he said, 'and that their works should be presented in the original versions.'

Zappa's music succeeded so well because of his instrumentation, which included classical instruments alongside the highly amplified electric instruments of a rock 'n' roll band. In this he partially achieved what Varèse had wanted all along: an extension of the traditional music-making line-up. In 1924 Varèse told the London *Evening News*: 'Stringed instruments are still the kings of orchestras, despite the fact that the violin reached its zenith in the early part of the eighteenth century. Why should we expect this instrument, typical of its period, to be able to carry the main burden of the expression of today? The rest of the conventional orchestra of today precludes the exploitation of the possibilities of different tone colours and range . . . It must not be forgotten that the division of the octave into twelve half tones is purely arbitrary. There is no good reason why we should continue to tolerate the restriction.'

Zappa didn't, though some of his recordings combining classical and electric instruments are more successful than others. 'Today is an age of speed, synthesis and dynamics,' Varèse told the *San Francisco News* in 1938. 'Consequently we expect contemporary forms to reflect those qualities.' Zappa's large, ever-changing line-ups did just that; it is one of the reasons his music endures. However, what Varèse and Zappa most desired was a sound machine that would remove the need for musicians altogether and play an accurate version of the composer's work at the touch of a button. Varèse never saw it in his lifetime, but Zappa did and used it a lot in later years.

It is probably just as well that Varèse and Zappa never met. They would have been at odds politically: Varèse was an old-style European leftist, a friend of Lenin, Trotsky and Diego Riviera who campaigned energetically to raise money for the Spanish Republican cause and was devastated when Spain, then France fell to the fascists. The long gap before Varèse's *Deserts* (1955) was not because, as Zappa said, 'he knew nobody was going to play it', but due to acute depression brought on by the Spanish Civil War, fears for his friends and family in occupied France, the horrors of the Holocaust, the bombing of Hiroshima and Nagasaki, and the constant threat of nuclear annihilation. For Varèse and his friends the dreams of a more just and equal society had been totally shattered. The desert he wrote about was the emotional desert of the soul. He despaired that humans could wreak such destruction and cause such suffering.

In contrast, Zappa had internalized the whole *Time-Life* anti-communist line to such an extent that he refused to perform in the Soviet Union when invited, and would not have understood the left-wing politics of someone like Varèse. Furthermore, he would have felt distinctly uncomfortable in Varèse's basement studio, where next to paintings by Miró, the gongs and the piano was a large NO SMOKING sign.

In addition to Louise Varèse, Zappa also met Nicolas Slonimsky, the world's leading expert on Varèse's work. He was the principal conductor for the Pan American Association of Composers, founded by Varèse, Henry Cowell and Carlos Chavez in April 1928. He performed *Intégrales* in Paris in 1931 and conducted the first Paris and Berlin performances of *Arcana* in 1932. He conducted the first American performance of *Ionisation* at Carnegie Hall on 6 March 1933 and the next month conducted it in Havana. He conducted the première of *Ecuatorial* at New York's Town Hall in 1934. No one knew more about the music of Varèse than Slonimsky.

When Zappa was invited to host the Edgard Varèse Memorial concert in New York, he said: 'I erroneously thought that since I was supposed to be introducing the works, that the audience would appreciate some background facts about his life . . . not realising the typical New York audience would be more "Hewy, Frank, Hey!" . . .

and not want to know .... So to prepare myself for this, I knew that Slonimsky lived in Los Angeles, and since he conducted the première of *Ionisation* I thought I would meet him and talk to him and get some inside information.' And so, one evening in the spring of 1981, Slonimsky was surprised by a telephone call from Zappa who said: 'I never realized you were in Los Angeles and I want so much to get in touch with you about your book of scales [his *Thesaurus of Scales and Melodic Patterns*].' They arranged to meet and Zappa sent his $60,000 chauffeur-driven black Mercedes limousine to collect him (Slonimsky asked the driver how much it had cost).

Zappa led the 87-year-old conductor to his basement studio and Slonimsky immediately asked how much he paid for his huge Bosendorfer piano. 'Seventy,' said Zappa. In his autobiography, *Perfect Pitch*, Slonimsky wrote: 'Zappa declared himself an admirer of Varèse and said he had been composing orchestral works according to Varèse's principles of composition with unrelated themes following in free succession. To substantiate this claim, he brought out three scores, in manuscript, each measuring 13 x 20 inches, beautifully copied and handsomely bound. Indeed, the configurations of notes and contra-puntal combinations looked remarkably Varèsian.'

Frank invited him to try out the Bosendorfer and Slonimsky played the coronation scene from Mussorgsky's opera *Boris Godunov*, which utilized the extra bass notes. Then Frank asked if he would play some of his own work. Slonimsky played the last part of his *Minitudes*, described as mutually exclusive triads that covered the entire key-board. Delighted, Zappa asked if he would play it at his next concert. Slonimsky asked when. 'Tomorrow,' said Frank. 'We can rehearse in the afternoon.'

In rehearsal Slonimsky ran through his piece, adding 16 bars to the coda, ending in repeated alternation of C major and F sharp major chords in the highest treble and lowest bass registers. He had not played an electric piano before, but quickly adjusted to it. The band picked up his music with no trouble. Slonimsky watched the concert from the wings, wearing earplugs provided by Smothers to protect him from the high decibel level. Slonimsky: 'Zappa sang and danced while conducting, with a professional verve that astounded me. A soprano soloist [Lisa Popeil] came out and sang a ballad about being a hooker, using a variety of obscenities. Then came my turn . . .'

Zappa introduced the frail octogenarian as 'our national treasure'. Slonimsky removed his earplugs and sat at the electric piano. Slonimsky: 'With demoniac energy Zappa launched us into my piece. To my surprise I sensed a growing consanguinity with my youthful audience as I played. My fortissimo ending brought out screams and whistles the like of which I had never imagined possible. Dancing Zappa, wild audience, and befuddled me – I felt like an intruder in a mad scene from *Alice in Wonderland*. I had entered my Age of Absurdity.'

18 Orchestral Manoeuvres

Zappa's turn towards more commercial albums (including the surprise hit 'Valley Girl') meant that he could finally afford to have his pieces recorded by a full orchestra. In 1982 he bought the Beach Boys' mobile recording truck; a remote facility with a hundred inputs, two 24-track Ampex machines, cables, stands and all the necessary gear. From then on, all of his concerts could be recorded on 24 tracks using three recorders; two for continuous recording in order not to run out of tape halfway through a song, and a third installed as a back-up.

In fact, from this moment on Zappa's albums are composed largely of material recorded at dozens of different venues, sometimes with the beginning of a song coming from one date and the end from another. At times Zappa boasted there were many more edits than that. On the title track from his next album, *Ship Arriving Too Late To Save a Drowning Witch*, there were 15 edits on the basic track, each recorded in a different city and some only two bars long. Zappa: 'It's a very hard song to play, so there was no one perfect performance from any city. What I did was go through a whole tour's worth of tape and listen to every version of it and grab every section that was reasonably correct, put together a basic track, and then added the rest of the orchestration in the studio.'

Zappa once characterized this sort of behaviour as 'obsessive overdubbage' and he was right. There was no reason to extract so many fragments from so many tapes – four or five would have sufficed – unless he was doing it out of pure enjoyment. Sitting there alone, razor blade in hand (this was before he could afford an electronic editing suite), he was in complete control: a master of space and time, in an environment designed totally to support him and his work. The lonely, gawky new kid in the schoolyard no longer needed friends; he had found happiness without them. And being Zappa, he had found a justification for his position which proved, at least to him, that his was the best approach to life. Zappa: 'Try to imagine what the opposite of loneliness is. Think of it. Everyone in the world loves you? What is that? Realize you are in isolation. Live it! Enjoy it! Just be glad that there aren't a bunch of people who want to use up your time. Because along with all the love and admiration that's going to come from the people that would keep you from being lonely, there is the emotional freight you have to bear from people who are wasting your time, and you can't get that back. So when you're lonely and all by yourself, guess what you have? You have all your own time. That's a pretty good fucking deal. Something you couldn't buy any place else. And every time you're out being sociable and having other people be "nice" to you so you don't feel "lonely", they are wasting your time. What do you get for it? Because after they're done being nice to you they want something from you. And they've already taken your time! Loneliness... is not a bad deal. It's a good deal.'

This was the self-justification of a workaholic; a sobriquet he naturally denied: 'Everybody uses that word on me – it's not true. A workaholic is a guy who works in an insurance agency, a bank, or a brokerage – brings his fucking briefcase home so he can climb up the ladder of success.' In fact, it is a clinical condition, usually associated with people with low self esteem. Zappa was proud of the long hours he worked and frequently alluded to it in interviews, as if to say: 'See how hard I work, don't you think that makes me a good person?' No other rock star or composer mentions how many hours a week they put in. Clinically, these are the symptoms of someone who has immunized himself against loneliness. Zappa had become a confirmed misanthrope who treated the outside world with extreme cynicism and scorn and restricted his human relations to as few people as possible, even within his working environment. He worked all day every day for years with his engineer Bob Stone, but kept him at a distance: 'My relationship with Bob is purely professional, and it's better that way. I know nothing about him, where he lives, if he has a woman or what. Hello, goodbye and that's it; only a couple of breaks for a bite to eat and to go to the toilet.' Of course, the people who wasted his time with 'emotional freight' were his family, and he saw as little of them as possible.

In his autobiography he described Gail as his best friend, but said that the only time they spoke was about business, if they had to, and the rest of the time they didn't talk at all. The children, also, were not allowed to disturb Frank's work. In this one important respect, the Zappa household was deeply conservative: it was the mother's role to bring up the children. Gail appears to have shared Frank's views on everything, including his unreconstructed attitude towards feminists. She told Victoria Balfour: 'I don't know why they're not at home taking care of the kids where they should be.'

Moon, in particular, has spoken of her resentment at spending so little time with her father: 'I did feel his presence in the house, but you didn't bother my father unless it was really important.' It was a strange upbringing for the children, like something from a Victorian novel; knowing their father was there, but not being allowed to see him, always having to be quiet in that part of the house. Zappa hardly ever went out: 'LA is a shitty city,' he said. 'I only stick my nose out of the door to go on tour.' He never took a walk around the block, and it would not have occurred to him to take the children on an outing or a vacation. 'I'm not a tourist,' he said. 'I don't travel for pleasure. I don't take vacations. I only leave the house when I have something to do.' This lack of consideration for his family mirrors his father's attitude: the old Sicilian patriarch just up and moved whenever he felt like it, breaking off his family's friendships and schooling without a second thought.

In all other respects the children were brought up in complete freedom. They were allowed to decide whether or not they felt like going to school on any given day and were encouraged to call their parents Frank and Gail. There was no parental supervision and no rules, leaving nothing to rebel against. Moon: 'I hated it. It always left me with an awful floating feeling . . . too much space, too many choices . . . I craved rituals and rules like my friends had. I prayed for curfews and strictly enforced dinner times.'

Zappa's theory was that children were just little people who happened to be a bit shorter than adults and lacking in verbal and manual skills, but that did not mean they were any less intelligent. In fact, young children are not as intelligent – their brains are still growing. They are dependent individuals and need boundaries and limits.

It was an eccentric household. Frank and Gail may not have been hippies, but they were certainly bohemian. When they lived at the Log Cabin, Gail would hitch hike barefoot and bra-less down to the Country Store on Laurel Canyon. Once, when a man approached Moon in the dairy section, the two-year-old already knew enough words to scream 'Fuck off, pervert!' Moon has a vague memory of a nanny who attempted to conceal the large areolae surrounding her nipples with black masking tape and coloured Magic Marker, and also recalls men with straggling beards, body odour and bad posture who crouched naked near her playthings, melting her coloured wax crayons to make candles in old milk cartons. She recalled one visitor had drilled a hole in his nose so he could whistle through it.

When she went to school she thought she was going there to help the teacher; she didn't know about education. She was surprised to find that none of the other children had names like Moon or Dweezil – though this being Hollywood, there were other unusual names. Nor did they dress like her – Moon sometimes wore her underwear on her head. Nor did they know anything about R&B or make Barbie and Ken fuck and orgasm loudly. They didn't find inflatable sex devices or pornographic cartoons lying around the living room, nor did they watch scary movies with their parents.

Sex was always out in the open. The Zappa children watched porn films with their parents and were encouraged in their own sexuality as soon as they reached puberty. When they became teenagers, Gail insisted they shower with their overnight guests in order to conserve water. Moon: 'There was so much nudity in the house that, of course, I would never be drawn to porn or doing something deviant, because there was no charge on that. I didn't do drugs because there were none around my house, but there was nothing to stop me. There was nothing to rebel against. Nothing had a charge on it.'

Moon loved spending time in her friends' houses because they seemed so normal: 'I remember I had a friend whose family had dinner together, and the mother would tuck you in at night and make breakfast in the morning. They even had a spare bike for a friend. It just seemed so amazing to me.' Though her friends often stayed over, Moon was always mortified in case they encountered Frank wandering around the house naked at night or overheard her parents having sex (her bedroom was next to theirs and they could be very noisy).

There was also the matter of Frank's lyrics. Moon: 'When you're a kid, it's "Why is he talking about those body parts?"' In an article in *Harper's Bazaar* she wrote: 'My dad's music had made me shy, almost repressed about my own anatomy, with his lyrics about ramming things up poop chutes and shooting too quick – this from my dad! He was always so open creatively that I was off in search of black turtleneck bathing suits with long sleeves.'

The imitation Tudor house on Woodrow Wilson Drive never recovered from having a recording studio built in its basement. The 48-track facility took up a large amount of space, as did the ancillary echo chambers and tape-storage vaults. Two-inch tape is bulky and tape boxes soon overflowed, filling cupboards and improvised shelf space beneath stairs, all securely protected by electronic combination locks and a closed-circuit television system that monitored the locked entrance gate and grounds. There was a guardhouse at the gate and security was tight; Frank and Gail were terrified the children might be kidnapped.

The house became a labyrinth as new rooms were added: a workshop for the two resident technicians, a film editing suite and film storage – film and video was almost as big a problem as storing the audio tapes – a huge storage vault under the front yard, an office for Frank above the bedroom, all on different levels in seemingly random architectural styles. Frank threw nothing away and the rooms filled with stage props, instruments, a stage wardrobe, out-of-date equipment, old furniture and artwork: there were four huge chests filled with concert posters, original artwork by Cal Schenkel, Zappa's drawings going back to his days as a greeting-card designer, notebooks, set lists and photographs. There were new rooms for the children: Dweezil finished up in a bedroom at the top of a wobbly outside spiral staircase. The new kitchen, the biggest room in the house and the hub of the family, was built in an odd shape so as not to disturb a large jacaranda tree next to the house.

Through the dim concrete passages lined with tape boxes and rooms piled high with old Movieolas and sports equipment scurried the staff: assistants, guitar tecs (including Gail's brother Midget Sloatman), engineers, musicians, accountants, roadies, drivers and film editors, each with a project or a mission. More and more of the business seemed to come Gail's way, yet on top of this she managed to oversee school runs for four children, as well as the usual children's parties and play visits.

Throughout the seventies, Zappa's children saw hardly anything of their father: he was on the road or rehearsing for six months each year, and spent the other six months in the studio. When he was around, they were usually asleep. Now that he had the UMRK and was touring less by the early eighties, he spent more time in the house. The children welcomed this, even though it meant they had to be quiet during the day when Frank was sleeping.

Some time between September 1980 and 1981, Moon slipped a note under Frank's studio door addressed to 'Daddy' (not 'Frank', as he liked to be called). She introduced herself: 'I'm 13 years old. My name is Moon. Up until now I have been trying to stay out of your way while you record. However, I have come to the conclusion that I would love to sing on your album . . .' She gave the house telephone number and asked him to contact her agent, Gail Zappa, and suggested that she might do her 'Encino accent' or her 'Surfer Dood Talk'. 'It was me saying "Pay attention to me!"' she told the *Sydney Morning Herald*. Moon's imitation of the Encino accent was a big hit around the house. 'I would go to bar mitzvahs and come back speaking Valley lingo that everybody at the bar mitzvah was speaking and the song came out of that.'

It was some time before Frank responded to her offer, then one night at 3 a.m., he and drummer Ed Wackerman were jamming in the studio on a riff that started off at a soundcheck about a year before. Zappa had been messing around with it for a long time. That night the track really came together, so Frank saved the tape and, little by little, over several days, they added other stuff to it, including some terrific guitar playing, and the 'Valley Girl' backing track was made.

Frank woke Moon in the middle of the night and brought her down to the vocal booth to record her monologue. She was seized by a fit of nerves, but managed to improvise a number of tracks, imitating actual phrases she had heard the girls use in the San Fernando Valley. The more Frank laughed, the more she knew she was coming up with the right stuff.

The bass line was the last thing to be added. Frank had mixed his very full guitar track down low, in order not to conflict with the vocal, and thought he could get away with not using a bass at all. Then engineer Bob Stone said: 'Aw, go ahead and put on a bass line.' Zappa was about to go out on tour, so one night and after rehearsal he brought bass player Scott Thunes up to the studio and about an hour and a half later the track was finished. Frank cut an acetate for Moon and went off to Denmark to begin his ill-fated 1982 European tour.

While he was away, Moon gave an interview to her favourite radio station KROQ-FM, taking along her acetate of 'Valley Girl'. They played it on the air and the switchboard lit up. The station held on to the acetate and kept playing it again and again. It was such an instant success that other stations taped it off the air in order to play it. Zappa had an unexpected hit on his hands and the record wasn't even out. 'Valley Girl' would appear on *Ship Arriving Too Late To Save A Drowning Witch*, which was released on 3 May, a week or so after

Zappa left the country. It was not the sort of album that would be broken by a teenage novelty record, consisting as it did of songs about male lust, industrial pollution and 'Teenage Prostitute', sung live in an overblown high operatic shriek.

Curiously, Zappa was slow off the mark to cash in the success of 'Valley Girl' and only belatedly released it on 5 July, and then only as a 12-inch dance single rather than a regular 7 inch. When it charted, Barking Pumpkin finally released it as a regular single on 30 August and it dragged *Ship Arriving Too Late To Save A Drowning Witch* up to Number 23 on the charts. It was Zappa's last big-selling record. 'Valley Girl' got him his second Grammy nomination, for Best Rock Performance by a Duo or Group with Vocal. Moon told *People* magazine: 'I had no idea it was going to be such a big hit. I just wanted to spend some time with my father.'

Zappa was irritated that his second hit single after 'Dancin' Fool' was also a novelty record and almost seemed to dissociate himself from it. Zappa: 'There are a couple of things about "Valley Girl" being a hit: first, it's not my fault – they didn't buy that record because it had my name on it. They bought it because they liked Moon's voice. It's got nothing to do with the song or the performance. It has everything to do with the American public wanting to have some new syndrome to identify with. And they got it. There it is. That's what made it a hit. Hits are not necessarily musical phenomena . . . we've hired a guy to make merchandising deals on that song.'

The song was a natural for merchandising and in November *Cashbox* reported that Barking Pumpkin Records had entered into an agreement with Stanford Blum Enterprizes for exclusive worldwide licensing rights to 'Valley Girl'. Barking Pumpkin said that 18 licences had already been sold for products carrying the Valley Girl name, and a special Valley Girl logo designed by Rod Dyer, including a doll, a clothing line, a cosmetics line, jewellery, ceramics, posters and greetings cards. A video game was in the planning stage. *Cashbox* reported that Zappa's Munchkin Music had already filed a suit in the Los Angeles Federal Court against Computer One Industries for manufacturing and selling a line of Valley Girl T-shirts.

By January 1983, Zappa was already in court, trying to stop production of the movie *Valley Girl* claiming that it would confuse the public about the true Valley Girl name. He claimed unfair competition, diluting his trademark and $100,000 in punitive damages, in addition to whatever the court granted in damages. His programme of Valley Girl clothing, cosmetics, key chains, dolls, greetings cards and other merchandise would be damaged. In another legal action he also stopped Bloomindales from opening a Valley Girl boutique.

He seemed ultimately resigned to the success of 'Valley Girl' and even edited Moon's *Official Valley Girl Coloring Book*, but as he told *Billboard*: 'People think "Valley Girl" is a happy kind of song, but it isn't. I've always hated the [San Fernando] Valley. It's a most depressing place.' He was even more depressed that record buyers seemed to think it was a celebration of the Valley Girl lifestyle. 'It was a joke,' he said. 'It just goes to show that the American public loves to celebrate the infantile. I mean, I don't want people to act like that. I think Valley Girls are disgusting.' On a more positive note, 'Valley Girl' made him enough money to have a full symphony orchestra play his classical compositions, and it made Moon rich enough to later buy a house on Woodrow Wilson Boulevard, the street she grew up on.

'Valley Girl' rather overshadowed *Ship Arriving Too Late To Save A Drowning Witch*, though certain critics were ready to pounce on Zappa's sexual attitudes in the album. 'Teenage Prostitute' gave them cause for concern. It is about a 17-year-old run-away whose pimp is shooting her full of smack. Zappa appears not to feel any compassion for her. The fact that her pimp would beat her if she tried to get away is treated as a joke. Did Zappa sympathize with girls who were forced into prostitution? Apparently not. He was quite happy to hire prostitutes for his own purposes. His attitude to them was like his attitude to everything: the pimp provided them, they provided a service and he was a consumer of that service. On the 1988 European tour he hired three prostitutes as prizes in a raffle at a party he gave for the band in Barcelona. Zappa: 'It was a straightforward business deal. It was like a "rent-a-girl" business.' He naturally sang about it on stage.

As far as Zappa was concerned this was the real world. Zappa: 'People don't like it when I remind them that in their attempts to get sexual gratification most Americans are so inept. People hate it when I tell them that, so they take their frustrations out on me. But I'm just a reporter – I tell people what I see, and I see ineptness and buffoonery going on.'

On 22 December Bob Dylan turned up at Zappa's house. He felt he had lost touch with recording technology and wanted a producer familiar with a state of the art studio. Seated at the piano in the basement, he played a number of songs that would later appear on *Infidels*. Frank liked them and agreed to do it, but Dylan evidently thought Zappa's percentage too large; after approaching Elvis Costello and David Bowie he co-produced himself with Mark Knopfler. We will never know what Zappa would have done with *Infidels*.

After the disastrous concert in Palermo in July 1982 Zappa took two years off to concentrate on his classical projects. He was confident that his 'serious' music had merit and deserved to be heard. Zappa: 'I think what I do in that realm is easily as good as anything else that anyone else has done or will do. I'm a good composer. I can write for orchestra, and I think up things that no one's ever heard of and you'll never hear of until I can get somebody to do it.'

First he spent three months in the UMRK putting together his next album, *The Man From Utopia* – to be released in March 1983 – and then began preparations for a full-scale orchestral recording of his classical pieces; aided by the huge influx of cash from 'Valley Girl'.

Zappa had been unlucky in getting his classical music performed and recorded. Back in 1976 he had lost $125,000 in copyist fees and travel and hotel expenses when a concert by the Vienna Symphony Orchestra fell through due to lack of funding. In 1980 arrangements for the Residente Orchestra from The Hague collapsed because Zappa had not realised the orchestra expected to be paid royalties on the recording. That time he lost $100,000. After similar experiences with two Polish orchestras, he decided to use an all-American orchestra and made a deal with the Syracuse Symphony Orchestra from upstate New York. Lincoln Center was booked for 30 January 1983, but then the orchestra's fee mysteriously doubled due to some obscure musicians' union regulations. The Syracuse Symphony were sent packing and Zappa looked to Europe again. He first thought of the BBC Orchestra, because 14 of their members had played with the Mothers of Invention at the Royal Festival Hall in 1968, but they were booked for the next five years. A full-size symphony orchestra consists of more than 100 players, plus supporting accountants, book-keepers, librarians, drivers and so on – like a rock band, only 20 times as big – and consequently they plan their time as far ahead as possible.

Fortunately for Zappa, the London Symphony Orchestra (LSO) had a two-week gap in their schedule. The LSO was founded in 1904 and shortly afterwards became a limited company, owned and managed by the players. The 107 musicians choose what they are going to record and who is going to conduct them and over the years have worked with the world's foremost composers and conductors. Zappa was probably familiar with their 1972 recording of Stravinsky's *The Rite of Spring*, conducted by Leonard Bernstein (the LSO's then president). The orchestra had planned on taking a winter break, but the players decided that Zappa's work posed an interesting challenge and accepted the booking. Zappa was remarkably lucky to get a world-class orchestra at only a few months' notice.

It is unclear what Zappa was looking for. If it was just accuracy in reading his scores (as his later comments about musicians and his work with the Synclavier suggest), he might have been better off hiring 100 session musicians. The LSO was famous for its creativity and the way this great collection of players could fuse into a single unit. Zappa might have been better suited to the Berlin Philharmonic Orchestra with its amazing technical assurance and intense performance, but of course, he hadn't known that orchestras have to be booked years in advance.

Having secured the LSO, he now had to find a conductor who would do justice to his scores. Pierre Boulez would have been his ideal choice, but (to the astonishment of the modern music establishment)

Zappa and Boulez were already engaged on a project and Boulez barely had time to devote to that.

Boulez had a formidable reputation. He compared himself to the Chinese Red Guards and the Bolsheviks: an autocrat who condemned Brahms as a 'bore', called Tchaikovsky 'abominable' and Verdi 'stupid, stupid, stupid'. Boulez was one of the most important and influential men in the modern music establishment. Arriving in Paris in 1942 as a Schoenbergian atonalist, his first public gesture was to boo loudly at an all-Stravinsky concert. Such was his influence that shortly after meeting him, Stravinsky took up twelve-tone writing, as did Aaron Copland. The moderns also came to his barbed attention: Webern was 'too simple', Berg was in 'bad taste', Stockhausen was 'a hippie', his own teacher, Olivier Messiaen, wrote 'brothel music' and his one-time ally John Cage had become a 'performing monkey'.

Boulez also disparaged American minimalists who had, he thought, a 'supermarket aesthetic', as well as American serialists with their 'cashier's point of view'. He admired Ligeti, Bartók, Birtwhistle, Varèse and Elliott Carter and was a composer in his own right. Critic Alex Ross wrote that Boulez 'set the profile of "modern music" as it is popularly conceived and as it is still widely practised – a rapid sequence of jabbing gestures, like the squigglings of a seismograph.'

Frank bought his first Boulez album when he was 17: *Le Marteau sans maître* conducted by Robert Craft. At 18 he obtained a copy of the score and saw that the performance was not very accurate. He later got Boulez's recording of the piece and noticed that he played it slower than the marked tempo, which he raised with Boulez when they met. At a June 1980 concert in Paris, Zappa dedicated his show to Boulez, who was in the audience. He sensed they had ideas in common; in particular that music is about sound, not feelings.

Some months later, Zappa had sent Boulez a selection of his scores – presumably things like 'Pedro's Dowry' from *Orchestral Favorites*, in which Zappa is at his most Varèsian: no melody, dense blocks of sound, rapid figuration contrasted against sustained notes, sweeping musical phrases which often begin on one instrument and are completed on another, and lots of percussion (Boulez also favoured percussion in his compositions). Frank asked if he would be interested in conducting them. Boulez replied to say that he could not because he did not have a symphony orchestra at his disposal in Paris. He did, however, have the Ensemble InterContemporain, a virtuoso ensemble of 28 musicians specialising in modern work, based at L'Institut de Recherche et Coordination Acoustique/Musique (IRCAM), his nine million pound music research facility housed in the Pompidou Centre in Paris. He commissioned Zappa to write a piece to suit their instrumentation and a delighted Zappa set to work.

Kent Nagano, the conductor of the Berkeley Symphony Orchestra (then a small part-time orchestra, not the large professional group it is now), happened to visit IRCAM and was surprised to see Zappa's name on the list of pieces that were to be performed in the future. Wasn't Frank Zappa a rock musician? A friend told him: 'Well, it seems he's written a number of serious compositions and he wanted the Ensemble to perform it, and Pierre Boulez has agreed to conduct it.'

Nagano lived in San Francisco, so when it was announced that Zappa would be playing there in December 1981, he contacted Zappa's manager Bennett Glotzer and asked if he would send him some of Zappa's scores. Instead he received a message from Zappa, asking to meet him during the intermission at one of the concerts. It was the first time Nagano had been to a rock concert; he bought some earplugs and went along to the San Francisco Civic Center. He was overwhelmed by the experience, which was everything he feared a rock concert would be.

At the intermission, Smothers found him and escorted him backstage to meet Frank. Kent Nagano: 'He showed me the scores he'd brought with him. He said, "Take a look at that. What do you think?" And I opened up the scores and they were really so complicated that I was a bit taken aback. I explained to him that I really didn't know what to make out of them. I had to take them home and study them a little bit before I could answer him. He said, "Okay, take the scores, go home and let me know what you think." So I studied the scores and I had a great time because they were so complicated. They were challenging to figure out. And I found to my great surprise that in this stack of scores were some pieces that were really great, really exciting wonderful pieces. That, not only were they complex, but they were well-written compositions.'

Nagano was surprised that anybody could write something so original who wasn't known in the classical music field. The scores interested him so much that he asked if the Berkeley Symphony Orchestra could perform some of them. Frank said he wanted time to think about it, adding that recent performances of his music were so poorly prepared he was now much more careful in choosing who would perform his music.

Nagano heard nothing for about four months. Then he received a phone call: Zappa had been looking for a conductor with a reputation for handling complex music and Nagano's name had come up, presumably for his work with the Berkeley Symphony on a cycle of Olivier Messiaen's orchestral pieces. Nagano: 'He said: "I've hired the London Symphony Orchestra. How would you like to come with me to London, do public concerts in London and record these pieces?" And at this point I was really unknown, I was just basically out of school and I was working with this orchestra that was having a tough time.

'This is one of the very few times in my life when I tried to be coy, 'cause I wanted to be cool. Of course I wanted to go and I liked the music a lot, but I said: "Well gee, I don't know. I have to think about it," and of course that was being dishonest. But I said it anyway and Frank said: "Hmm, well I tell you what. I'll give you fifteen seconds to think about it, and after fifteen seconds you either say yes or no and if you don't say anything at all, I'll just go to another conductor." So I said: "Well actually Mr Zappa I am, I am interested." And that was the last time that I actually ever tried to be coy, because when you're dealing with people who are really serious, there's really no room to play games. I mean people who are really concerned about making music, just want to make good music, so in a way he taught me a lesson very early on in my career.'

Zappa planned to take percussionist Ed Mann and drummer Chad Wackerman with him, as well as David Ocker to play the clarinet solo on 'Mo 'n' Herb's Vacation', a piece commissioned from Zappa by Ocker in lieu of an increase in wages. Zappa had used some of his 'Valley Girl' money to buy a Sony PCM-3324 digital recording system to go with the PCM-1610 two-track digital audio mastering system already installed at UMRK – making him one of the few recording artists in the world to own a completely digital system. Mark Pinske, the engineer who made the live recordings of the last tour, used it to make the first ever digital recordings of the LSO.

Kent Nagano flew to LA to do some initial rehearsals at Zappa's house. They were a good match: Nagano had an excellent ear, both for rhythmic count and textural accuracy (Zappa's obsession). Nagano: 'I knew that for him it was just as important to have music performed as close to perfection as possible as it was for me. That's one reason why I got my reputation – both negatively and positively – because I rehearse until its really very, very accurate.'

The idea of an infallible score to be scrupulously realized by musicians did not exist until the Romantic period. Before then many crucial details were left up to the performers. The idea of the note-perfect performance so prized by Zappa and by music conservatories was unknown; players were expected to add whatever embellishments they could, depending on skill and ability. Frank was following in the tradition of the very music academies he so reviled when he demanded a studiously inexpressive, note-perfect rendering.

Zappa normally spent between two and four months rehearsing seven or eight musicians for a rock 'n' roll tour, and even then he made an enormous number of edits to the live recordings of these groups before releasing them. However, because of the time constraint he rehearsed the LSO for just four and a half days. He then expected them to perform three albums of his music without mistakes. Had he concentrated on just one, he might have had the accuracy he wanted, but it was not to be. Zappa, David Ocker, Chad Wackerman and Ed Mann flew to London on 4 January 1983 to begin rehearsals at the Hammersmith Odeon, ready for the concert on 11 January.

Kent Nagano: 'I think it's fair to say that the London Symphony, when they heard they were doing Frank Zappa's music, had no idea what that really meant in terms of the complexity. But I will say that they were really quite phenomenal; they worked so hard and I really fell in love with the orchestra, just as a group.'

Nagano described Zappa's music as technically some of the most difficult music for the conductor to count ever written. It also exercised little-used upper and lower ranges of the instruments that were difficult to play, particularly in such unusual time signatures. Fortunately, the players quickly came to grips with it, aided by Nagano who had good control of the time-keeping.

Nagano: 'It was a wonderful experience. Frank Zappa is a great musician. He has ears that can hear things that are just phenomenal: extremely complex textures . . . I could call a lot of wrong notes, but actually so could he. He could hear these incredibly complex orchestrations and identify what wasn't working right. And because of that, he earned my great respect and the London Symphony's respect.'

In 1982 the LSO was appointed resident orchestra at the Barbican Arts Centre, giving its first performance there on 3 March 1982. The stage at the Barbican is quite small, but they quickly found the optimum seating arrangement. Zappa, of course, thought he knew better.

David Ocker: 'As soon as the project was confirmed, Frank started redesigning the layout of the orchestra to achieve maximum recording separation. He made charts and graphs of who should sit where. Orchestra seating is very standardized and Frank was making radical changes. My advice against it was met with deaf ears. As soon as rehearsals started certain sections of the orchestra began complaining – each rehearsal had some different changes to the seating arrangement. It became a very chaotic issue which was complicated by the Barbican stage, which wasn't really big enough for a 100-piece band. Changes were being made as late as the day of the concert. After the concert, Frank gave up on the idea and had the recordings done in conventional set-up. All in all, I think he did it backwards. The concert and rehearsals would have gone much better in standard set-up while the recordings – in that huge room – could have been recorded in virtually any layout without much problem.'

In *The Real Frank Zappa Book*, six years after the event, Frank described the LSO concert as a disaster, claiming the stage was too small to hold the full orchestra; to his disgust, some musicians had to be sent home and still got paid. This, of course, was because he interfered with the seating arrangements. The LSO performed 90 to 100 concerts a year on that stage without anyone going home. Zappa also said that many LSO members got drunk ('roasted') in the backstage bar during the intermission and 'roasted' his music. Kent Nagano – who would have noticed a deterioration in their playing – said he was unaware of anything wrong. David Ocker saw drinking, but not to excess: 'I never saw anyone drink during rehearsal or concert, only before and after (and intermissions). I saw a back-stage bar in use before a concert at the Queen Elizabeth Hall as well as the Barbican, so I concluded that must be a common thing. I suspect, however, that this is a cultural difference between Britain and the US.'

It was a culture clash: in Puritan America drinking alcohol is seen as sinful, whereas in Europe it is an acceptable part of everyday life. Zappa was shocked at finding a bar backstage at the Barbican – though there is a backstage bar at the Hammersmith Odeon, a venue he played many times. The backstage bar is for the use of players and they are responsible enough not to misuse it, but Zappa believed that when he was paying for someone's time they belonged to him and even one drink made him furious, though he was powerless to prevent it. For Zappa the control-freak it was an intolerable situation and he complained about it for the rest of his life whenever an interviewer mentioned the LSO.

In any case, Zappa was not very interested in the live perform-ance of his music; his wanted only to get his dots down on tape. Zappa grumbled: 'I'm glad people liked it [the concert], but it wasn't a very accurate performance of the music. There were a lot of wrong notes in the show and the acoustics of the place were really shitty.' Aside from the composer, most people judged the concert to be a great suc-cess – including the critics, Kent Nagano and the LSO, who gave him a standing ovation at the end, a rare accolade from an orchestra.

Zappa bestowed an even rarer accolade on David Ocker: 'After the première in London I got a big hug from him – a very unusual event!' This was for his brilliant clarinet solo in 'Mo 'n' Herb's Vacation', a piece that Ocker had asked him to write. Ocker: 'Frank started "Mo 'n' Herb's Vacation" because I asked him to write a solo clarinet piece. He was dubious about the idea, but he did it – eventually it was called "Mo's Vacation", but he didn't like it so he added a simultaneous drum solo called "Herb's Vacation". He still wasn't happy so he added three more clarinets and four bassoons, bass and a few other audio events. I guess it was still not big enough, so he added two more movements for huge orchestra – becoming the '"Mo 'n' Herb's Vacation" on the LSO album. He finally liked it at that stage, because it was only then that he expressed any thanks to me for asking him to write the piece.'

Zappa grudgingly accepted that the concert could have been worse: 'The LSO has an air of professionalism about it that goes above and beyond most other orchestras that I've been associated with, which is not a lot, but I've been associated with a few. I like the attitude of the LSO and whatever the liabilities might be from some of the individual performers, or the attitude of some guys in the orchestra, the net result of working with them was really positive. They got into it, they took it seriously, they did it like it was a professional job and some of them actually loved it. Then there were other people in the orchestra who couldn't care less because they're doing this as a job . . . In spite of the fact that it wasn't as accurate as it should have been, that evening was a fantastic event. It was a miracle; people should appreciate that.'

It might have made more sense to spend longer in rehearsal and record the LSO concert at the Barbican, but Frank wanted maximum separation on the tracks to allow him to edit the tape and, as the venue he had originally booked was unsuitable, there had been a flurry of activity as they tried to find a hall to use as a recording studio. Frank did not want to use the Hammersmith Odeon because you could hear the electrical transformer backstage, and virtually every other suitable hall was booked; mostly with Christmas shows. The LSO have of course recorded dozens of highly acclaimed albums at the Barbican, but Frank, as ever, knew best and they finished up in an acoustically dead sound stage at Twickenham Film Studios, home of the James Bond movies.

Recording began the day after the concert. Frank hired the Island

Records mobile studio and set to work. The technical problems he encountered during recording are recounted in loving detail in his autobiography, in a section filled with patronising remarks about musicians, including their supposed love of alcohol.

Recording lasted for three days: 12–14 January. Kent Nagano: 'The idea was to get as many pieces as we possibly could as close to perfection as we could ... We produced three albums during that period.' Because of the restricted time available and the huge amount of music Frank wanted to record, the orchestra was worked very hard, which inevitably led to stress among some players. Nagano: 'In all fairness to the orchestra, the music is humanly very, very difficult, and when you're doing two – sometimes three – sessions a day, it's pretty hard to keep your chops going.'

A session is three hours, with a short rest period each hour, so it comes as no surprise to hear that on the final day, some of the trumpet players took a break in the pub across the road. If Zappa had had more experience with orchestras he would have known what to expect. Paul McCartney: 'Trumpets are notoriously the guys who go to the pub because you need to wet your whistle, you need plenty of spittle. So there's a traditional role for them.' But Frank was furious. He claims they returned 15 minutes late and made so many mistakes and played so badly that it required 40 edits to make seven minutes of music accurate enough to release.

In fact, this is perfectly normal. There are hundreds of edits in all orchestral recordings, but Zappa was so put out that even on the liner notes to the second volume of *Frank Zappa: London Symphony Orchestra*, written in 1987, he was still petulantly complaining about the missing 15 minutes, the 'glowing' brass section, and making sarcastic references to 'fine British craftsmanship'. In one interview he claimed: 'To put that record together, I had to edit the tape about 8,000 times. That's based on each roll of splicing tape having about 2,000 splices on it, and I used four rolls on that sucker.' That is almost three edits every second (the album lasts 52 and a half minutes); an absurd exaggeration.

As it was, he was lucky to get two entire albums – 90 minutes of material – out of three days' recording with only four and half days rehearsal; four and even five months' rehearsal is common for a major classical piece. The orchestra played some fiendishly difficult music: 'Bob In Dacron', 'Sad Jane', 'Mo 'n' Herb's Vacation', 'Envelopes', Pedro's Dowry', 'Bogus Pomp' and 'Strictly Genteel', but they were used to playing difficult work and rose to the occasion.

Although Zappa was a hard taskmaster, the LSO clearly enjoyed working on the material, and were particularly delighted to meet Kent Nagano. On the last day of recording, one of the players removed a sign from an electrical transformer that warned: DANGER LIVE CONDUCTOR and hung it on his podium. Nagano: 'I still have that plaque. But they really gave 100 per cent, and they appreciated Frank's music; at the end they gave him an ovation that was for Frank and for his music. It was wonderful.' Sadly Zappa kept aloof and claimed the ovation was just for Nagano. He could not join in the camaraderie of the project. He wanted to hear his music played by an orchestra, but his personal demons prevented him from getting real pleasure out of it. He never got emotionally involved; he just wanted to hear what the dots sounded like.

19 Wives of Big Brother

Before leaving for London for the LSO project, Zappa had to endure the boredom of the Christmas holidays: the children were home from school and they expected (or at least hoped) to see him and there were even family meals that he was encouraged to attend. Zappa: 'During the holidays it's hard to get people to work. I mean people who are employed by me in the studio: an engineer and two maintenance guys. While they're off on vacation, I think "What am I going to do?" So I put the typewriter in my bedroom and spent a few days doing these things.' These 'things' were film scripts and sketches. He told *Sounds*: 'I've got a stack of film treatments over there that I did during the Christmas holidays, treatments for three films and a Broadway show. I cranked them all out in one week, now I'm going to go out and try to sell them.'

Frank's idea of writing consisted mostly of vaguely humorous sketches along the lines of those performed on *Saturday Night Live*, a TV show he particularly enjoyed. To produce three treatments and a show in seven days suggests they were little more than first drafts, especially as Zappa was a one-finger typist. He never gave his lyrics and sketches the care and attention that he lavished on his music and they are superficial in comparison. Zappa rarely went beyond his immediate preoccupations with ordinary everyday events, things seen on TV or stories of life on the road. Generally, even these stories were second hand. They were provided by band members at the Morning Briefing, where they were expected to recount tales of debauchery and excess for his delectation and future use.

One of the Christmas holiday scripts was *Thing-Fish*, yet another song cycle, described as: 'An evil prince called Fish Thing wants to rid the world of all unwanted highly rhythmic individuals and sissy boys. The prince invents this disease and puts it in the water supply. He also puts it in bottles of cologne called Galoot Cologne – pronounced ko-long-nuh. His object is to make the Broadway musical safe once again for boring productions like *Hello Dolly* and *Peter Pan*. I mean, have you ever been to a Broadway show?' UPI described it as moving through 'a fantastic world of gay liberation, women's liberation, Reaganomics, conspiracy theories and biological warfare.' Zappa told them, 'It's a joke.'

Not surprisingly, he was unable to find the $5 million needed to take *Thing-Fish* to Broadway. Had he found the money, would he have really wanted to mount a Broadway musical; especially as he must have known it was one of his least substantial works? Perhaps he was testing the water: his live audiences had been diminishing and his experience of the classical music world had not been good. He had always been interested in stage shows, from his days of making puppets and costumes at Edgewood to the Hollywood musical structure of *200 Motels*, and he may have been investigating that world to see if there were any opportunities.

'We composers are forced to use, in the realisation of our works, instruments that have not changed in two centuries,' said Edgard Varèse in a lecture given at the University of Southern California in 1939. 'Personally, for my conceptions, I need an entirely new medium of expression: a sound-producing machine (not a sound-reproducing machine) . . . Whatever I write, whatever my message, it will reach the listener unadulterated by "interpretation".

'It will work something like this: after a composer has set down his score on paper by means of a new graphic, similar in principle to a seismographic or oscillographic notation, he will then, with the collaboration of a sound engineer, transfer the score directly to this electric machine. After that, anybody will be able to press a button to release the music exactly as the composer wrote it . . . exactly like opening a book.'

Varèse expected this new machine to liberate music, to offer him an 'unsuspected range in low and high registers, new harmonic splendours obtainable from the use of sub-harmonic combinations now impossible, the possibility of obtaining any differentiation of timbre, of sound combinations, new dynamics far beyond the present human-power orchestra . . .' He expected that 'the machine would be able to beat any number of desired notes, any subdivision of them, omission or fraction of them – all these in a given unit of measure or time which is humanly impossible to obtain.'

Varèse did not live to see such a machine, but Frank Zappa did and it transformed the way he worked. The Synclavier (manufactured by New England Digital) essentially did away with the need for musicians. Zappa: 'It allows me to do music the way I always wanted to do it, just go in there and do it. You can play that in, just blast it in there and then edit and tweak it.'

Zappa's Synclavier work received an unexpected first airing. Every Monday evening at the Los Angeles County Museum a group of musicians called the Ear Unit put on concerts of contemporary music. They wanted to play 'While You Were Out', which appeared on the *Guitar* album, and asked Zappa if he could provide an arrangement for two percussion, two keyboards, flute, clarinet and cello.

Though Zappa had attended none of their concerts, he agreed to their request. When the Ear Unit went to the house to collect the parts, he played an electronic realisation of the music on the Synclavier to show them how it should sound. They were startled and said they didn't have time to rehearse anything so complicated (they were already committed to play two other difficult pieces including one by Elliott Carter). Frank insisted they play it correctly or not at all. The performance had already been announced in the programme, so they were in a quandary.

Frank then suggested an ingenious way out. 'Here's what we'll do,' he said. 'I'll have the computer simulate the sound of all the instruments in your group, and I'll make a digital recording of the piece.' All they had to do was mime. Zappa printed out the parts for each musician on the Synclavier, then the computer made an analogue tape cassette of each part, so each musician would know what he was supposed to be playing. Zappa: 'That frees the performer to do what he really wants to do, which is to look good on stage. He doesn't have to worry about a single note, because the machine takes care of that.' He was delighted by the idea. It was, as he put it: 'The only time a composer ever got a perfect performance of a brand new piece at its première.' Varèse would have envied him.

Zappa gave the Ear Unit the master tape on a Sony PCM-F1 cassette, which plays back through a video player. Unfortunately they didn't know the difference between VHS and Beta, and they were unable to play it. Instead they used one of the practice analogue cassettes, which sent a wall of hiss into the audience. No one in the audience suspected anything, because the other pieces also used amplification; certainly nobody noticed that the ensemble was not actually playing. In fact, the Los Angeles Times reviewer noted that the group 'played modern music with such vibrance'. Frank did not attend the concert, but he was suitably disgusted by the reports of the hiss and by the fact that professional music critics could be so easily fooled.

When the final volume of the ten-volume Grove Dictionary of Music and Musicians (5th edition) was published, several people, including David Ocker, looked to see if Zappa was listed. He wasn't, but there was an entry for Francesco Zappa, a little known eighteenth-century Italian cellist and composer from Milan who was active between 1766 and 1788.

Ocker tracked down numerous examples of Francesco Zappa's work and Frank's secretary sent off for photocopies of those in US libraries. Soon they were inundated with bundles of trio sonatas, written in eighteenth-century musical notation as individual parts, not scores, and very hard to read. Frank was quite excited by this discovery, though he laughingly dismissed the suggestion that he might be a reincarnation of the 200-year-old composer.

However, he immediately set Ocker to work entering the music into the Synclavier. He initially attempted to make the music sound authentic, using synthesized string-like sounds, adding crescendos and diminuendos to approximate an eighteenth-century trio of cello and two violins. Frank liked to play them to visitors to the UMRK.

Once Ocker had entered all of the musical notation into the Synclavier, Frank's only creative input was to decide which sound settings to use when the machine played them. Ocker: 'I never did understand what he was trying to do with it, but he picked some very rich synthetic sounds that served to obscure the eighteenth-century music ... When it came to recording them, the sound was far too staid and old-fashioned for Frank. He started substituting the most uproarious synthesizer sounds then available (this was before sampling) onto the three parts, instantly obscuring all the nuances I'd added and blurring much of what Francesco himself had written. Some of the combinations he tried in the studio were even more outlandish than what ended up on the record.'

Zappa described it as 'nice and real melodic ... Basically it's typical of music of that period, except it doesn't sound typical when it comes out of the Synclavier.' The result, not surprisingly, sounded like a computer playing classical music: mechanical, soulless, lifeless. It was not a project Zappa cared a great deal for and, according to Ocker, Zappa dashed it off 'super quickly' compared with other albums, sharing time with other projects between March and April 1984. As a musical artefact, the album *Francesco Zappa* ranks alongside George Harrison's *Electronic Sound* (1969), in which the listener gets to hear the Beatle learning to play the Moog synthesizer; here the listener hears Zappa test the limits of the Synclavier.

The Synclavier was heard again on *The Perfect Stranger*, an album combining solo synthesizer work played by Zappa and three live tracks recorded by the Ensemble InterContemporain on 10–11 January 1984 with Pierre Boulez conducting. The project with Boulez had finally been scheduled. It consisted of a concert on 9 January 1984 at le Théâtre de la Ville of three pieces written in the late seventies and early eighties: 'Dupree's Paradise', 'Naval Aviation In Art?' and the world première of 'The Perfect Stranger', written specifically for the Ensemble InterContemporain. This was followed by two days recording at the IRCAM studios beneath the Pompidou Centre with Zappa producing.

Working with Boulez was not especially enjoyable. Zappa liked to be in charge, but he was no match for Boulez, who dominated the French modern music scene – a rarefied world of arrogant and disdainful intellectuals. Boulez lectured, composed and conducted, and was a consummate administrator, sucking up virtually all the available government money for experimental music for IRCAM. Zappa had never encountered the rigorous arguments and deadly seriousness of the Parisian intellectual scene; he was out of his depth. Even at lunch Zappa did not recognize the dish Boulez appeared to be enjoying, so asked what it was.

'Sliced nose of the cow,' Boulez replied (*palais de bœuf*) and offered him some. Zappa stuck to his American-style steak.

Nevertheless Frank enjoyed experimenting with the amazing facilities on offer at IRCAM, which included the famous 4X digital processor, invented by their in-house Italian computer genius Giuseppe di Giugno. Frank used it to make last-minute modifications to 'The Perfect Stranger'.

The unspoken rule is that if a piece is commissioned, the composer has to sit and watch the première and pretend it was terrific. In Zappa's opinion the three pieces were under-rehearsed. He sat on a chair to the side of the stage during the concert and it seemed to him that the players were having difficulties. In his autobiography he wrote: 'I hated that première. Boulez virtually had to drag me onto the stage to take a bow.' However, unlike the LSO recordings, Zappa never suggested the pieces were performed inaccurately, either at the concert or on the album.

Boulez would not have played Zappa's music if he did not regard it as having merit, but he never actually said that he liked it. He thought it was a useful exercise for the Ensemble InterContemporain. 'I found a kind of vitality,' he said, 'and it was very good for our musicians to do that: they were not accustomed at all to it, and that's good to work on it.' However, in 1987 he told the newspaper *Libération*: 'I reserve judgement about all the qualities of Zappa's music.' Boulez was a great supporter of Varèse and had been the first person to perform his work in France after the war.

In an article on the influence of Varèse, Boulez wrote: 'I knew Frank Zappa quite well. His great interest was Varèse's music. It certainly had a great influence on his thinking and on his material. It was very interesting to watch how someone like Zappa was hypnotized by Varèse. Though Zappa was in a different world, Varèse's music was still influential in an osmosis kind of way. It is not immediately appreciable, nonetheless still very acute.'

For 'The Perfect Stranger' Zappa used all his most effective devises, the marimba giving way to harp at the end of a phrase and staccato blocks of sound contrasting with rapid runs. This is probably the best example of his music being based upon speech patterns, transcribed for musical instruments. Boulez brought a new level of meaning to the other two tracks; both audience favourites. But *The Perfect Stranger* is a strangely uneven album, because the remaining tracks are computer-generated. They sound very mechanical compared with the Ensemble InterContemporain ones, especially when there is a run of identical fast notes on a marimba-like setting. This was made before the Synclavier could sample sounds, so everything is electronically generated.

This classical interlude ended, for the time being, with 'A Zappa Affair': two nights at the Zellerbach Auditorium in Berkeley on 15–16 June 1984, when Kent Nagano conducted the Berkeley Symphony Orchestra in ballet versions of 'Bob In Dacron', 'Sad Jane', 'Mo 'n' Herb's Vacation', 'Pedro's Dowry', 'Sinister Footwear' and something listed as 'a spontaneous minimalist composition'. Members of the Oakland Ballet used huge marionettes borrowed from the San Francisco Miniature Theater as part of their costumes.

Though he gave no live concerts during his two years in the world of modern music, Zappa continued to release rock 'n' roll albums. On 28 March 1983 he put out two albums: *Baby Snakes*, the historic Zappa Halloween show recorded live at the Palladium, New York 28–31 October 1977, and a new studio album, *The Man From Utopia*.

This contained the usual songs about his latest gripes: 'Cocaine Decisions' criticized the widespread use of coke in the music industry – a veiled reference to his war with Warners. Though sung in Frank's best treacly Hollywood voice, it is entirely humourless. 'Stick Together' was his perennial complaint about unions. 'Sex' described his preference for larger ladies and 'The Jazz Discharge Party Hats' made a further exploration of his obsession with women's underwear, in what biographer Neil Slavin described as 'probably the most tasteless song in Frank's whole catalogue'.

The most interesting track, 'The Dangerous Kitchen', is essentially a catalogue song, like a Walt Whitman poem: half-chanted, half-sung in the *Sprechstimme* manner (a method also used to brilliant effect on 'The Radio Is Broken'). Here he extemporized on the contents of his kitchen (they were about to build a new one). This is Zappa the lyricist at his best: taking common ordinary incidents and expanding them, investing them with meaning, to stand for the human condition. Steve Vai transcribed Zappa's vocal part and overdubbed it as an acoustic guitar track on the live tape. It showed that Zappa could indeed write a song about anything. *The Man From Utopia* had a particularly repellent album sleeve by Tanino Liberatore, creator of the comic-book hero Ranxerox. It shows Zappa as Ranxerox surrounded by mosquitoes and swirling teargas at his last Italian gig. The album fared badly.

Two months later, Zappa released *Them Or Us*, a double-album of much the same thing. It includes some very high-quality tracks, but also a few fillers that might not have made it onto vinyl if Zappa had had someone to bounce ideas off. As it was, Barking Pumpkin was beginning to look like a family label; the new album included vocals from Moon, a guitar solo from Dweezil and a song title by Ahmet. Moon sings on 'Ya Honza', which contains extracts from 'Sofa No 2' rendered mostly in German, as well as 'Lonely Little Girl' and Moon's out-takes from 'Valley Girl'. The whole vocal track is played backwards, making it a sonic experience unaffected by lyrical meaning. Dweezil plays classic heavy metal guitar on a very slow version of 'Sharleena' and 'Frogs With Dirty Little Lips' came from a song Ahmet had made up.

It seemed Zappa had been revisiting his collection of fifties R&B records, as there are numerous references to older songs throughout *Them Or Us*, beginning with a straightforward cover version of the Channels' 'The Closer You Are' and continuing with 'In France', a piece of American Francophobia sung by none other than Johnny 'Guitar' Watson who, sadly, was not given a guitar solo. It was a well-balanced album, ranging from novelty numbers like 'Baby Take Your Teeth Out' and 'Frogs With Dirty Little Lips' to the Allman Brothers 'Whipping Post', which Zappa had been using as a surprise encore, partly because it was about the least likely number any audience would have expected him to play.

Now that the UMRK was running at full capacity, Zappa began an ambitious re-issue programme. He planned to release his entire catalogue as a series of five boxes with seven albums in each, beginning with *Freak Out!*

MGM/Verve had returned all his master tapes at the conclusion of their lawsuit, but they had been badly stored and the oxide had fallen off the original stereo mixes – in places you could see right through the tape, making it impossible to go from the quarter-inch masters to digital. In these instances he had to return to the original eight-track and twelve-track masters and re-mix them.

It is hard to believe he didn't have his own safety copies, as he had all the multi-track tapes and out-takes. Even so, why didn't he instigate a search for copy masters and safety masters? MGM pressed in both New York and Los Angeles, as well as Germany, Italy, Great Britain, Japan, Australia and New Zealand. The masters for these pressings were made locally by the record companies, which is why there are sometimes differences in foreign pressings. Presumably many of these tapes were still stored in MGM vaults worldwide and could have been used.

The two-inch multi-track masters were in good condition and the fact is that if one track on a multi-track is all right, then so are the others, but once Zappa had the two-inch tapes on his machine he was tempted to 'improve' them.

Zappa: 'I decided that I would add new digitally recorded drums and bass. That's been done to *We're Only In It For The Money* and *Ruben and the Jets* . . . There was no way to leave it alone because the original masters had been trashed.' *Freak Out!* and *Absolutely Free* were re-equalized from the two-track mix, but *We're Only In It For The Money* was remixed from the original masters, with brand-new digitally recorded drums and bass added. Zappa: 'We took off the original mono drum set and put on classy drums and all that. We did the same thing on *Ruben and the Jets*. On *Lumpy Gravy* we used a combination of the original two-track masters plus newly overdubbed material.'

Zappa hired Chad Wackerman to redo the drums and Arthur Barrow to overdub the new bass parts. Barrow: 'I did try to talk Frank out of it the best I could. I said, "Are you sure you want to do this?" He said, "I don't like the old bass and drums."' . . . Actually, how could the oxide be falling off the tape on one track and not on other tracks? The other tracks sounded perfect to me . . . . As for *Ruben and the Jets*, I kinda think that's bad too. Because one of the coolest things about that album originally was the tape-loop for the drums . . . It was a great sound.' Instead, Zappa dubbed on punchy seventies disco-sounding bass and drums that changed the whole character of the album.

Even worse was the way Barrow borrowed the Knack's 'My Sharona' riff for 'Flower Punk.' He was just kidding around but Zappa liked it and insisted that it stay in. 'My Sharona' was not recorded until twelve years after *We're Only In It For The Money*, and was a new wave song, rather than from the hippie period, so the psychedelic pastiche was destroyed.

Ruben and the Jets was an even greater travesty, because Zappa had originally gone to great pains to achieve the correct fifties ambience.

The digitally clean alien-sounding rhythm tracks destroyed all that. He later relented and re-issued *We're Only In It For the Money* on CD in its original form, but at the time of writing the only available version of *Ruben and the Jets* is the ghastly remix.

Zappa told *Ice* magazine: 'The master tapes for *Ruben and the Jets* were in better shape, but since I liked the results on *We're Only In It For The Money*, I decided to do it on *Ruben* too. But those are the only two albums on which the original performances were replaced. I thought the important thing was the material itself. I'm not necessarily enthralled with the level of musicianship or technical capability of my recordings done in 1967.'

Fans were outraged. Imagine if Lennon and McCartney had decided later on to replace Ringo with some smooth session musician. Zappa forgot (or more likely didn't even consider) that the early fans loved the Mothers of Invention, not just Zappa. In the sixties the Mothers were seen in the same light as the Stones, the Doors or Love. Zappa was the front man, but for many Mothers fans Jimmy Carl Black was just as important and it was seen as the ultimate in arrogance to replace him. It only helped to confirm Zappa's reputation as a monomaniac.

He must have recognized the potential danger, at least, because he kept the original musicians' names on the albums. In January 1985, just as *The Old Masters Box One* was about to be released, Jimmy Carl Black, Bunk Gardner and Don Preston heard about it and began a $13 million lawsuit against Zappa for unpaid royalties on Mothers of Invention albums released on Verve and Bizarre Records. They were soon joined by Ray Collins, Art Tripp and 'Motorhead' Sherwood and the claim was increased to $16.4 million.

They said they had received no royalties since 1969. Zappa was furious at their impertinence and tried every way he could to stop the suit. Interviewers soon learned to tiptoe around this delicate subject. As far as Zappa was concerned it was all *his* music – the musicians were just hired hands. He preferred to forget that without the original Mothers he would probably never have had a career at all; the early fans did not know or care who wrote the stuff, it was the humour and group attitude that counted and much of that came from the other members of the line-up.

Eventually it was settled out of court and none of the ex-Mothers have broken their agreement to keep silent about its outcome. They received something, but it was nothing like the amount they had tried to claim.

The first intimations of Zappa's *Thing-Fish* project appeared when Zappa directed a 'celebrity sex fantasy' photo shoot for the April 1984 issue of *Hustler*, Larry Flynt's hardcore porn magazine. Frank picked Ample Annie up from the Faces book and spent hours auditioning her on the phone before she flew to LA from Las Vegas for the shoot. He wanted to use her in the stage production he was planning. He wanted her to play a domineering housewife with a high-pitched shrieking voice, and had her repeat 'Harvey, yer a worm,' over and over again. Frank was premature in casting *Thing-Fish*, as he didn't have the money to put on a show. However, first he had Ample Annie appear in a photo-feature version of the *Thing-Fish* libretto in *Hustler*. She went to the house and met Gail and the children and Frank explained what she had to do.

Larry Flynt put up $55,000 for the feature, which included a *Thing-Fish* mask that cost $7,000 to make (Zappa used it on the album sleeve). The background consisted of the suburban house of 'an unknown Italian, somewhere in New Jersey', with fake snow and pink flamingos in the front lawn. Someone had found a Polaroid of Pat Boone with his penis hanging out and sold it to Larry Flynt. It amused Zappa so much he blew it up to poster size to use in the set.

Annie's hair was dyed white and backcombed and ratted out to about a foot around her head. She wore a dog collar, strange glasses that had boxes with naked legs hanging out of them and a scar was painted on her well-endowed chest. Annie: 'Naturally I stripped through the pages of the magazine. I started out in a Santa Claus outfit and went slowly down to a pencil and a briefcase.' It was in fact a pen, six feet long, that she had to straddle naked. She was paid $2,000 a day for three days and *Hustler* got 21 pages out of it. Annie: 'As usual, I was underpaid given the results.'

The shoot took place just before Thanksgiving. Larry Flynt and his wife and several assistants visited Frank at his home. Zappa deplored the attempts by the courts to suppress the magazine and gave his full support to Flynt in his crusade for freedom of speech. He wrote a statement that appeared in the January 1984 issue of *Hustler*: 'PLEASE BE ADVISED: YOUR RIGHT TO THINK FOR YOURSELF HAS NOT YET BEEN CANCELLED. YOU CAN STILL DO IT: AND IT IS GOOD FOR YOU. IT IS ALSO GOOD FOR AMERICA. THE FORMULA FOR THE CONTROL OF A TOTALLY SUBMISSIVE WORKFORCE, AS IT IS BEING ADMINISTERED TODAY, IS A SHORTSIGHTED SOLUTION TO COMPLEX ANTHROPO-MORPHIC PROBLEMS. UNIFORMITY IS NEITHER DESIRABLE NOR ENFORCEABLE, AND ESPECIALLY IN THE CASE OF A "FREE SOCIETY", IT IS NOTHING TO ASPIRE TO.'

Frank's feature appeared in the April 1984 issue, but it is hard to imagine what *Hustler* readers made of it: like a Cal Schenkel collage, the shots are cluttered with props and the bizarre libretto of *Thing-Fish* is printed across the top of each page. Annie was naked in many of the shots, but the set-ups were weird and perverse. Presumably Frank found them erotic, but how many other people did? The average *Hustler* reader probably thought it was a waste of space.

Zappa remained friends with Larry Flynt until his death. Flynt told the *New Yorker*: 'Frank was a genius, a rebel, and Frank and I in all our conversations had a very honest dialogue. We were never really out of synch politically or socially. There were always things to talk about, but never really anything to argue about. Frank really, really liked me a lot.' Gail agreed: 'Frank loved Larry. Frank and Larry were kindred spirits.'

Zappa never got the funding together for *Thing-Fish* as a Broadway musical. Instead it was released as a triple-album in November 1984. Even Zappa's most devoted fans found it hard going, and many people never got beyond the second album. As well as recycling songs from *Zoot Allures*, *Tinseltown Rebellion*, *Ship Arriving Too late To Save A Drowning Witch* and *You Are What You Is*, the lyrics managed to revisit all of Zappa's favourite themes: government population-control experiments, organized religion, Miss Pinky, and Zappa's fascination with homosexuality, which he always depicted as sado-masochistic. His return to the 'Bobby Brown' scenario once again transcended anything that could be interpreted as parody: a man finds a feminist so threatening it causes him to turn gay.

All of this was sung (beautifully) by Ike Willis in a brilliant imitation of Kingfish, the character played by Tim Moore in *The Amos and Andy Show* (the first US TV show with an all-black cast). Kingfish had a bogus stereotype black accent, which Zappa reproduced with 'den', 'dey', 'der', 'dat', 'gwine', and so on; even Willis has trouble keeping up with it. There are so many lyrics that they dominate the album, the story-line of which makes little sense unless followed in the libretto. As it was, in Zappa's words, just something he knocked off when his engineer was on holiday, few people bothered to make the effort. *Thing-Fish* is best summed up by the character Harry. When Rhonda asks him: 'Is this entertainment?' He replies: 'This is a disaster, a complete and utter disaster!'

In 1980 Karl Dallas asked Zappa if he had a special liking for writing stupid songs. 'I absolutely do,' said Zappa. 'I've said it many times before, and I'll say it again, like hydrogen, stupidity is one of the building blocks of the universe. As you come to grips with the splendour of stupidity itself, the process of being alive not only becomes more tolerable, but can even be enjoyable.'

Rehearsals began in May for a twentieth anniversary world tour. The line-up now consisted of Napoleon Murphy Brock on sax and vocals; Ike Willis on guitar and vocals; Ray White on guitar and vocals; Bobby Martin on keyboards and vocals; Brad Cole on keyboards; Scott Thunes on bass and Chad Wackerman on drums, but even before the tour began, Brad Cole was replaced by Allan Zavod, and Napoleon Murphy Brock was fired after the eleventh gig for using drugs (Zappa announced this on television, which many thought was a finkish thing to do; the equivalent of informing the cops).

The six-month tour began in July and ran until 23 December. They opened with six nights at the Palace Theater in LA, and various ex-Mothers and members of Zappa's line-up sat in, including George Duke, Johnny 'Guitar' Watson, Aynsley Dunbar, Bruce Fowler and Denny Walley. Dweezil sat in on two nights and also on the final gig. The tour took in the States and Canada, plus eleven European countries. By Christmas Zappa was exhausted, but the money came in useful.

There was a problem with Frank's manager, Bennett Glotzer. Gail told Don Menn: 'In about 1984 we'd gotten into a situation where we were subsidising Frank's manager. He owed us a lot of money, and so in order to keep the business going we were taking care of all his outstanding debts and I was getting very agitated with that. Things weren't working in an efficient way, Frank was on the road, and the shit hit the fan. He fired the manager, and I took over the business, and the first thing I did was fire everybody that worked for us. The lawyers, accountants – I just said, "That's it. I don't want any help from any of these people," and went out and found replacement parts. I took over in 1985, and it was trial by fire. It took several years to get through the outstanding nasties.'

Things were so tight she had to take out a $12,000 bank loan to buy two computers. Over the years Barking Pumpkin had always kept a list of the people who wrote to them and this now became a direct mail list. She sent out a questionnaire, offering a Barking Pumpkin T-shirt for sale and got the $12,000 back right away. Zappa named the mail-order company Barfko-Swill. Gail hired her sister and a guy who worked for Frank in production and the three of them sat on the floor of the living room, stuffing T-shirts into envelopes.

They switched record distributors when they found discrepancies in CBS Records' accounting and signed with MCA for the States, EMI for the rest of the world. The CBS problem had caused a backlog of 'product', resulting in four albums being released during Zappa's 1984 tour: on 23 August *Boulez Conducts Zappa: The Perfect Stranger* was released on Angel, one of EMI's classical labels; Barking Pumpkin released *Them Or Us* on 18 October and both *Thing-Fish, Original Cast*

Recording and *Francesco Zappa* on 21 November, giving Zappa's fans a wide variety of styles to choose from.

A perfect foil for Zappa's acerbic wit, self-righteous indignation and fighting spirit now presented itself in the form of the Parents' Music Resource Center (PMRC), a group of influential Washington wives seeking to clean up popular music by introducing a labelling system for records similar to that used by the film industry.

Tipper Gore (the wife of Tennessee Senator Al Gore) bought a copy of Prince's *Purple Rain* for her eleven-year old daughter and was appalled to find that one verse in 'Darling Nikki' appeared to be about masturbation. Horrified, she set about using her influence to put a stop such filth. In February 1985 a leadership committee was formed consisting of Tipper Gore, Pam Howar (the wife of powerful real-estate developer Raymond Howar), Susan Baker (a devout Christian with a liking for Country & Western and wife of Treasury Secretary James Baker), and Sally Nevius (the wife of a prominent Washington businessman). The four women put together a blue-chip mailing list of 2,000 names from their Christmas-card roster and were soon joined by Ethelynn Stuckey, the wife of a former Georgia Congressman.

They received a $5,000 grant from the Reagan-supporting Beach Boy Mike Love's Love Foundation, and in April 1985 set up the PMRC, a non-profit foundation with a job to do. According to *People* magazine: 'Practically overnight the group emerged as rock's most potent critics' as they hit the TV and radio talk-show circuit.

They compiled a system of classification for songs that offended them: 'X' for 'profane or sexually explicit'; 'V' for violence; 'D/A' for songs which advocated the use of drugs or alcohol; and 'O' for songs with an 'occult' content. The PMRC assembled a list of songs they found offensive – the so-called 'filthy fifteen' – and sent it to Stanley Gortikov, president of the Recording Industry Association of America (RIAA), expressing their outrage. They demanded a rating system for lyrics and for warning labels to be slapped on albums.

It was a weird list, consisting of everything from Top 40 hits to thrash metal. Top of the list was Prince's 'Darling Nikki' for its sexually explicit lyrics. Second came Sheena Easton's 'Sugar Walls', then Judas Priest's 'Eat Me Alive', Vanity's 'Strap On Robby Baby', Mötley Crüe's 'Bastard' (it 'glorified violence'), AC/DC's 'Let Me Put My Love Into You' ('sexually explicit'), and Twisted Sister's 'We're Not Gonna Take It' ('violent', though 'political' might have been a better definition). Madonna entered the list at number eight with 'Dress You Up'. W.A.S.P. got an X-rating for 'Animal'/'Fuck Like A Beast', whereas Def Leppard only managed a 'D/A' for 'High 'n' Dry'. Danish group Mercyful Fate managed a rare 'O' for 'Into the Coven', whereas Black Sabbath only rated a 'D/A' at twelve with 'Trashed'. The PMRC discovered sexually explicit lyrics in The Mary Jane Girls' Top 10 hit 'In my House' and Venom at number 14 received a coveted 'O' for 'Possessed'. At 15, Cyndi Lauper's ode to masturbation 'She-Bop' rated 'X', even though, as the lyrics claimed, there 'ain't no law against it yet'.

The PMRC were a non-profit organisation, so could not lobby for legislation; they had to be content with 'industry self-regulation' – voluntary censorship on the part of the record companies.

It so happened the record companies had a piece of legislation of their own that they very much wanted to get passed: a tax on home taping. HR2911, the so-called 'Mathias' bill, had to get through the Thurmond Committee. This proposal was written by the RIAA and provided for a 10–25 per cent tax on all tape-recorders and a one cent per minute tax on blank cassettes. The money would be collected by the government and distributed to 'copyright owners': the giant record companies and music publishers. It was a classic special-interest bill written specifically for Warners, CBS, Polygram, MCA, RCA and Capitol/EMI, which controlled more than 80 per cent of all recorded music in the States.

The PMRC letter to the RIAA was signed by 20 women, many of whom were married to congressmen. Senator Al Gore, Tipper's husband, was a co-sponsor of HR2911 and one of the signatories was the wife of Strom Thurmond (Republican, South Carolina). The implications of not taking the PMRC seriously were obvious. The President of the RIAA caved in immediately. He recommended appeasement, suggesting a notice on potentially 'unacceptable' records and even went along with the PMRC's concerns about hidden messages and backward masking on records (a long time obsession of the fundamentalist Christian right).

He called the PMRC's recommendations 'reasonable' and indicated that 'a new policy of sensitivity, discretion and reasonableness be applied in recording and releasing practices . . . Artist contracts, new and old, might be examined to assure that future content makes such company discretion possible.' In other words, he suggested a blacklist of artists deemed unacceptable to the Washington wives.

In early August, the major record companies agreed to print the warning 'Parental Guidance: Explicit Lyrics' on records that might cause offence, but this wasn't enough for the PMRC or their new allies, the influential National Conference of Parents and Teachers (PTA). They wanted a whole raft of demands enacted and managed to get a congressional hearing tabled.

As the wives appeared on TV and radio talk shows, denouncing everything from 'Dancing In The Street' to Bruce Springsteen's 'I'm On Fire', the Press went into a frenzy over 'porn rock'. The PMRC claimed there was a causal link between rock music and a variety of social ills from teenage pregnancies and suicide to rape, murder, sexual perversion and devil-worship. A spokeswoman said: 'It is our contention that pervasive messages aimed at children which promote and glorify suicide, rape and sado-masochism have to be numbered among the contributing factors.' The liberal press launched a counter-attack and TV stations invited rock musicians to have their say.

Zappa was quick to give an opinion on almost any subject – from education to TV evangelism – but he rarely ventured into politics, other than to condemn the Republican Party and the lunatic Right. During the Vietnam War, for instance, unlike many of his contemporaries Zappa refused to be drawn into anti-war protests or demonstrations. Typically, when he decided to launch a counter-attack on the PMRC, he did it as an individual rather than joining any of the organisations that sprang up in defence of recording artists. The fight was led by the Musical Majority, a coalition organized by Gold Mountain Records' chief Danny Goldberg that included John Cougar Mellencamp, Don Henley, Hall and Oates, the Pointer Sisters, members of Kiss, REO Speedwagon and many others.

Zappa cared passionately for freedom of speech and the First Amendment, but the idea of working with other people and not being in complete control was so abhorrent that he preferred to spend more than $70,000 of his own money rather than co-ordinate his activities with his fellow artists. Over the next two years he sent out press information packs and clippings and gave as many as 300 interviews.

At times this suggested an element of personal publicity in the whole project. When Peter Werbe at WRIF-FM in Detroit asked him about the Musical Majority, Zappa more or less dismissed them: 'Yeah, I have no connection with them. That's Danny Goldberg, another record company owner, and he's got a . . . I don't know whether it's the artists themselves or their managers who are signatory to his proclamation or whatever it is.' Perhaps his opposition to the PMRC would have been more effective if he had known.

Most of the PMRC's suggestions were unenforceable. For instance it was unrealistic to compare the record business with the movie industry: each year there were a little more than 300 films released, but the record companies issued more than 25,000 songs; who was going to monitor and categorize them? What if there was disagreement? More importantly, as Zappa put it: 'People who act in films are hired to "pretend". No matter how the film is rated, it won't hurt them personally. Since many musicians write and perform their own material and stand by it as their art (whether you like it or not), an imposed rating will stigmatize them as individuals.'

In addition, several large record-store chains announced they would not handle any records with a sticker. Then the Camelot chain of 400 stores was told by the Shopping Malls Association that if they allowed any stickered albums into their stores they would lose their leases. It was obvious that stickering would result in any 'questionable' records being unavailable in most of the country.

Pressured by their wives, the congressmen held an 'impartial forum' to investigate the sorry state of the record industry. Senator

Hollings (whose wife was a signatory to the RIAA letter) said: 'If I could do away with all of this music constitutionally, I would . . .' The Senate hearing on 19 September 1985 was fixed in favour of the PMRC. The five-hour event was a media circus with 35 television feeds, 50 photographers, plus reporters and members of the public.

At the Senate hearing, Zappa was by far the most eloquent speaker, though he undermined his credibility by imitating the southern accents of some of the PMRC wives. Dee Snider from Twisted Sister proved to be far more articulate than the PMRC had expected and was able to contradict much of their testimony; but it was John Denver who did the most damage to the PMRC cause. Clean-cut and all-American, he held fast to the First Amendment, telling the chairman: 'Sir, we *cannot* have any kind of censorship whatsoever.'

Dee Snider described Denver's testimony: 'And here they were, falling all over themselves, complimenting him about the work he'd done for world peace and hunger and all his good efforts, and saying, "But Mr Denver, don't you think we could have just a *little* bit, maybe some ratings on records?" And he says, "Absolutely *not*." He wouldn't budge. He had everything backed up. He was devastating. But to watch the press coverage, you wouldn't even know that John Denver was there for the most part. He was the most damaging, they gave him the least press.'

Frank, however, received wide coverage and surpassed himself in a brilliant speech (available in his autobiography and on the Internet). His testimony was well researched and factually accurate, giving him a solid base from which to stray into flights of rhetoric to please the media and ensure that his views were reported: 'Ladies, please be advised: the $8.98 purchase price does not entitle you to a kiss on the foot from the composer or performer in exchange for a spin on the family Victrola. Taken as a whole, the complete list of PMRC demands reads like an instruction manual for some sinister kind of "toilet-training program" to house-break all composers and performers because of the lyrics of a few. Ladies, how dare you?'

He noted that country music had been excluded from the labelling proposal and joked that Tipper and her husband, Al Gore, the Senator from Tennessee, were trying to boost sales of Nashville music: 'Shouldn't the ladies be warning everyone that inside those country albums with the American flags, the big trucks and the atomic pompadours there lurks a fascinating variety of songs about sex, violence, alcohol and the devil, recorded in a way that lets you hear every word, sung for you by people who have been to prison and are proud of it? Is the PMRC attempting to save future generations from sex itself? The type, the amount, and the timing of sexual information given to a child should be determined by the parents, not by people who are involved in a tax-scheme cover-up.'

Most of all he objected to the moral superiority of the wives: 'The PMRC's proposal is most offensive in its "moral tone". It seems to enforce a set of implied religious values on its victims. Iran has a religious government. Good for them. I like having the capital of the United States in Washington, DC, in spite of recent efforts to move it to Lynchburg, Virginia. Fundamentalism is not a state religion. The PMRC's request for labels regarding sexually explicit lyrics, violence, drugs, alcohol and especially occult content reads like a catalogue of phenomena abhorrent to practitioners of that faith. How a person worships is a private matter, and should not be inflicted upon or exploited by others. Understanding the fundamentalist leanings of this organisation, I think it is fair to wonder if their rating system will eventually be extended to inform parents as to whether a musical group has homosexuals in it. Will the PMRC permit musical groups to exist, but only if gay members don't sing, and are not depicted on the album cover?

'The PMRC has demanded that record companies "re-evaluate" the contracts of those groups who do things on stage that they find offensive. I remind the PMRC that groups are comprised of individuals. If one guy wiggles too much, does the whole band get an "X"? If the group gets dropped from the label as a result of this "re-evaluation" process, do the other guys in the group who weren't wiggling get to sue the guy who wiggled because he ruined their careers? Do the founders of the tax-exempt organisation with no members plan to indemnify record companies for any losses incurred from unfavourably decided breach of contract suits, or is there a PMRC secret agent in the Justice Department?'

Zappa's war against the 'cultural terrorists' as he called them in a *Cashbox* guest editorial took up the best part of a year, but he got an album out of it. Treating the hearings as an anthropological event, he incorporated sections of the them into a twelve-minute track called 'Porn Wars' on an album called *Frank Zappa Meets The Mothers of Prevention*. Zappa: 'It uses the actual voices of the senators and Reverend Jeff Ling and Tipper Gore from the Senate hearing saying the things that made them famous during the hearing, and that makes the music.'

Initially, most of the clips from the hearings are presented unaltered, but as the track progresses Frank has a wonderful time speeding them up, altering their pitch and tone so that their voices become a sound collage in the manner of Luciano Berio's tape pieces, aided by sombre Synclavier music, snorks and fragments of under-the-piano conversation left over from the *Lumpy Gravy* sessions. Though the track works perfectly well as a piece of music, even if you don't know the source of the material, Zappa deemed it so American that Canadian and European listeners got replacement tracks when *Frank Zappa Meets The Mothers of Prevention* was released; a pity, because it was a superb piece of work.

Most of the other tracks were instrumentals, often bubbling over with notes rather like the mid-fifties hits of Les Paul and Mary Ford. One track, however, drew even more attention than Zappa's sampling of the senators. Zappa was still seething at having to part with money in unpaid royalties to the former members of the Mothers of Invention and his anger and resentment seems to have been expressed in an extraordinary anti-sixties youth-culture track called 'We're Turning Again'. It contained a mean-spirited putdown of hippies, described as being totally empty, living useless lives and lacking a sense of humour! He attacked their political activism – saying they were full of shit – and made a tasteless reference to the police at Kent State mowing down Allison Krause, the girl who had pushed flowers into gun barrels the previous day.

Zappa, of course, had done nothing to try to stop the Vietnam

War. He put down the peaceniks for believing in all the newspapers and magazines that (he claimed) defined their folklore. But a lot of this folklore had been written by Frank Zappa or pronounced by him in dozens of interviews in the underground press. He now completely dismissed the entire sixties youth movement, its politics and its music, in one bad-tempered hissy fit.

Zappa then went on to 'joke' about the deaths of a roster of sixties rock stars who never did him any harm: he attacks Jimi Hendrix (who he was happy to have on the sleeve of *We're Only In It For The Money*); Mamma Cass (a friend from Kirkwood Drive days – here he perpetuates the myth that she choked to death on a sandwich); Keith Moon (whose fame Zappa was pleased to exploit to help sell *200 Motels*); Jim Morrison (who he sometimes jammed with on the Strip); and Janis Joplin (who he was happy enough to sleep with). Tommy Mars, who played keyboards on the track, found it extremely tasteless and so did many fans. This nasty, vicious song exposed Zappa as a cold nihilist with no emotions and no feelings for anybody else.

Rarely did he allow this side of him to come through in such an undisguised manner. It looked as if he were heading in the same direction as the father of Gonzo journalism, Hunter S. Thompson, who famously erected a huge statue in his garden of a large fist with middle finger raized: giving the finger to everyone, indiscriminately.

20 One More Time for the World

Zappa's world was changing. Within a few short years he went from rock 'n' roll musician to businessman: commuting to Moscow, briefcase in hand, and briefly becoming the trade representative for the Czechoslovakian government in the States (a career move no one could have predicted!). But first, he needed to sort out his business at home.

With his pioneering interest in digital recording, Frank was keen to have his albums released on compact disc when that format was introduced in 1982. His distributors, EMI-Capitol, were cautious about CDs (as they had been in signing the Beatles) and were the last of the major labels to introduce them. Even then, they were manufactured in Japan, making them expensive compared with cassette or vinyl.

However, Rykodisc (founded in 1983) was a new company that saw CDs as the future. When their chief A&R man Don Rose proposed releasing his back catalogue on CD Frank jumped at the chance; especially as he was offered complete control over the release programme, which was initially limited to 24 titles. The deal was announced in January 1986 and the CDs began appearing that autumn.

Prior to this, Zappa's only CD had been *The Perfect Stranger* on the classical Angel label. Also in January 1986 came a European-only release *Does Humor Belong In Music?*, recorded live by the UMRK

24-digital truck on the 1984 world tour. It was the quintessence of that tour, live recordings with no studio overdubs, and yet this concert did not exist. Zappa had no respect for the integrity of the performance. Instead he combined sections of each song as performed in several different venues, usually dropping in the best solo he could find.

It was the first time he did this to an entire live album and some of the dropped-in solos jar a little as the atmosphere of the performance suddenly changes. However, it meant he could present as-close-to-perfect-as-possible renderings of each of the songs: 'Lets Move To Cleveland', for instance, not only has a superb piano solo from Allan Zavod, but an outstanding drum solo from Chad Wackerman and a wonderfully inventive guitar solo from Zappa. The intro came from Los Angeles; the piano solo from St Petersburg, Florida; the drum solo from Vancouver; and the guitar solo from Amherst College, returning to Los Angeles for the out chorus!

It is a fine example of one of Zappa's best line-ups in full flight. Zappa is in his element, mooching about the stage, listening attentively to the playing, smoking a cigarette, reading messages handed up from the audience, collecting panties, sometimes dancing a little on the spot, relaxed – on one track he can barely stop laughing enough to sing the lyrics. This was where he was happiest: on-stage in some stadium or college auditorium far from home, a well rehearsed, tight band at his command, listening to his music, an audience roaring approval and, best of all, in complete control!

He enjoyed that tour: 'We had a lot of laughs. For example, one night in Seattle, in the middle of the show, Ike Willis started to do an imitation of the Lone Ranger, blurting out "Hi Ho Silver!" I still don't know why it happened, but I cracked up every time he did it. It must have been road fatigue. He'd keep yelling in the most inappropriate places. The whole show was riddled with bad Lone Ranger jokes and me not being able to sing the right words. I enjoyed that night.'

Frank's audience was an important part of his life; many fans travelled widely to see him as often as possible when he was on tour and he commanded a fierce loyalty. Zappa: 'They are part of the act. They're the reason why we're there. You see, my function on the stage is that of middleman between audience and the musicians. I pay their salary and I make sure they're there to deliver the goods to the people who require the entertainment. I act as a referee during that show. We have many thousands of kids in that hall who are waiting to be entertained. They want to get their rocks off. I'm the ring master.'

His preference was for a rowdy New York audience. Although he complained that his music was too subtle for his audiences to understand or that people missed the music because they were too involved with the lyrics and spectacle, when people did actually sit and listen as they did in Britain, he hated it. Zappa: 'People who come to a concert here just want to watch it . . . They don't get involved in it . . . It's like playing to a bunch of cardboard cut-outs. It's like a room full of voyeurs . . . They're not involved with what you're doing so there's no energy exchange between the audience and the band. Whereas in New York it's different.'

Frank liked to get members of the audience up on-stage to dance or read messages passed to him from the audience. He also collected panties for the on-stage washing line. Zappa: 'We used to have two guys in the band who were panty fetishists. It was a way to make them happy and to make the girls in the audience happy too. I also think it's a good look for the stage. I think a stage with a clothesline full of women's underwear has a certain aroma to it. You know what I mean. We even have an underpants roadie – the same guy who takes care of the Synclavier.'

Zappa tailored his shows to the audience: 'I make music that I make for an audience that has a special affinity for that kind of stuff. It's for them. A lot of the people who make the music are also part of the audience for the music and they need to be serviced, so it's not self-indulgence.'

The hundreds of interviews he gave to fight the PMRC had increased Zappa's public recognition and he was invited to give talks. He lectured the students of Wesleyan University in Lincoln, Nebraska, on the dangers of censorship and discussed art, morality and censorship on WGBH, Boston. He gave a lecture at Tony Bill's restaurant in Venice, California (where he also slipped in a preview of his new album *Jazz From Hell*), and he appeared at the At My Place club in Santa Monica for a panel discussion on censorship. He lectured at the Northridge campus of the University of California and made an appearance at the Audio Engineering Society convention at the LA Hilton to discuss the Synclavier and play selections of his work.

Frank extended his political lobbying to testify before the State Senate Judiciary Committee in his home state, Maryland, where they were considering a ban on sexual imagery in music, and where he had some success in preventing another pointless law entering the statute books. On the commercial front he appeared, incongruously, as a drug-dealer in the then trendy cop show *Miami Vice*. Suddenly Zappa was a public figure.

In 1987 he tried to use his new-found fame to sell the idea of a television series called *Night School* to the ABC network. It was designed to appear five nights a week in order to counteract bias in news reporting, but since much of this biased news originated with ABC in the first place the idea was rejected.

This was a bad year for Zappa's projects: an attempt to float Intercontinental Absurdities as a public company on the stock exchange failed, as did his religion: the Church of American Secular Humanism (CASH), which he established in Montgomery, Alabama, but then could not really find a use for. Fox invited him to be fill-in host on the *Late Show* (Joan Rivers had just been fired), but all of Zappa's suggestions for guests (Daniel Schorr from National Public Radio, Gerard Thomas Straub, producer of TV evangelist Pat Robertson's *The TV Club*) were rejected and they eventually transmitted a rerun.

All but one of the tracks on *Jazz From Hell* (released in November 1986) were composed on the Synclavier – and sounded like it: the mechanical repetition of the percussion, a strange rhythm on one track that sounded like a mechanical version of a musical saw, the lack of decay in the long drawn-out notes and wobble introduced to some notes to make them sound less computer-generated just seemed like tape slippage.

The contrast between these tracks and the live instrumental recorded at St Etienne in France is enormous. The way Chad Wackerman intuitively knows where Zappa is going in his guitar solo and provides the perfect accompaniment for each bar is uncanny: an example of telepathy at work and, of course, all too human, unlike the cold hard surface of the other tracks.

Ironically, this mild, unthreatening and totally instrumental album was later given a Parents Advisory sticker when the record industry finally introduced them – presumably on the basis of its title: further proof of the idiocy of the scheme. On a more positive side, *Jazz From Hell* garnered Zappa two Grammy nominations, one of which, for Best Rock Instrumental Performance (Orchestra, Group or Soloist), he won. A rival for the award was his son Dweezil, whose 'Wipe Out' from the soundtrack to *Back To The Beach*, recorded with Herbie Hancock and Terry Bozzio, had also been nominated.

The little Zappas were growing up and naturally wanted to get involved with their father's life in music and films. Moon was the first and had sung on several other tracks since 'Valley Girl', but she showed little inclination to become a musician. Instead she appeared in a series of bit parts in *Nightmares* (1983); *National Lampoon's European Vacation* (1985) and *Boys Next Door* (1986); she was in a 1982 episode of *Chips* and in the TV series *Fast Times At Ridgemont High* (1986). After leaving school at 15 she was adrift in the town of hype and tinsel. She tried to use her quirky humour as an actress and stand-up comic, but really she was not intellectually prepared or trained to do anything serious. As she put it: 'As a child I was given free rein; now I am only employable as an empress of the universe or something in "the arts".'

Dweezil had more direction. He idolized his father and wanted to join the family firm. He released his first single 'My Mother Is A Space Cadet' in December 1982, played guitar with Frank on-stage during the 1984 World Tour, and in August 1986 released his first album *Havin' A Bad Day*, produced by Frank and UMRK engineer Bob Stone. That year he also worked as a VJ on MTV. His proud father spoke to *Rolling Stone* about it: 'If his fan mail is any indication, they got the right guy for the job. The thing that's cool about Dweezil is he's just turned seventeen. He is a kid. He's not a guy pretending to be a kid. He's the age of the audience, and he's a genuine music fan. He knows something about the groups he's putting on. And he also knows them as individuals. The little stories he tells don't come off like showbiz stories.' Dweezil was also dating and Zappa suddenly found the house filled with Hollywood starlets, including Kate Wagner and Molly Ringwald.

Even 12-year-old Ahmet was getting in on the family act. In October 1986 he auditioned for the role of Stinky in a Showtime sitcom. Zappa told *Rolling Stone*: 'He's not afraid to say anything to anybody. He was reading in this room for the producers, and there were these howls of laughter. Ahmet came out, and my wife asked what happened. "Well," he said, "they liked me. They said they were going to bring me back to read again. I told them, 'I hope to God it's not written by the guy who wrote this crap.'"

Zappa took his children out of the education system as fast as he could and all of them took the California equivalency test at 15, rather than stay on in high school. He viewed the system as designed entirely to dumb-down people and turn them into passive consumers. Zappa: 'I tend to view the whole thing as a conspiracy. It is no accident that the public schools in the United States are pure shit. It is no accident that masses of drugs are available and openly used at all levels of society. In a way the real business of government is the business of controlling the labour force. Social pressure is placed on people to become a certain type of individual, and then rewards are heaped on people who conform, to that stereotype . . . You celebrate mediocrity, you get mediocrity . . . Few people who do anything excellent are ever heard of. You know why? Because excellence, pure excellence, terrifies the fuck out of Americans because they have been bred to appreciate the success of the mediocre.'

It is all the more peculiar, then, that Zappa did not let his children go to college. In one interview he said that he wouldn't stop them going, but they would have to pay for themselves. To many of his friends this was inexplicable. Moon wasted years appearing in bit parts in third-rate movies and TV sit-coms before finally finding her *métier* as a writer. She would have benefited enormously from studying English Literature at a good university; both her journalism and her first novel *America the Beautiful* reveal her to be an extremely talented writer. Blame must be laid at Zappa's door for imposing his own bizarre ideas about the American education system on his children. Maybe he didn't want her to become one of them 'college-educated women' he wrote about in 'The Illinois Enema Bandit'.

Now that he could talk to the children Zappa had even less reason to go out or make friends. He had ready-made company, everything he needed was at home: his family, his Synclavier, his studio, his staff, coffee, cigarettes, two dogs, six cats, a snake and a turtle. He was 'the only complete man in the industry', as William Burroughs once put it.

But Zappa needed more material to release and as usual he wanted to record it live. This meant another tour, the first in four years. He assembled his favourite musicians: Ike Willis on guitar and vocal; Mike Keneally on guitar, synthesiser and vocal; Bobby Martin on keyboards and vocal; Ed Mann on percussion; Scott Thunes on bass and Chad Wackerman on drums. To this he added a horn section: Walt Fowler on trumpet; Bruce Fowler on trombone; Paul Carman on alto sax; Albert Wing on tenor sax and Kurt McGettrick on baritone sax.

Flo and Eddie showed up for some of the early rehearsals. They had a successful radio show on WXRK New York in the drivetime slot and after seeing the lyrics to some of the songs on the set-list they decided that further association with Zappa would harm their new middle-of-the-road career.

Zappa had the band learn over 100 songs – more than eleven and a half hours of music. It took four months of rehearsals; even the horns were in rehearsal for two and a half months; eight hours a day, five days a week. It would have been an enormous extravagance for a tour, where normally the band learns a set list and maybe a half dozen songs for encores or to vary the programme. Three weeks' rehearsal would have been enough for a big show in those days. The reason for the huge repertoire was so that Zappa could record the group at live rates rather than paying union studio rates. The players were each on $500 a week plus a per diem when they were actually on the road (Zappa had finally bowed to normal practice), which was good deal less than a session musician cost.

Scott Thunes was given the difficult job of running the band and conducting rehearsals. Mike Keneally: 'Scott has a way of expressing dissatisfaction which is not particularly tactful. Simply put, if somebody hadn't learned their part properly, Scott was a pain in the ass . . . Most of the other guys in the band (who were older than Scott, and jazz musicians to boot) didn't wish to have Scott in their face all the time.' Tommy Mars was in the original line-up, but found working with Scott Thunes so difficult he left before the tour.

This should have rung alarm bells for Zappa, but he was not at many rehearsals and didn't notice the problems within the band. He thought Thunes was ideal. For instance, on the 1981 tour during a song called 'Envelopes' there were 32 bars before the bass part began, so Thunes used to invent things to do while waiting to come in. At the concert in Salt Lake City he ripped off his shirt and using a little plastic spatula he coated his chest and arms with mayonnaise from a canister for the sandwiches backstage. Then he strapped the bass back on and came in exactly on the beat. That kind of thing amused Frank greatly; in Frank's mind it made Thunes 'roadable'.

At the beginning of the 1988 tour Frank was really happy; he took his family with him and they joined in – the kids doing cartwheels across the stage. The encore consisted of three elements: a hilarious Beatles medley made up of three tunes telling the story of disgraced TV evangelist Jimmy Swaggart; a reggae version of Led Zeppelin's 'Stairway To Heaven' – Jimmy Page's guitar parts cleverly rewritten for the brass section and ending with the riff from 'Teddy Bear's Picnic' – and finally, that old chestnut popularized by the movie *10*, Ravel's *Bolero*. Zappa told Charles Amirkhanian: 'I always liked Bolero. I think that it's really one of the best melodies ever written. Most people in the audience have heard it in one form or another over the years, so if you're going to conduct an experiment in arranging technique and this is a reggae version of Bolero, it's nice to be arranging a tune that people are already familiar with.'

During the US segment of the tour, Zappa always had a voter registration booth at the back of the hall. There were problems, of course: in Philadelphia, the registrar of voters for the Tower Theater neighbourhood told them 'We already have enough registered voters' and refused to send any registration slips. In Washington DC they said 'We don't know about his politics, so we're not going to send anyone over,' and withheld the forms (the Citizens' Action Group provided some). The League of Women Voters would not help because they objected to the banner that read: *Lick Bush in 88*. Registration was already closed in Chicago, and in Detroit they would have had to have a registrar from each suburb.

Despite all this, Zappa managed to get 11,000 people to register to vote, an idea that was picked up by other rock 'n' rollers on the road with John Cougar Mellencamp, Sting and Earth Wind and Fire all following his example. Zappa told *Overseas* magazine: 'I was on a four-month tour while the primaries were going on, so I thought it would be natural to get involved with voter registration. The United States is the least registered industrial country on Earth. Something like a mere 15 per cent of the eligible voters between 18 and 24 cast ballots in the 1984 elections. It's pathetic! I don't believe an American has a right to complain about the system if he can vote and doesn't.'

Keyboard player Robert Martin: 'One of the most wonderful things about that tour was that on any given night, whatever had happened that day in the news, or the night before in the hotel, or that day on the airplane could, and probably would, come out in the concert in some way. Frank would change some lyrics around and we would follow ... There were a lot of laughs on stage, in the hotels, on the planes; we laughed a lot of the time.' But being on the road was never like being in a real band because Frank was hardly ever with them. Arthur Barrow: 'Any time we were in a place like London, Paris or New York, Frank would stay at some ritzy place and we'd be at a Holiday Inn or something. It was never really much of a band hanging out ... It's never really a band with Frank.'

Ed Mann was the one who first had a problem with Scott Thunes, and during the tour the other players began to agree. Scott was clearly a difficult person to get along with. Even a laudatory article about Thunes in *Bass Player* magazine felt compelled to say: 'His résumé doesn't mention that his musical career could be seen as one endless mêlée, or that he's been fired from as many bands as he's quit. And Scott admits most of the people he has worked with will never call him again.' Mike Keneally described Scott: 'He's very abrasive. He's very honest. He's brutal. He's blunt. And when he was in charge of running the rehearsals in Frank's absence, all these qualities came to the fore, but it was in the service of getting the job done.'

When the tour reached the East Coast, the band presented their problems to Frank. Scott took it badly. In the hothouse atmosphere of a touring party, little things become important and minor acts of vandalism began to occur: someone scratched Thunes's face off his laminate pass and when one promoter presented the band with a cake with all their names on it, someone had wiped off Scott's name.

Scott Thunes: 'Every night on-stage I was surrounded by daggers and completely lost my concentration. For three months I was a wreck and the music suffered because of my mistakes. Frank's only enjoyment was playing guitar solos, and those fell apart; he ended up not doing any. We also ended up not doing any more three-hour soundchecks. We'd play just two songs and then he'd get out of there. He couldn't stand being in the same room with us. It was the worst possible combination of events for him.'

Frank really liked Thunes and told *Society Pages*: 'He's a fabulous guy. I felt really upset that the other people in the band chose to hate him, and chose to hate the way he played, thereby bringing about the demise of the band. That's really unfortunate.'

At the end of the European section of the tour, with ten more weeks of gigs in the US to come, Frank asked the band if they would continue playing with Scott in the band. All but Mike Keneally said no, assuming that Frank would hire a new bass player. (A reasonable assumption, since Frank would have kicked out Scott if he had been found with drugs.) Zappa was not happy. He told *Musician* magazine: 'I don't like having a whole band ganging up on me, forcing me to get rid of a bass player I liked. I enjoy playing with Scott.'

So Frank sacked everybody and that was the end of the tour. They had a whole summer's worth of gigs booked, most of them in the $50,000 a night range, so the financial loss was enormous. Frank claimed to have lost $400,000, but most of that expense came from rehearsing more than 100 songs for four and half months. He told Charles Amirkhanian: 'I didn't have any choice. There was no time to replace anybody, whether it was the bass player or anybody else, because there was no time to put in another four months of rehearsal before I did the gigs in the US. So, we just ended the tour in Genoa, Italy.'

There was no need for four months of rehearsal and had he reduced the repertoire to something more realistic, he could have brought a new bass player up to speed in the two or three weeks before the summer gigs, adding new numbers as the tour progressed. But that would mean the band had won. Cancelling the tour was a petulant act. Furious at having his authority challenged, Zappa would rather lose $400,000 than be seen to back down. In any case, the loss was smaller than that because he recorded enough songs to fill several CDs. It was an extraordinary move and showed just how far he would go when he felt threatened.

Zappa may have regretted it; there is a rueful note in his statement to *Musician* magazine: 'If that band had stayed together all this time, not only would it have been the most outrageous touring band on the planet, but I'd still be playing guitar.' As it was, he never toured or played the guitar again (with the exception of two occasions in Eastern Europe where he briefly joined musicians on stage).

With the tour cancelled, Zappa turned to another project that had been on hold. He had been commissioned to write an autobiography and hired writer Peter Occhiogrosso to work with him on it. They taped interviews throughout July and Occhiogrosso took them away to transcribe and organize into chronological order.

Zappa found the result very dull. He spent August chopping up the material and reorganising it into a jokey children's-type book instead of a conventional ghosted autobiography, which would have exposed Frank to the critics. He did however add his opinion on the separation of Church and State, his thoughts on what he called 'Practical Conservatism', as well as his jaded opinion of orchestras, musicians, unions and the Californian education system. He also included ideas for TV shows and for a system to download music over the telephone (years before the Internet). The book was padded out with long transcripts of the PMRC hearings and the breach of contract case against the Royal Albert Hall.

The Real Frank Zappa Book was published by Poseidon Press in May 1989. It is a fascinating document, but it is regrettable that Zappa never wrote a proper autobiography, because the brief snatches of memoir are fascinating. By jumbling up the biographical information, he managed to give nothing away about himself that wasn't already known and positioned the book firmly in the pop artefact market.

In 1988 he released the first two volumes of his *You Can't Do That On Stage Anymore* series. The first consisted of tapes from all over, the second was the complete 22 September 1974 concert recorded in Helsinki, Finland. That October Zappa also released *Broadway The Hard Way*, the first album of tracks recorded live earlier that year by his auto-destruct band. A double CD from the same tour, *The Best Band You Never Heard In Your Life*, appeared in April 1991.

With enough music recorded to last for many years and disinclined to go on the road again, Zappa settled down to compose on his Synclavier. However, much as he enjoyed typing notes into the keyboard, he became restless, so when Dweezil decided to visit Moscow to help set up a joint Soviet venture with a friend of Frank's, Dennis Berardi, owner of Kramer Guitars, Zappa went along to help.

In the seventies, Zappa had been invited to take his group to the Soviet Union for a six-week tour in a cultural exchange with a children's theatre group, but he turned it down. Zappa joked about it in *High Times*: 'I like potatoes, but a person can eat only so many potatoes, and I respect cockroaches, because they've been around longer than people and I think they must know something that keeps them on top, but I don't want to spend six weeks surrounded by potatoes and cockroaches.'

Zappa had swallowed the propaganda about Communism that his father and the media had fed him. He was wary enough of the US authorities, so the idea of being in a situation where Soviet bureaucrats had some control over him was anathema. Later he was proud that his music had helped to topple Communism, but he had not been prepared to visit Russia while it was Communist. Now the situation had changed.

Berardi was thinking of opening a guitar factory in Russia. The deal fell through, but Frank was fascinated by the changing situation in Russia. He returned five times to set up business deals through his 'international licensing, consulting and social engineering' company called Why Not?. This business consultancy took 5 per cent if a deal was concluded. He attempted to raise funds for a Russian horror film, which, considering his lack of success financing his own movie ambitions was obviously doomed to failure. He also used his trips to Russia to negotiate with Melodia, the state-owned record company, to release *Guitar, Jazz From Hell* and *Broadway The Hard Way*. The Financial News Network hired him to talk about how to develop trade with the Soviet Union on their cable station and asked him to go to Moscow with a video crew and make an hour-long documentary

Frank had been commissioned to write the score for a TV documentary made by the Cousteau Society called *Outrage At Valdez*, about the 24 March 1989 oil spillage from the Exxon oil tanker off the coast of Alaska, which caused unprecedented ecological damage. It was composed entirely on the Synclavier and, surprisingly, was Frank's first TV score. Zappa: 'My wife and I have long supported the Cousteau Society. Without this organization to remind citizens, corporations and lazy governments all over the world of environmental dangers, we would be in a lot worse shape than we are. I consider it an honour to have been asked to participate in this special.'

As a further gesture of support he donated his composition fee back to the society. However, it turned out that he had not been given the final edited version to work from and all the picture cues were wrong. It meant that two days before leaving for Moscow he had to change all the cues and re-mix the music, because Ted Turner's WTBS needed it in a hurry. Zappa: 'That was two of the worst days of my life. It was so fuckin' painful that at the end of it I was so exhausted that I couldn't take the flight. I just crashed for a day, and then got on the plane for Russia . . . It was just an emergency job.' He arrived a day late and missed a day's worth of appointments.

Zappa: 'On my first trip to Moscow I went to this place called the Stosnomic Centre in Gorky Park. This guy Starsdarnen had created facilities where rock 'n' roll bands from all over the country could rehearse and he would help them get record deals and so on and in one of the rooms was a Siberian R&B band. I walked in and I thought the guy was going to have a heart attack; he couldn't speak for spluttering. Through an interpreter he says "Look at this" and he opens his wallet, shows me a photo of his house in Siberia. He's got all of my records on the rack, posters of me on the wall, and I was looking because I didn't know how the fuck it ever happened!'

In Moscow with his video crew Frank filmed the Luzhniky Sports Complex that he thought western food and beverage vendors would be interested in developing along with the adjacent river front property, which he saw as a shopping mall and entertainment centre. He filmed the Ginsing Co-operative Beauty Centre and attended a meeting at the Global Forum on Environment and Development for Survival at the Soviet Academy of Sciences. He also worked on a deal of his own to broker Russian distribution of Ben and Jerry's ice cream. He already represented MPI, a Chicago-based home video company, and was looking to set up TV licensing and mail-order distribution of their film catalogue across Eastern Europe.

Then, quite unexpectedly, came one of the biggest surprises Zappa ever had; he got involved in the Velvet Revolution. On his way back from Moscow he intended to stop off in Prague, where keyboard player Michael Kocáb had arranged for him to meet President Václav Havel.

In 1989 Kocáb was brought to Zappa's house by someone Frank was at school with in Lancaster but hadn't seen in 20 years who called up out of the blue and said that his next-door neighbour was married to a Czechoslovakian and they had someone visiting from Czechoslovakia who wanted to meet him. Frank's manager was reluctant to ask Frank, thinking he wouldn't be interested, but finally a meeting was arranged.

Kocáb: 'Obviously I was very nervous. After all, Frank is one of my biggest idols ... Frank gave us a cool welcome, and I started to believe the things they say about famous stars. We went into his work room, which featured a big fireplace, along with various digital recording equipment. He offered us a beer, and while he was eating a hamburger, he asked us what we wanted.' They discussed the possibility of a performance of his classical music in Prague, but Frank immediately asked if they had $250,000, which they hadn't, so the subject was dropped. He played 'Sinister Footwear' and asked for their opinion. Kocáb: 'I told him what I thought about it, and for the first time I thought I had broken the barrier, as we proceeded to discuss classical music while listening to more recordings. I played for him a recording from *Odysseus*, and I believe that he liked it.'

At this point the mood changed completely; Zappa realized he was dealing with a professional, the leading composer in Czechoslovakia, and Zappa even suggested he might release *Odysseus* on Barking Pumpkin records. Kocáb played him more of his own music and showed him videos of his group, Prague Selection. The visit lasted for six hours. Kocáb: 'Before I left we made arrangements to keep in contact in the future. At the end of our meeting, Frank mentioned that he might even change his stance of not travelling to Eastern Europe.'

Zappa: 'I was visited at my house by a man who at that time was a famous Czech rock musician. His name was Michael Kocáb and he invited me to Prague to have some of my orchestral music played. Then, a few months later, there was a revolution and he was not only a rock musician but a Member of Parliament.'

The old Czechoslovakian administration fell on 24 November 1989 and the new one was filled with rock musicians and music journalists: Jarda Koran, the new Lord Mayor of Prague, had previously played with Jazz Section; Pavel Kantor moved from being a rock singer to becoming the new head of protocol.

The first Czechoslovakian underground band was the Plastic People of the Universe, named after Zappa's song. They were imprisoned in 1976. They were loud, surreal, irreverent and not very good, but their incarceration politicized members of their largely apolitical, apathetic generation. Václav Havel and three fellow journalists were so outraged at their treatment that they petitioned for their release, which inspired Charter 77.

Kocáb's band, the Jazz Section, fared better. Party bureaucrats looked kindly on jazz as it had been a means of protest against Nazi occupation during the war. Jazz Section played jazz rock and fusion without a problem, and even a version of punk rock. It was not until they began to publish books and underground texts that the communist bureaucracy threw them in jail. This gave their newly politicized followers a cause; petitions were drawn up, posters and flyers circulated, and calls made for democracy, undermining the state apparatus.

In November 1989 the hard-line communists were swept from power and the Civic Forum took over the government. Kocáb was one of the leaders of the Civic Forum and when free elections were held he became an MP. He had the unenviable job of overseeing the withdrawal of Soviet troops from Czechoslovakia, negotiating with the Czechoslovakian Politburo, the Politburo in Moscow and the KGB.

On 20 January 1990 Zappa, suffering from a nasty cold, took an Aeroflot flight from Moscow accompanied by his video crew. It began as an ordinary business trip, but he arrived to a rockstar welcome with 5,000 cheering fans waiting at Prague's Ruzyne airport. They climbed on the roof and packed out the lobby, carrying hand-made signs and chanting 'Zappa! Zappa!' Some even hung onto his bus as it drove away.

Zappa: 'It was unbelievable! Never in my 25 years in the rock 'n' roll business have I gotten off an aeroplane and seen anything like this. They were totally unprepared for the situation, there was no security, but the people were just wonderful! When I managed to inch my way through the airport, and once we got out the front door of the airport, it took about half an hour to go forty feet from the curb to the bus because

of the people that were just piling on top of us. It was unbelievable.'
Zappa had met some Czechoslovakian fans during the 1988 tour; they
had travelled to Vienna for the concert. They told him about the Frank
Zappa Society of Czechoslovakia, but he had no idea of the extent of his
popularity, which was all the more extraordinary considering none of
his music had been officially released there.

It was in every way like a state visit. He was put up at the
Intercontinental Hotel, a top luxury hotel on namesti Curieovych,
overlooking the River Vltava in the city centre, and his first official
engagement was to meet the Mayor of Prague at the Baroque Troja
Chateau. This was followed by a press conference in the Knights' Hall
and meetings with members of the Zappa fan club – Zappastrope – in
the garden restaurant.

He met with underground artists at the Krivan Hotel, twelve of
whom had painted a series of murals in his honour (sadly the manager
ordered them destroyed a month later). Frank met with members of the
Plastic People of the Universe, and sang a couple of songs with them.
For these musicians, who had spent years in jail for their opposition
to the communist regime, finally meeting Zappa must have seemed
unreal.

He appeared at 'TV Youth Club' where he delivered a monologue
accompanied on the piano by Kocáb, and he made an appearance at
the White Horse where he played with local musicians and sang two
songs, including 'Love Of My Life' over a playback of *Tinseltown
Rebellion*. Speaking on BBC Radio he said: 'We taped some interviews
with some of the kids who were fans there. One of the stories they told
me was that the secret police liked to catch people who had my records
and they would say that they were going to beat the Zappa music
out of them. There were two guys who said they had that particular
experience with the Stasi.'

On 22 January Zappa was taken to see the Loretto church with its
famous seventeenth-century cloisters, where he played on the glock-
enspiel previously played by Franz Liszt. From here it was a short
walk to the Prague Castle where he saw the changing of the guard
– and marched along after them, followed by the FNN video crew and

a Czechoslovakian TV team. Photographs of this event show Zappa looking more Eastern European than any of the Czechoslovakians, marching along in his huge black greatcoat, his bristling moustache and briefcase, imitating the soldiers' goosestep.

At Prague Castle he finally met Václav Havel, the newly elected president of the republic. Havel was casually dressed in jeans and a blue sweater and, like Frank, was a chain smoker. Zappa spoke with Havel on behalf of FNN, the video crew still filming. He asked what sort of foreign investment Czechoslovakia was looking for, but Havel said these were questions that should be addressed to his financial ministers. Instead Havel told him that he had several Mothers of Invention albums and especially enjoyed listening to *Bongo Fury* with Captain Beefheart. He apologized for not being familiar with Frank's later releases. Frank made light of this, saying: 'The measure of being well informed should not be tied to how many of my albums a person has.'

Havel was to make a state visit to the US and asked if Zappa would be there. 'There will be meetings with artists and so on,' he said, 'and maybe the Rolling Stones will play, because they wrote one song for me. And I will be very glad if Joan Baez is there, she helped us when we needed it. I don't know how well artists collaborate in the United States. Maybe you can help?'

Zappa: 'So there I was in the Oval Office or something and the President is talking about Captain Beefheart and rock 'n' roll and I'm thinking, "Is this *The Twilight Zone* or what?"'

In fact, Havel was under a lot of stress. He and Kocáb were preparing for a major confrontation in parliament the next day when Kocáb was to make the speech, requesting that the Soviet Union pull their troops out of Czechoslovakia. However, the President still found time to show Frank around the ancient castle and the fourteenth-century cathedral of St Vitus, which sits within its walls.

They met again for lunch in the castle along with Havel's wife Olga, the vice-minister for economy and ecology, and the deputy Prime Minister Valtr Komarek, leader of the new economic team. They discussed how the country could increase its income and the conversation continued later that day over dinner, also in the castle. At Frank's request, Milan Lukes, the Minister of Culture, was also present. Zappa made a number of useful suggestions, including the proposal that instead of digging up their ancient cities and stringing telephone lines everywhere, they start straight off with a cellular phone network and give everyone a mobile phone. This was in the light of AT&T charging Italy $30 billion to rewire the phone system in 1989. He also proposed a method of burning low-grade coal – which was abundant in Czechoslovakia – where the emissions are cleaned and used as a turbocharger to create electricity – something he picked up by sitting next to a lobbyist from the system's manufacturer on a plane.

Havel, a playwright, was busy contacting artists and intellectuals all over the world as part of his campaign to gain support for his democratic reforms. He had already met the Dalai Lama and Zappa was followed shortly after by Allen Ginsberg and other American beat poets in Prague for a literary conference. Zappa told the *Nation*: 'Havel and his ministers know they need some Western investment, but they don't want all the ugliness that often invades a country with Western investment. The easiest way to keep the lid on that is to have someone involved whose primary concern is culture, who can reject or modify a project if it's going to have a negative impact on society.'

Zappa told Swedish radio: 'Havel said, "We are all people from art and culture. We must make the policy better than the politicians."... I support that aspect of what he's trying to do and he's a very nice man and an honest man and he's suffered a lot to get where he is . . . he's one of the good guys.'

After dinner Milan Lukes, the Minister of Culture, went on television and announced that Zappa would be representing Czechoslovakia on trade, tourism and cultural matters. Zappa was given a letter, signed by the deputy Prime Minister, which had been typed up in English in the middle of the night and was handed to him in his hotel in the morning. It read:

Dear Sir, I entrust you with leading negotiations with foreign partners for preparation of preliminary projects, possibly drafts of trading agreements directed to participation of foreign firms. It concerns tourist, agricultural and other enterprises in Czechoslovakia. I am very obliged to you for the help offered in this respect and I am looking to further co-operation.

VALTR KOMAREK

On 23 January Zappa visited Parliament and met with members of the government. At one meeting he told them, 'I've come to Czechoslovakia to see Communism die, but it's still kicking. It's necessary to put an end to it.' (This was the day Kocáb asked the Russians to remove their troops.)

Zappa left the country with a contract to issue five albums and CDs, having arranged for *The Real Frank Zappa Book* to be translated into Czechoslovakian, and for his company Why Not? to be a consultant for the Czech government in matters of trade, tourism and cultural exchange. He told the Canadian Broadcasting Company: 'I will also function as a headhunter on their behalf, in order to find people to do things that they need to have done in that country. So I've got a new job now.'

He flew from Prague to Paris, where he had hired a video-editing suite. He commuted by stretch limo between the George V and the studio and edited his 25 hours of videotape down to a 27-minute sample-bite reel to be delivered to FNN by Concorde the following day. He also found time to do a press conference with Jacques Cousteau to support his society, and to film an interview between himself and Pierre Boulez. (They had remained in touch and on 23 May the previous year had appeared on-stage for 'An Evening with Pierre Boulez and Frank Zappa in Conversation', held at Schoenberg Hall in the UCLA music department. This time Zappa dominated the proceedings with his wisecracks and a hall full of fans.)

Back in the States on 26 January, he presented *Frank Zappa's Wild Wild East* show on FNN and showed more footage of his travels. He felt completely at home on a financial show. As he told Mike Zwerin during his stopover in Paris: 'I have been an enthusiastic capitalist for years. There are articles and interviews to prove it.' Later in the month Zappa stood in for Bob Berkowitz, the host of the FNN business talk show *Focus*, for three days and took part in a live phone-in.

Fans found it hard to understand why Zappa – who complained that he never had enough time to oversee concerts of his classical work or to edit his tapes – would now spend his time trying to sell frozen muffin mix to the Russians. But for Zappa there was complete 'conceptual continuity', as he explained in conversation with Boulez: 'If you take any lump of musical *stuff*, rhythms, melody, harmony, whatever you want to, it falls into that category, and that's your raw material. You can make, from this raw material, a composition by organizing it. If you use that concept on anything else, any other material in any other field, you can use the same musical imagination to organize other ideas, objects, procedures, whatever. So if I'm working within the field of business, like I'm doing some stuff in Russia, it is like doing a composition. You find things that go together with other things that work and you organize them. It has been my experience, since starting in this direction, that the people that I'm working with are a lot nicer, a lot more honest, and it's a refreshing change from the music business.'

As required by US law, Zappa filed as an agent for a foreign power and set to work. He approached Young and Rubicam, and suggested they take on the new Czechoslovakian government as a client to help them build tourism. The deal didn't go through, because Zappa didn't know of the problems Young and Rubicam had had with the Jamaican government over their tourist account. He lined up a Soviet partner for Bake 'n Joy, who marketed frozen muffin batter, but despite Soviet interest Bake 'n Joy got cold feet and dropped out. There were similar problems with many of his other ideas.

Within six weeks, Zappa's role in Czechoslovakia had changed dramatically. During his luncheon with Havel, he had spoken his mind on a number of matters. Zappa: '[Havel] was talking about how Dan Quayle was coming to visit them, and I expressed the opinion that I thought it was unfortunate that a person such as President Havel should have to bear the company of somebody as stupid as Dan Quayle for even a few moments of his life. And the next thing I know, Quayle doesn't come, James Baker III re-routes his trip to Moscow, so that he can come blasting into Prague, and literally lays down the law to the Czechoslovakian government. He says you can either do business with the United States or you can do business with Zappa. What'll it be?'

Following the February visit to Prague by Secretary of State James A. Baker, the Czechoslovakian government reduced Frank's role to that of an unofficial cultural emissary. Baker had never forgiven Zappa for calling his wife (a co-founder of the PMRC) a 'bored housewife'. Havel's press secretary Michael Zantovsky reluctantly issued a statement saying: 'We like Frank Zappa, but he is not authorized to negotiate any trade agreements with our government.' The Czechoslovakians, having finally rid themselves of the Russians, now had to deal with equally arrogant Americans. Frank quietly bowed out. When he was invited to Prague for the presidential election in the summer of 1990 he politely sent his regrets. He told *Business World*: 'I really support Havel's idea of establishing a government that has an aesthetic, as well as an economic, ethic. But right now the best thing I can do is to stay away.'

However, when he was invited again, to celebrate the final withdrawal of Soviet troops from both Czechoslovakia and Hungary, he accepted. Zappa was uncharacteristically apprehensive about this trip, telling *Musician* magazine: 'I'm faced with a bit of a dilemma which is going to smack me right in the face on Thursday. I'm going to Czechoslovakia and Hungary and I've been invited because they're having big celebrations. The last Russian soldier leaves Czechoslovakia on June 24th and Hungary on the 30th, and they want me to bring my guitar over and play. And I haven't touched it for years. I don't have any calluses! I don't know what to do with that fucking thing. And if I don't take it along with me, I know a lot of people will be disappointed, but I know if I plug it in they're going to be even more disappointed 'cause I can't play anymore.'

On 24 June 1991 Frank and Gail flew to Prague where they joined 150,000 people in the streets to celebrate the departure of Soviet military forces. There was a rock concert at the Prague Sports Hall with a laser show, headlined by Kocáb's Prague Selection, and at one point Zappa joined them on-stage, strapping on his blond Strat to trade licks with Kocáb on an instrumental reggae number. Before the music began, Zappa addressed the audience, which included President Havel, from the stage. He told them: 'I'm sure you already know it, but this is just the beginning of your new future in this country, and as you confront the new changes that will take place, please try to keep your country unique. Don't change into something else, keep it unique.'

All across Eastern Europe the hard-line Communist regimes were collapsing and Zappa next made his first visit to Hungary, this time at the invitation of the mayor of Budapest, Gabor Demszky. They had lunched together in LA on 19 April at Century City, after which, much to Zappa's delight, Gabor had an appointment just around the corner with Ronald Reagan. On 29 June Frank and Gail accompanied Mayor Demszky and Arunas Toras, the mayor of Vilnius, Lithuania, on a state pleasure cruise on the Danube, as part of Hungary's celebrations at the withdrawal of Soviet troops. The Zappas met Hungarian Vice President Dornbach Alajossal, as well as Hungarian poets, musicians, politicians, and, of course, the Press. Despite the presence of every important cultural and political person in the country, Zappa seemed the star attraction.

At a celebratory concert at Tabán, the site of many music festivals, Frank once again strapped on his guitar to join four Hungarian jazz musicians on-stage, telling the audience: 'Finally I get to perform in your country. You know, it's been three years since I touched my guitar. At the end of the tour in 1988, I put my guitar in its case, and I haven't seen it since then. The first exception to that was on the 24th in Prague when I played one song, and that's what I intend to do tonight in Tabán. Believe it or not, it's an exciting experience, because it isn't easy to match with other folks' arrangements and not interfere. In both Budapest and Prague, I decided to congratulate you people in the name of friendship. The Soviets completed their withdrawal from Hungarian territory, and I think that's really good news. It's really fortunate and heartening . . . but we'll see what's going to happen to music.'

21 On Out

On 27 May 1990 Frank was due to give the keynote speech at the Fifth International Music and Media Conference in Amsterdam with a talk entitled 'Rock Around the Bloc'. It never happened. Frank had been feeling sick for a number of years, but his doctors could find nothing wrong. Then he suddenly took a turn for the worse and was rushed to the hospital emergency room with an intestinal blockage. Tests showed he was suffering from prostate cancer. A malignant tumour had been growing undetected for between eight and ten years. By the time they found it, it was inoperable.

Frank told *Playboy*: 'When I went into the hospital, the cancer had grown to where I could no longer take a piss. In order for me just to survive, they had to poke a hole in my bladder. I spent more than a year with a hose coming out of my bladder and a bag tied to my leg.' He was given radiation treatment – a series of twelve shots designed to reduce the size of the tumour – but the side-effects were such that after the eleventh he was so sick he said he couldn't go back again. By this time the radiation had shrunk the tumour to the point where he could get rid of the bag, but he was still very ill.

This was the real reason he had not attended the presidential elections in Prague, and why he cancelled a June appearance at the

Meeting Of The World music festival in Finland. Zappa: 'The minute somebody tells you you have cancer, your life changes dramatically, whether you beat it or you don't . . . It complicates your life because you have to fight for your life every single day, besides doing your shit. To do the music is complicated enough, but to think of doing things that involve travel and other kinds of physical stress is too much. Whatever medication you take fucks you up, too.'

Zappa had planned to attend the fourth Biennale de la Dance festival in Lyons where five nights (20–24 September) were devoted to 'Dancing Zappa'. Unfortunately he was not there to see Kent Nagano direct ballet performances of his work performed by the Orchestre de l'Opéra de Lyons and the Lyons Opera Ballet.

Frank had to rely on his family more than ever before. Moon devoted the next few years to caring for him, driving him to the hospital for his radiation treatments, cooking his meals and overseeing his medication. For her it was a chance to finally get close to him, to bridge the emotional gap between them, but whenever she tried to discuss anything personal he clammed up. Moon: 'He said, "I'm sorry. I can't talk to you about these things. I'm just in too much pain." It put a cap on how much further our relationship could go.'

Frank was sometimes overwhelmed by feelings beyond his control, which irritated him immensely, and he went to great lengths to deny their existence. He was especially annoyed to have his emotions manipulated by a Broadway show. He told Bob Marshall: 'I can literally hate the show and find myself crying because of something that happened in there. And I know that the fact that liquid comes out of my eyes has got nothing to do with reality. I'm sitting there consciously thinking that this show is a piece of shit and I'm crying, and I'm saying to myself, "Well, at least I have some sort of average-scale, average-size, average-vulnerability human factors working." But at the same time I'm sitting there going "Why?" . . . I just know that what people normally think of as human feelings are not what they think they are. I see chemistry here.'

The extraordinary collapse of Communism in Eastern Europe gave Zappa a new interest in politics and he began to express his opinions in interviews, often forcefully. Zappa: 'I just think that the whole way in which we conduct ourselves on an international level is very old fashioned. It's arrogant, and we're gonna be left in the dust because we need to rethink the whole way in which we relate to the other nations of the world . . . We shouldn't be the world's policeman. Nobody asked us to be the world's policeman.'

He always began with the position that 'The Emperor's not wearing any clothes, never has, never will.' After that, everything fell into place, albeit in a rather simplistic way. Zappa: 'Everything bad in the USA now is Reagan's fault. Disastrous economic policy, all kinds of scandals that involve the administration, it's all his fault. He was an idiot, but he knew how to tell a good joke. The people around him were devils, they enriched their friends and left the average American citizen with no hope for the future. Reagan was an imperialist president, with television and the rest of the media in his pocket . . . Why bother to bend over backwards to have anything that resembles brotherhood, when after the Reagan administration years, it was officially announced by the government that greed is good? Well, if the government says so, then why do I need to look out for anybody else when the most important thing on the planet to do is to look out for yourself?'

If an actor could become president of the United States and a playwright could become president of Czechoslovakia, Zappa saw no reason why a rock musician and composer should not run for office. In April 1991 he felt well enough to investigate this possibility. He told Charles Amirkhanian: 'I'm pissed off enough that I'm at the stage where I'm considering running, and I'm taking concrete steps to look into it . . . because if I do it, I would do it to win, not just to go out there and be symbolic.'

He talked about running for president in several interviews, but he never announced his candidature. A combination of ill-health and a realization that the vast majority of Americans had never heard of him (and if they had, they didn't like what they heard), made him reconsider.

Back on the home front, the new decade opened with another lawsuit, this time against Zappa. In April the six original Mothers re-opened their 1985 suit, but this time they claimed defamation of character because Zappa had publicly dismissed their earlier suit as 'the product of chemically-altered emanations'. Zappa eventually settled out of court in February 1991 for an undisclosed amount, paying their legal fees. This held up the release of *Ahead Of Their Time*, a 1968 live recording of the original Mothers performing with members of the LSO at the Royal Festival Hall. Frank knew it would be popular with his fans, but he hated the idea of having to give the ex-Mothers even more royalties. After a delay of eight months, financial common sense won out and Zappa released *Ahead Of Their Time* in June 1991.

Moon and Dweezil got a deal for a TV sitcom called *Normal Life*. Zappa: 'I won't say it's based on this family, but there are certain similarities to the way this household runs.' It could have been a forerunner for *The Osbournes*, but by the time it began transmission in June 1990 the original idea had been so changed by the CBS executives that the life had been drained out of it and it flopped. Probably the most successful enterprise was the 1989 opening of Joe's Garage, a rehearsal facility managed by Gail, which was quickly booked solid. Gail told *Billboard*: 'It has very charming surroundings which I think that people who work hard in this business deserve, because usually they get the sleaziest, most horrible situations to have to work in.'

Zappa's cult reputation made him an obvious target for bootleggers. There were probably more Zappa bootlegs in circulation than even Dylan or the Beatles, largely because there was more material. He played such a huge repertoire there were enough new songs for a dozen bootlegs on each tour.

Though the fans who bought them almost certainly had a complete set of his official recordings, Zappa was enraged that someone was making money from his work. He came up with a unique and controversial solution. He did a deal with Rhino to start a subsidiary label called Foo-eee to bootleg the bootlegs, including their artwork and titles. Tom Brown at Foo-eee/Rhino Records sent bootlegged tapes and lists of possible releases to Barking Pumpkin Records. Zappa claimed not to have listened to the bootlegs, but somebody at Barking Pumpkin did because the lists were narrowed down and Brown was told: 'Frank says that these are okay and these aren't.' It seems likely it was Zappa who made the selection, in case the tracklist impinged on some future official release.

Zappa: 'All I'm saying is if a person needs to own a bootleg, buy 'em from Foo-eee, because Foo-eee will at least pay the royalties for the writing and publishing.' The bootlegs were tweaked a bit at the UMRK, but Frank's staff were under instructions not to find the original hi-fidelity tapes that he almost certainly had in his tape vault. Instead they were to use the poor-quality audience recordings. Two groups of CDs were released: an eight-CD box set, *Beat The Boots*, came out in July 1991, followed by a seven-CD box set in June 1992.

Zappa: 'I haven't heard them myself, nor do I intend to. I make no claim that any of the material contained on these records is of any musical value whatsoever. Besides if you want crap, now you can get fully authorized, affordable crap, and maybe put some sleazebag out of business.' But unless fans bought them as box sets, there was no way to tell they were bootlegs – it did not say on them and they were soon available separately. The result was that many unsuspecting fans bought terrible quality recordings thinking they were legitimate, and the big European record chains sold them for the same high price as the rest of Zappa's catalogue. Fans felt ripped off – they *were* ripped off.

Zappa's reputation for caring about the sound quality of his releases was destroyed forever. Also, while he got his publishing and writing royalties, the musicians who played on the bootlegs received nothing. When one of them telephoned the house to ask if any royalty payments would be forthcoming, Gail told him to 'Fuck off!'

As usual, it was all about control. Zappa had to be in control of his own release programme; he had to 'get back at those guys', even if it meant alienating thousands of fans.

Zappa's Universe was a series of three concerts (beginning on 7 November 1991) organized by conductor Joel Thome, who assembled the Orchestra of Our Time to present an evening of Zappa's work at the Ritz in New York. Mike Keneally and Scott Thunes were joined by other ex-Zappa sidemen Steve Vai, Denny Walley and Dale Bozzio among many others. The concert was filmed for video release and featured orchestral versions of a wide range of Zappa's songs, including 'Waka-Jawaka' and 'Brown Shoes Don't Make It'. Zappa was expected to attend.

At an afternoon press conference at the Ritz on the day of the first concert, Moon – flanked by Dweezil, Zappa's publicist Sean Mahoney and promoter John Scher – faced dozens of microphones and cameras to make an announcement: 'We're here to make a statement on behalf of our family. Although Frank was looking forward to being here, and really intended to be here, unfortunately he's not here. As many of you know, he's been diagnosed by journalists as having cancer. We'd like you to know his doctors have diagnosed prostate cancer, which he's been fighting successfully and he has been feeling well and working too hard and planned to attend. Up until the last minute we were still hoping he would feel well enough to get on a plane and come here. There are occasional periods when he's not feeling as well, and it's unfortunate it happened to coincide with this event. He's thrilled people are performing his music. The more the merrier. And we're thrilled. And we're here to participate in this event . . .'

Frank did get as far as the airport, where he was to take a small charter jet to New York, but just before boarding he and the other passengers were informed that mechanical problems would delay take-off by several hours. Then Frank saw the name of the jet – 'La Bamba' – and decided to wait until the next day, not wanting to 'do a Ritchie Valens'. But the following day he felt terrible with flu and could not make the flight. Rumours had been circulating for some time, but now it was official. Some reporters had him in hospital with only weeks to live. In fact, he was in the studio preparing the final volumes of *You Can't Do That On Stage Anymore*.

In 1991 the German film-maker Henning Lohner – who directed a documentary about Zappa called *Pee-Fee-Yatko, the Man and His Music* – suggested to Dr Dieter Rexroth, director of the Frankfurt Festival, that they should commission a major orchestral piece from Zappa for the summer of 1992. When Frank proved to be unenthusiastic about writing for so many players, they proposed instead that he write for the Ensemble Modern, an 18-piece group specializing in modern music. In May Rexroth, Andreas Mölich-Zebhauser, the musical director of the Ensemble Modern, and his predecessor Karsten Witt, flew to LA to put their case. Zappa was not familiar with the Ensemble Modern's work, but he was won over after listening to a CD of them playing music by Kurt Weill and Helmut Lachenmann. He liked their attitude and style, and was impressed by the high level of technical ability.

The Ensemble Modern travelled to LA in mid-July to spend a fortnight working with Zappa so that he could get a feeling for their strengths and individual capabilities. He had each member of the group play and took samples for his Synclavier, so he could 'play them' after they had returned to Germany and write arrangements to suit the individual players. Rehearsals took place in a hall provided by the Los Angeles Philharmonic and sessions were held both at the UMRK and in the big room at Joe's Garage, where Frank had installed a conductor's podium.

Zappa: 'I had a chance to see individually what the players could do, what their specialities were, what kind of special things they could do on their individual instruments, and when you know what a musician can do, it helps when you are writing a piece.'

As well as happily tackling pieces of formidable complexity, the group went along with Zappa's humour as well. He had Hermann Kretzschmar sit under the piano at Joe's Garage and read aloud from *PFIQ*, a body-piercing magazine, using a strangled Dr Strangelove voice. At the actual concert Kretzschmar read from a US immigration form that Zappa had found in the pocket of an airplane seat, while Frank dropped musical clusters around his phrases.

One of the players, Catherine Milliken, was Australian and played the didgeridoo, as well as the oboe and English horn. The sound of it made Frank crack up and in the piece 'Food Gathering In Post-Industrial

America' she stuck it into a spittoon of water with Vermiculite floating on the surface to make a terrible gurgling sound. Zappa: 'One of the things I like about the Ensemble Modern is that they're interested in sound just for its own sake. At one rehearsal, one of the horn players picked his horn up off the floor, and it scraped and made a noise. And I said, "Do it again," and the next thing you know, we had the entire brass section taking their instruments and scraping the bells back and forth across the floor, making this grinding, grunting sound.'

Some of the numbers were to be accompanied by La La La Human Steps, a dance troupe from Canada. Zappa: 'I saw a videotape of what they did, and I thought they were special and I thought that the style of their performance fit in with what we were doing. So I asked Andreas [Mölich-Zebhauser], the director of the group, to contact them and see if they could work something out, and they did.'

Standing next to the fireplace, among the clutter of souvenirs, artwork, instruments and old stage props that lined the walls of Zappa's basement, was a large, yellow, fibreglass fish carved from a surfboard. It was made by Mark Beam, who sent it anonymously to the Zappa family as a Christmas gift in 1988. When Andreas Mölich-Zebhauser saw the fish, he immediately seized upon it as the symbol for the event. He wanted to call the concert the *Yellow Shark*. Zappa had no real objection, unless people thought that it was the name of the piece. He presented the shark to Mölich-Zebhauser, who had become very attached to it, and gave him a note of ownership, in case he had trouble getting it through customs.

On 13 July, accompanied by Gail and Moon, Frank flew to Germany and spent a further two weeks in rehearsal with Ensemble Modern, resulting in a 90-minute programme spanning all of Zappa's diverse styles, from 'Uncle Meat' and 'Dog Breath Variations,' the Varèse-like 'Times Beach II' to the difficult piano work of 'Ruth Is Sleeping'. The *Yellow Shark* concerts were held at the Frankfurt Alte Oper 17–19 September, and continued on to Berlin's Philharmonie for the 22–23, finishing at the Konzerthaus in Vienna on 26–28 September.

Zappa was thrilled: 'I've never had such an accurate performance at any time for that kind of music that I do. The dedication of the group to playing it right, and putting the eyebrows on it is something that – it would take your breath away. You would have to have seen how gruelling the rehearsals were, and how meticulous the conductor, Peter Rundel, was in trying to get all the details of this stuff worked out.'

Two thousand people a night packed the opera houses and the applause lasted for 20 minutes. It was the pinnacle of Zappa's 'serious' music career. Sadly, he was unable to attend all of the performances. Though he conducted 'G-Spot Tornado' on the opening night, he had to sit down to do so, and just walking on-stage was very uncomfortable for him. At the finale of 'Pentagon Afternoon' the rest of the band pulled out rayguns and shot the string section – there was typical Zappa humour even in an opera house. At the end, there were flowers for everyone, including Frank.

He could only attend the first and third performances in Frankfurt. Zappa: 'I got sick and had to fly home. If I hadn't been sick, the experience would have been exhilarating. Unfortunately, I felt so excruciatingly shitty that it was hard to walk, to just get up onto the stage, to sit, to stand up. You can't enjoy yourself when you're sick, no matter how enthusiastic the audience.'

Frank's illness changed his way of life completely; no longer the night owl, he was usually in bed by six or seven in the evening, rising at 6.30 a.m. to do a little work before his studio staff arrived at 9.30. He was 40 pounds overweight because his medicine made him retain water. He told *Playboy*: 'Some days you can do more of it than others. Part of the problem is that it hurts to sit some days, and this work is done sitting at a computer terminal. I used to be able to work sixteen, eighteen hours a day and just get up from my chair and go to sleep and go back to work, and it was fine. But some days I can't work at all. Some days I can work two hours. Some days I can work ten.'

The medication took its toll. After a particularly painful episode, Frank was hospitalized for three days where they gave him morphine to numb the pain. It took him ten days to get over the effects of the opiates – something he never wanted to experience again. Some days he was clear-headed, other days his mind was clouded by the medicine; it became hard to know which was the more confusing, the drugs or the disease – and Zappa the control freak hated drugs. He told *Playboy*: 'You can't trust your own decisions because you don't know, chemically, what's happening.'

The news that Zappa was seriously ill provoked yet another reconciliation between him and Don Van Vliet. Zappa: 'Don calls me about once a week, and he's still painting away. He's had some problems with his health. He's had some trouble walking, recently, but I think he's getting better. He calls me up and turns on a cassette machine and plays me some . . . he has some of the rhythm and blues records that we used to listen to in high school, songs like "Tell Me Darling" by the Gaylarks. The phone will ring and there'll be this cassette machine on the other end with this song playing on it.'

Even Tipper Gore (co-founder of the PMRC) made a gesture of reconciliation. 'She sent me a sweet letter when she heard I was sick,' said Zappa, 'and I appreciate that.'

Zappa's musical taste had always been eclectic, ranging from Arab music to Bulgarian folk songs, from Doo Wop to Varèse. Zappa: 'I think my playing is probably more derived from the folk music records that I heard; Middle Eastern music, Indian music, stuff like that. For years I had something called *Music On The Desert Road*, which was an album with all kinds of different ethnic music from the Middle East. I used to listen to that all the time – I liked that kind of melodic feel. I listened to Indian music, Ravi Shankar and so forth . . .'

Traditional Irish music was not part of his early musical experience, but when Zappa encountered the Chieftains, he was immediately captivated. They first met in 1988 when Frank and Paddy Moloney both appeared on a BBC World Service programme, and again in 1991 when they were guests on Libby Purves's *Midweek* show on BBC Radio 4. They liked each other and Frank asked Moloney to call him when he was next in LA.

The call came on 24 June 1992. Frank was delighted to hear from Paddy and insisted he bring the Chieftains and their instruments over to the house right away and do some recording at the UMRK. One of

Zappa's great skills was to bring out the hidden talents in a player, and he appreciated what Moloney had done with the Chieftains. He told Irish journalist Joe Jackson: 'I love the sounds these guys make. I love the melodies and the chord changes, and especially the way their music is performed. Each member of the group is an expert on his instrument, not just in terms of technique, but in terms of the concept they have of what the final ensemble product is supposed to sound like.'

Comparing the Chieftains with the more famous Irish rock band U2, Zappa asked: 'Which would you rather have? Mediocre invention or a direct linear descent from Celtic culture, which is what I hear in the music of the Chieftains? The Chieftains are their own culture and I hear traces of not only Celtic history, but global history in their work, echoing back to the beginning of time.'

Frank wanted to try out some experimental recording techniques with the Chieftains that he and engineer Spence Chrislau were working on. Zappa stood them around a circular stand, four feet in diameter and covered in microphones, and had them play one of his new compositions. Paddy Moloney told John Glatt: 'Frank Zappa's a genius. To me he's a hundred years ahead of his time. I think his music is incredible.' By midnight they were finished with Frank's project, but he was enjoying himself enormously and suggested that they use the studio to record something of their own.

The Chieftains had been rehearsing some pieces for *The Celtic Harp*, an album to celebrate the 200th anniversary of the traditional music collector Edward Bunting. The band were jetlagged and wanted to get back their hotel, but Paddy Moloney realized that they could save a lot of expensive studio time by recording some of the tracks at the UMRK.

Frank asked Kevin Conneff to sing 'The Green Fields of America', but he really didn't want to. He told Moloney: 'Paddy, my voice is gone. It's twelve o'clock for God's sake.' But Zappa and Moloney were insistent. Conneff tried it three times, but was not satisfied with his performance. Then Zappa had Spence Chrislau arrange a microphone in the purpose-built echo-chamber at the back of the studio and Conneff gave it another go. He told John Glatt: 'After a couple of false starts – because I had a slight sore throat and was totally exhausted and couldn't think straight – I sang "The Green Fields of America". And apparently it floored him.'

This beautiful nineteenth-century acapella song of emigration is one of the finest examples of the tradition, and Connett sang it with heart-rending clarity. But he thought he could do better and wanted to try another take. Frank said: 'No, no. I really like the first take. I think it's great.' And that was the take Moloney used on *The Celtic Harp*. That night they had recorded five tracks – more than half the album – before the exhausted musicians headed home at 2 a.m. They finished the album two months later at the Windmill Lane Studio in Dublin.

The prostate cancer spread to his bones and Frank finally accepted the fact that he had a terminal illness. Sometimes he could not work at all and had to spend the day in bed, other days were more productive. He told *Playboy*: ' You get to be very time-budget conscious . . . I have a low tolerance for wasting time. I try not to be irritable about it, but it's my main concern. I'm trying to live my life the same way that I lived it before, without indulging in any of the things that would waste time.' But it was uncomfortable for him to work and he found himself tempted to sign off on something when normally he would have devoted more time to it. During one period of severe pain, he let a number of pieces go before they were ready. Then, as he enjoyed a respite, as they had not yet been released, he was able to work on them again and finish them properly.

He spent most of his time working on *Civilisation: Phase III*, a follow up to *Lumpy Gravy*. It featured 'N-Lite' a piece he had worked on intermittently for more than a decade. He was still making final adjustments to *Civilisation Phase III* weeks before his death. Gail told the *LA Times*: 'I think it's very much about finishing his life. He said that after he finished this, he had nothing more to do. I asked him, "Is there anything else you want to tell me about?" He said, "No, I've done everything that I can."'

One problem with writing for the Synclavier – a machine now

only found in synthesizer and keyboard museums – was that Zappa naturally exploited its many wonderful features. He was able to extend a wide array of instruments way above and below their actual range, making the music impossible to play live in the future; similarly, the machine enabled him to use time signatures so complex that no human could ever play them. Effectively he ensured that his Synclavier music would not be performed live after his lifetime, at least not in the form he composed it.

There is also the problem of using complex technology that is state of the art at the time, but ages quickly. After enjoying an enormous burst of sales, New England Digital, the manufacturers of the Synclavier, saturated their market – there were a limited number of artists and studios who could afford a $100,000-plus system. This, combined with the rapid rise of sophisticated personal computers able to duplicate many of the Synclavier's features at a fraction of the price, resulted in New England Digital going bust in 1992. Synclaviers are now antiques of the early digital age, and it will become increasingly difficult to find people who can provide spares and maintenance for them. This means that much of Zappa's Synclavier music will only ever be available in the recordings he made of it.

A number of the tracks on *Civilisation: Phase III* are by the Ensemble Modern, but significant passages played by the Synclavier mean that future concert performances are out of the question. The 19 tracks were released in funereal packaging on two matt-black CDs. They are interspersed with left-overs from the *Lumpy Gravy* recordings of people under the piano at Apostolic. To these Zappa added even more absurdist dialogue concerning pigs and ponies, including the voices of Moon and Frank's Synclavier assistant Todd Yvega.

These snatches of dialogue quickly become irritating, but some of the other tracks are among the most remarkable Zappa ever released, such as 'Beat the Reaper', a title that indicates Zappa's urgency in bringing the project to completion. The highlight is 'N-Lite', of which the *LA Times* said: 'It is likely that no piece of music in history contains so much densely packed, meticulously arranged, diverse sound. The composer described the work simply as "a frightening son-of-a-bitch".'

The name 'N-Lite' betrayed its computer origins: one group of notes in front form a sequence that sounded like the Village People's 'In The Navy' and a sonic cluster that had the computer label 'Thousand Points of Light'.

Gail believes Zappa intended *Civilisation: Phase III* to be his 'master work'. Gail: 'It's called mortality. I think it has a lot to do with Frank knowing that he wasn't going to be able to realize a lot of the things that he wanted to. So then you do what you can. Part of it is an expression of that. I don't think he was in a hurry, as much as he was pragmatic and said, "I can do this." I see it as a big-time "Thanks for the memories", in some ways.'

As Frank weakened, Gail tried to cheer him up by organizing regular Friday night soirées in which people from the band, other musicians, plus a few people from the arts and film worlds would come over to talk, drink margaritas and play music. 'We would have these wonderful eclectic conglomerations of people,' recalled keyboard player Bobby Martin. One evening, in January 1993, these included Phil Abrams, the Amazing Bubble Man, who entertained by blowing bubbles; documentary film-maker Chris Sykes; and a trio of Tuvan throat singers from South Siberia (Kaigal-ool Khovalyg, Anatoly Kuular and Kongar-ool Ondar, members of Huun-Huur-Tu), complete with translators, who were touring the United States for the first time.

Frank was intrigued by their music and had sampled their voices for his Synclavier at the UMRK a few days before. He also recorded some of their music. Now he presented them with a tape of their performances, along with 'something extra', a solo track by Anatoly Kuular onto which Spence Chrislau had overdubbed a funky bass and drum track – 'Using calculus!' Zappa repeated many times, mysteriously.

After a dinner of Tuvan pizza (lamb with onions), the Simpsons creator Matt Groening turned up. It was his thirty-ninth birthday, so a half-eaten chocolate log was transformed into a birthday cake and Gail, Moon, Frank and guests all serenaded him with 'Happy Birthday', complete with Tuvan throat-singing. Afterwards in the studio, Frank got the Tuvans to improvise over one of his heavy metal pieces, but it didn't work out so he gave it up. He was just too tired. After a rest, he rejoined the group for a snack before retiring to bed at 8 p.m.

The BBC filmed one of Zappa's Margarita Fridays in January 1993 for a *Late Night Show* documentary on his life and work. The guests that night were the Chieftains, Johnny 'Guitar' Watson, L. Shankar, Terry Bozzio and the members of Huun-Huur-Tu. Unfortunately, Frank was not feeling at all well for the filming, but the Chieftains managed to put a smile on his face with some rousing traditional Irish music. Frank just loved the sound of Paddy Moloney's slide whistle and drone pipes. He liked to introduce people from entirely different musical traditions and see what happened when they played together. But despite the wonderfully diverse line-up, he was too exhausted to do much with it and Moloney discreetly took over.

Even though it was obvious Zappa was too sick to undertake any more large projects, his friends at the Ensemble Modern had booked 27 May 1994 for a concert in Cologne. Andreas Mölich-Zebhauser, the musical director, wanted to commission Zappa to make a 22-minute film, assembled from his extensive bank of video images, to accompany the music. They also planned an evening of Zappa's theatrical works like *Billy the Mountain* and 'Brown Shoes Don't Make It' arranged for a classical ensemble, to be performed in May 1995. Both ideas excited and encouraged Frank, but he knew he would never see them.

The Chieftains' next project was *The Long Black Veil*, a more commercial offering to balance the tribute to Edward Bunting. They were recording tracks with Mick Jagger, Sting, Sinéad O'Connor, Van Morrison and other famous names. Moloney telephoned to ask Frank if they could use the UMRK to record 'Tennessee Waltz' with Tom Jones. He agreed, but when they showed up a few days later, he was having a bad day and was getting ready to visit the hospital for another blood transfusion.

Frank let Paddy and Spence Chrislau get on with it. Then Frank heard the 'Tennessee Mazurka' (a little number Moloney had written two days before for the session) coming from the studio and went to investigate. When Tom Jones arrived he was shocked to see Zappa looking so sick. Frank left for the hospital in the middle of the session, but before he went he made some suggestions on how to improve the arrangement: new phrasing for the song, a new intro for the bass player, all of which Moloney used.

Spence Chrislau told John Glatt: 'He was just doing an arrangement. It was really funny because although he had said he wasn't interested, it turned out in fact that he was very interested and very instrumental in the end result.' Gail had filled the fridge in the pool room with German beer, and after recording the Chieftains and Tom Jones relaxed so much that Tom missed his flight to New York and had to take the next one, arriving just in time to appear on David Letterman's *The Late Show*.

Zappa's late-blooming friendship with the Chieftains invigorated and encouraged him in the final months of his illness. Gail told John Glatt: 'I'll be eternally grateful to all of them for that beyond anything else. It's something that transcends everything to have a friendship that starts through music and then moves beyond that. It's amazing.' It is sad that it took a terminal illness to make Frank enjoy friendship and companionship; the weekly soirées could have begun years before, when he was in good health.

As Frank's illness progressed he became bed-ridden, though Spence Chrislau made regular visits to his bedside to report on what was happening in the UMRK. Zappa spent his final months listening to his beloved R&B and Doo Wop records. Kevin Conneff's 'The Green Fields of America' became his favourite song during the last few days of his life. Gail told John Glatt: 'It's still very hard for me to listen to it because it was recorded in our studio and Frank loved it so much. Frank and I used to listen to it together and the two of us were just in tears. I will never forget that. It was so extraordinary.'

Frank knew he was dying and began to contact his old friends to say goodbye. Ike Willis recalled: 'In the fall of '93, when I talked to Frank on the phone ... he told me, "Ike, if you have any travel plans in the near future, I suggest you come down and see me, things are getting close and I want to talk to you before it's too late."' He encouraged Ike to go out and 'Go for the gusto, Ike, if you can keep it alive, go ahead and do it, 'cause I can't do it anymore.'

Though not prepared to reveal his feelings, Zappa approached death with stoicism and courage. Moon: 'I wanted the best relationship with him, but I realized that when you are with someone who is passing away, it's as good as it gets at that moment. It's a horrible realization, but also a beautiful one. He bore his death with wonder.'

The Chieftains arrived in LA in December on a 13-city US tour, and Paddy Moloney called Gail to arrange to meet Frank. She said he was very ill, but suggested they come for Sunday lunch. Instead of visiting Zappa, they arrived on the Sunday to pay their condolences.

Frank Zappa died on Saturday, 6 December 1993, just before 6 p.m. He was awake and had Gail and all the children with him, but his mother and his siblings were not called until after his death. The death of a child is about the hardest thing a parent can suffer and Rose Marie was hurt by Gail's decision not to allow her to see her son a final time.

Moon: 'When he died, we got to put him in his coffin. Normally someone else gets to do that, but we put him in ourselves. We treated it like he was going on tour, and put in his espresso machine and some cayenne pepper and various other things that he would need. I thought it was going to be really scary when he died, but it just wasn't. I felt so lucky to be there.'

Zappa was buried the next day at Westwood Village Memorial Park. Gail told Howard Stern: 'We wanted to keep it private and, you know, the minute that you file the death certificate, which you have to do in order to get the burial permit, it's picked up by the Press. So they were very kind to us and they kept the certificate there with the mortuary on the phone until we actually got there, and then they filed it, so we could bury him right away and that's what he wanted, anyway.' At Zappa's request Kevin Conneff's 'The Green Fields of America' was played at his funeral. 'It's one of the biggest compliments I was ever paid,' Conneff told John Glatt.

Zappa's grave is unmarked. It is located in section D, plot 100, of the Pierce Bros Westwood Village Memorial Park, a tranquil little graveyard hidden away behind the skyscrapers of Wilshire Boulevard near UCLA, at 1018 Glendon Avenue. It is the final resting place of dozens of Hollywood stars. Marilyn Monroe has a simple wall plaque with her name and dates; Natalie Wood's grave is marked with a Russian Orthodox cross; and among the flowering trees and shrubs are the graves of Jack Lemmon, Walter Matthau, George C. Scott, Burt Lancaster and Dean Martin.

Frank joined singers Peggy Lee, Mel Torme, Minnie Riperton and Beach Boy Carl Wilson, and his grave is a short distance from that of Roy Orbison, which is also unmarked. Zappa's plot is located to the immediate right of character actor Lew Ayers', beneath the overhanging boughs of a tree that sheds its leaves onto his grave. The walls to the east and north sides of the graveyard are made up of crypts (Monroe's ashes are interned in one) which, in the Californian sunshine gives the place a European atmosphere; it could almost be in Sicily.

22 Afterword

Zappa's impact on twentieth-century music was considerable, and in many different areas. He was celebrated for his guitar playing; his ability as a band leader; and, of course, his musical compositions, which ranged from jagged atonality to the gorgeous harmonies of Doo Wop, crossing from pop into the classical repertoire. He was remembered as a social reformer, a social historian and journalist. His lyrics could be both challenging and funny and aside from his music he is remembered for his irascible political views and some witty epigrams.

His astonishing abilities as a guitarist were sometimes obscured by the humour, the rants and the trademark moustache. He took enormous risks in a solo, but when all went well he ranked alongside Hendrix, Clapton, Beck; Zappa was a real sixties guitar-hero. Certain songs particularly suited his style: 'Watermelon In Easter Hay', 'Sexual Harassment In the Workplace' and 'Black Napkins' contain guitar solos so moving that members of the audience were often in tears.

Zappa was a brilliant band leader, working in the tradition of Art Blakey or Miles Davis as a finishing school for musicians. He wrote pieces to showcase their individual talents and tested the limits of their abilities. His work was difficult to play; it stretched his musicians, but having played in a Zappa line-up was very good for their CV, and many of his players went on to greater things.

Zappa's favourite compositions, as told to *Guitar World* in 1980, were: 'Oh No', the theme from *Lumpy Gravy*, 'The Eric Dolphy Memorial Barbecue', 'Uncle Meat', 'Brown Shoes Don't Make It', 'Dinah-Moe Humm' and 'Who Are The Brain Police?'. He described 'Peaches en Regalia' as a classic: 'That's probably the ultimate across the board Frank Zappa song of all time. It's the only thing I've never heard anybody say they didn't like.' Talking about his recent work a few days before his death, he said: 'My best things are like "The Jazz Discharge Party Hat" or "Dangerous Kitchen". The former comes close to Schoenberg, with its jazz accompaniment to a *Sprechgesang* text presentation, and the latter – the lyrics were written, but the pitched recitation was something that was done free-form on stage, with the band following.'

A Zappa Top 10 – as selected by hardcore fans in the Zappa fanzine *T'Mershi Duween* – went as follows: 'Watermelon In Easter Hay', 'Inca Roads', 'Peaches en Regalia' / 'Black Napkins', 'Yo Mama', 'Willie the Pimp', 'What's New In Baltimore?', 'The Black Page', 'King Kong', 'The Torture Never Stops' and 'G-Spot Tornado'.

'King Kong' was another of Zappa's favourites. It has been chosen by many small ensembles to play in classical settings because, unlike some of his work, it is relatively easy to play. Zappa: 'It's simple, really easy. It's a D minor vamp. In fact I would say that 80 per cent of the things that we have that have solos in them are in the same key. Reading the same changes. I just love D minor vamps. D Minor with a major forechord. Gives you a nice modal effect.' From the Doo Wop songs on *Ruben and the Jets* to the intricate sonic clusters of 'Dupree's Paradise', Zappa left a musical legacy with something for everyone.

He began life as a drummer and moved on to the guitar, but his work was always very concerned with time signatures and unusual rhythmic patterns. His guitar playing influenced his composition: there are many repeated notes, many very fast notes and clusters of sound like guitar chords.

It was a strange decision to give up the guitar in 1988 and concentrate entirely on keyboard composition using the Synclavier. Many of Zappa's compositions had their origins in guitar solos, forged in the heat and excitement of being on-stage, which were later transcribed and used as melodies. To go from this to the slow picking out of notes on a computer keyboard inevitably led to less exciting music (some of his ex-band members dismissed it as completely sterile). But there is no way of knowing what Zappa would have done with it had he lived long enough to use today's technology. He was restless for change and would not have stayed still. At the time of his death he was beginning to explore world music.

As so much of his work was journalistic or broadly anthropological, it is impossible to separate Zappa's politics and philosophy from his music. It was all one; all part of his 'conceptual continuity'. As he told Bob Marshall after a long discussion about philosophy: 'The conceptual continuity is this: everything, even this interview, is part of what I do for, let's call it, my entertainment work. And there's a big difference between sitting here and talking about this kind of stuff, and writing a song like "Titties and Beer". But as far as I'm concerned, it's all part of the same continuity. It's all one piece.' To let his audience know this, he dropped a few references to poodles here and there for fans to find like an Easter-egg hunt, but the real intention was more serious.

Zappa is an iconoclast in the male American tradition of Neal Cassady, Hunter S. Thompson, William S. Burroughs, Ken Kesey, Allen Ginsberg, Lenny Bruce and the early Norman Mailer. His is a writer's viewpoint, rather than a musician's, and his views are known to his public as much through interviews as through his lyrics. Sceptical and witty like Lenny Bruce, Frank presented himself not as an outside agitator, but as an informed insider. Bruce was the cool hipster; Zappa the freak – or, as he could be more meaningfully dubbed, a bohemian.

Zappa was never a hippie, more of a late-arriving Beat. He was a loner, very much a solo act, but if we try to locate him anywhere it would probably be as a bohemian; the artist as a romantic genius. The Romantic movement, a response to the Industrial and French Revolutions, encouraged the view that artists are fundamentally different from the rest of society. According to Elizabeth Wilson, author of *Bohemians, the Glamorous Outcasts*: 'The Romantic Genius is the artist against society – he or she embodies dissidence, opposition, critical of the status quo, these may be expressed politically, aesthetically or in the artists' behaviour and lifestyle. Components of the myth are transgression, excess, sexual outrage, eccentric behaviour, outrageous appearance, nostalgia and poverty – although wealth could contribute to the legend provided the bohemian treated it with contempt, flinging money around instead of investing it with bourgeois caution.'

This description fits Zappa pretty well. His attempt to change the world by Freaking Out was a naive continuation of an artistic bohemian tradition that dates back at least as far as Courbet and embraces much of the European avant-garde, from the Surrealists to the Existentialists. Zappa would have undoubtedly agreed with Picasso's statement: 'We must wake people up. Upset their way of identifying things. It is necessary to create unacceptable images. Make people foam at the mouth. Force them to understand that they live in a mad world. A disquieting world, not reassuring. A world which is not as they see it.' This was what Zappa was trying to do, with some success.

However, although we might situate him in an artistic tradition, he had little interest in such things. 'I didn't have that kind of an education,' he once said. 'I have no knowledge of the history of art or poetry, or any of that kind of stuff. It never interested me. I think that it's nice that it's there for people who want it, but I never studied it. I don't know anything about that. I just did my own stuff. If it happens to be similar to other things that other people have done, fine.' He was a fellow traveller, on a parallel course, alone.

He was a cynic in Los Angeles, where to be perceived as a cynic is the kiss of death. Nothing must be allowed to deflate the enormous egos of LA or to undermine the importance of 'the Work' (usually something like rewriting a second-rate sitcom) or to suggest that celebrity is not the highest achievement possible on Earth. Zappa was irreverent in a country where right-wing fundamentalist Christians rule the airwaves and the government and most of the population believe the Bible to be literally true. He was a natural outsider, a loner like the heroes of Sam Fuller's movies.

Zappa's cynical eye fell like a searchlight on every trace of foolishness. Nobody was immune from his gaze, from the racist Southern redneck of 'Lonesome Cowboy Burt' to the mendacious TV evangelists of 'Heavenly Bank Account' and 'Jesus Thinks You're a Jerk'. The right-wing fundamentalist Christians were the subject of much of his fury, but he also pinned down L. Ron Hubbard and the Scientologists, the Maharishi, and gurus in general. He spoke about the idiocy of the drug laws; the vacuity of music business executives and the arrogance of American military interventionism.

He railed against the dumbing-down of the school system to create an America of near-illiterates hypnotized by TV and celebrity, who believe all the lies the politicians tell them; an acquiescent workforce who buy all the junk pushed at them by the advertisements that fill so much of American life: TV, radio, billboards, magazines and newspapers; on clothing, buildings, buses and cabs; even the public benches in LA are covered with adverts, while light aircraft fly overhead towing commercial messages. Zappa used them as raw material.

Many of his targets were stereotypes: sex-obsessed Catholic girls; vacuous Valley girls; rapacious Jewish Princesses; strident women's libbers; the fetishistic equipment of the bondage and rubberwear gay scene; spaced-out hippies and incoherent drug users; and, of course, road-fatigued rock 'n' roll musicians (himself included). His vision of the world was savagely satiric. Zappa the journalist pointed at all this and said: 'Look, these things exist!'

Zappa had much in common with that other great Baltimore reporter, H. L. Mencken, who in August 1925 complained of 'our growing impatience with the free play of ideas, our increasing tendency to reduce all virtues to the single one of conformity, our relentless and all-pervading standardization ... No other nation of today is so rigorously policed. The lust to standardize and regulate extends to the most trivial minutia of private life.' Zappa saw the same danger signals and continued to warn us: championing the rights of the individual to the very last.

Of course, Zappa's reliability as a reporter was sometimes damaged by his misanthropy (something Mencken was also accused of), which tended to colour his world view. Many interviewers saw him as arrogant, which he could be. The truth was that Zappa did not like many people. 'I have an expression I use,' he said, 'It's not as good as "Shoot low – they're riding Shetlands," but I try and remember this all the time – you can use it yourself – like a mantra: "People suck."'

Zappa read little and professed to have no interest in the arts or literature, but nonetheless regarded himself as an intellectual. When asked if he felt on a higher intellectual level than most people, he agreed that he did. Asked if he ever met people with whom he could communicate on an equal basis, he said no. This was said to provide good newspaper copy, but, with a few exceptions, Zappa did see himself as superior.

Not that he had any illusions about the status of intellectuals in America. He told Fabio Massari: 'Here a Ministry of Culture doesn't exist. And you know why? There is no culture. There are two words that can't be used here: . . . "Culture" and "intellectual". If you mention support for so-called culture, the Right is on your back immediately. Here, however, an intellectual is a baldie, the ugly little guy who never gets sucked off by women. I can say I am an intellectual, but the basic model the USA requires is that of a poor bastard. That's the way it is, otherwise the real America is the one with the fat guy who guzzles beer.' Zappa was an intellectual by default.

Intellectuals coin epigrams and Zappa came up with three, often quoted, which will surely enter the canon. On stupidity: 'Scientists claim that hydrogen is the basic building block of the universe because it is so plentiful. I say that there is more stupidity than hydrogen, and *that* is the basic building block of the universe.' On rock critics: 'People who can't write, doing interviews with people who can't talk, for people who can't read.' And his credo at the end of *Joe's Garage*: 'Information is not knowledge. Knowledge is not wisdom. Wisdom is not truth. Truth is not beauty. Beauty is not love. Love is not music. Music is the best.'

'If "Love is not music," what is love?' he was once asked. Zappa replied: 'It's chemical, merely chemical.' His father always wanted him to be a chemist.

Zappa became a wealthy man, but not mega-rich like some of his contemporaries. Rhino offered $12 million for the Zappa back catalogue. Rykco bid $22 million, leaving the Zappa Family Trust comfortably off. Rykco sold part of the company to do it and went bust (it was bought by Chris Blackwell's Palm Records).

Zappa complained endlessly about not being played on the radio, but as the owner of numerous record labels he knew that to get air-play you need a commercial single and to pay so-called 'independent' music pluggers to promote it (so the payola can't be traced back to the record company). But Frank did not make commercial singles. His two biggest hits, 'Don't Eat the Yellow Snow' and 'Valley Girl', were recognized as such not by him but by DJs. Zappa always lacked a commercial ear, which is ironic considering he started off making comedy records with Paul Buff.

Zappa found fame: he was fêted by Václav Havel, praised by Pierre Boulez, and bedded by numerous groupies. But he was much more than a rock 'n' roll star. Groups like the Omnibus Wind Ensemble in Stockholm recorded brass arrangements of his music and the Ensemble Ambrosius in Helsinki made a CD of Zappa pieces arranged for baroque instruments. Even the President's own Marine Corps band in Fairfax, Virginia, wanted to play 'Dog Breath Variations'. Two gunnery sergeants in the band were fans so Zappa sent them the music.

Another proof of fame is that things get named after you and Zappa is no exception. There is a gene (ZapA Proteus mirabilis); a fish (*Zappa confluentus*); a jellyfish (*Phialella zappa*); a mollusc (*Amauratoma zappa*); and a spider (*Pachygnatha zappa*). And finally, taking Zappa's song 'Help I'm A Rock' literally, a tiny planet orbiting between Mars and Jupiter was named Zappafrank – after the International Astronomical Union's Minor Planet Center was subjected to the largest lobbying effort ever seen in the naming of more than 3,000 asteroids.

If Zappa had one ultimate message, one over-riding idea: 'It's that the Emperor's not wearing any clothes, never has, never will.' It is even more relevant today than when he first said it.

Notes

See Bibliography for publishing details of cited books

1 Baltimore

Partinico: General description: Mary Taylor Simeti, *On Persephone's Island: a Sicilian Journal* (New York: Alfred A. Knopf, 1986); 'Golden Triangle': 'Italy: Godfather's Strike Gold As Wines Go To Pot' by Bruce Johnson, *Daily Telegraph* (4 September, 2001).

Baltimore: www.livebaltimore.com; 'Baltimore, Maryland – Hairdo Capital of the World' in John Waters, *Shock Value*; Alexander D. Mitchell IV, *Baltimore Then and Now*; Interviews with Rose Marie Zappa, Maria Colimore and Frank Zappa (FZ) on his life in Baltimore in 'Frank Zappa: I Never Set Out to be Weird' in Rafael Alvarez, *Hometown Boy, the Hoodle Patrol and Other Curiosities of Baltimore*; FZ interviewed by Kurt Loder in *Bat Chain Puller: Rock & Roll In The Age of Celebrity*.

Childhood memories: FZ with Peter Occhiogrosso, *The Real Frank Zappa Book*.

Family finances: David Walley, *No Commercial Potential: The Saga of Frank Zappa*.

Chronology: The Zappas moved around a great deal, but no matter how one arranges the chronology, one would have to contradict FZ's own account of the family history. In his autobiography and in numerous interviews, he says that the family moved straight from Baltimore to Edgewood. In his autobiography, FZ also states that 'it was still World War II' when the family moved to Opa-locka in Florida. As FZ was four years old when the war ended, Florida clearly came first.

Edgewood: Suzanne Marshall, PhD, 'Chemical Weapons Disposal and Environmental Justice' (Kentucky Environmental Foundation, November 1996).

Childhood memories: FZ, *The Real Frank Zappa Book*.

Fishing: Michael Gray, *Mother! The Frank Zappa Story*.

Catholicism: Peter Occhiogrosso, *Once a Catholic*.

Baltimore catechism: FZ interviewed by John Swenson, *High Times* (No 55. March 1980); FZ interviewed by David Sheff, *Playboy* (April 1993).

2 California

Chemistry set: FZ interviewed by Keith Altham, *NME* (5 February 1972).

Snare drum: FZ interviewed by Steve Rosen, *Guitar Player* (January 1977).

'Mice': FZ interviewed by John Colbert, 'Frank Zappa' *Musicians Only* (28 January 1980). It is unlikely that piece was ever written down.

Spike Jones: sleevenotes by Joop Visser to *Strictly For Music Lovers*, 4 CD box set by Spike Jones and His City Slickers (Proper Records: Properbox 5, 1999); FZ interviewed by Charles Amirkhanian, KPFA-FM (15 April 1991); FZ interviewed by Jeff Newelt, 'Be a Little Civic Hellraiser' in *34th Street*, Philadelphia (18 April 1991).

Claremont: FZ, '50s Teenagers and 50s Rock', *Evergreen Review* (Number 81, August 1970).

Arab music: Biography in *Cashbox*, 3 August 1974 (also Kurt Loder, *Bat Chain Puller*).

Doo Wop: 'Gee' on the radio quoted *T'Mershi Duween* 15; The Velvets: 'I' on Red Robin 122 (December 1953); The Crows: 'Gee' on Rama 5 (1953); Hank Ballard and the Midnighters: 'Annie Had a Baby' on Federal 12195 (September 1954); The Chords: 'Sh-Boom' on Cat 104 (April 1954).

Rhythm and Blues as main influence: WXPN Philadelphia, 'Totally Wired' show (17 December 1986).

Record player: Nigel Leigh interview, BBC-TV.

The Gaylords: 'The Little Shoemaker' on Mercury entered the US charts in July and stayed for 18 weeks.

The Robins: 'Riot in cell Block Number 9' on Spark 103 (1954).

First public appearance: CBS Records Press release, May 1981.

Hank Ballard and the Midnighters: 'Work With Me Annie' on Federal 12177 (April 1954).

Look magazine article on Varèse: Greg Russo, *Cosmik Debris: The Collected History and Improvisions of Frank Zappa*.

Mission Bay High School: FZ, '50s Teenagers and 50s Rock', *Evergreen Review* (Number 81, August 1970); FZ interviewed by Les Carter, on KPPC-FM, Pasadena (27 November 1968).

'Teenage hoodlum types': Unidentified interview on 'The Conversation Disc Series' ABCD016. n.d. n.p. (England)

'I Was A Teenage Malt Shop': quoted in David Walley, *No Commercial Potential: The Saga of Frank Zappa* and by Ben Watson in *Frank Zappa the Negative Dialectics of Poodle Play*.

Sleeve notes by Finkelstein: Ibid.

'I loved Stravinsky . . .' FZ, *The Real Frank Zappa Book*.

Boston Symphony Orchestra: Greg Russo, *Cosmik Debris: The Collected History and Improvisions of Frank Zappa*.

Varèse and the Robins: Kurt Loder, *Bat Chain Puller*.

The Jewels: 'Angel In My Life' on Imperial 5351 (April 1955).

'Parallel Fourths': FZ, *The Real Frank Zappa Book*.

Music notation: FZ interviewed by David Sheff, *Playboy* (April 1993); FZ interviewed by Don Menn, *Guitar Player* magazine (1992).

Elwood's playing: Nigel Leigh interview, BBC TV.

Fired from the Ramblers: Quoted in a CBS Records press release, 1981.

Couldn't dance to it: FZ interviewed by David Mead, 'Unholy Mother', *Guitarist* magazine (June 1993).

Elwood's brother: United-Mutations website.

San Diego bands: FZ interviewed by Sally Kempton, 'Zappa and the Mothers, Ugly Can Be Beautiful', *Village Voice* (1967).

Whitfield: Wilbur Whitfield & the Pleasers: 'P. B. Baby' was Alladin 3381.

3 Lancaster, CA

Lancaster: Glen A. Settle, *Lancaster Celebrates a Century 1884–1984* (City of Lancaster, 1983); Patrice 'Candy' Zappa, *My Brother Was A Mother*. David Walley: *No Commercial Potential: the Saga of Frank Zappa, Then and Now*.

Okies with cars: *Rock Late* (1970)

Natty dresser: FZ to author, 1969.

Cheerleaders: FZ interviewed by Jerry Hopkins, *Rolling Stone* (1968). Included in MGM-Verve press pack. Reprinted in *The Rolling Stone Interviews*.

Cultural opportunities: FZ interviewed by David Sheff, *Playboy* (April 1993).

Cultural wasteland: FZ interviewed by Steve Rosen, *Guitar* magazine (January 1977).

'Motion': CBS London Press release, 1981. Note: The work of Barbara Rubin used a similar system: her method was to swing the camera around her head, though she did often superimpose such images on fixed-view shots.

Call to Varèse: FZ, 'Edgard Varèse: Idol of My Youth. A Reminiscence and Appreciation.' *Stereo Review* (June 1971). Reprinted in Dominique Chevalier: *Viva! Zappa*. FZ always mentioned that he was particularly pleased when Varèse told him he was working on a piece called *Deserts*, which he could immediately relate to because he was living in the Mojave Desert. But when FZ turned 15 he was still living in Mission Bay, San Diego. FZ said that Varèse was away in Brussels working on his *Poème électronique* for the 1958 World Fair when he first telephoned and he did not actually speak to the composer until a later date. As *Poème électronique* was not commissioned from Varèse until 1956, Zappa must have made the call from Lancaster, on the occasion of his sixteenth birthday, 21 December 1956. This would also connect better with Zappa's attempt to meet the composer in July 1957, a meeting they discussed during the phonecall. Incidentally, Varèse wrote *Deserts* between 1950 and 1954, so it was already completed at the time of both FZ's fifteenth and sixteenth birthdays; but if Varèse asked the young fan where he was calling from and FZ had explained that Lancaster was in the desert, this would have been an easy connection for Varèse to make.

No rock in Lancaster: FZ interviewed by David Sheff, *Playboy* (April 1993).

Big Jay McNeely: Larry Benicewicz: Big Jay McNeely Part 2, *Blues Rag* (September 1997).

Night in jail: FZ interviewed by David Sheff, *Playboy* (April 1993).

They didn't like me: FZ interviewed by Don Menn, *Guitar Player* (1992). Reprinted in *A Definitive Tribute to Frank Zappa* (*Guitar Player*, May 1994).

Sports: FZ interviewed by Dan Ouellette, *Pulse!* (August 1993).

Dissonant results: FZ interviewed by Andy Gill, *Q* (December 1989).

The twelve-tone system: Wellesz in his pamphlet *Arnold Schoenberg* (1945), quoted in *The Concise Oxford Dictionary of Music* (London, 1964). And see John Rockwell, *All American Music*.

Motorhead: Motorhead interviewed by Billy James, *T'Mershi Duween* 31 (June 1993).

Girlfriend: FZ interviewed by Bob Marshall for *The Canned Ham*, San Jose, CA (21–22 October 1988).

Watson's tone: FZ interviewed by David Mead, *Guitarist* magazine (June 1993).

Nigel Leigh: BB2 interview quoted by Neil Slaven.

Letter to Aunt Mary: Quoted by Rafael Alvarez, *Baltimore Sun* (12 October 1986).

Relatives shocked: FZ interviewed by Rafael Alvarez, *Baltimore Sun* (12 October 1986).

'I was a jerk in high school': CBS Records press release (May 1981).

Don Van Vliet: Eliot Wald, 'Conversation with Captain Beefheart', *Oui* (July 1973).

Hutzler's tearoom: Ibid.

Formal musical education: Warners press-kit for the *Waka/Jawaka*, Hot Rats album.

Juilliard: CBS Press release, 1981.

Junior college: David Walley, *No Commercial Potential: the Saga of Frank Zappa, Then and Now*.

Harmony book: FZ interviewed by Don Menn, *Guitar Player* (1992). Reprinted in *A Definitive Tribute to Frank Zappa* (*Guitar Player*, May 1994); FZ interviewed by David Mead, *Guitarist* (June 1993).

'Lost In A Whirlpool': FZ interviewed by Eric Buxton, Rob Samler, Den Simms, *Society Pages* (22 December 1989); 'Lost In A Whirlpool' CD notes: Frank Zappa, *The Lost Episodes*.

4 Ontario

Ontario: David Allen, 'In Claremont, Zappa's family takes a trip down memory lane', Ontario *Daily Bulletin* (8 November 2003).

Family Problems: Patrice 'Candy' Zappa, *My Brother Was A Mother*.

Garden of Eden: FZ interviewed by David Sheff, *Playboy* (April 1993).

Refused to go to Mass: Peter Occhiogrosso, *Once a Catholic*.

I was interested in Zen: *East Village Other* (March 1967).

Gregorian chant: Peter Occhiogrosso, *Once a Catholic*.

Taboo words: FZ interviewed by Susan Shapiro, *Sounds* (18 December 1976).

Psychiatrists: *East Village Other* (March 1967).

314 West G Street: Candy Zappa talking to Peter MacCay: http://www.cableaz.com/users/lantz/other.html.

Telecaster: FZ to David Mead, *Guitarist* (June 1993).

Folk music: 'LA Country Rock – A Personal History' by Chris Darrow, *Discoveries for Record and CD Collectors*, archived at Madmeg.net. No date given.

Greeting cards: FZ interviewed by Don Menn, *Guitar Player* (1992). Reprinted in *A Definitive Tribute to Frank Zappa* (*Guitar Player*, May 1994)

Green window project: Splat's Zappa Page website.

Timothy Carey: interviewed by Mike Murphy and Johnny Legend, origin unknown, reprinted on Splat's Zappa Page website.

'Tiptoe Through The Tulips': FZ interviewed by Frank Kofsky: *Jazz & Pop* (September 1967).

'It was rancid': David Walley, *No Commercial Potential, the Saga of Frank Zappa, Then and Now*.

'Take Your Clothes Off When You Dance': On FZ, *The Lost Episodes* (1996).

'World's Greatest Sinner': *Pomona Progress-Bulletin* (9 March 1962).

5 Cucamonga

Paul Buff: Buff interviewed by Drew Wheeler, *Billboard* (10 May 1990). Note: Buff also produced Rene and Ray's 'Queen Of My Heart' for Del-Fi/Donna; Terri and Johnnie's 'Your Tender Lips' on Donna; and bands like the Esquires, a surfing band from Pomona, whose two-sided instrumental 'Flashin' Red' was recorded at Pal and released January 1964 as Durco 1001.

Paul Buff credo: www.paulcbuff.com website. See also his interview with Bryan Thomas in the liner notes to FZ, *Cucamonga*, Del-Fi DFCD71261.

8-Track: The first recording made on Atlantic's new eight-track recorder was 'Splish Splash' Atco 6117 (19 May 1958).

Pal Studio: Drew Wheeler, *Billboard* (10 May 1990).

Pal Studio Record heads: 'Absolutely Frank', *EQ Magazine* (March 1994).

Ray Collins: Interviewed by Roy Harper, *Outer Shell* Internet magazine.

'Love Of My Life': Zappa quoted in CBS Records press release for *Tinseltown Rebellion*, 1981.

Little Julian Herrera: David Porter interview with Ray Collins, KPFK-FM (12 August 1989).

Rip Rense: Liner notes to Ryko RCD 40573. FZ, *The Lost Episodes* (1996).

Rene and Ray: 'Queen Of My Heart', Donna (May 1962). Rene was Pablo Venezuela of Glendora, and Ray was Ray Quinones. The songwriting credits go to both, but the song is a steal from Jesse Belvin's 'The Girl Of My Dreams'. Ray Quinones also released a song, 'So Dearly' on the Donna label as Rosie and Ron, which may also have been recorded at Pal.

Bob Keane: Aka Bob Keene, born Robert Kuhn, started Del-Fi in 1957, specialized in recording 'Pachucos', as the Mexican-Americans of East LA were called. His biggest hit was 'Donna' by Ritchie Valens, which reached Number Two. After Valens' death, Del-Fi moved into surf music. Zappa's involvement with the Del-Fi/Donna label – including cuts sold by him – was as follows: Paul Buff: 'Slow Bird'/'Blind Man's Buff' Donna 1376; Baby Ray and the Ferns: 'How's Your Bird?'/'The World's Greatest Sinner.' Donna 1378; The Pauls: 'Cathy My Angel'/"Til September' Donna 1379; Bob Guy: 'Dear Jeepers'/'Letter From Jeepers' Donna 1380; The Heartbreakers: 'Everytime I See You'/'Cradle Rock' Donna 1381.

'How's Your Bird?': Ray Collins quoted in the liner notes to the *Rare Meat* EP from Del-Fi 1983.

Snorks: Paul Buff disputes this. In a conversation with Patrick Neve posted at the United Mutations website. Buff said: 'I wasn't aware of Dick Barber – aka the Snorker – and have to take full credit for myself being the godfather of snorks and other such early Zappa noises.'

Cyclophony: 'Ontario Composer, Steve Allen To Play Wacky Duet', *Pomona Progress-Bulletin* (26 March 1963). The show was aired the next day.

'The World's Greatest Sinner': Dick Barber interviewed in *Society Pages* Number 5 said: 'It was was Frank, me, Ray Collins, and who else? Motorhead maybe, playin' the baritone sax. The group was called Baby Ray and the Ferns . . . We did "The World's Greatest Sinner" . . . "Twist" and "Cheebop-a-Dooly Bop".' These last two numbers have not been released.

'Love Of My Life': David Porter interview with Ray Collins, KPFK-FM (12 August 1989).

Playing bicycle: FZ to Susan Shapiro, *Sounds* (18 December 1976).

'Memories of El Monte': Steve Propes interview with Ray Collins, KLON-FM (13 August 1989).

Art Laboe's Memories of El Monte: The original vinyl release on Starla has little in common with Laboe's CD release with the same title and sleeve. Most of the original tracks are missing from the CD and have been replaced with padding from the seventies. The original, which was regarded by Zappa as an almost perfect compilation, consisted of: The Paragons, 'Let's Start All Over Again'; Marvin and Johnny, 'Cherry Pie'; Chuck Higgins, 'Pachuko Hop'; Don and Dewey, 'Leavin' It All Up To You'; Roy Holden, 'I Love You So'; Jim Balcon, 'Corrido Rock'; The Shields, 'You Cheated'; Gene and Eunice, 'This Is My Story'; Sonny Knight, 'Dedicated To You'; Julie Stevens, 'Blue Moon'; The Jacks, 'Why Don't You Write Me'; and Little Julian Herrera, 'I Remember Linda' (featuring Ray Collins), only six of which appear on the 20-track CD.

Penguins line-up: FZ told Mick Watts of *Melody Maker*: 'The rest of those Penguins were just a bunch of guys from the car wash.' Not so.

Studio Masters: This is sometimes given as Stereo Masters Studio.

Cradle Rock: The guitarist that sounds like FZ is Richard Provincio. For the session the Heartbreakers were backed by Don Cardenas, sax player for the Blendells, Andy Tesso, lead guitarist with the Romancers – he and FZ both drew heavily on Johnny 'Guitar' Watson – and two other members of the Romancers.

The Vigah! label scam: Paul Buff in conversation with Patrick Neve (16 March 1998), posted on the United Mutations website.

'The Big Surfer': Capitol 4981 (27 May 1963).

Mount St Mary's College: Matt Groening, *Guitar Player* (1992). Reprinted in *A Definitive Tribute to Frank Zappa* (*Guitar Player*, May 1994).

The Soots: FZ to Mark Williams, *IT* (1970).

Vic Mortenson on drums: Liner notes to *Grow Fins*.

Ray Collins praise: FZ to J. P. Cantillon in *Sh-Boom* magazine (March 1990).

'Puff the Magic Dragon': FZ to Dan Ouellette, *Pulse!* (August 1993). 'Puff the Magic Dragon' was in the charts in April 1963.

Troubadour: FZ to Les Carter, KPPC-FM, Pasadena (27 November 1968).

'Go on and sing': *IT* (March 1977).

'Mr Clean': Original Sound OS 40 (July 1964).

The Rotations: Original Sound OS 41 (July 1964).

Dot Records: The date given for the rejection letter in the liner notes to *Frank Zappa: The Lost Episodes* is incorrect.

Fuzz bass: 'Absolutely Frank', *EQ* Magazine (March 1994).

Split with Kay: Candy Zappa interview on idiotbastard website; Patrice 'Candy' Zappa, *My Brother Was A Mother*.

6 Studio Z

Studio Z: FZ interviewed by the Salvos, *Melody Maker* (January 1974).

Beefheart on his name: *IT* 26 (16 February 1967).

Motorhead on Studio Z: Interviewed by Rip Rense for the liner notes of *Frank Zappa, The Lost Episodes*.

Go-go girls: FZ interviewed by Steve Rosen, *Guitar Magazine* (January 1977).

Singing at the Saints and Sinners: Ibid.

The (Ontario) Daily Report: Saturday 27 March 1965.

San Bernardino County Jail: FZ interviewed by Lon Goddard, *Melody Maker*

(7 June 1969); FZ quoted by Nigey Lennon in *Being Frank, My Time With Frank Zappa*.

Soul Giants: Ray Collins interviewed by David Porter on KPFA-FM (8 December 1989); FZ to Jerry Hopkins, *Rolling Stone* (1968): issued as part of Verve press pack with no date given. Reprinted in *The Rolling Stone Interviews* (New York: Paperback Library, 1971); Jimmy Carl Black interviewed by Steve Moore, Internet posting; Jimmy Carl Black interviewed by Graham Halliday, *Chunky Yet Funky Zine*, n.d. Internet.

Lambs: FZ interviewed by Les Carter, KPPC-FM, Pasadena (27 November 1968).

Long-term plan: FZ interviewed by Dan Ouellette: *Pulse!* (August 1993).

7 The Strip

Grubby little place: FZ in *Cashbox* (1974).

Aldous Huxley: *After Many A Summer* (London: Chatto & Windus, 1939).

Ski jacket: Jimmy Carl Black interviewed by Steve Moore, Internet posting.

Victor Maymudes: 'It Is Good To Look Back', obituary posted on the Internet (6 February 2001).

'Mafia undertakers': FZ interviewed by Jerry Hopkins, *Rolling Stone* (1968). Reprinted in *The Rolling Stone Interviews* (New York: Paperback Library, 1971).

Teen Set: *Teen Set* (December 1966).

Starvation to poverty: *The Real Frank Zappa Book*.

Vito Paulekas biography: Richard Goldstein, 'The Head Freak Awaits A New Son', *New York Magazine* (1967). Reprinted in *Richard Goldstein's Greatest Hits*; Barney Hoskyns, *Waiting For The Sun*; Pamela Des Barres, *I'm With The Band: Confessions of a Groupie*; Barney Hoskyns, 'The Strip', *Mojo* 3 (January / February 1994).

Karl Franzoni biography: *Last of The Freaks: The Karl Franzoni Story*; Karl Franzoni interviewed by John Trubee, Internet posting.

Watts Riots: Various Internet sources. FZ interviewed by Bob Marshall and Dr Carolyn Dean, for *The Canned Ham*, San Jose, CA (1988).

FZ songs at the time: FZ biography written for *Cashbox* (1974).

Alice Stuart: FZ in *Hit Parader* (June 1968).

Henry Vestine. FZ interviewed in *Hit Parader* (June 1968).

'Like A Rolling Stone': Quoted by Clinton Heylin in *Bob Dylan: Behind the Shades* (London: Viking, 2000).

8 Freak Out!

The Strip: Roy Trakin, 'A Special Time in Rock: 1966 On The Sunset Strip', *Los Angeles Times* (date unknown).

Discovery of Canter's: Karl Franzoni interviewed by John Trubee, 'Last of The Freaks: The Karl Franzoni Story', Internet posting.

The Trip: FZ interviewed by Jerry Hopkins, *Rolling Stone* (1968). Reprinted in *The Rolling Stone Interviews*.

Lenny Bruce: Adam Gopnik, 'Standup Guys', *The New Yorker* (12 May 2003); Albert Goldman: *Ladies and Gentlemen, Lenny Bruce!!*; Lenny Bruce, *The Essential Lenny Bruce*.

Marijuana: Ray Collins interviewed by David Porter, KPFK-FM (12 August 1989).

San Francisco: *Cashbox* (1974).

'Difference between freaks and hippies': FZ interviewed by Jerry Hopkins, *Rolling Stone* (1968). Reprinted in *The Rolling Stone Interviews* (New York: Paperback Library, 1971).

Vestine leaving: Jimmy Carl Black: liner notes to *Who Could Imagine* by the Grandmothers.

FZ on line-up: *Cashbox* (1974).

Steve Mann: FZ in *Hit Parader* (June 1968).

Recording dates: www.globalia.net.

Mac Rebennak: *Under a Hoodoo Moon*.

'Brain Police': FZ in *Cashbox* (1974).

'Go Cry On Somebody Else's Shoulder': Ray Collins interviewed by David Porter, *KPFK* (12 August 1989).

Counter-Culture: FZ interviewed by Jón Benediktsson (23 March 1992), Icelandic Radio.

Honolulu trip: Jimmy Carl Black interviewed by Graham Halliday, *Chunky Yet Funky Zine*, Internet.

'Untalented bores': Lou Reed quoted in Victor Bockris, *Lou Reed, the Biography*.

John Judnick: Later designed the PA for the Rolling Stones 1972 World Tour, so he was well equipped for the task.

9 Laurel Canyon

Ridpath Drive: Chapter 16 of Jac Holzman's *Follow the Music* is filled with details of the Ridpath scene, as is Michael Gray's *Mother: The Frank Zappa Story*. See also John Collis, *Van Morrison: Inarticulate Speech of the Heart*; David Crosby, *Long Time Gone, the Autobiography of David Crosby*; Pamela Des Barres, *I'm With The Band: Confessions of a Groupie*; Barney Hoskyns, *Waiting For The Sun: Strange Days, Weird Scenes and the Sound of Los Angeles*; James Riordan and Jerry Prochnicky's *Break On Through: The Life and Death of Jim Morrison*.

Billy James interviewed by Jerry Hopkins in *Royal's World Countdown* (date unknown).

Crabs: Pamela Zarubica to Michael Gray in *Mother! The Frank Zappa Story*.

Michael Vosse: At *Teen Set* (December 1966).

John Densmore: *Riders On the Storm* (London: Bloomsbury, 1991).

Burt Ward: Recorded 9–10 June 1966. FZ arranged both A and B sides of the single and presumably the other four unreleased tracks.

Eric Burdon: Quoted in 'The Animals, Britain's Greatest R&B Band' by Peter Doggett, *Record Collector* (October 1994).

Gail Sloatman: Al Kooper with Ben Edmunds, *Backstage Passes: Rock 'n' Roll Life In the Sixties*.

No Bra: Victoria Balfour, *Rock Wives*.

Gail Zappa: Interviewed by Connie Bruck, *The New Yorker* (25 January 1999); Gail Zappa interviewed by Drew Wheeler, *Billboard* (19 May 1990).

Bobby Jameson: 'Gotta Find My Roogalator' Penthouse 503. Recorded 21 June 1966 at H&R Studios, LA. Released 8 August 1966.

GUAMBO: Jerry Hopkins, 'GUAMBO Is an Act of Love – Mothers, Happenings, Dancing', *Los Angeles Free Press* (29 July 1966).

Suzy Creamcheese text: *Los Angeles Free Press* (16 September 1966).

Zeidler & Zeidler response: *Los Angeles Free Press* (28 October 1966).

Air Hostess: Tom Brown interviewed by Vladimir Sovetov, Internet.

Nesmith: Harold Bronson (ed), *Hey, Hey, We're the Monkees*.

FZ July 1968: Unattributed quote in *Twenty Years of Rolling Stone, What a Long Strange Trip It's Been*.

Ingber: Ray Collins interviewed by Dave Porter, KPFK-FM (12 August 1989).

Absolutely Free was recorded at TT&G 15–18 November 1966 in four double sessions.

'Plastic People': FZ in *International Times* 18 (31 August 1967).

'Brown Shoes Don't Make It': Ibid.

10 New York City

Richard Goldstein's 'The Pop Bag' column in the *Village Voice*. Reprinted without a date in *The Lives and Times of Zappa and the Mothers*.

Robert Shelton: 'Son Of Suzy Chreamcheese', *New York Times* (25 December 1966).

Dali: Eve Babitz, *Eve's Hollywood*.

Lumpy Gravy designed to be released as Capitol STAO-2719 on 7 August 1967. The sleeve notes state recording as being done in February 1967; FZ interviewed by the *Society Pages* team (22 December 1989); FZ interviewed by John Stix, *Guitar World* (September 1980).

Hotel Van Rensselaer: Gail Zappa interviewed by Drew Wheeler, *Billboard* (19 May 1990).

Garrick: The Mothers played 23 March–3 April; from 6–19 April; 24 May–5 September 1967 (with breaks); Jimmy Carl Black interviewed by Roland St Germain, *T' Mershi Duween* 29 (1993); FZ interviewed by Jerry Hopkins, *Rolling Stone* (27 April 1968); liner notes to Sandy Hurvitz, *Sandy's Album Is Here At Last*.

Marines: FZ to Frank Kofsky, *Jazz & Pop* (September 1967). Reprinted in Pauline Rivelli and Robert Levin (eds), *Rock Giants*.

Happenings: Allan Kaprow, 'The Legacy of Jackson Pollock', *Art News* (October 1958).

Suburban fans: FZ in *Cashbox* (1974).

Comedy: FZ to J. Marks in J. Marks and Linda Eastman, *Rock and Other Four Letter Words*.

Hendrix: Zappa interviewed by Noël Goldwasser in *Guitar World* (April 1987); the Jimi Hendrix Experience played the Café au-Go-Go 21–23 July.

Groupies: *Rolling Stone* 27 (15 February 1969); the 'groupie issue'.

Janis Joplin: Joel Selvin, *Summer of Love*.

Ian Underwood: Meeting with FZ recreated live on stage at the Falkoner Theatret Copenhagen, 27 September 1967, and appears on *Uncle Meat* as 'Ian Underwood Whips It Out'.

We're Only In It For The Money: recorded 2–9 August at Mayfair. Unknown dates in September. October dates at Apostolic. Gary Killgren the engineer from Mayfair appeared on the cut-out insert sheet as a school safety patrol lieutenant.

Marketing the Mothers: FZ interviewed by Nick Jones, *Melody Maker* (26 August 1967).

'gear our product': FZ interviewed by Dave Griffiths, *Record Mirror* (2 September 1967).

Paul McCartney on the sleeve: in conversation with the author, February 2003.

Zappa on *Sgt Pepper*: Sheraton Hotel press conference, Oslo, 1988.

Cal Schenkel on the sleeve: interview with the author, February 1994

Jerrold Schatzberg on the sleeve: interview with the author, February 1994.

Gail Zappa on the sleeve shoot: Gail to Steven Roby in *Black Gold*.

FZ marries Gail Sloatman: The Romàn Garcia Albertos website gives 21 September as the date, but this is only two days before the Royal Albert Hall concert with the London Philharmonic Orchestra, and Zappa would certainly have needed more than one afternoon to rehearse and get over jetlag.

Gary Killgren's whispers: Tribute 'Absolutely Frank' in *EQ* magazine (March 1994).

European tour: The group photograph in *Melody Maker* (11 November 1967) shows Sandy pouting and Pamela Zarubica smirking, as if they objected to being placed next to each other in the line-up.

Piano people: *Arrows* 98. 1969.

'Pigs and Ponies': Jerry Hopkins, *Rolling Stone* (27 April 1968).

FZ on *Lumpy Gravy*: FZ interviewed on 1976 Australian tour.

Clapton: FZ interviewed by Steve Rosen, *Guitar* (January 1977).

Monkees: Mike Nesmith to Harold Bronson (ed), *Hey, Hey, We're the Monkees*.

Dolenz: Bill Holdship, 'Head' *Mojo* 103 (June 2002).

Cal Schenkel on Ruben: Interview with the author, February 1994.

All one album: FZ interviewed by Jerry Hopkins, *Rolling Stone* (27 April 1968).

MGM's test pressing: Ibid.

Plaster-Casters: 'The Groupies & Other Girls' special issue: *Rolling Stone* (15 February 1969); 'Penis Landscape', *Q* magazine (March 2000).

11 The Log Cabin

The Log Cabin: Tiny Tim, etc. Pamela Des Barres, *I'm With The Band: Confessions of a Groupie*.

GTOs' first gig: Pamela Des Barres indicates that it was at the Whiskey a Go-Go, presumably the day of or the day before her journal entry for 10 August 1968, which describes it. But the Mothers were in Milwaukee for this date. The Whiskey gig must have been the Mothers' 23 July appearance.

Burdon: Eric Burdon: *I Used To Be an Animal But I'm Alright Now*.

Eric Clapton: FZ interviewed by Steve Rosen, *Guitar* magazine (January 1977).

'**Oh No**' is on *Weasels Ripped My Flesh; Ahead Of Their Time; You Can't Do That On Stage Anymore Vol. 1; Roxy & Elsewhere* and *Make A Jazz Noise Here.*

'**Would You Like A Snack?**' was recorded on 5 June 1968. It is unrelated to the song of the same name on *200 Motels*. Grace Slick: *Somebody to Love? A Rock and Roll Memoir;* Ralph J. Gleason, *The Jefferson Airplane and the San Francisco Sound.*

NT&B: FZ interviewed by Edwin Pouncey, *Sounds* (29 January 1983).

Log Cabin: In 2002 the Log Cabin site was still a ruin, but work appeared to be going on in other parts of the estate.

Ahead of Their Time: The Royal Festival Hall concert was on 25 October 1968, not 28 October as stated on the CD. There were two shows, at 6.15 and 9 p.m. Presumably the CD contains the performances taken from both shows; Rehearsal: FZ to the author, November 1970.

'**A Pound For a Brown**': FZ to the author.

Vito: Julie Russo, 'Vito Heads For Haiti', *Los Angeles Free Press* (6 December 1968).

Zappa on Ruben: FZ interviewed by the author, August 1969; *IT* (11 September 1969).

Wild Man Fischer: FZ interviewed by Sandy Robertson, *Sounds* (28 January 1978); FZ interviewed by the *Ann Arbor Argus* (19 June 1969); Cal Schenkel interviewed by the author.

Howard Kaylan: *Voxpop.*

FZ: 'The Incredible History of the Mothers' in *Hit Parader* 48 (June 1968).

Jimmy Carl Black: Jimmy Carl Black interviewed by Graham Halliday, *Chunky Yet Funky*, Internet.

Alice Cooper: Joe Smith, *Off The Record, An Oral History of Popular Music.*

FZ: 'The Oracle Has It All Psyched Out', *Life* magazine; Alice Cooper, *Me, Alice.*

Cynthia Plaster-Caster: Peter Margasak, 'It Ain't Hummel', *Chicago Reader* (28 November 1997); Mary Wisniewski, 'Cynthia Plaster-Caster', *Triplefastaction . . . Velocity.* 1.2; The cast list for sixties and seventies acts: Joe Coplin, friend; Al Hernandez, friend; Jimi Hendrix; Noel Redding, bass player with Jimi Hendrix Experience; Don Ogilive, Hendrix roadie 1968; Bob Pridden, Who chief roadie; Eric Burdon, then vocalist with the Animals; Richard Cole, Led Zeppelin roadie; Dennis Thompson, drummer with MC5; Wayne Kramer, guitarist with MC5; Frank Cook, drummer and manager; Fritz Richmond, Jim Kweskin Jug Band; Michael Vesty, record producer; Bob Grant, DJ; Anthony Newley, singer-songwriter; Daney West, manager Iron Butterfly; Eddie Brigati, lead singer, Young Rascals; Barry Bono, Young Rascals roadie; Harvey Mandel, guitarist;

Lee Mallory, singer-songwriter; Doug Dillard, Dillards; John Barr, bass player; Tony Stevens, bass player, Savoy Brown; Keef Hartley, drummer Keef Hartley Band; Keith Webb, drummer, Terry Reid Band; Bob Henri, drummer, Argent, the Kinks; Zal Yanovsky, Lovin' Spoonful; Ainsley Dunbar, drummer, the Mothers, Journey; Ricky Fataar, drummer, the Rutles, the Beach Boys; Smutty Smith, Rockats; John Smothers, Frank Zappa's bodyguard; etc.

Beefheart: *Captain Beefheart* by Mike Barnes is the standard work on Beefheart and is used here. See also Rudy Vanderlans, *Cucamonga*.

Brainwashing: 'Yeah, I'm happy. Happy as a clam', by Dave DiMartino, *Mojo* 2 (December 1993).

Arranging: Ibid.

Rehearsed to death: FZ in *International Times* (March 1977).

Ethnic recording: *Guitar Player* 'Zappa! Special' (1993).

Whitney studios: *Sounds* (5 December 1970).

Album finished: Ibid.

Enjoy the music: FZ in *International Times* (March 1977).

12 Bizarre/Straight

Breakup: Don Preston interviewed by Steve Moore (January 2001), Internet; FZ interviewed by Jerry Hopkins, *Rolling Stone* (18 October 1969); FZ interviewed by Larry Kart, *Downbeat* (30 October 1969). Zappa told Neil Slaven, author of *Zappa, Electric Don Quixote*: 'Here's Duke Ellington, after all these years in the business . . . begging the road manager of the tour for a $10 advance. And the guy wouldn't give it to him.' This seems even more unlikely than Zappa's official story, as Duke Ellington's personal road manager was his son, Mercer; Jimmy Carl Black interviewed by Alex Wünsch, *T'Mershi Duween* 24 (March 1992); Don Preston, ibid.; Jimmy Carl Black interviewed by Andy Greenaway on 23 June 2000 at idiotbastard website; Neil Flavin, *Electric Don Quixote*; Weasels: FZ interviewed by Jay Ruby at *Jazz & Pop*.

Oldies album: FZ in conversation with the author, July 1969; 'Rubber Biscuit' by the Chips (Josie: 45-803) 1956; 'The Girl Around The Corner' by Lee Andrews and the Hearts (Lana: L-l 12) 1956? (reissued 1957).

Unreleased albums: Records awaiting release in October were: *Before the Beginning, The Cucamonga Era, Show and Tell, What Does It All Mean, Rustic Protrusion, Several Boogie, The Merely Entertaining Mothers of Invention Record, The Heavy Business Record, Soup and Old Clothes, Hotel Dixie, The Orange County Lumber Truck* and *The Weasel Music* (some of them had been re-titled since the summer).

LSE: FZ interviewed by Mitch Howard, *IT* 56 (13 June 1969); (unknown interviewer) *Arrows* 98 (1969); FZ interviewed by Larry Kart, *Down Beat* (30 October 1969).

Don 'Sugarcane' Harris: Don & Dewey's 'Leaving It All Up To You' appeared on Art Laboe's *Memories of El Monte* collection (vinyl version only).

Johnny Otis: FZ to unknown interviewer (13 September 1970).

Kenny and Ronnie: 'Kenny's Booger Song' and 'Ronnie's Booger Song' appear on *The Lost Episodes*.

'The Story of Willy the Pimp' later appeared on the *Mystery Disc* where the sleeve notes (not by FZ) confusingly say it was recorded in 1972 – three years after *Hot Rats*. It clearly comes from the Garrick Theater period.

The Four Deuces' 'WPLJ' was issued as Music City 790 in 1955; Jackie & the Starlites' 'Valerie' was released as Fury 1034 in 1960 (Zappa always misspelled the title).

King Kong: FZ as producer: FZ to the author, in conversation 1970. Buell Neidlinger: FZ quoted by Leonard Feather, *King Kong* sleeve notes. The dead quality of the sound may be down to the studio; no details are given as to where *King Kong* was recorded and possibly World Pacific used their own studios. It might come down to bad microphones or a lack of EQ facilities.

Dick Kunc: FZ interviewed in 'The Sounds Talk-In', *Sounds* (5 December 1970).

Burnt Weeny Sandwich: Bizarre/Reprise RS6370. Some sources give a release date of 9 February 1970, but Zappa played a finished pressing to the author early in December 1969 and it seems likely that copies would have been shipped as soon as possible for the Christmas season.

Amougies: FZ interviewed by Marc Didden, *Humo* (15 November 1973).

Aynsley Dunbar: *Still Fumin' News* (Spring/Summer 2001).

Zubin Mehta: FZ interviewed by Jay Ruby, *Jazz & Pop* (1970).

Haskell Wexler: well known for his cinematography on *The Savage Eye* (1960), *Studs Lonigan* (1960), *The Loved One* (1965) and *Who's Afraid of Virginia Woolf?* (1966).

Jeff Simmons: *Lucille Has Messed My Mind Up* was released as Straight STS 1057 on 16 February 1970, produced by LaMarr Bruister.

Flo and Eddie: Jim Pons interviewed by Steve Moore for *Throttlejammer* (April 2000); Mark Volman interviewed by 'Ronnie' for *Ear Candy* Internet site; Mark Volman interviewed by Michael Wale in *Vox Pop*; Mark Volman and Howard Kaylan interviewed by Co de Kloet on 30 October 1990 for the Radio NOS (Netherlands) programme 'Supplement' to commemorate FZ's fiftieth birthday. Reprinted in *Society Pages* 9 (25 May 1992) and 10 (24 August 1992).

Sex: *Nuggets* (April 1977).

Joni Mitchell: FZ interviewed by the author, November 1970.

Vienna: FZ in conversation with Nigey Lennon, reported in *Being Frank, My Time With Frank Zappa*.

13 200 Motels

200 Motels: FZ interviewed by the author, November 1970; Theodore Bikel, *Theo, the Autobiography of Theodore Bikel* (New York: HarperCollins, 1994); Jim Pons interviewed by Steve Moore for *Throttlejammer* (April 2000); Keith Moon interviewed by Jerry Hopkins, *Rolling Stone* (21 December 1972); Ringo Starr interviewed in *Circus* (November 1974); Tony Palmer, 'Frank Zappa, the Royal Philharmonic and Me . . .', London *Observer*, 28 March 1971; *200 Motels* press kit.

Royal Albert Hall: Peter Waymark, 'Obscenity in banned pop show is denied', *The Times* (9 February 1971); FZ interviewed by Dave Perkins, *The Eyeopener* (22 November 1973), Toronto.

Fillmore East: John Lennon interviewed by Jan Wenner, *Lennon Remembers* (London: Verso, 2000); John Lennon interviewed by Howard Smith, WPLJ-FM, New York (6 June 1971); Howard Smith interviewed by Albert Goldman, *The Lives of John Lennon*; Howard Smith in conversation with the author, New York, 1971; Don Preston interviewed by Steve Moore, January 2001: Steve Moore website.

The Soldier's Tale: Igor Stravinsky's sleeve notes to the February 1961 Columbia recording of the ballet, which he conducted.

Cal Worthington FZ interviewed by Mick Farren, *NME* (26 April 1975).

Billboards: FZ interviewed in *The Eyeopener* (22 November 1973), Toronto.

Diebenkorn: *The Art of Richard Diebenkorn*, Whitney Museum of American Art, New York 1997.

Zoological: David Sylvester, describing Walter Sickert, wrote: 'So extreme is his detachment that he sees them as if he is not so much a psychologist as a zoologist – though one fancies that zoologists tend to feel more empathy and wonder.'

Los Angeles: FZ interviewed by the author, 29 January 1979; FZ interviewed by Frances Lynn, *Blitz* (1983).

Nigey Lennon: *Being Frank, My Time With Frank Zappa*.

Miss Pamela: Pamela Des Barres, *I'm With The Band: Confessions of a Groupie*.

European Tour: Dick Barber interviewed by Bruce Burnett, *Society Pages 4*.

Thrown off Stage: Jim Pons interviewed by Steve Moore for *Throttlejammer* (April 2000); *Rolling Stone* (6 January 1972); *Rolling Stone* (27 April1972); FZ interviewed by Dave Perkins *The Eyeopener* (22 November 1973), Toronto; Mark Volman in *Musician* (February 1994), the Frank Zappa 1940–1993 Special.

14 Waka/Jawaka

FZ's day: FZ interviewed by Danny Holloway, *NME* (2 September 1972).

Bitches Brew was recorded 19–21 August 1969 in New York City.

Ruben & The Jets: Motorhead interviewed by Pete Feenstra in the CD sleeve notes to Ruben & the Jets, *For Real*.

'Big Swifty': *Warners Circular*, October 1972 (published monthly by the press office).

Nigey Lennon: interviewed by Andy Greenaway (15 June 2000), Idiotbastard website.

Wazoo line-up: FZ interviewed by Danny Holloway, *NME* (2 September 1972).

Tychobrahe: Tychobrahe Sound took a three-quarter page ad in the *Cashbox* 'Frank Zappa After Ten Years' profile (3 August 1974).

Flo and Eddie: Ibid.

Recycled ideas: Howard Kaylan interviewed by Co de Kloet for Radio NOS (30 October 1990), Netherlands.

'Inca Roads': Tom Fowler interviewed for *T Mershi Duween* (24 April 1996).

Bruce Fowler: FZ interviewed in *Musician* Magazine (November 1991).

Showmanship: *Warners Circular*, October 1972.

Authoritarian person: FZ interviewed by Marc Didden, *Humo* (15 November 1973).

Bolic Studios: FZ quoted from unknown source by Simon Prentis in 'Anything anywhere anytime for no reason at all', *Society Pages* 45 (May 1989).

Dental floss: *Cashbox* 'Frank Zappa After Ten Years' profile (3 August 1974).

Censorship: The best survey of US censorship laws is Edward de Grazia's *Girls Lean Back Everywhere, the Law of Obscenity and the Assault on Genius*. Lawyer Grazia fought the *Tropic of Cancer, Naked Lunch, I Am Cuirious – Yellow* trials.

Saying the unsayable: *Cashbox*, 'Frank Zappa After Ten Years' profile (3 August 1974).

Deep Throat: Linda Williams, *Hard Core, Power, Pleasure and the 'Frenzy of the Visible'*.

Mennon Foot Spray: FZ interviewed by Dave Perkins, *The Eyeopener* (22 November 1973), Toronto.

Per Diem: Sal Marquez, *Musician* (February 1994); 1940–93 tribute issue.

Chess players: FZ interviewed by David Fudger, *Disc* (26 April 1975).

Ponty leaving: Jean-Luc Ponty interviewed by Alain Le Roux, *Le Jazz* webzine (22 April 1997).

Ruth Underwood: *Musician* (February 1994); 1940–93 tribute issue.

Ahmet: Victoria Balfour, *Rock Star Wives*.

15 On the Road

Bickford: FZ interviewed by Barry Hansen, *Rolling Stone* (4 July 1974).

Royal Albert Hall case: FZ to Pete Erskine, *NME* (14 September 1974); FZ interviewed by Mick Farren, *NME* (26 April 1975); FZ interviewed by Dave Perkins, *The Eyeopener* (22 November 1973), Toronto.

DiscReet: FZ interviewed in *Disc* (26 April 1975).

Beefheart: FZ interviewed by Dave Perkins *The Eyeopener* (22 November 1973). Toronto; FZ interviewed by David Fudger, *Disc* (26 April 1975); FZ interviewed by Mick Farren, *NME* (26 April 1975).

Brainiac: FZ to Edwin Pouncey, *Sounds* (29 January 1983).

Royce Hall: Pamela Goldsmith to Bill Lantz: Bill Lantz's website homepage.

FZ versus Vliet: Jimmy Carl Black interviewed by Andy Greenaway (23 June 2000) on idiotbastard website.

FZ versus Herb Cohen: FZ to author, 24 November 1976.

Ed Sanders: Germaine Greer, *The Madwoman's Underclothes*.

Mo Ostin: 'Oh God! Not Another Frank Zappa Bio . . .' Warners press release, September 1976.

'Black Napkins': FZ interviewed by Susan Shapiro *Sounds* (18 December 1976).

Indemnifying Warners. FZ to author, 24 November 1976.

Grand Funk: *International Musician*, February 1979.

Bozzio: FZ interviewed by Susan Shapiro *Sounds* (18 December 1976).

Solos: FZ interviewed by Steve Rosen, *Guitar* (January 1977)

16 Dr Zurkon's Secret Lab in Happy Valley

Case against Herb: 'Zappa Seeking To Zap Discreet Label', *Billboard* (30 July 1977).

Läther: FZ interviewed by the author, 29 January 1979; Chris Welch, *Melody Maker*, 19 February 1977. FZ interviewed by Paul Rambali, *NME* (28 January 1978); FZ interviewed by Karl Dallas, *Melody Maker* (28 January 1978). The tape boxes reproduced in the *Läther* CD booklet show Zappa's safety copies, not the master tapes, of the box set. The speed given is 15 inches per second, not the 30 ips of the masters. This means that though two boxes show EMI as the client and two show Arista, this only indicates who the Record Plant was going to bill for making a tape copy; it does not necessarily mean the tapes were intended for those companies (though EMI was offered *Läther*). For instance, an Arista act may have used some blank tape already charged to Zappa one night and this was to pay back the cost, a fairly common practice in studios at that time. The idea that Arista would release a four-album box set is amusing as it was Clive Davis, head of Arista, who first told Zappa that the Mothers had 'no commercial potential'.

Tits: FZ interviewed by Susan Shapiro, *Gig* (February 1977).

'Lady': FZ interviewed by Tony Bacon, *International Musician* (March 1977).

Louisville audience: FZ interviewed by Pete Lopilato, *Primo Times*, an Indiana magazine of popular culture (December 1977).

Jumping jacks: FZ interviewed by Susan Shapiro *Sounds* (18 December 1976).

Rock critics: FZ interviewed by Sandy Robertson, *Sounds* (28 January 1978).

Sleep Dirt: FZ interviewed by the author, 29 January 1979.

Nova Convention: James Grauerholz to author, 29 October 2001.

Studio: FZ interviewed by the author, 29 January 1979. In order to get more accurate playing it is common studio practice to record difficult piano parts at half speed on the low notes of the piano then speed the tape up to the correct octave.

London studios: FZ interviewed by the author, 29 January 1979.

Pseudonyms: Paul McCartney, George Harrison, Eric Clapton, FZ himself; most big names have done it at some point. The author heard the Van Morrison version at the Town House and it is without doubt superior to FZ's own track. It was a tactical mistake to ask Warners.

Bebe on plane: Bebe Buell (with Victor Bockris): *Rebel Heart*.

Singers: *IT* (March 1977).

Tower of Power: FZ interviewed on *Nightlife*, Swedish radio interview *c*.1980.

'Jewish Princess': FZ interviewed by John Swenson, 'Frank Zappa: America's Weirdest Rock Star Comes Clean', *High Times* No 55 (March 1980); FZ interviewed by Michael Branton, 'Frank Zappa vs The World!', *Bam* (5 October 1979); FZ interviewed by Clark Peterson, *Relix*, v6 No 5 (November 1979); FZ interviewed by David Sheff, *Playboy* (April 1993).

Fist: Peter Schjeldahl, 'Time Pieces' *New Yorker* (27 October 2003).

Camp: Susan Sontag, 'Notes on Camp', *Partisan Review* XXXI: 4 (New York: Fall, 1964).

UMRK: John Swenson, 'Frank Zappa: The Myth of *Joe's Garage*', *Rolling Stone* (13 December 1979).

Writing Joe's Garage: *Rolling Stone* (26 July 1979).

The garage: John Swenson, 'Frank Zappa: The Myth of *Joe's Garage*', *Rolling Stone* (13 December 1979); FZ interviewed by David Mead, *Guitarist* (June 1993).

Joe's Garage: FZ interviewed 12 January 1991 in *Society Pages* 7 (September 1991).

Sex Life: FZ interviewed by Karl Dallas, *Melody Maker* (26 January 1978).

17 Days on the Road

Grammys: *Rolling Stone* (16 March 1980).

Baby Snakes: Tom Carson, *Village Voice* (7 January 1980); FZ interviewed by Chris John, BBC Radio Forth (Scotland) 1980.

Tinseltown Rebellion: CBS press release (May 1981).

Love: Gail Zappa interviewed by George Petros in *Seconds* magazine, n.d.

Not speaking: Gail interviewed by Victoria Balfour in *Rock Wives*.

Sexual attitudes: FZ interviewed by Michael Branton, *Bam* (5 October 1979).

Genesis of songs: Gail interviewed by George Petros in *Seconds* magazine, n.d.

Punk: FZ interviewed by Karl Dallas, *Melody Maker* (26 January 1978).

Sabotaging songs: FZ interviewed by Dan Forte, *Musician* (1982).

Emotion in music: FZ interviewed by Tim Schneckloth, Down Beat (18 May 1978); Igor Stravinsky, *An Autobiography*.

Shut Up And Play Your Guitar: FZ interviewed by Michael Branton, *Bam* (5 October 1979); FZ interviewed by John Dwenson, *Guitar World* (March 1982); *Guitar Player* (November 1982).

Drugs: 'Frank Zappa: America's Weirdest Rock Star Comes Clean', FZ interviewed by John Swenson, *High Times* #55 (March 1980).

JCB: Jimmy Carl Black interviewed by Alex Wünsch, *T'Mershi Duween* 22 (January 1992).

Palermo: FZ interviewed by Roman Kozak, *Billboard* (28 August 1982); 'The Frank Zappa Interview Picture Disc' (Summer 1984); FZ interviewed by Fabio Massari, *Sonora* 4 (1994, recorded 1991).

Varèse: *Rolling Stone* (16 April 1981); FZ interviewed by John Dwenson. *Guitar World* (March 1982).

Pre-Bach: Varèse interviewed in *Musical Courrier* (20 May 1955).

Traditional instruments: 'The Music of Tomorrow' Varèse interviewed in London *Evening News* (14 June 1924).

Age of speed: Varèse interviewed by *San Francisco News* (10 January 1938).

Slonimsky: FZ interviewed 22 December 1989, *Society Pages* 2, n.d. (1990); Nicholas Slonimsky, *Perfect Pitch, A Life Story*.

18 Orchestral Manoeuvres

Edits: FZ interviewed by Tom Mulhern, *Guitar Player* (February 1983).

Loneliness: FZ interviewed by Batya Friedman and Steve Lyons, *Progressive*.

Workaholic: FZ interviewed by Frances Lynn. *Blitz* (1983).

Bob Stone: Guido Harari, 'FZ and Me', *Sonora* 4 (1994).

Balfour: Victoria Balfour, *Rock Wives*.

Not to bother FZ: Moon Zappa, *People* (2 October 2001).

Bother dad: Moon interviewed by *People* (2 October 2001).

LA shitty city: FZ interviewed by Frances Lynn, *Blitz* (1983).

Friend's houses: Moon Zappa interviewed by Christopher Goodwin, London *Sunday Times* (6 August 2000).

Shy: Moon Zappa, 'Confessions of a Metalhead', *Harpers Bazaar* (April 1998).

Kidnapped: Moon Zappa interviewed by Christopher Goodwin, London *Sunday Times* (6 August 2000).

Moon's note: *Sydney Morning Herald* (25 November 2000). Reproduced in the CD liner notes to *Ship Arriving Too Late To Save a Drowning Witch*.

Encino accent: Moon Zappa interviewed by Michael Goldberg, *Creem* (November 1982).

Hit: Moon interviewed by *People* (2 October 2001).

Not my fault: FZ interviewed by Tom Mulhern, *Guitar Player* (February 1983); *Washington Post* (30 August 1984).

Merchandizing: *Cashbox* (20 November 1982); *UPI* (13 January 1983).

Prostitutes: FZ interviewed by Dem Simms and others, *Society Pages* 1 (April

1990); FZ interviewed by Brett Milano in a New Haven local paper, summer 1984. Reprinted in *Mother People* 26.

Composer: FZ interviewed by Karl Dallas, *Melody Maker* (26 January 1980).

Paris concert: Palais des Sports, Paris (11 June 1980).

Pierre Boulez: 'The Godfather' by Alex Ross, *New Yorker* (10 April 2000).

Kent Nagano: Ken Nagano interviewed by Martin Hansson at Swedish Radio P2. c.1992; Kent Nagano interviewed by Andy Greenaway, *T'Mershi Duween* 16 (December 1990).

Trumpets: Paul McCartney interview with the author, 12 October 1992.

Zappa-LSO: FZ interviewed by Edwin Pouncey, *Sounds* (29 January 1983); *The Real Frank Zappa Book*; liner notes to *The London Symphony Orchestra: Zappa Vol I & II*.

8,000 edits FZ interviewed by Brett Milano for a New Haven, Connecticut, newspaper, n.d. Reproduced in *Mother People* 26 (November 1984).

19 Wives of Big Brother

Vacation writing: FZ interviewed by Frances Lynn, *Blitz* (1983); FZ interviewed by Edwin Pouncey, *Sounds* (29 January 1983).

Thing-Fish: *UPI* (24 January 1985).

Synclavier: *Musician* 96 (October 1986).

Francesco Zappa: FZ interviewed by Steve Birchall, *Digital Audio* (October/November 1984).

Boulez: *Libération* (18 November 1990); and on Varèse: Deutsche Grammophon website.

Stravinsky: Igor Stravinsky, *Poetics of Music*, trans by Arthur Knodel and Ingolf Dahl.

Remix: FZ interviewed by Steve Birchall, *Digital Audio* (October/November 1984); Arthur Barrow interviewed by Tink Troccoli, Slev Uunofski and Tom Brown, *T'Mershi Duween* 28 (November 1992); *Ice* magazine quoted, but without details in *Society Pages* 4, n.d. (1990).

Thing-Fish: Annie Ample autobiography (details unknown, taken from Internet postings).

Larry Flynt: *New Yorker* (25 January 1999).

Stupid Songs: FZ interviewed by Karl Dallas, *Melody Maker* (26 January 1980).

Restructuring: Gail Zappa interviewed by Don Menn.

PMRC: *People* (16 September 1985); Barking Pumpkin Z-Pack; PMRC press releases.

PTA: *The Washington Post* (29 August 1985).

PMRC: Susan Baker quoted in *Village Voice* (8 October 1985).

Musical Majority: FZ interviewed by Peter Werbe, WRIF-FM, Detroit (28 October 1985).

John Denver. Dee Snider interviewed by *Hard Rock Video* 5 (February 1986).

20 One More Time for the World

Lone Ranger: FZ interviewed in *Pulse* (April 1993).

Audiences: FZ interviewed by Chris John, *BBC Radio Forth* (1980).

Panties: FZ interviewed by Kurt Loder, *Rolling Stone* (February 1988).

Audiences: FZ interviewed by Karl Dallas, *Melody Maker* (26 January 1980).

Moon Unit: Foreword to Chelsea Cain (ed), *Wild Child, Growing Up In the Counterculture*.

Dweezil: FZ interviewed by *Rolling Stone* (6 November 1986).

Ahmet: FZ interviewed by *Rolling Stone* (6 November 1986).

Education: FZ interviewed by *Progressive* (November 1986).

Thunes: Keneally, taken from the Internet and reprinted in *T'Mershi Duween* 42 (January 1995).

Bolero: FZ interviewed by Charles Amirkhanian, KPFA-FM (15 April 1991).

Votes: *Overseas!* (February 1990).

Hanging Out: Arthur Barrow interviewed by *T'Mershi Duween* 28 (November 1992).

Thunes: Thomas Wictor, 'Scott Thunes: Requiem for a Heavyweight', *Bass Player* (March 1997); Mike Keneally interviewed by *Society Pages* 6 (June 1991); Scott Thunes interviewed by Thomas Wictor, *Bass Player* (March 1997); FZ interviewed by *Musician* (November 1991); FZ interviewed by Charles Amirkhanian, KPFA-FM (15 April 1991).

Russia: FZ interviewed by John Swenson, *High Times* 55 (March 1980); FZ interviewed 12 January 1991, *Society Pages* (September 1991); FZ interviewed by Gary Steel, New Zealand (12 May 1990).

Michael Kocab: FZ on 'Midweek' with Libby Purvis, BBC Radio 4 (3 July 1991).

Jazz Section: 'Rock Around the Revolution', *The Economist* (3 February 1990).

Prague: FZ interviewed by CBS, Canada (24 January 1990); FZ interviewed by Mike Zwerin, *International Herald Tribune* (30 January 1990); FZ on 'Midweek' with Libby Purvis, BBC Radio 4 (3 July 1991); FZ interviewed by *The Nation*

(19 March 1990); FZ interviewed by Swedish Radio (21 December 1990); FZ interviewed by CBS, Canada (24 January 1990).

Capitalist: FZ interviewed by Mike Zwerin, *International Herald Tribune* (30 January 1990).

Business: 'An Evening with Pierre Boulez and Frank Zappa', UCLA (23 May 1989).

Baker: FZ interviewed by Lawrence Joseph, *Business World* (10 July 1990); FZ interviewed on *The Late Show*, BBC TV (11 March 1993).

Y&R: Cleveland Horton, 'Zappa Pitches for Czechs', *Advertising Age* (5 March 1990).

No calluses: FZ interviewed by *Musician* (November 1991).

21 On Out

Chemicals: *T'Mershi Duween* 12 (April 1990).

Normal Life: *T'Mershi Duween* 11 (February 1990).

Cancer: FZ interviewed by David Sheff, *Playboy*, (April 1993).

Emotional distance: Moon Zappa interviewed by *People* (2 October 2001).

World's policeman: FZ interviewed by *Society Pages* (22 December 1989).

Reagan: FZ interviewed by the *Compact Sonora* 4, Sao Paulo (1991).

Brotherhood: FZ interviewed by Volpacchio on 16 May 1991 in *Telos* (Spring 1991).

Prez: FZ interviewed by Charles Amirkhanian, KPFA-FM (15 April 1991).

Bootlegs: FZ interviewed by Tom Troccoli, Cynthia Littlejohn and Den Simms, *Society Pages* 5, (26 May 1991); FZ interviewed by Zjakki Willems, Frankfurt (21 July 1992). Reprinted in *Society Pages* 10 (August 1992).

'Do a Ritchie Valens': Ritchie Valens, whose biggest hit was 'La Bamba' / 'Donna' died in an aeroplane crash.

LA visit: FZ press conference, Hotel Frankfurter Hof, Frankfurt (21 July 1992).

Sound for own sake: FZ interviewed by Rip Rense, *Los Angeles Times* (1 October 1992).

La La La: FZ press conference, Hotel Frankfurter Hof, Frankfurt (21 July 1992).

On the performance: FZ interviewed by Rip Rense, *Los Angeles Times* (1 October 1992).

Illness: FZ interviewed by *Pulse*, Scotland, 1993; interviewed by David Sheff, *Playboy*, (April 1993).

Beefheart: FZ interviewed by Charles Amarkanian, FPFA-FM.

Eastern music: FZ interviewed by David Mead, *Guitarist* (June 1993); FZ interviewed by Joe Jackson, *The Irish Times* (10 December 1993).

The Chieftains: John Glatt, *The Chieftains, the Authorized Biography*.

Civilisation Phase III: Gail interviewed by *Los Angeles Times* (6 December 1994).

Rose Marie Zappa: Rose Marie outlived her son by a decade, dying in a Burbank nursing home at the age of 91 on 29 January 2004.

FZ death: Moon interviewed by Rachel Halliburton, *Independent Weekend Review* (19 August 2000); Gail interviewed by Howard Stern, *Howard Stern Show* (10 December 1993); John Glatt, *The Chieftains: the Authorized Biography*; Moon interviewed by *Sydney Morning Herald* (25 November 2000).

22 Afterword

Favourite songs: FZ interviewed by John Stix, *Guitar World* (September 1980).

Best Things: FZ interviewed by Joe Jackson, *Irish Times* (10 December 1993).

Fans' favourite albums: Poll results in *T'Mershi Duween* 45.

King Kong: FZ in conversation with the author, November 1970.

Conceptual continuity: FZ interviewed by Bob Marshall for the *Canned Ham* show, San Jose, California (22 October 1988).

Bohemians: Elizabeth Wilson, *Bohemians, the Glamorous Outcasts*.

Wake people up: André Malraux in conversation with Pablo Picasso in André Malraux, *La Tête d'obsidienne* (Paris: NRF, 1974).

People suck: FZ interviewed by *NME* (17 April 1976).

No education: FZ interviewed by Bob Marshall for the *Canned Ham* show, San Jose, California (22 October 1988).

Intellectual: FZ interviewed by Sandy Robertson, *Sounds* (28 January 1978); FZ interviewed by Fabio Massari (July 1991); 'Talking with Frank', *Sonora* (April 1994), Sao Paulo.

Emperor's new clothes: FZ interviewed by Bob Marshall for the *Canned Ham* show, San Jose, California (22 October 1988).

Bibliography

Alvarez, Rafael: *Hometown Boy, the Hoodle Patrol and Other Curiosities of Baltimore*. The Baltimore Sun, Baltimore, 1999

Amaya, Mario: *Pop As Art*. Studio Vista, London 1965

Amburn, Ellis: *Pearl, the Obsessions and Passions of Janis Joplin*. Warner, New York, 1992

Andrews, Bob and Jodi Summers: *Confessions of Rock Groups*. Spi, New York, 1994

Aquila, Richard: *That Old Time Rock & Roll, A Chronicle Of an Era, 1954–1963*. Schirmer, New York, 1989

Balazs, André: *Chateau Marmont Hollywood Handbook*. Universal, New York, nd

Balfour, Victoria: *Rock Wives*. Beech Tree, New York, 1986

Bane, Michael: *White Boy Singin' the Blues: The Black Roots of White Rock*. Penguin, Harmondsworth, 1982

Barnes, Mike: *Captain Beefheart*. London, Quartet, 2000

Battock, Gregory [ed]: *The New Art*. E. P. Dutton, New York, 1966

Bikel, Theodore: *Theo, the Autobiography of Theodore Bikel*. HarperCollins, New York, 1994

Blesh, Rudi and Harriet Janis: *They All Played Ragtime*. Oak, New York, 1971 [fourth revised edition]

Bockris, Victor: *Lou Reed, the Biography*. Hutchinson, London, 1994

Bronson, Harold (ed): *Hey, Hey, We're the Monkees*. General Publishing/Rhino, Santa Monica 1996

Bradford, Perry: *Born With the Blues, Perry Bradford's Own Story*. Oak, New York, 1965

Brewster, Bill and Frank Broughton: *Last Night a DJ Saved My Life: the History of the Disc Jockey*. Grove, New York, 2000

Brooks, Ken: *Captain Beefheart, Tin Teardrop*. Agenda, Andover, Hamps. 2000

Bruce, Lenny: *The Essential Lenny Bruce*. Ballentine Books, New York, 1967

Buell, Bebe [with Victor Bockris]: *Rebel Heart*. St. Martin's, New York, 2001

Burdon, Eric: *I Used To be An Animal, But I'm All Right Now*. Faber and Faber, London 1986

Cain, Chelsea [ed]: *Wild Child, Growing Up In the Counterculture*. [forward by Moon Zappa] Fusion, London, 2000

Caserta, Peggy: *Going Down With Janis*. Dell, New York, 1973

Christgau, Robert: *Any Old Way You Choose It. Rock and Other Pop Music, 1967–1973*. Penguin, Baltimore, 1973

Clayson, Alan: *Ringo Starr, Straight Man Or Joker?* Sidgewick & Jackson, London, 1991

Collis, John: *Van Morrison: Inarticulate Speech of the Heart*. Little Brown, London, 1996

Cooper, Alice: *Me, Alice*. Putnam's, New York, 1976

Crosby, David, with Gottlieb, Carl: *Long Time Gone, the Autobiography of David Crosby*. Heinemann, London, 1989

Dalton, David: *Janis*. Stonehill, New York, 1972

Dawes, Amy: *Sunset Boulvard, Cruising the Heart of Los Angeles*. Los Angeles Times, Los Angeles, 2002

Densmore, John: *Riders On the Storm*. Bloomsbury, London, 1991

Des Barres, Pamela: *I'm With The Band, Confessions of a Groupie*. Beech Tree, New York, 1987

Des Barres, Pamela: *Take Another Little Piece of My Heart: A Groupie Grows Up*. William Morrow, New York, 1992

Eastman, Linda and J. Marks: *Rock and Other Four Letter Words*. Bantam, New York, 1968

Echols, Alice: *Scars of Sweet Paradise, The Life and Times of Janis Joplin*. Henry Holt, New York 1999

Frame, Pete: *Rock Family Trees*, Omnibus, London, 1979

Friedman, Myra: *Janis Joplin, Buried Alive*. William Morrow, New York, 1973

George, Nelson: *The Death of Rhythm and Blues*. Pantheon, New York, 1988

George, Nelson: *Where Did Our Love Go?* St. Martins, New York, 1985

Gillett, Charlie: *Making Tracks, the History of Atlantic Records*. Granada, London, 1975

Gillett, Charlie: *The Sound of the City*. Outerbridge and Dienstrey. New York, 1970

Gleason, Ralph: *The Jefferson Airplane and the San Francisco Sound*. Balentine, New York, 1969

Glatt, John: *The Chieftains, the Authorized Biography*. St. Martins, New York, 1997

Goldman, Albert: *Freak Show*. Atheneum, New York, 1971

Goldman, Albert: *Ladies and Gentlemen, Lenny Bruce!!* Random House, New York, 1971

Goldman, Albert: *Sound Bites*. Turtle Bay, New York, 1992

Goldstein, Richard: *Goldstein's Greatest Hits, a Book Mostly About Rock 'n' Roll*. Prentice-Hall, Englewood Cliffs, NJ, 1970

Gonzalez, Fernando L.: *Disco–File. The Discographical Catalog of American Rock & Roll and Rhythm and Blues Vocal Harmony Groups 1902–1976*. New York [2nd edition] 1977

de Grazia, Edward: *Girls Lean back Everywhere, the Law of Obscenity and the Assault on Genius*. Random House, New York, 1992

Greer, Germaine: *The Madwoman's Underclothes*. Picador, London, 1986

Groia, Philip: *They All Sang On the Corner: New York City's Rhythm and Blues Vocal Groups of the 1950's*. Edmund, Setauket, New York, 1974

Holzman, Jac, and Gavan Daws: *Follow the Music*. First Media, Santa Monica, 1998

Hopkins, Jerry and Danny Sugarman: *No One Gets Out Of here Alive*. Plexus, London, 1980

Hoskyns, Barney: *Waiting For The Sun: Strange Days, Weird Scenes and the Sound of Los Angeles*. St. Martin's, New York, 1995

Hoskyns, Barney: *Ragged Glories*. London, Pimlico, 2003

Huddleston, Judy: *This Is the End … My Only Friend. Living and Dying With Jim Morrison*. Shapolsky, New York, 1991

Joplin, Laura: *Love Janis*. Villard, New York, 1992

Kennealy, Patricia: *Strange Days, My Life With and Without Jim Morrison*. Dutton, New York, 1992

Kooper, Al, with Ben Edmunds: *Backstage Passes: Rock 'n' Roll Life In The Sixties*. Stein and Day, New York, 1977

Landau, Deborah: *Janis Joplin, Her Life and Times*. Warner, New York, 1971

Leigh, Spencer: *Baby, That Is Rock and Roll. American Pop 1954–1963*. Finbar International, Folkestone, 2001

Loder, Kurt: *Bat Chain Puller. Rock & Roll In The Age of Celebrity*. St. Martin's, New York, 1990

Marks, J and Linda Eastman. *Rock and Other Four Letter Words*. Bantam New York 1968

McCartney, Linda: *Sixties, Portrait Of an Era*. Pyramid, London, 1992

Miles, Barry: *In The Sixties*. Jonathan Cape, London, 2002

Mitchell IV, Alexander D.: *Baltimore Then and Now*. San Diego: Thunder Bay, 2001

Muir, John [ed]: *The Lives and Times of Captain Beefheart*. Babylon, Manchester, 1977

Nite, Norm N.: *Rock On. The Solid Gold Years*. Thomas Y Crowell. New York 1974

O'Brien, Glenn: *Soapbox*. Imschoot, Gent, Belgium.

Occhiogrosso, Peter: *Once a Catholic*. Houghton Mifflin, Boston, 1987

Ouellette, Fernand: *Edgard Varèse, a Musical Biography*. Grossman, New York, 1968

Picardie, Justine and Dorothy Wade: *Atlantic and the Godfathers of Rock and Roll*. Fourth Estate, London, 1993

Pichaske, David: *A Generation In Motion, Popular Music and Culture in the Sixties*. New York, Schirmer, 1979

Rebennak, Mac: *Under A Hoodoo Moon*. St. Martin's, New York, 1994

Revill, Davis: *The Roaring Silence. John Cage: a Life*. Arcade, New York, 1992

Rivelli, Pauline and Robert Levin [eds]: *Rock Giants*. World, New York, 1970

Riordan, James and Jerry Prochnicky: *Break On Through: The Life and Death of Jim Morrison*. William Morrow, New York, 1991

Roberts, Jonathan: *How To California*. Dell, New York, 1984

Roby, Steven: *Black Gold, the Lost Archives of Jimi Hendrix*. Billboard, New York, 2002

Rockwell, John: *American Music: Composition in the Late Twentieth Century*. Knopf, New York, 1983

Rogan, Johnny: *Timeless Flight, the Definitive Biography of The Byrds*. London, Square One, 1990

Selvin, Joel: *Summer of Love*. Dutton, New York, 1994

Slick, Grace: *Somebody to Love?* A Roll and Roll memoir. Warner, New York, 1998

Slonimsky, Nicholas: *Perfect Pitch, A Life Story*: Oxford University, Oxford, 1988

Smith, Joe: *Off The Record, An Oral History of Popular Music*. Warner Books, NYC, 1988

Starr, Kevin: *Material Dreams: Southern California Through the Twenties*. Oxford University, New York, 1995

Stravinsky, Igor: *An Autobiography*. 1936; reprinted Calder and Boyars, London, 1975

Stravinsky, Igor: *Poetics of Music*, trans by Arthur Knodel and Ingolf Dahl. Harvard University Press, Cambridge, Massachusetts, 1970

Tate, Greg: *Flyboy In the Buttermilk*. Simon & Schuster, New York, 1992

Vanderlans, Rudy: *Cucamonga*. Sacramento: Emigre, 2000

Wale, Michael: *Vox Pop, Profiles Of the Pop Process*. Harrap, London 1972
Waters, John: *Shock Value*, Dell, New York, 1981
Waters, John: *Trash Trio, Three Screenplays*. Fourth Estate, London, 1988
Wenner, Jan [ed]: *Groupies and Other Girls*. Bantam, New York, 1970
Wenner, Jan, [ed]: *Twenty Years of Rolling Stone, What a Long Strange Trip It's Been*. Straight Arrow, New York, 1987
Williams, Linda: *Hard Core, Power, Pleasure and the 'Frenzy of the Visible.'* University of California Press, Berkeley, 1989
Wilson, Elizabeth: *Bohemians, the Glamorous Outcasts*. I. B. Tauris. London, 2000
Witts, Richard: *Nico, the Life and Lies of an Icon*. Virgin, London, 1993
Zappa, Moon Unit: *America the Beautiful*. Review, London, 2000
[Eds of *Rolling Stone*] *The Rolling Stone Interviews*. Paperback Library, New York, 1971

Further Reading

Brooks, Ken: *Frank Zappa, A Strictly Genteel Genius Rides Again*. Agenda, Andover, Hamps. n.d
Chevalier, Dominique: *Viva! Zappa*. Omnibus, London, 1986
Colbeck, Julian: *Zappa, a Biography*. Virgin, London, 1987
Courrier, Kevin: *Dangerous Kitchen, The Subversive World of Frank Zappa*. ECW. Toronto, 2002
Dister, Alain: *Frank Zappa et les Mothers of Invention*. Albin Michel, Paris, 1975
Doruzka, Petr: *Suplík Plny Zappy*. Paseka a Práce, Prague, 1993
Gray, Michael: *Mother! The Frank Zappa Story*. Plexus, London, 1993
Gwerder, Urban: *"Alla Zappa"* Painting Box, Zurich, 1976
Harris, Suzannah Thana: *Under the Same Moon. My Life With Frank Zappa, Steve Vai, Bob Harris, and a Community of Other Artistic Souls*. Mastahana, New Castle, CO, 1999
James, Billy: *Necessity Is . . . The Early Years of Frank Zappa & the Mothers of Invention*. SAF, London, 2001
Kostelanetz, Richard [ed]: *The Frank Zappa Companion*. Schirmer, New York, 1997
Lennon, Nigey: *Being Frank; My Time With Frank Zappa*. California Classics, Los Angeles, 1995
McPherson, Neil: *Zappafax, a Catalogue of Information on Frank Zappa and the Mothers*. Zappafax, Wolverhampton, 1977
Miles [Barry][ed]: *Frank Zappa In His Own Words*. Omnibus, London 1993
Miles [Barry]: *Frank Zappa: a Visual Documentary*. Omnibus, London, 1993

Muir, John [ed]: *The Lives and Times of Frank Zappa*, Babylon, nd. np. [Manchester, 1978]

Obermanns, Norbert: *Zappalog, the First Step of Zappalogy*. 2nd ed. Rhino, Los Angeles, 1981

Russo, Greg: *Cosmik Debris: The Collected History and Improvisions of Frank Zappa*. Crossfire, Floral Park, New York, [revised edition] 1999

Slaven, Neil: *Zappa: Electric Don Quixote*. Omnibus, London 1996

The Torchum Team: *Zappa: The Torchum Never Stops*. Vol 1. np. [Germany] 1991

The Torchum Team: *Zappa: The Torchum Never Stops*. Vol 2. np. [Germany] 1991

The Torchum Team: *Zappa: The Torchum Never Stops*. Vol 3. np. [Germany] 1991

The Torchum Team: *Zappa: The Torchum Never Stops*. Vol 4. np. [Germany] 1992

Walley, David: *No Commercial Potential, the Saga of Frank Zappa, Then and Now*. E. P. Dutton, New York, 1972, revised 1980

Watson, Ben: *Frank Zappa the Negative Dialectics of Poodle Play*. Quartet, London, 1994

Weissner, Carl [ed]: *Frank Zappa, Plastic People Songbook*. Zweitausendeins. Frankfurt-am-Main, 1977

Zappa, Frank [w/ Peter Occhiogrosso]: *The Real Frank Zappa Book*. Poseidon, New York, 1989

Zappa, 'Candy' Patrice: *My Brother Was A Mother*. California Classics, Los Angeles, 2003

Discography

Album collections are indicated by bold typeface

1 *Freak Out!* (June 1966)

1 Hungry Freaks, Daddy
2 I Ain't Got No Heart
3 Who Are the Brain Police?
4 Go Cry on Somebody Else's Shoulder
5 Motherly Love
6 How Could I Be Such a Fool
7 Wowie Zowie
8 You Didn't Try to Call Me
9 Any Way the Wind Blows
10 I'm Not Satisfied
11 You're Probably Wondering Why I'm Here
12 Trouble Every Day
13 Help, I'm a Rock
14 It Can't Happen Here
15 The Return of the Son of Monster Magnet

2 *Absolutely Free* (June 1967)

1 Plastic People
2 The Duke of Prunes
3 Amnesia Vivace
4 The Duke Regains His Chops
5 Call Any Vegetable
6 Invocation and Ritual Dance of the Young Pumpkin
7 Soft-Sell Conclusion
8 Big Leg Emma
9 Why Don'tcha Do Me Right?
10 America Drinks
11 Status Back Baby
12 Uncle Bernie's Farm
13 Son of Suzy Creamcheese
14 Brown Shoes Don't Make It
15 America Drinks & Goes Home

3 *We're Only In It For The Money* (March 1968)

1 Are You Hung Up?
2 Who Needs the Peace Corps?
3 Concentration Moon

4 Mom & Dad
5 Telephone Conversation
6 Bow Tie Daddy
7 Harry, You're a Beast
8 What's the Ugliest Part of Your Body?
9 Absolutely Free
10 Flower Punk
11 Hot Poop
12 Nasal Retentive Calliope Music
13 Let's Make the Water Turn Black
14 The Idiot Bastard Son
15 Lonely Little Girl
16 Take Your Clothes Off When You Dance
17 What's The Ugliest Part of Your Body? (reprise)
18 Mother People
19 The Chrome Plated Megaphone of Destiny

4 *Lumpy Gravy* (May 1968)

Part One:
1 The Way I See It, Barry
2 Duodenum
3 Oh No
4 Bit of Nostalgia
5 It's from Kansas
6 Bored Out 90 Over
7 Almost Chinese
8 Switching Girls
9 Oh No Again
10 At the Gas Station
11 Another Pickup
12 I Don't Know If I Can Go Through This Again

Part Two:
1 Very Distraughtening
2 White Ugliness
3 Amen
4 Just One More Time
5 A Vicious Circle

6 King Kong
7 Drums Are Too Noisy
8 Kangaroos
9 Envelops the Bath Tub
10 Take Your Clothes Off

5 *Cruising With Ruben & The Jets* (December 1968)

1 Cheap Thrills
2 Love of My Life
3 How Could I Be Such a Fool
4 Deseri
5. I'm Not Satisfied
6 Jelly Roll Gum Drop
7 Anything
8 Later That Night
9 You Didn't Try To Call Me
10 Fountain of Love
11 "No. No. No."
12 Anyway the Wind Blows
13 Stuff Up the Cracks

6 *Mothermania* (March 1969)

1 Brown Shoes Don't Make It
2 Mother People
3 Duke of Prunes
4 Call Any Vegetable
5 The Idiot Bastard Son
6 It Can't Happen Here
7 You Are Probably Wondering Why I'm Here
8 Who Are the Brain Police?
9 Plastic People
10 Hungry Freaks, Daddy
11 America Drinks and Goes Home

7 *Uncle Meat* (April 1969)

1 Uncle Meat: Main Title Theme
2 The Voice of Cheese
3 Nine Types of Industrial Pollution
4 Zolar Czakl

5 Dog Breath, In the Year of the Plague
6 The Legend of the Golden Arches
7 Louie Louie (At the Royal Albert Hall in London)
8 The Dog Breath Variations
9 Sleeping In a Jar
10 Our Bizarre Relationship
11 The Uncle Meat Variations
12 Electric Aunt Jemima
13 Prelude To King Kong
14 God Bless America (Live at the Whiskey A Go Go)
15 A Pound For a Brown on the Bus
16 Ian Underwood Whips It Out (Live on stage in Copenhagen)
17 Mr. Green Genes
18 We Can Shoot You
19 "If We'd All Been Living in California . . ."
20 The Air
21 Project X
22 Cruising For Burgers
23 Uncle Meat Film Excerpt Part I
24 Tengo Na Minchia Tanta
25 Uncle Meat Film Excerpt Part II
26 King Kong Itself (as played by the Mothers in a studio)
27 King Kong (its magnificence as interpreted by Dom DeWild)
28 King Kong (as Motorhead explains it)
29 King Kong (the Gardner Varieties)
30 King Kong (as played by 3 deranged Good Humor Trucks)
31 King Kong (live on a flat bed diesel in the middle of a race track at the Miami Pop Festival . . . the Underwood ramifications)

8 *Hot Rats* (October 1969)

1 Peaches En Regalia
2 Willie the Pimp
3 Son of Mr. Green Genes

4 Little Umbrellas
5 The Gumbo Variations
6 It Must Be a Camel

9 *Burnt Weeny Sandwich* (February 1970)

1 WPLJ
2 Igor's Boogie, Phase One
3 Overture to a Holiday in Berlin
4 Theme from Burnt Weeny Sandwich
5 Igor's Boogie, Phase Two
6 Holiday in Berlin, Full-Blown
7 Aybe Sea
8 The Little House I Used to Live in
9 Valarie

10 *Weasels Ripped My Flesh* (August 1970)

1 Didja Get Any Onya?
2 Directly from My Heart to You
3 Prelude to the Afternoon of a Sexually Aroused Gas Mask
4 Toads of the Short Forest
5 Get a Little
6 The Eric Dolphy Memorial Barbecue
7 Dwarf Nebula Processional March & Dwarf Nebula
8 My Guitar Wants to Kill Your Mama
9 Oh No
10 The Orange County Lumber Truck
11 Weasels Ripped My Flesh

11 *Chunga's Revenge* (October 1970)

1 Transylvania Boogie
2 Road Ladies
3 Twenty Small Cigars
4 The Nancy & Mary Music
5 Tell Me You Love Me
6 Would You Go All the Way?
7 Chunga's Revenge

14 Keep It Greasy
15 Outside Now
16 He Used to Cut the Grass
17 Packard Goose
18 Watermelon In Easter Hay
19 A Little Green Rosetta

30 *Tinsel Town Rebellion*
(May 1981)

1 Fine Girl
2 Easy Meat
3 For the Young Sophisticate
4 Love of My Life
5 I Ain't Got No Heart
6 Panty Rap
7 Tell Me You Love Me
8 Now You See It - Now You Don't
9 Dance Contest
10 The Blue Light
11 Tinsel Town Rebellion
12 Pick Me, I'm Clean
13 Bamboozled By Love
14 Brown Shoes Don't Make It
15 Peaches III

31 *Shut Up 'n Play Yer Guitar*
(May 1981)

32 *Shut Up 'n Play Yer Guitar Some
More* (May 1981)

33 *Return Of The Son Of Shut Up
'n Play Yer Guitar* (May 1981)

1 five-five-FIVE
2 Hog Heaven
3 Shut Up 'n Play Yer Guitar
4 While You Were Out
5 Treacherous Cretins
6 Heavy Duty Judy
7 Soup 'n Old Clothes
8 Variations on the Carlos Santana
Secret Chord Progression
9 Gee, I Like Your Pants

10 Canarsie
11 Ship Ahoy
12 The Deathless Horsie
13 Shut Up 'n Play Yer Guitar Some
More
14 Pink Napkins
15 Beat It With Your Fist
16 Return Of The Son Of Shut Up 'n
Play Yer Guitar
17 Pinocchio's Furniture
18 Why Johnny Can't Read
19 Stucco Homes
20 Canard Du Jour

34 *You Are What You Is* (September
1981)

1 Teen-age Wind
2 Harder Than Your Husband
3 Doreen
4 Goblin Girl
5 Theme From The 3rd Movement Of
Sinister Footwear
6 Society Pages
7 I'm a Beautiful Guy
8 Beauty Knows No Pain
9 Charlie's Enormous Mouth
10 Any Downers?
11 Conehead
12 You Are What You Is
13 Mudd Club
14 The Meek Shall Inherit Nothing
15 Dumb All Over
16 Heavenly Bank Account
17 Suicide Chump
18 Jumbo Go Away
19 If Only She Woulda
20 Drafted Again

35 *Ship Arriving Too Late To Save A
Drowning Witch* (May 1982)

1 No Not Now
2 Valley Girl

3 I Come From Nowhere
4 Drowning Witch
5 Envelopes
6 Teen-age Prostitute

36 *The Man From Utopia*
(March 1983)

1 Cocaine Decisions
2 SEX
3 Tink Walks Amok
4 The Radio Is Broken
5 We Are Not Alone
6 The Dangerous Kitchen
7 The Man From Utopia Meets Mary Lou
8 Stick Together
9 The Jazz Discharge Party Hats
10 Luigi & the Wise Guys
11 Mõggio

37 *Baby Snakes* (March 1983)

1 Intro Rap/Baby Snakes
2 Titties & Beer
3 The Black Page #2
4 Jones Crusher
5 Disco Boy
6 Dinah-Moe Humm
7 Punky's Whips

38 *London Symphony Orchestra Vol. I* (June 1983)

48 *Vol II* (September 1987)

1 Bob In Dacron, First Movement
2 Bob In Dacron, Second Movement
3 Sad Jane, First Movement
4 Sad Jane, Second Movement
5 Mo 'n Herb's Vacation, First Movement
6 Mo 'n Herb's Vacation, Second Movement

7 Mo 'n Herb's Vacation, Third Movement
8 Envelopes
9 Pedro's Dowry
10 Bogus Pomp
11 Strictly Genteel

39 *Boulez conducts Zappa: The Perfect Stranger* (August 1984)

1 The Perfect Stranger
2 Naval Aviation In Art?
3 The Girl In the Magnesium Dress
4 Dupree's Paradise
5 Love Story
6 Outside Now Again
7 Jonestown

40 *Them Or Us* (October 1984)

1 The Closer You Are
2 In France
3 Ya Hozna
4 Sharleena
5 Sinister Footwear II
6 Truck Driver Divorce
7 Stevie's Spanking
8 Baby, Take Your Teeth Out
9 Marque-son's Chicken
10 Planet of My Dreams
11 Be In My Video
12 Them Or Us
13 Frogs With Dirty Little Lips
14 Whipping Post

41 *Thing–Fish* (November 1984)

1 Prologue
2 The Mammy Nuns
3 Harry & Rhonda
4 Galoot Up-Date
5 The 'Torchum' Never Stops
6 That Evil Prince
7 You Are What You Is

Weasels Ripped My Flesh
Chunga's Revenge
Fillmore East, June 1971
Just Another Band From L.A.
The 'Mystery Disc' (see album 68)

47 *Jazz From Hell*
(November 1986)

1 Night School
2 The Beltway Bandits
3 While You Were Art II
4 Jazz From Hell
5 G-Spot Tornado
6 Damp Ankles
7 St. Etienne
8 Massaggio Galore

48 *London Symphony Orchestra Vol. II)* (see album 38)

49 ***The Old Masters Box Three***
(December 1987)

Waka/Jawaka
The Grand Wazoo
Over-Nite Sensation
Apostrophe (')
Roxy & Elsewhere
One Size Fits All
Bongo Fury
Zoot Allures

50 *Guitar* (April 1988)

1 Sexual Harassment In the Workplace
2 Which One Is It?
3 Republicans
4 Do Not Pass Go
5 Chalk Pie
6 In-a-Gadda-Stravinsky
7 That's Not Really Reggae
8 When No One Was No One

9 Once Again, Without the Net
10 Outside Now (Original Solo)
11 Jim & Tammy's Upper Room
12 Were We Ever Really Safe In San Antonio?
13 That Ol' G Minor Thing Again
14 Hotel Atlanta Incidentals
15 That's Not Really a Shuffle
16 Move It Or Park It
17 Sunrise Redeemer
18 Variations On Sinister #3
19 Orrin Hatch On Skis
20 But Who Was Fulcanelli?
21 For Duane
22 GOA
23 Winos Do Not March
24 Swans? What Swans?
25 Too Ugly For Show Business
26 Systems of Edges
27 Do Not Try This at Home
28 Things That Look Like Meat
29 Watermelon In Easter Hay
30 Canadian Customs
31 Is That All There Is?
32 It Ain't Necessarily the Saint James Infirmary

51 *You Can't Do That On Stage Anymore Vol. 1* (May 1988)

1 The Florida Airport Tape
2 Once Upon a Time
3 Sofa #1
4 The Mammy Anthem
5 You Didn't Try To Call Me
6 Diseases of the Band
7 Tryin' To Grow a Chin
8 Let's Make the Water Turn Black / Harry, You're a Beast / The Orange County Lumber Truck
9 The Groupie Routine
10 Ruthie-Ruthie
11 Babbette
12 I'm the Slime

18 Society Pages
19 I'm a Beautiful Guy
20 Beauty Knows No Pain
21 Charlie's Enormous Mouth
22 Cocaine Decisions
23 Nig Biz
24 King Kong
25 Cosmik Debris

55 *The Best Band You Never Heard In Your Life* (April 1991)

1 Heavy Duty Judy
2 Ring of Fire
3 Cosmik Debris
4 Find Her Finer
5 Who Needs the Peace Corps?
6 I Left My Heart In San Francisco
7 Zomby Woof
8 Bolero
9 Zoot Allures
10 Mr. Green Genes
11 Florentine Pogen
12 Andy
13 Inca Roads
14 Sofa #1
15 Purple Haze
16 Sunshine of Your Love
17 Let's Move To Cleveland
18 When Irish Eyes Are Smiling
19 "Godfather Part II" Theme
19 A Few Moments With Brother A. West
20 The Torture Never Stops Part One
21 Theme From "Bonanza"
22 Lonesome Cowboy Burt (Swaggart Version)
23 The Torture Never Stops Part Two
24 More Trouble Every Day (Swaggart Version)
25 Penguin In Bondage (Swaggart Version)
26 The Eric Dolphy Memorial Barbecue
27 Stairway To Heaven

56 *Make A Jazz Noise Here* (June 1991)

1 Stinkfoot
2 When Yuppies Go To Hell
3 Fire And Chains
4 Let's Make the Water Turn Black
5 Harry, You're a Beast
6 The Orange County Lumber Truck
7 Oh No
8 Theme From Lumpy Gravy
9 Eat That Question
10 Black Napkins
11 Big Swifty
12 King Kong
13 Star Wars Won't Work
14 The Black Page (new age version)
15 T'Mershi Duween
16 Dupree's Paradise
17 City of Tiny Lights
18 Royal March from "L'Histoire du Soldat"
19 Theme From the Bartók Piano Concerto #3
20 Sinister Footwear 2nd mvt.
21 Stevie's Spanking
21 Alien Orifice
22 Cruisin' For Burgers
23 Advance Romance
24 Strictly Genteel

57 *You Can't Do That On Stage Anymore Vol. 4* (June 1991)

1 Little Rubber Girl
2 Stick Together
3 My Guitar Wants To Kill Your Mama
4 Willie the Pimp
5 Montana
6 Brown Moses
7 The Evil Prince
8 Approximate
9 Love of My Life Mudd Club Version

66 *Frank Zappa Plays The Music Of Frank Zappa, a Memorial Tribute* (October 1996)

1 Black Napkins
2 Black Napkins "Zoot Allures" album version
3 Zoot Allures
4 Merely a Blues In A
5 Zoot Allures "Zoot Allures" album version
6 Watermelon In Easter Hay
7 Watermelon In Easter Hay "Joe's Garage" album version

67 *Have I Offended Someone?* (April 1997)

1 Bobby Brown Goes Down
2 Disco Boy
3 Goblin Girl
4 In France
5 He's So Gay
6 SEX
7 Titties 'n Beer
8 We're Turning Again
9 Dumb All Over
10 Catholic Girls
11 Dinah-Moe Humm
12 Tinsel Town Rebellion
13 Valley Girl
14 Jewish Princess
15 Yo Cats

68 *Mystery Disc* (September 1998)

1 Theme from "Run Home Slow"
2 Original Duke Of Prunes
3 Opening Night at "Studio Z" (Collage)
4 The Village Inn
5 Steal Away
6 I Was a Teen-Age Malt Shop
7 The Birth of Captain Beefheart

8 Metal Man Has Won His Wings
9 Power Trio from the Saints 'n Sinners
10 Bossa Nova Pervertamento
11 Excerpt from the Uncle Frankie Show
12 Charva
13 Speed-Freak Boogie
14 Original Mothers at the Broadside (Pomona)
15 Party Scene from "Mondo Hollywood"
16 Original Mothers Rehearsal
17 How Could I Be Such a Fool?
18 Band introductions at the Fillmore West
19 Plastic People
20 Original Mothers at Fillmore East
21 Harry, You're a Beast
22 Don Interrupts
23 Piece One
24 Jim/Roy
25 Piece Two
26 Agency Man
27 Agency Man (Studio Version)
28 Lecture from Festival Hall Show
29 Wedding Dress Song/The Handsome Cabin Boy
30 Skweezit Skweezit Skweezit
31 The Story of Willie the Pimp
32 Black Beauty
33 Chucha
34 Mothers at KPFK
35 Harmonica Fun

69 *Everything Is Healing Nicely* (December 1999)

1 Library Card
2 This Is a Test
3 Jolly Good Fellow
4 Roland's Big Event/Strat Vindaloo
5 Master Ringo
6 T'Mershi Duween
7 Nap Time

8 9/8 Objects
9 Naked City
10 Whitey (Prototype)
11 Amerika Goes Home
12 None Of The Above (Revised & Provided)
13 Wonderful Tattoo!

70 *FZ:OZ* (August 2002)

1 Hordern Intro (Incan Art Vamp)
2 Stink-Foot
3 The Poodle Lecture
4 Dirty Love
5 Filthy Habits
6 How Could I Be Such a Fool?
7 I Ain't Got No Heart
8 I'm Not Satisfied
9 Black Napkins
10 Advance Romance
11 The Illinois Enema Bandit
12 Wind Up Workin' In a Gas Station
13 The Torture Never Stops
14 Canard Toujours
15 Kaiser Rolls
16 Find Her Finer
17 Carolina Hard-Core Ecstasy
18 Lonely Little Girl
19 Take Your Clothes Off When You Dance
20 What's the Ugliest Part of Your Body?
21 Chunga's Revenge
22 Zoot Allures
23 Keep It Greasy
24 Dinah-Moe Humm
25 Camarillo Brillo
26 Muffin Man
27 Kaiser Rolls (Du Jour)

71 *Halloween* (February 2003)

1 NYC Audience
2 Ancient Armaments

3 Dancin' Fool
4 Easy Meat
5 Magic Fingers
6 Don't Eat the Yellow Snow
7 Conehead
8 "Zeets"
9 Stink-Foot
10 Dinah-Moe Humm
11 Camarillo Brillo
12 Muffin Man
13 Black Napkins (The Deathless Horsie)

Tricks Or Treats:

14 Suicide Chump (Video)
15 Dancin' Fool (Video)
16 Radio Interview

Beat the Boots box sets

Beat the Boots I (July 1991)

1 *As An Am*
2 *The Ark*
3 *Freaks & Motherfu*#@%!*
4 *Unmitigated Audacity*
5 *Anyway The Wind Blows*
6 *'Tis The Season To Be Jelly*
7 *Saarbrucken 1978*
8 *Piquantique*

Beat The Boots II (June 1992)

1 *Disconnected Synapses*
2 *Tengo Na Minchia Tanta*
3 *Electric Aunt Jemima*
4 *At The Circus*
5 *Swiss Cheese/Fire!*
6 *Our Man In Nirvana*
7 *Conceptual Continuity*

Compilations

1 *The Cucamonga Years*
(December 1991)

2 *Strictly Commercial, the best of
Frank Zappa* (August 1995)

3 *Strictly Genteel, a "classical"
introduction to Frank Zappa*
(May 1997)

4 *Cheap Thrills* (April 1998)

5 *Son of Cheep Thrills* (April 1999)

6 *Threesome No. 1* (April 2002)

7 *Threesome No. 2* (April 2002)

8 *Zappa Picks by Jon Fishman of
Phish* (October 2002)

9 *Zappa Picks by Larry LaLonde of
Primus* (October 2002)

Films and Books

Films and Videos

1 *200 Motels* (October 1971)
2 *Baby Snakes* (December 1979/ October 1987)
3 *Dub Room Special* (October 1984)
4 *Does Humor Belong In Music?* (March 1986)
5 *Video From Hell* (October 1987)
6 *True Story of 200 Motels* (January 1989)
7 *Uncle Meat* (January 1989)
8 *The Amazing Mr Bickford* (January 1990)

Books

1 *Them Or Us (The Book)* (1984)
2 *The Real Frank Zappa Book* (1989)

Index

Black-Outs II, the, 61–2, 69
Blackwell, Chris, 387
Blakey, Art, 381
Bley, Carla, 134
Blondie, 268
Blood, Sweat and Tears, 111
Bloomindales, 305
Blue Notes, the, 29
Blue Whale, 197
Blues Project, the, 125
blues, 24, 42–3, 49, 89, 111; country blues, 102, 121; jealousy as theme, 285; urban blues, 181
Bock, Dick, 194–5
Bolan, Mark, 155
Bond, Christopher, 239
Bonds, Gary US, 21
Boogie Men, the, 60, 63
Boone, Pat, 77–8, 328
bootlegs, 199, 261, 366–7
Bostic, Earl, 51
Boston, 5, 162, 228
Boston, Mark, 181
Boston Symphony Orchestra, 26
Boulez, Pierre, 307–9, 322–3, 359, 360, 387
Bowie, David, 306
Bozzio, Dale, 277, 368
Bozzio, Terry, 246, 253–5, 263–4, 266, 271, 344, 377
Brahms, Johannes, 308
Bramble, Wilfred, 209
Branson, Richard, 270
Brentwood, California, 74
Brewer, Don, 254
Brinson, Ted, 71–2
Britain: Establishment, 212; obscenity laws, 245; success of Hot Rats, 194; word 'product' not used, 150; Zappa disillusioned with, 223; Zappa interviewed in, 290
Brock, Napoleon Murphy, 240, 246, 330
Brown, Arthur, 155, 221
Brown, Clarence 'Gatemouth', 29, 37, 42, 49
Brown, Tom, 367
Browne, Jackson, 120
Bruce, Denny, 134
Bruce, Lenny, 96, 106–8, 118, 169; album released on Bizarre, 174; as American iconoclast, 383; birthday party, 176; death, 234; as Zappa's mentor, 285
Bruck, Connie, 126
Bryant, Denis, 239
Buckley, Tim, 120, 169, 229, 238
Budapest, 362
Buell, Bebe, 270
Buff, Allison, 79, 80, 82
Buff, Paul, 63, 64, 66, 73, 178; Pal Studio collaborations, 69, 72, 73, 76, 78–9, 76, 78, 387; sets up Pal Studio, xi, 66–7; records Surfaris hit, 67–8; music publishing companies, 76; moves to Original Sound, 79, 80, 102; Zappa acknowledges debt, 81; bails Zappa, xi, 86
Buffalo Springfield, 135
Bunny and Bear, 126
Bunting, Edward, 373, 377
Burdon, Eric, 123, 167
Burgan, Kenny, 60, 63
Burroughs, William S., 235, 346, 383; celebration and birthday party, 268; Naked Lunch, 139, 233, 268, 275
Burton, Gary, 184
Bush, George, 107, 147
Business World, 361
Butcher, Pauline, 156, 165–7, 179
Butler, Anya, 124–5
Butterfield, Paul, 113, 120
BYG Records, 196
Byrds, the, 94, 97–9, 100, 120–1, 125, 146
Byrne, David, 217

Cadets, the, 42
Cage, John, 160, 168, 308
Cameo label, 73
Camp, 276
Canned Heat, 111
Capitol Records, 74, 140–1, 157, 260, 261, 333, 340
Captain Beefheart and His Magic Band, 180–3, 194, 197, 248; Trout Mask Replica, 49, 182–3, 197; see also Vliet, Don
Caraeff, Ed, 194
Caravan, 197
Carey, Timothy, 61–2, 64, 65, 70–1
Carlin, George, 96
Carman, Paul, 346
Carson, Tom, 282
Carter, Elliott, 308, 319

227; Gibson ES-5 Switchmaster, 81; Gibson Les Paul, 190; Jimi Hendrix's, 248; Ovation acoustic, 267; Tychobrahe Octavia fuzz/octave divider, 229; Zappa's solos, 287–9, 381, 383

Guy, Bob, 73

Haden, Charlie, 134
Haeny, John, 120
Hall and Oates, 335
Hamburg, 105, 219
Hammond, John, 103
Hancock, Herbie, 344
Happening artists, 146
Hardin, Tim, 120
Harkelroad, Bill, 167, 181
Harper's Bazaar, 301
Harris, Bill, 142
Harris, Bob, 283
Harris, Don 'Sugarcane', 193, 196, 197
Harris, Jeff, 52
Harrison, George, 260, 321
Hauer, Josef Matthias, 41
Havana, 294
Havel, Vaclav, 353, 355, 357–8, 360, 362, 387
Hawaii, 124, 223, 237, 255
Hayden, Victor, 181
Heartbreakers, the, 73
Heckstall-Smith, Dick, 197
Heery, Gary, 253
Heinlein, Robert, 148
Hellman, Monte, 55
Helsinki, 243, 245, 351, 387
Hendrix, Jimi, 107, 162, 381; burnt Stratocaster, 248; effects equipment, 229; oil painting of, 280; Zappa and, 148, 152, 156, 339
Henley, Don, 335
Henske, Judy, 97
Herman, Woody, 162
Herrera, Little Julian, and the Tigers, 68
Heydorn, Amy, 51
Higgins, Chuck ('Pachuko Hop'), 71
High Times, 273, 290, 351
Hillman, Chris, 125
hippies, 95; early scene, 98, 101, 105; Zappa and, 107, 156, 338, 383, 385
Hiroshima, 294
Hit Parader, 170

Hite, Bob ('the Bear'), 102, 111
Holland, 194, 237
Hollings, Senator, 335–6
Holly, Miss, 57
Hollywood: children's names, 300; dress, 95; F. K. Rockett studios, 82; glamour, 276; Studio Masters, 73; Vista-Continental Theater, 70–1; Wallach's Music City, 61, 92–3; Zappa begins to visit, 66, 77, 79; Zappa moves to 90–3
Holocaust, 294
Honolulu, 116
Hopkins, Jerry, 112, 161
Hopkins, Nicky, 179
Hot Rats band, *see* Mothers of Invention
Houdini, Harry, 164
Houston, Joe, 24–5, 37, 42
Howar, Pam, 332
Howell, Trevor Charles, 222–3
Howlin' Wolf, 24, 26, 49, 77, 102, 247
HR2911 ('Mathias') bill, 333
Hubbard, L. Ron, 385
humour, 108, 203–4, 371, 381; American, 238–9; Mothers', 171, 202, 327; toilet, 286; *see also* parody; satire
Humphrey, Paul, 192
Humphrey, Ralph, 232, 237, 240
Hungary, 361–2
Hunt, Ray, 88–9
Hunter, Tab, 77
Hurvitz, Sandy, 142, 147–8, 154, 169–70
Hustler magazine, 328–9
Hutton, Danny, 113
Huun-Huur-Tu, 376, 377
Huxley, Aldous, 92

Ice magazine, 327
Ikettes, the, 232, 237
Ingber, Elliot, 111, 113, 134
Intercontinental Absurdities, 177–8, 343
International Astronomical Union's Minor Planet Center, 387
International Composers' Guild, 25–6
International Musician, 266, 289
International Times, 156
Iran, 108, 277, 337
Island Records, 314–15
Italian-Americans, 6–7, 11
Italians, 273–4

Italy, 3, 5, 7, 11, 237, 291, 358

critics, 265–6, 286, 320, 386; Cyclophony, 70; film, 115; folk, 60, 103, 147, 372; harmony, 48, 57; heavy-metal, 147, 255; humour in, 163; Hungarian, 39; hurdy-gurdy, 5; Indian ragas, 121, 173; industry, 162, 324; Irish, 372; labelling, 332–8; Middle Eastern, 372; minimalism, 308; movie, 196; oral tradition in, 29; Renaissance, 180; sea shanties, 39; School of Vienna composers, 72; serialism, 41, 48, 308; sexual content in pop, 244; Stravinsky on, 287; surf, 67, 72, 117, 161; Tibetan, 39; time-shifting, 279; Tuvan throat-singing, 376–7; twelve-tone, 27, 41, 308; world, 383; *see also* blues; Doo Wop; jazz; R&B; rock 'n' roll

Musical Majority, 334, 335, 349

Musician magazine, 240, 349, 350

Musicians' Union, 97, 107, 155, 193, 307

Mussolini, Benito, 7

Mussorgsky, Modest Petrovich, 295

Muthers, the, 84, 85

Nagano, Kent, 309–13, 316, 323

Nagasaki, 294

naming, 189, 274–5

Naples, 3

Nash, Graham, 120

Nashville, 81

Nation, 358

National Conference of Parents and Teachers, 334

Ned and Nelda, 75, 82, 216

Neidlinger, Buell, 194

Neil, Fred, 123

Nelson, Oliver, 39

Nesmith, Mike, 133, 158

Nevius, Sally, 332

New Mature World Theater, 236

New York: albums recorded in, 160; art scene, 218, 268; audiences, 342; difference from Los Angeles, 117; dirt and pollution, 142; Halloween concerts, 243, 257, 270, 292, 324; Italian neighbourhoods, 5; Zappa living in, 141–2, 148–9;
LOCATIONS: Apostolic Studios, 157–8, 159, 172, 180, 190, 375; Balloon Farm, 137–8; Carnegie Hall, 219, 294; City Hall, 153;

Felt Forum, 228, 243, 257; Fillmore East, 198, 204, 212, 223; Garrick Theater, 140, 142–3, 146–50, 155, 158, 160, 171, 196, 201, 264, 275; Greenwich Village, 36, 46–7, 139, 141–2, 144, 146–7, 205; Hilton, 162; Hotel Chelsea, 149; Limelight Club, 268; Lincoln Center, 307; Madison Avenue, 138; Madison Square Garden, 255; Metropolitan Opera House, 212; Palladium, 263, 292, 324; Ritz, 368; Tenth Avenue, 259; Town Hall, 294; Ukrainian Ballroom, 268; Victoria Theater, 282

New York Times, 137

New York Wind Ensemble, 25

New Yorker, 126, 276, 329

Nice, the, 197

Nichols and May, 107

Nico, 120

Nifty Tough & Bitchen (NY&B), 169

Nixon, Richard, 107, 147, 184, 264, 280

NME, 219, 266

Northridge, California, 343

Norway, 237, 273

Nugent, Ted, 239

Nun, Bobby, 22

Oakland Ballet, 323

Occhiogrosso, Peter, 13, 350

Ocker, David, 261, 271, 310–14, 320–1

O'Connor, Sinéad, 377

Odense, 219, 220

Odetta, 96

Offerrall, Lucy (dancer), 164–6, 208–10

O'Hearn, Patrick, 255, 266, 271

Old Town label, 188

Oldenburg, Claes, 146, 275

Olympics, the, 42, 213

Omens, the, 61

Omnibus Wind Ensemble, 387

Ono, Yoko, 213–14

Opa-locka, Florida, 7

Orbison, Roy, 380

Orchestra of Our Time, 292, 368

Orchèstre de l'Opéra de Lyons, 364

Orchids, the, 49

Original Sound studios, xiii, 78–81, 102; label, 76

Original Staples Singers, the, 57

Orioles, the, 45

157, 168, 171; on break-up of original Mothers, 185, 187; Dweezil named after, 189; with reformed Mothers, 198; monster act, 199–200; in *200 Motels*, 208; on concert with John Lennon, 213–14; at Montreux, 220; with fusion band, 226; on Zappa's appropriation of ideas, 230; joins 'Tenth Anniversary' tour, 240; sues Zappa, 327

Previn, Dory, 243

Prince, 333

Puckett, Gary, and the Union Gap, 60

Pudsey, Yorkshire, 244–5

puppets, 11, 22, 54

Quayle, Dan, 360

R&B, 55, 63, 89, 193, 300, 378; Art Laboe's recordings, 71; on *Burnt Weenie Sandwich*, 195; *Cruisin' with Ruben and the Jets* as pastiche, 172; dominance of saxophone, 41; Dot Records copies, 77 fifties' soundtrack, 24; influence on Zappa, 21–2, 26, 29, 72; and jealousy, 285; New York, 119; records, 41, 43, 45, 58, 77, 102, 188; revival, 225; Zappa's collection, 30, 36, 72, 80, 84, 92, 118, 172, 189, 325; Zappa's early groups, 37, 42, 69

Ramblers, the, 28, 51

Rasputin Productions, 169

Rauschenberg, Robert, 146, 275

Ravel, Maurice, 347

Raven, the, 166, 167

Ray, Aldo, 133

RCA, 19, 26, 333

Reagan, Ronald, 95, 292, 332, 362; Zappa's criticisms of, 107, 147, 162, 365

Rebennak, Mac, 112–13

Record Mirror, 150, 157

recording: CDs, 340; close-miking, 67, 79; digital, 311, 340; eight-track, 67; fuzztone, 79; Kepex Noise Gate, 81; Rec-O-Cut lathe, 67, 81; stereo, 67, 77, 173; Zappa's tape archive, 190, 258, 258, 367; 'xenochrony', 271

Recording Industry Association of America (RIAA), 332, 333, 336

Redding, Noel, 155

Reed, Lou, 72, 116–17

Reiner, Rob, 262

Relix magazine, 273

Rene and Ray, 69

Renzy, Alex de, 236

REO Speedwagon, 335

Reprise label, 173, 180

Residente Orchestra, 306

Return to Forever, 225

Rexroth, Dr Dieter, 369

Rhino label, 366–7, 387

Rhinoceros, 160

Richards, Keith, 268

Ringwald, Molly, 345

Riperton, Minnie, 380

Rivers, Joan, 343

Rivers, Johnny, 94, 101, 127

Riviera, Diego, 294

Robertson, Pat, 343

Robins, the, 22, 27, 42

rock 'n' roll, 93–4, 103, 121, 125, 137; as art form, 266; blamed for social ills, 334; concept albums, 114; critics, 265–6, 286, 386; double-albums, 114; jazz-rock, 194, 355; journalism, 265–6; lifestyle, 105; musicians, 385; operas, 81–2, 277, 279; punk, 281, 283–4, 355; Tony Palmer book, 206–7; triplets, 173

Rock, George, 19

Rockin' Brothers, the, 37

Roddy, Joseph, 23

Rogers, Milt, 77–8

Rolling Stone, 149, 163, 179, 266, 292, 344–5

Rolling Stones, the, 90, 120, 152, 264, 281, 327, 357

Roman, Ron, 70

Romanticism, 286, 311, 383–4

Ronstadt, Linda, 120

Rose, Don, 340

Ross, Alex, 308

Rost, Doug, 60, 63

Rotations, the, 79

Rothchild, Paul, 120

Rotterdam, 219

Route 66, ix, 66

Roxy Music, 256

Royal Philharmonic Orchestra, 206, 211

Ruben and the Jets, 225

Rundel, Peter, 371

Russell, Mr, 48

sound, 323; obsolescence, 375; samples
Tuvan throat singers, 376
Syracuse Symphony Orchestra, 307

Talking Heads, 217
Talmy, Shel, 124
Taplin, John, 212
Taylor, Cecil, 39, 103, 115, 194
Taylor, James, 243
Tchaikovsky, Pyotr Ilyich, 308
Teen Queens, the, 42
Teen Set, 97, 122, 153, 179
television, 124, 236–7, 318, 330, 365, 385;
advertising, 276, 279, 385; *The Amos
and Andy Show*, 330; *Batman*, 123; BBC
Late Night Show, 377; evangelism, 99,
107, 147, 264, 291, 334, 343, 347, 385; *Fast
Times at Ridgemont High*, 344; Financial
News Network (FNN), 352, 356–7, 359;
Focus, 359; *Frank Zappa's Wild Wild
East*, 359; *The Joe Pyne Show*, 99; *Late
Show*, 343, 378; *Miami Vice*, 343, MTV,
344; news, 100, 343; *Outrage at Valdez*,
352; *Saturday Night Live*, 263, 317; *The
Untouchables*, 113
Tempe, Arizona, 20
Terri and Johnnie, 69
Terry, Sonny, 96
Texas, 262
The Hague, 228, 306
Them, 118, 122
Third Story Music, 169
Thomas, Ernie, 37
Thome, Joel, 292, 368
Thompson, Chester, 240, 246
Thompson, Hunter S., 339, 383
Thomson, Virgil, 216
Thornton, Bianca, 255
Three Dog Night, 113, 121
Thrillers, the, 188
Thunes, Scott, 303, 330, 346–9, 368
Thurmond, Strom, 333
Time-Life, 294
Times, The, 211
Titans, the, 51
Took, Steve Peregrine, 155
Topanga Canyon, California, 282
Toras, Arunas, 362
Tork, Peter, 121

Torme, Mel, 380
Toronto, 162, 219, 268
Torrance, California, 90, 215
Tossi, Ernest, 48
Townley, Gilly, 158
Townshend, Pete, 155, 203, 209
Towson, Maryland, 5
Trade Mark of Quality bootleg label, 199
Travis, Merle, 68
Tripp, Arthur Dyer, III, 160, 168, 187, 194,
327
Trotsky, Leon, 294
Turner, Ike, 231–2
Turner, Ted, 353
Turner, Tina, 231–2, 237
Turtles, the, 121, 175, 201–2, 205, 209, 229
Twisted Sister, 333, 336
Tyrannosaurus Rex, 155

U2, 373
Underwood, Ian, 166, 168, 170; musical
ability, 149, 187; Dweezil named after,
189; plays on *Hot Rats*, 192; plays with
Jean-Luc Ponty, 194, with Hot Rats band,
197; with reformed Mothers, 198; with
new Mothers, 200–1; with Grand Wazoo
Orchestra, 227; leaves Zappa, 231, 240;
rejoins Zappa, 231, 237
Underwood, Ruth (née Komanoff), 168, 196,
208, 231; with Grand Wazoo Orchestra,
227; leaves Zappa, 237; refuses to take
solos, 240; tribute to Zappa, 240
United Artists, 206
University of Southern California, 318
Upland-Ontario, California, ix, xi, 54, 58,
60–1, 277; *Daily Report*, xi, xii, 84, 86;
Zappa brothers run restaurant, 75–6
Urueta, Chano, 247
Utah, 15
Utility Muffin Research Kitchen (UMRK),
283, 302, 306, 321, 325, 369; Zappa builds
and occupies studio, 269, 279–80; bootleg
edits, 367; digital recording, 311, 340–1;
Chieftains record at, 372–3; Tuvan throat
singers record at, 376; Tom Jones records
at, 377–8

Vai, Steve, 283, 324, 368
Valens, Ritchie, 69, 368